'As I was walking in the fields,' said Robert McCheyne, close to the final days of his life, 'the thought came over me with almost overwhelming power, that every one of my flock must soon be in heaven or hell. O how I wished that I had a tongue like thunder, that I might make all hear; or that I had a frame like iron, that I might visit every one, and say, "Escape For thy life!" Ah sinners! You little know how I fear that you will lay the blame of your damnation at my door.'

His frame was not like iron, and he soon died at the age of twenty-nine, now over a hundred and fifty years ago. It was with this disrupting awareness that people 'must soon be in heaven or hell' that young McCheyne preached to his audience of over a thousand week by week in Dundee, Scotland.

Recently I stood in the place where this man preached the very sermons that are in this book. I admit some inner trembling at the demands that his saintly life brought to my mind at that time. Here is a man who lived and died well, painfully aware of his own failures and foibles as a man, yet transported in his preaching and his living like few have ever been.

McCheyne was a Christian, a real Christian, in the highest sense of that word. And his preaching, an extension of his life, his tears and his biblical knowledge, changed lives. They are the declarations that preceded genuine revival and they were God's instrument for sustaining that mighty work of revival as well. Can you imagine what it would have been like to have heard McCheyne at St. Peter's on a Lord's Day preaching what one man called these 'solemn and searching' sermons?

To have McCheyne's unpublished sermons in our hands is, without question, a great privilege. I am thankful for the labours of Michael McMullen in bringing them to our view at a time when models of biblical and passionate expositions are so desperately needed. Without this labour, and the surprising providence of God in uncovering them, they would yet be on dusty library shelves. As you read, pray fervently, in the spirit of McCheyne, that you will experience what hearers did so long ago.

Jim Elliff
President of Christian Communicators Worldwide
Resident Consultant For the Midwestern Center for Biblical Revival
Kansas City, USA

This volume is dedicated to our family's close friends,
Neil, Pat, Jocelyn, Emery and Annaliese Olcott.

Though there are now many miles between us,
they can never diminish the love and respect we have for you all.

And our constant prayer for you all is:

That you will know the Blessing of God which makes rich
And adds no sorrow at all!

The Passionate Preacher

Sermons of
Robert Murray McCheyne

Edited by
Michael McMullen

Christian Heritage

ISBN 1 85792 410 X

© Christian Focus Publications
First published in 1999
by
Christian Focus Publications
Geanies House, Fearn,
Ross-shire, IV20 1TW, Great Britain

Cover design by Owen Daily

Contents

Preface

Scotland has been a nation greatly blessed of God. There have been great moves of God in revival in this land: amongst these were the revivals in the time, and under the anointed preaching, of the young and godly John Livingstone in the 1600s. There were also the sweeping awakenings which took place in Cambuslang and Kilsyth, through the 18th and 19th centuries. Besides Livingstone, God raised up many great men who preached fearlessly and faithfully the gospel of life, men such as Knox, Hamilton, Wishart, the Haldane brothers, William Chalmers Burns and the preacher of these sermons, Robert Murray McCheyne.

McCheyne was born on 21st May 1813. After training for the Ministry, he had only been licensed a very short time when he was given charge of St. Peter's in Dundee. This was a challenging and very demanding position, but God blessed McCheyne's faithfulness and godliness with many conversions. It is recorded that even at his evening trial sermon, when he preached as a candidate on 14th August 1836, the blessing of God fell on two souls as he preached from the book of Ruth. St. Peter's was regularly filled to overflowing, with more than 1,100 attending and that in an area of only 4,000 souls.

McCheyne had a wonderful close friend in Andrew Bonar. Very soon after McCheyne's untimely death in 1843, Bonar produced what would soon become one of the Church's most treasured possessions, the *Memoir and Remains of the Rev Robert Murray McCheyne*. It sold in vast quantities and still remains a firm favourite with Christians of all denominations. McCheyne is a wonderful example of what God calls us to be, holy and committed to him in all things. McCheyne enjoyed the blessing of God because he enjoyed the holiness of God. He longed to become more like his Lord and he constantly urged his people to do likewise.

His *Memoir* contains a selection of his sermons and other writings, and other sermons are also still in print. This present volume is an addition to that corpus, but a very special addition, for it contains, to the best knowledge of the editor, sermons taken directly from the manuscripts of McCheyne and sermons, therefore, which have never before been published. This has been a labour of love and as one reads these pleadings from the heart of McCheyne they still carry the conviction and urgency which characterised his preaching. On one occasion he met his good friend Andrew Bonar, and on discovering that on the previous Sunday Bonar had preached on hell, McCheyne asked him whether he had been able to do so with tenderness.

It is clear from this collection, as well as from previous collections of McCheyne's sermons, that he had had a small number of favourite themes. Among these one would have to include, his desire to seek and win the lost for Christ. This call is illustrated in a poem McCheyne wrote concerning a family member who chose the world rather than have Christ. The poem was entitled: *That she was determined to keep by the world.* Other central themes of his preaching included, the centrality and holiness that should characterise the Lord's Day; the degree of commitment and type of behaviour that God expects of his people; and last but by no means least, revival. There are also several of his sermons that clearly display his love for the Jews, and it is obvious from his sermons on this particular subject, that his mission to Israel had a profound effect upon him. The editor also feels it incumbent upon him, to point out that on page 227, where McCheyne has some hard comments about socialists, he is not meaning that a Christian cannot be a socialist. McCheyne was obviously a man of his time, and these comments must be seen in the context of his day. There was a particular agitation at this time in the early 1800s and these are his comments on that situation.

The reader will find that these particular sermons of McCheyne have been placed in Bible book order, rather than in the order in which he preached them. This should help those who are interested in working through particular books or themes. It must also be said, that some of the sermons are clearly still in outline, while others are almost fully written out. It seems that on some occasions, especially when revivals were in full flow, McCheyne would simply not have time to write his sermons out in full, and he preached from the barest of notes. As time passed and he had more time, he would often take the opportunity to use some of his outlines, to produce much more completed sermons.

McCheyne was never robust in health and on the advice of doctors, he took part in the Mission to the Jews of Europe and Palestine that the Church of Scotland sent out in 1839. Only four years later, McCheyne would be dead. But through his writings and his godly reputation, McCheyne has continued to influence the lives of

Christians, great and small. When informed of the project to produce
new material from McCheyne, the editor received many testimonies
to that influence. Here are just three examples:

> 'It was over fifty years ago that, shortly before our marriage, my wife
> gave me a copy of the Bonar *Memoir and Remains*. I read it through at
> once with great profit, both for spiritual life and ministry. Over the years
> I have turned to passages from time to time, and always derived
> encouragement and inspiration, if not without some soul-searching. A
> question that has been with me in relation to this brief life and ministry
> is whether, with much that our churches now do, we not only fall short
> of the whole-hearted dedication that McCheyne achieved but also provide
> poor substitutes for the type of ministry that he exemplified, and that the
> power of the Word and Spirit, with prayer, does the real work that it is
> our privilege and responsibility to do. God has different tasks for different
> people and gives different gifts. We cannot all be McCheynes. But we
> can all learn from the devotion, both to Christ and his people, which he
> displayed and from the spiritual goals and methods which characterised
> his ministry.'
>
> Prof. Geoffrey W. Bromiley,
Emeritus Senior Professor of Church History and Theology,
Fuller Theological Seminary, California.

> 'I simply wish to record a deep indebtedness to my reading, at an early
> stage of my Christian life, his *Memoir and Remains*. They were a strong
> formative influence on my desire to live a holy life, my evangelistic
> passion, and in my call to ministry. They have since continued to have
> been read and reread as a source of inspiration and challenge throughout
> the course of my ministry.'
>
> Rev Douglas J. Hutcheon,
Superintendent, Baptist Union of Scotland.

> 'The words of McCheyne are of great value today, as the kind of
> evangelical and spiritual outlook he stood for is badly needed again in
> Scotland.'
>
> Rev. Prof. T. F. Torrance,
Professor Emeritus,
Edinburgh University.

These sermons have been transcribed directly from McCheyne's
own sermon manuscripts, which are held in the collections in a
Scottish University. They were 'discovered' as the editor was
researching the life of one of McCheyne's close friends, William

Chalmers Burns. The sermons remain almost entirely as McCheyne himself wrote them, all that has been added is the occasional word or phrase to give a sentence better sense for the reader. In the form in which these manuscript sermons were found, McCheyne had never intended them for publication. This means that where his writing is not altogether clear, the editor takes full responsibility for any words which may have been wrongly transcribed. The editor is currently working on more of McCheyne's unpublished material and the hope is that all that McCheyne wrote that has not been published will, quite soon, be made available for the Church to continue to benefit from and grow thereby.

McCheyne passed to his reward in glory more than 150 years ago, but his enduring example to believers continues to testify to the greatness and grace of his Lord. And it is that same Lord who continues to call to his Church to be holy because he is holy. Scotland has not seen the Lord move in revival for quite some time. Oh! that he would raise up many more McCheynes – that not just Scotland, but that the whole world might experience once again, the rich blessing of God through the preaching of his Word through his godly servants.

> When this passing world is done,
> When has sunk yon glaring sun,
> When we stand with Christ in glory,
> Looking o'er life's finished story,
> Then, Lord, shall I fully know
> Not till then how much I owe.
>
> Oft the nights of sorrow reign
> Weeping, sickness, sighing pain,
> But a night Thine anger burns
> Morning comes, and joy returns:
> God of comforts! Bid me show
> To Thy poor, how much I owe.

Robert Murray McCheyne

Dr. Michael D. McMullen
Midwestern Baptist Theological Seminary
Kansas City, USA

1. God's Covenant (2 Samuel 23:5)

Although my house *be* not so with God; yet he hath made with me an everlasting covenant, ordered in all *things*, and sure: for *this is* all my salvation, and all *my* desire, although he make *it* not to grow.

The sayings of dying believers are often very sweet and precious. Their eye is often made very clear, their heart is made single, they are weaned from the world and Christ is often very near them, as David himself sang, 'even in the valley'. Here we see the eye of David resting on three things: (1) The sin and wickedness of his house; (2) The covenant; (3) The nature of that covenant.

1. The sin of his house

'Although my house be not so with God.' In the verses before he had been describing what a good and righteous king ought to be – and what the Lord Jesus really is – 'he that ruleth over men must be just, ruling in the fear of God. And he shall be as the light of the morning.'

1. It was the sin of his house that cast him down

It was not only a sinful nature he felt: 'Behold I was shapen in iniquity and in sin did my mother conceive me'; it was not only a wicked heart, the positive sins of his life considered by themselves; but it was the sins of his house. He remembered his adultery with Bathsheba and the example he had set before his house. He remembered how he had been like Eli in not restraining his children. He remembered the crimes of his children: Amnon's lust and Absalom's rebellion. The scenes of iniquity that his palace had witnessed all crowded upon the eye of the dying man – and yet he had peace in Jesus.

2. It was the state of his house before God

Man perhaps might have excused or justified David, but God looketh on the heart. Many times David's house presented a lovely scene to the eye of man; when he gathered his family round him and led them on the harp to sing the praise of God. But he felt he was going into the presence of the heart-revealing God, that God and not man was to be his judge. And he therefore looks at his house in the light of God's countenance and condemns it. 'Although my house be not so with God.'

Learn

How great the sins of the house are. Perhaps in health and strength David thought little of the sins of the house and yet when dying they appeared to him infinite. I will mention some family sins:

1. Not worshipping God in your family

Wherever Abram went he built altars to the Lord. Job also used to offer sacrifice for his children. Joshua said, 'As for me and my house, we will serve the LORD (Josh. 24:15).' And no doubt David maintained the family altar. But many of you will have this to look back upon from your deathbed, that your house has not been so with God. Perhaps you have many reasons to offer just now why it is not so. You have not time or you have not courage, but in that day your excuses will appear to be nothing and your guilt will stare you in the face. Ah! it is no slight sin to be a family that does not own God, that asks no blessing on the day, no guardian care for the night.

2. Not setting a holy example

This was David's sin. He gave the example of sin to his children, which they were not slow to follow. This lay heavy on his heart. So with many here. Your children see you neglect prayer and the Bible and learn to do likewise. They see you profane the Sabbath by idle talk or the newspaper. They hear your swearing and profanity and filthy language and may learn it. Perhaps they see still darker scenes than these: the coarse debauch of the Saturday night; the wicked company; the lewd songs; and they learn your ways. They grow up around you, pictures of yourselves. Alas! will this be no bitter thought on your dying bed? 'Although my house be not so with God.'

3. No family government

God said of Abram, 'I know him that he will command his children.' It was Eli's sin that his sons made themselves vile and he restrained them not. This was David's sin. He seems not to have restrained them and therefore they turned out vile. So many of you will doubtless have this to reflect upon that your house is not so with God, that you have brought up children but not ruled them. So that they have got over your head and are your shame and misery. This sin will lie upon you on your dying bed.

4. Worldliness

David said in Psalm 101: 'I will walk within my house with a perfect heart. I will not know a wicked person; mine eyes shall be upon the faithful of the land.' Many of your families are not conducted on these principles. Many of your families are especially worldly. *Listen to the conversation* in most of your families. Is it of eternity? Of Christ? Of heaven? Of hell? You are journeying together towards that eternal world, and yet is not the very name of Christ vanished from your discourse?

Look at the company that is kept in your family. Can you say, 'I will not know a wicked person'? Surely if a man may be known by the company he keeps, many of you may be known to be on the road to destruction. How many are vain-talkers, busybodies, like flies that feed on carrion, hawks that live on rotten flesh? How often swearers, profane persons, lewd persons are suffered in your houses?

Look at the occupations of your leisure moments. What books are read in your houses? Are they full of unsearchable riches or of sin? What games? How do you spend Saturday night? Ah! these are the things that make a deathbed terrible.

2. David's comfort: 'Yet hath he made with me an everlasting covenant.'

1. The covenant here spoken of is without doubt the covenant of grace, made from eternity between God the Father and God the Son. 'I have finished the work which thou gavest me to do' (John 17:4). The work was just the work of this covenant, to do all and suffer all that sinners should do and suffer. It was a most holy, wise and infinitely glorious agreement entered into by the persons of the Godhead.

2. He hath made it with me

God makes the covenant with a sinner when he brings the sinner to lay hold on Christ; then the covenant made with Christ is put into the sinner's hand, its conditions being all fulfilled already by Jesus. It was God that brought David to lay hold on that covenant. By his almighty power he softened David's heart, changed his will, and made him gladly cleave to Christ as his covenant-head.

3. The wonder is on the word 'yet'.

Although my house be so wicked and vile, yet he came near it, and though I was the vilest in it, yet he made the covenant with me. He did not look on my wicked example, he did not look at Amnon's sin and Absalom's wickedness. He came over the mountains.

Learn:

1. That God alone can bring you into the covenant. Your heart is hard. Your mind so dark that no power on earth can bring you to lay hold on the covenant. 'I will give him for a covenant of the people.' He hath made it with me. A Sovereign Almighty Jehovah must do it or it will be left undone.

2. That God can do it though you live in an ungodly house. 'YET', precious 'yet'. You often make this objection, 'I live....' Answer: wherever you live, God is able to reach you. God loves to come over difficulties, like the gazelle. God can both choose and wash and sanctify you out of an ungodly house.

3. The covenant only can give peace in dying. Not sanctification but Christ.

3. The Nature of the Covenant

1. Ordered in all things

A sacrifice ordered in all things is one when there is the altar, the wood, the fire and the lamb. A feast ordered in all things is where there is enough for all and for every want of the guests. So the covenant is ordered in all things. There is everything in Christ that a sinner requires.

i. A Redeemer provided: 'I have laid help on one that is mighty.'
(a) *Blood for pardon*, the blood of the Son of God.
(b) *A robe of righteousness* to justify.
(c) *All grace to sanctify.*
(d) *Grace to enable us* to lay hold on Christ.

2. Everlasting

Its pardon is for ever and ever. The fountain flows by the path of life so that all our journey we may wash and be clean. Nay, in eternity we shall be eternally clothed in nature dipped in blood. When millions of ages have passed away, this will be the only reason still that we are in glory – Christ has died.

Its righteousness, everlasting righteousness (Daniel 9) shall not be abolished. Angel robes may wear dim but this never.

Its supplies of grace, everlasting, the life cannot dim, the living water cannot dry up. Through eternal ages Jesus will be our life, and we shall be holy as long as he is the fountain of holiness.

3. Sure

It is certainly efficacious. Will it not give way upon trial? May I venture my soul upon this covenant? Answer: it is sure. Sure as God's Word can make it, and his faithfulness, that whosoever lays hold has life. *This is a faithful saying.* Lay hold, sinner, it is sure.

2. Elijah the Tishbite (1 Kings 17:1-6)

And Elijah the Tishbite, *who was* of the inhabitants of Gilead, said unto Ahab, *As* the LORD God of Israel liveth, before whom I stand, there shall not be dew nor rain these years, but according to my word. And the word of the LORD came unto him, saying, Get thee hence, and turn thee eastward, and hide thyself by the brook Cherith, that *is* before Jordan. And it shall be, *that* thou shalt drink of the brook; and I have commanded the ravens to feed thee there. So he went and did according unto the word of the LORD: for he went and dwelt by the brook Cherith, that *is* before Jordan. And the ravens brought him bread and flesh in the morning, and bread and flesh in the evening; and he drank of the brook.

1. The time of his appearance
The reign of Ahab (16:29). When the enemy came in like a flood, God lifted up a standard. From Jeroboam the ten tribes had fallen away. Use: so take courage in times of a flood of iniquity, to pray that God would lift up men like Elijah (Isaiah 59:19). There were sixty years since the death of Solomon.

2. His Name
It means 'Thy God is Jehovah' or 'my strength is Jehovah'. Names are full of meaning, e.g. Methuselah. Elijah was a man of like passions, here was all the difference. So with Christians now. This only makes them overcome the world.

'The Tishbite', of village of Tishba, among the mountains of Gilead. We are told no more of his birth. Learn that God brings some of his noblest instruments from obscurity, the apostles etc. Not many wise (1 Corinthians 1:26ff.).

3. His message
'As the Lord God....'

1. His own condition: 'before whom I stand.'

a. This implied reconciliation to God (Rom. 5). e.g. servants of Solomon (1 Kgs. 10:8); their angels (Matt. 18:10). Do you stand before the Lord?

b. His willingness to obey the Lord. With twain, they did fly (Isa. 6).

2. His message
See James 5:17. He had come from his knees, therefore he was bold, and he knew that God sent him. Probably all nature was fresh and green [when he first spoke]: the hills of Samaria; the valleys; the mountains with brooks leaping down. The heavens became brass. Pray that ministers may thus come from their knees. Pray that the rain may fall.

3. God's Command to Elijah (1 Kings 17:1-6)

1. Elijah's command from God
How it came: When Elijah was in perplexity. 'The word came to him', unasked, uninvited. Verse 3, 'Get thee hence.'

Use: God still directs his children that watch for his leadings. *Inwardly*, by clearing it up to their mind that this is best, especially after prayer. *Outwardly*, by shutting up every other door.

2. Elijah's Obedience
The command required faith that God would hide him, provide him with water and food. Elijah believed God like Abraham and went.

3. Elijah's solitude
He dwelt there for a whole year, a solitary glen; the wild trees hanging over; the hanging woodbine; the dashing brook.

What would he do?
1. He had God's Word
2. His God
3. His own heart
4. All nature, the ravens and the brook.

Learn that God may often send his best ministers into solitude.
Learn that there is much to be done alone.

But did God feed him? All the promises of God are yea. God is faithful and never will let his children want.

4. The Trials of Elijah (1 Kings 17: 7-16)

And it came to pass after a while, that the brook dried up, because there had been no rain in the land. And the word of the LORD came unto him, saying, Arise, get thee to Zarephath, which *belongeth* to Zidon, and dwell there: behold, I have commanded a widow woman there to sustain thee. So he arose, and went to Zarephath. And when he came to the gate of the city, behold, the widow woman *was* there gathering of sticks: and he called to her, and said, Fetch me, I pray thee, a little water in a vessel, that I may drink. And as she was going to fetch *it*, he called to her, and said, Bring me, I pray thee, a morsel of bread in thine hand. And she said, *As* the LORD thy God liveth, I have not a cake, but an handful of meal in a barrel, and a little oil in a cruse: and, behold, I *am* gathering two sticks, that I may go in and dress it for me and my son, that we may eat it, and die. And Elijah said unto her, Fear not; go *and* do as thou hast said: but make me thereof a little cake first, and bring *it* unto me, and after make for thee and for thy son. For thus saith the LORD God of Israel, The barrel of meal shall not waste, neither shall the cruse of oil fail, until the day *that* the LORD sendeth rain upon the earth. And she went and did according to the saying of Elijah; and she, and he, and her house, did eat *many* days. *And* the barrel of meal wasted not, neither did the cruse of oil fail, according to the word of the LORD, which he spake by Elijah.

1. Elijah's Trial
The brook dried up. Elijah is perplexed, cast down, deserted. So many are tried as if God had forgotten to be precious.

2. His relief
By another command.
Zarephath, the country of Jezebel, a widow. What widow?

1. The length of the journey
2. The place
3. A poor widow
4. Unknown

God still tries faith
'He arose and went'.

3. Elijah's reception (Isaiah 41:17; 42:16)
Sarepta is thankfully situated. Hungry and thirsty, Elijah climbed the hill. The woman appeared very poor.

He finds her perhaps a believing woman. Sometimes we meet a child of God where you do not expect it. There are such even in Sarepta.

Luke 4:25,26: God often takes the gospel away from those who despise it, to those who are despised. God is sovereign in his grace. So God may do in Scotland.

5. 'Thy people shall be willing' (Psalm 110:3)

Thy people *shall* be willing in the day of thy power, in the beauties of holiness from the womb of the morning: thou hast the dew of thy youth.

There are three things contained in the words, 'Thy people shall be willing':

1. A people given him by the Father, given to Christ before the world was.
When Paul was in Corinth and his soul was sinking within him, for he saw the people given over to lust and idolatry and drunkenness, the Lord appeared to him in a vision and said, 'Be not afraid, but speak: and hold not thy peace for I am with thee, and no man shall set on thee to hurt thee: For I have much people in this city' (Acts 18:9-10). So it is still. Christ, I do hope and believe, has still much people in this city yet in their sins and in the shadow of death. Perhaps some of you that today are biting your lip with contempt and mockery, are yet to be made his praying people. Ah, this is my hope in speaking to you. If I thought that all Christ's people had been gathered out of this place I would leave you tomorrow to seek souls somewhere else.

2. Christ has a day of power

The days in which he sheds down the Spirit peculiarly are his days of power. Pentecost was a day of Christ's power. Jesus, being by the right hand of God exalted, shed forth the Spirit like a mighty rushing wind, first on his own children, then on the multitudes, pricking their hearts and there filling them with gladness, and 3,000 souls were born in a day.

Such a day has been in New England under the ministry of Edwards and among the Indians under the preaching of Brainerd. Such a day has been in Scotland in Cambuslang, Kilsyth and Moulin. Such a day has been in Germany of late years under the preaching of Martin Boos. Such a day we have good tokens of in our own land at this hour. These are the days of Christ's power when his rod has been a rod of strength. As Moses' rod was strong to bring water out of the flinty rock, so the rod of Christ's Word has become strong to bring tears of awakening and of faith out of dead souls. Oh, that this day might be a day of Christ's power!

3. Christ's people shall be willing in that day

All that have been given to Christ shall be willing in that day of an outpoured Spirit. As many as are ordained to eternal life shall be made willing: willing to lose their own righteousness, willing to submit to the righteousness of Jehovah-Jesus, willing to give themselves and their all to the Lord. Oh, what a sweet sight our parishes will be in that day when we shall join hand in hand saying: 'Come and let us join ourselves to the Lord in a perpetual covenant that is not to be forgotten.' The Lord hasten it in his time.

Doctrine: *Christ's people shall be willing in the day of his power.*

1. Willing to feel themselves lost and undone

1. Secure sinners

I believe that the most are quite unwilling to hear the simple statements of the Bible, as applied to themselves.

    a. 'By the deeds of the law there shall no flesh living be justified.'

    b. 'All have sinned and come short of the glory of God.'

    c. 'Every mouth must be stopped and all the world become guilty before God.'

    d. 'Cursed is everyone that continueth not in all things.'

e. 'He that believeth not is condemned already.'

Now, unconverted persons are very willing to hear these Scriptures but they are not willing to submit to them. I believe that most of you, if you really attended to what we say, would go away in a rage. I believe that if you thought more seriously about what we say out of the Bible, you would gnash upon us with your teeth and say, 'It is not fit that such a fellow should live.'

2. *Awakened sinners* struggle hard to keep from feeling lost and undone. When a man's conscience is awakened he is obliged to confess that he is a sinner, but he struggles hard to do something to atone for his sins. God says every mouth must be stopped. He says, 'Not quite, I will try and say something in my defence.' God says, 'No flesh living can be justified.' He says, 'I will try what a little amendment and prayers will do.' God says, 'Ye are dead.' He says, 'I will try and do something rather than to go to hell.' For he does not feel it a gone case. He is not willing to admit that God is true and that he is infinitely condemned.

3. *What happens in the day of Christ's power?* Answer:
When Christ really takes the rod of his strength in hand, the soul is made willing, willing to be lost and undone. Not that the soul is willing to go to hell, no one can ever be really willing to go there if he is in his senses. But the soul perceives the truth of what the Bible says about his lost condition and submits: 'It must be true; I am infinitely lost; I never can do anything to save myself; my past efforts appear to be utter folly, like a fly trying to remove a mountain.'

If a man were lying beneath a weight that he could possibly throw off, as long as he thought he could lift the weight away he would struggle very hard, he would exert every muscle and nerve of his body. But if you convinced him of the Word of God who cannot lie, that the mountain was infinite and that it is clear impossible for him to lift it away, he would struggle no more. Not another heave afresh would he waste, he would say, 'It is done, it is all done now, I never can do anything to lift the load away.' So is it with an awakened soul in the day of Christ's power. He finds that repentance, reformation, prayer, good works, will not lift past sins away, that all his struggles are just in vain. He believes the Word, 'In thy sight no flesh living can be justified.' He sets his seal that God is true: 'we are all as an unclean thing and all our righteousness are as filthy rags.'

Learn it is Christ's power that must make you willing. It is Christ's rod that must go forth with strength to bring water out of that flinty rock. It is not the argument of a man or of a book. It is the rod of a risen Saviour. It is the Spirit shed down forth from the Saviour that alone can prick your hearts and make you feel undone.

Learn not to despair of any man or woman in the world. It is plain to me that this is not a day of Christ's power, yet I do not despair. We are perplexed but not in despair. I will trust to that word, 'I have much people in this city.' And oh, when Christ lifts the rod I know the proudest of you will bow. The most worldly money-worshippers among you will tremble. The most sensual wretches will feel undone. I will not despair of one of you all.

Oh, pray for a day of Christ's power. Nothing else will do. Cry for an outpoured Spirit. I have stood by two deathbeds since I saw you last and I could not but think, 'Ah, what will become of most of my poor parishioners if they were to lie thus.' Pray for a day of Christ's power before another die.

2. Willing that Christ be Surety

1. All unconverted persons are unwilling to receive Christ as their surety, 'they being ignorant'.

a. *They do not think so badly of themselves as to feel any need of a righteousness better than their own.* 'I am better than most of my neighbours. I am not so bad as I once was. I will be better yet I hope, before I die.'

b. *They do not think so highly of God.* They do not know that he is of purer eyes than to behold evil. They think if a man do the best he can God will accept him. They do not know his purity, that no imperfect thing can ever stand in his sight. They feel no need of Christ.

c. *They do not know the righteousness of Christ.* They do not know that he lived and died as a surety. They see no beauty in him, no form, no comeliness, that they should desire him.

2. Awakened persons are unwilling

Ye will not come unto me that ye might have life. You would think that awakened souls would fly quickly to Christ, but no! I believe they will go anywhere rather than to Christ.

a. *The awakened soul quarrels with God.* He is so strict and holy, his heart rises against God. He is suspicious of God and because Christ is the Saviour provided by God, therefore he will not come to him to have life.

b. *He cannot believe that Christ is provided for him.* He thinks that it may be for others but cannot be for him, that he must make himself better in some way before he comes to Christ. Ah, some of you know that there is no end to the pride and doubts of an awakened soul.

How can such be made willing?

3. In the day of Christ's power

The Spirit comes like a rushing mighty wind, unfelt, unseen, yet almighty. He makes Jehovah-Jesus glorious and the way of salvation by him. He reveals the beauty of Immanuel, God's fellow, God's equal Son, the Surety of sinners. He convinces the soul that though in himself no sinner living can be justified, yet in Jesus the chiefest of sinners may be justified. All this shines out of the Bible as if printed with sunbeams. There is a glory and a brightness in it. The soul cries like that poor woman in Germany: '*I cannot do otherwise, I must believe.*' Just as a sick child, that cannot stand nor go, is entirely willing to lie back in the arms of its mother, so is the conceived soul entirely willing to lie in Jesus for righteousness. The soul is just willing to stand before God, not in himself, but in Jesus. The soul is filled with peace which passeth understanding. Do you know this peace? Has this been done in your soul? Has Christ been revealed in you? If not, you may be rich and gay and merry and full of the pleasure of sin, but you are a poor, unpardoned soul for all that.

Awake! It is Christ's rod that must bend you to submit to the righteousness of God. It is not all the arguing in the world that will do it. He only can melt your heart into a sweet willingness to be formed in Christ, to count all but loss for the excellency of the knowledge of Christ. Paul was as proud a Pharisee as any of you, but a touch of Christ's rod so melted his heart that he gladly received the Word.

Oh, pray for a day of Christ's power, that our burdened souls may be released, that deep wading souls may be brought into a wealthy place, that souls may be brought out of prison, that they may fly like a cloud, that Christ, the glorious city of Refuge, may be filled for, oh, the gates are open night and day and yet there is room.

3. Christians are a willing people in a day of Christ's power
In dry days like the present, Christians can hardly be said to be a willing people.

1. It is only at times that they seem to realise the peace of believing. It is only now and then that they are willing to lie down condemned in themselves but infinitely complete in Jesus. Christians nowadays seem only to see glimpses of the divine face of Immanuel. They do not gaze steadily upon him, therefore there is little steady peace.

2. Christians are not willing to yield themselves to God.
They do not like to trust their souls into the hands of God to keep them from falling and to fill them with all the fullness of God. They are not willing to be carried to any height in grace. They wish to keep in with the world. They are often not willing to read the Word, not willing to hear, not willing to pray; they are unwilling people.

Not willing to submit to God in providence. To trust their all, blood, body, soul and friends for time and eternity. In prosperity they are for relying upon a hoard or upon their own forethought, but not willing to trust him, no not for a crumb. When trials come they are angry because of their gourd, like Jonah; and when God says, 'Doest thou well to be angry?' they say, 'Yes, I do well to be angry.' Some of you, this is, in fact, your case.

3. Christians are filled with a sweet submission to the righteousness of God.
The soul is willing to be guilty and condemned for ever as it is in itself, eternally willing to rest in Christ for ever. The soul is filled with a divine tranquil complacency in resting on Christ, a peace that passeth understanding, a joy that is unspeakable and full of glory.

The soul is willing to yield itself to God. It feels that Word drawing it, 'Return unto me, for I have redeemed thee.' The soul longs to know more of God, to be nearer to him, to be filled with the fullest measures of the Spirit, to be in the beauties of holiness. The desire to be holy fills the whole soul.

The soul trusts all to God, Leaves all upon him, father, mother, sister, brother, money, fame, health, life. The soul is without carefulness for he feels that God cares for him. The soul is filled with a sweet submissiveness saying, 'Though he slay me, yet will I trust in him.'

One of Brainerd's converts, when Brainerd asked her, 'What if God should take away your husband from you?', she replied, 'He belongs to God and not to me, and my infant it belongs to him; he will take care of it.' The soul cries out, 'When thou wilt, what thou wilt, how thou wilt.'

Oh, for such a day amongst you. Ah, it is too plain that the rod of Christ's power is not uplifted now:

1. Where is that sweet melting under the Word that tells of Jesus?
Where is that sense of your infinite vileness in yourselves and that sweet rest and complacency in a divine surety? Where are your longing desires after Christ? Where are your delights under his shadow?

2. Alas, you do not yield yourselves unto God
Have I not to weep over some of you and say ye have gone backward and not forward? How little leaning on the beloved, strengthened with all might in the inner man, pressing forward. Have I not to weep over some that mind earthly things?

3. Where are your sweet submissions of all to him, in sunshine and in shade?
Oh, for a day of his power! Oh, long for such a day! Another Pentecost! I charge you, pray for it. Set apart peculiar times for preparing for it. For the sake of your own souls, so barren and cold, for the sake of poor, weary, heavy-laden sinners, for the sake of dead souls, pray for a day of Christ's power. Awake, awake, Oh arm of the Lord! Awake, why sleepest thou? Plant thine hand out of thy bosom. Amen.

6. The Stone the Builders Refused (Psalm 118:22-24)

The stone *which* the builders refused is become the head *stone* of the corner. This is the LORD's doing; it *is* marvellous in our eyes. This is the day *which* the LORD hath made; we will rejoice and be glad in it.

1. *The stone here spoken of is the Lord Jesus Christ.* God often foretold the coming of Jesus under the figure of a stone. 'Behold I lay in Zion a stone, a tried stone, a sure foundation.' He came to be a foundation for poor, guilty, hell-deserving sinners to rest on.

2. *The builders refused him.* The Jewish priests who ought to have been the builders of God's house would not have him. The nation too, 'He came unto his own and his own received him not.' They killed him and cast him out of the vineyard. They buried him in a cave and rolled a stone to the mouth of the cave.

3. *God raised him to the head of the corner.* This is the Lord's doing. When the work of redemption was completed, God highly exalted him and gave him a name that is above every name. God has made him to be head over all things to the Church.

4. *The day on which he did so is the Lord's day* (v. 24). It was on the first day of the week, while it was yet dark, that Jesus rose. From that time it became the Christian Sabbath because Christ entered into his rest that day.

Doctrine: All believers love the Lord's day

1. Because it is the Lord's day
Verse 24: 'This is the day which the Lord hath made....' and again Revelation 1:10: 'I was in the Spirit on the Lord's day.' It is the Lord's day in two ways:

1. It is his by example. It is the day in which he rested from all his works, wherefore God blessed the Sabbath day and hallowed it. So the Lord Jesus rested on this day from all his agony and pain and humiliation. Therefore, it is the Lord's day.

2. It is his property, just as the Lord's Supper is the supper belonging to Christ. All the bread and wine in the world are Christ's but only the bread and wine of the communion table are the Lord's Supper. It is his table. He is the bread. He is the wine. He invites the guests. He fills them with joy and the Holy Ghost. So is it with the Lord's day. All days of the year are Christ's but he hath marked out one in seven as particularly his own.

He hath made it or marked it out. Just as he planted a garden in Eden, so he hath fenced about this day and calls it his own. The believer loves it – 'we will rejoice and be glad in it.' A true believer loves everything that is Christ's.

He loves his Word – 'if a man love me he will keep my sayings' (John 14:23). They are sweeter than honey, they are all golden sayings.

We love his house, 'I had rather be a door-keeper.' It is a trysting place with Christ. It is his audience chamber where he comes to commune with us from the mercy-seat.

We love his table. It is his banqueting house, where he feasts the souls of his own. It is the place where he makes our hearts burn.

We love his people, because they are his. All members of his body, all like him, filled with his Spirit.

And in the same manner, we love the Lord's day because it is his. It is the day he rose from the dead for our justification. It reminds us of his work and of his love. It all tells of him and his finished work. And we may boldly say that a man does not love Jesus that does not love the Lord's day.

Oh Sabbath breaker, you are a sacrilegious robber. When you steal the hours of the Sabbath for business or pleasure, you steal the precious hours which Jesus claims. What would you say of a man who should break through the fence of the Lord's Table and turn it into a common meal and eat and drink? Such is the sin of the Sabbath breaker when you take God's day for your health or recreation. 'Cursed is that gain, cursed is that recreation, cursed is that health which is gained by criminal encroachments on this sacred day.'

2. Because it is a relic of paradise and type of heaven
The first Sabbath dawned on the start of a sinless Paradise. When Adam was created in the image of his Maker, he was put into the garden to dress it and to keep it. Of vast extent, this no doubt called forth all his energies. To train the luxuriant vines, to gather the fruit

of the fig tree and palm, to conduct the water to the flowers and fruit trees required all his time. Man was never made to be idle. Still, when the Sabbath day came round, his rural implements were laid aside. The garden no longer was his care. His calm, pure mind looked beyond things seen. He walked with God, seeking deeper knowledge of Jehovah and his ways and burning more and more with holy love. Even in Paradise man needed a Sabbath. The Sabbath, then, is a relic of a sinless world.

It is also the type of heaven. When a believer lays aside his business, his pen or his loom, brushes aside his cares and anxieties, leaves them all behind him with his week-day clothes, and comes up to the house of God, it is a picture of the time when we shall come out of great tribulation into the Kingdom of God.

When he sits under the preaching of the Word and hears the voice of the Shepherd leading and feeding his soul, it reminds him of the day when 'the Lamb which is in the midst of the throne....'(Rev. 7:17). When he sings the praises of God with a glad heart, it reminds him of the day when we shall sing the song of Moses the servant of God and the song of the Lamb, where congregations never break up and Sabbaths have no end. When he retires and in secret meets with God and pours out his heart before him, it tells him of the time when he shall be a pillar in the house of his God.

Is it so with you, dear friends? Do you call the Sabbath a delight? Do you feel a holy, well-spent Sabbath to be heaven begun? It is heaven below to have a day with God. Oh, let your Sabbaths be wholly given to him then. Spend the whole time in the public and private exercises of God's worship. Rise early on the Sabbath morning and sit up late that you may have a long day with God. Fill up all your time with him.

Some of you know well that you will never be in heaven. A holy Sabbath you abhor. It is a kind of hell to you to be with those that are strict in keeping the Sabbath. You are restless and uneasy. When will the Sabbath be gone? Ah soon, soon, and you will be in hell. Hell is the only place for you. There is no Sabbath there.

3. Because it is a day of blessings

1. When God instituted the Sabbath in Paradise it is said, 'God blessed the Sabbath day and hallowed it.' He not only sanctified it or set it apart as a sacred day but blessed it, that is, he made it a day of blessing.

2. Again, when Jesus rose from the dead, that same day he revealed himself to the two disciples going to Emmaus and made their hearts burn.

3. The same evening he came and stood in the midst of the disciples and said, 'Peace be unto you....'

4. Again, after eight days (the next Lord's day), Jesus again stood in the midst and revealed himself to Thomas.

5. It was on the Lord's day also that the Spirit was poured out at Pentecost (see Leviticus 23:15,16), that beginning of all spiritual blessings. That first revival of the Christian Church was on the Lord's day.

6. It was on the same day that John, in the rocky Isle of Patmos, far away from the help of man, was filled with the Spirit and received his heavenly revelation. 'I was in the Spirit on the Lord's day' (Rev. 1:10). So that in all ages from the beginning of the world and in every place where there is a believer, the Sabbath has been a day of double blessing. It is so still. God is a God of free grace and confines himself to no time and place; but still he doth oftenest bless the Word on his own day. Jesus comes in on that day and reveals himself. The Spirit is poured down on that day. Men like John are filled with the Holy Ghost on that day. Dear saints get their deepest, fullest views into the eternal world [on that day].

Awakened sinners, be careful of your Sabbath days. This is the day that Jesus revealed himself so frequently and does so still. This is the day of the conversion of the 3,000. Ah, do not pollute his Sabbaths, do not go with your regardless friends. One polluted Sabbath may quench the Spirit with regard to your soul.

Believers in darkness, improve your Sabbaths. This is the day Christ revealed himself to Thomas.

Dear saints, who are panting after fuller revelations of Christ, seek these on the Sabbath. It was on that day Christ revealed himself to John so that he fell at his feet as dead.

Question: How shall we keep the Lord's day?

1. Testify against public profanations of it

1. The keeping open of the Exchange Reading Room
I am told that at all hours of the Lord's day you may find a man of business turning over the newspapers within its walls. And on Sabbath

evenings it is said to be more crowded than the Churches. Ah unhappy men! If any of them are here I would say you show too plainly that you are on the road to hell. If you were a murderer or an adulterer, you would perhaps allow this. Ah, do you not know that the same God who said, 'Thou shalt not kill', said also, 'Remember the Sabbath day?' The Sabbath breaker and the murderer are one in the eye of God.

2. There is that Railway
The Directors of this Railway are the only ones in Scotland who have submitted to the running of a mail train on the Sabbath day. While I am speaking perhaps it is rolling on, defiant against the Maker of heaven and earth and crying for judgement. Ah unhappy men! If any of them were here, I would say, ye know not what ye do.

Ye are robbers. Ye rob God of his holy day.

Ye are murderers of the souls of your servants. God said, 'Thou shalt not do any work, thou nor thy servant,' but you compel your servants to break God's law and ruin their souls.

Ye are traitors to your country. Was it not for Sabbath breaking that God cast Israel away? Ye are striving to bring down that worse on our beloved land.

Ye are suicides, stabbing at your own soul, proclaiming to the world that ye are not the Lord's people, hurrying on your own soul to meet the Sabbath breaker's doom.

Dear brethren, pray that their hearts may be turned or else if that may not be, that the Railway may be swept off the face of the earth.

3. The public houses
4. The public walking

2. Avoid sin on this day
You that are God's children should avoid sin every day, but more especially on this day. It is a day of double cursing, as well as double blessing. How many sin with the tongue on this day? How much idle talk, gossip, flattery and vile talking there is on this day! How many spend this day in drinking, [or in] sin that cannot be named? You will have to answer dreadfully for sin of holy time.

3. Spend it as a day in heaven
Lay aside the world. Get near to Christ. Be filled with the Spirit.
Spend much in praise and in works of mercy.

Concluding Points:
1. Can you name one godly minister of any denomination in all
Scotland, who does not hold the entire sanctification of the Lord's
day? I know not one.

2. Did you ever meet with a lively believer, one who loved Christ
and lived a holy life, who did not love to keep holy to God the Lord's
day? I never met one in any country of the world.

3. Is it wise to take the interpretation of God's will about the
Lord's day from infidels, scoffers, men of unholy lives, men who
cannot blush, men who are sand-blind by divine things, men who are
enemies of all righteousness, who quote Scripture as Satan did to
deceive and betray?

4. If you sin against the uniform testimony of God's wisest and
holiest servants in all ages, against the plain warnings of the Word of
God, against the loud remonstrances of living ministers, against the
very words of your catechism learned by your mother's knee, against
the voice of your outraged conscience, will this not be sinning against
light? Will you not repent it in the Judgement Day?

7. The Sabbath is the Lord's Day (Psalm 118:24)

This is the day *which* the LORD hath made; we will rejoice and be glad in it.

As a servant of God in this dark and cloudy day, I feel constrained to
lift up my voice on behalf of the entire sanctification of the Lord's
Day. The daring attack that is now made by some of the Directors of
the Edinburgh and Glasgow Railway on the Law of God and the
peace of our Scottish Sabbath, the blasphemous motion which they
mean to propose to the Shareholders in February next, and the wicked
pamphlets which are now being circulated in thousands, full of all
manner of lies and impieties, call loudly for the calm, deliberate
testimony of all faithful Ministers and private Christians on behalf
of God's holy day. In the name of all God's people in this town and
in this land, I commend to your dispassionate consideration the
following *reasons why we love the Lord's Day.*

1. Because it is the Lord's Day.

'This is the day which the LORD hath made; we will rejoice and be glad in it' (Psalm 118:24). 'I was in the Spirit on the Lord's day' (Rev. 1:10). It is his, by example. It is the day on which he rested from his amazing work of redemption. Just as God rested on the seventh day from all his works, wherefore God blessed the Sabbath Day and hallowed it, so the Lord Jesus rested on this day from all his agony, and pain, and humiliation. 'There remaineth therefore the keeping of a Sabbath to the people of God' (Heb. 4:9). The Lord's Day is his property, just as the Lord's Supper is the supper belonging to Christ. It is his table. He is the bread. He is the wine. He invites the guests. He fills them with joy and with the Holy Ghost. So it is with the Lord's Day. All days of the year are Christ's, but he hath marked out one in seven as peculiarly his own. 'He hath made it', or marked it out. Just as he planted a garden in Eden, so he hath fenced about this day and made it his own.

This is the reason why we love it, and would keep it entire. We love everything that is Christ's. We love his Word. It is better to us than thousands of gold and silver. 'O how we love his law, it is our study all the day.' We love his House. It is our trysting-place with Christ, where he meets with us and communes with us from off the mercy-seat. We love his Table. It is his banqueting-house, where his banner over us is love, where he looses our bonds, and anoints our eyes, and makes our hearts burn with holy joy. We love his people, because they are his, members of his body, washed in his blood, filled with his Spirit, our brothers and sisters for eternity. And we love the Lord's Day, because it is his. Every hour of it is dear to us, sweeter than honey, more precious than gold. It is the day he rose for our justification. It reminds us of his love, and his finished work, and his rest. And we may boldly say that that man does not love the Lord Jesus Christ who does not love the entire Lord's Day.

Oh Sabbath-breaker, whoever you be, you are a sacrilegious robber! When you steal the hours of the Lord's Day for business or for pleasure, you are robbing Christ of the precious hours which he claims as his own. Would you not be shocked if a plan were deliberately proposed for breaking through the fence of the Lord's Table, and turning it into a common meal, or a feast for the profligate and the drunkard? Would not your best feelings be harrowed to see the silver cup of communion made a cup of revelry in the hand of the drunkard? And yet what better is the proposal of our Railway Directors? 'The Lord's Day' is as much his day as 'the Lord's Table' is his Table. Surely we may well say in the words of Dr. Love, that eminent servant of Christ, now gone to the Sabbath above: 'Cursed is that gain, cursed is that recreation, cursed is that health, which is gained by criminal encroachments on this sacred day.'

2. Because it is a relic of Paradise and type of heaven.

The first Sabbath dawned on the bowers of a sinless Paradise. When Adam was created in the image of his Maker, he was put into the garden to dress it and keep it. No doubt this called forth all his energies. To train the luxuriant vine, to gather the fruit of the fig-tree and palm, to conduct the water to the fruit-trees and flowers, required all his time and all his skill. Man was never made to be idle. Still, when the Sabbath Day came round, his rural implements were all laid aside; the garden no longer was his care. His calm [was] eternal realities. He walked with God in the garden seeking deeper knowledge of Jehovah and his ways, his heart burning more and more with holy love, and his lips overflowing with seraphic praise. Even in Paradise man needed a Sabbath. Without it Eden itself would have been incomplete. How little they know the joys of Eden, the delight of a close and holy walk with God, who would wrest from Scotland this relic of a sinless world!

It is also the type of Heaven. When a believer lays aside his pen or loom, brushes aside his worldly cares, leaving them behind him with his week-day clothes, and comes up to the house of God, it is like the morning of the resurrection, the day we shall come out of great tribulation into the presence of God and the Lamb. When he sits under the preached Word, and hears the voice of the Shepherd leading and feeding his soul, it reminds him of the day when the Lamb that is in the midst of the throne shall feed him and lead him to living fountains of waters. When he joins in the psalm of praise, it reminds him of the day when his hands shall strike the harp of God. 'Where congregations ne'er break up, and Sabbaths have no end.' When he retires, and meets with God in secret in his closet, or, like Isaac, in some favourite spot near his dwelling, it reminds him of the day when 'he shall be a pillar in the house of our God, and go no more out'.

This is the reason why we love the Lord's Day. This is the reason why we 'call the Sabbath a delight'. A well-spent Sabbath we feel to be a day of heaven upon earth. For this reason we wish our Sabbaths to be wholly given to God. We love to spend the whole time in the public and private exercises of God's worship, except so much as is taken up in the works of necessity and mercy. We love to rise early on that morning, and to sit up late, that we may have a long day with God.

How many may know from this that they will never be in Heaven. A straw on the surface can tell which way the stream is flowing. Do you abhor a holy Sabbath? Is it a kind of hell to you to be with those who are strict in keeping the Lord's Day? The writer of these lines once felt as you do. You are restless and uneasy. You say, 'Behold, what a nuisance it is. When will the Sabbath be gone, that we may sell corn?' Ah! soon, very soon, and you will be in hell. Hell is the only place for you. Heaven is one long, never-ending, holy Sabbath Day. There are no Sabbaths in hell.

3. Because it is a day of blessings.

When God instituted the Sabbath in Paradise, it is said, 'God blessed the Sabbath Day, and sanctified it' (Gen. 2:3). He not only set it apart as a sacred day, but made it a day of blessing. Again, when the Lord Jesus rose from the dead on the first day of the week before dawn, he revealed himself the same day to two disciples going to Emmaus, and made their hearts burn within them (Luke 24:32). The same evening he came and stood in the midst of the disciples, and said, 'Peace be unto you, and he breathed on them and said, Receive ye the Holy Ghost' (John 20:19, 22). Again, after eight days, that is, *the next Lord's Day,* Jesus came and stood in the midst, and revealed himself with unspeakable grace to unbelieving Thomas (John 20:26). It was on the Lord's Day, also, that the Holy Spirit was poured out at Pentecost (Acts 2:1, compare Leviticus 23:15, 16). That beginning of all spiritual blessings, that first revival of the Christian Church, was on the Lord's Day. It was on the same day that the beloved John, an exile on the sea-girt isle of Patmos, far away from the assembly of the saints, was filled with the Holy Spirit, and received his heavenly revelation. So that in all ages, from the beginning of the world, and in every place where there is a believer, the Sabbath has been a day of double blessing.

It is so still, and will be though all God's enemies should gnash their teeth against it. True, God is a God of free grace, and confines his working to no time or place; but it is equally true, and all the scoffs of the infidel cannot alter it, that it pleases him to bless his Word most on the Lord's Day. All God's faithful ministers in every land can bear witness that sinners are converted most frequently on the Lord's Day, that Jesus comes in and shows himself through the lattice of ordinances oftenest on his own day. Saints, like John, are filled with the Spirit on the Lord's Day, and enjoy their calmest, deepest views into the eternal world.

Unhappy men, who are striving to rob our beloved Scotland of this day of double blessing, ye 'know not what ye do'. Ye would wrest from our dear countrymen the day when God opens the windows of heaven and pours down a blessing. You want to make the heavens over Scotland like brass, and the hearts of our people like iron. Is it the sound of the golden bells of our ever-living High Priest on the mountains of our land, and the breathing of his Holy Spirit over so many of our parishes, that has roused up your Satanic exertions to drown the sweet sound of mercy by the deafening roar of railway carriages? Is it the returning vigour of the revived and chastened Church of Scotland that has opened the torrents of blasphemy which you pour forth against the Lord of the Sabbath? Have your own withered souls no need of a drop from heaven?

May it not be the case that some of you are blaspheming the very day on which your own soul might have been saved? Is it not possible that some of you may remember, with tears of anguish, in hell, the exertions which you are now making against light and against warning, to bring down a withering blight on your own souls and on the religion of Scotland?

To those who are God's children in this land, I would now, in the name of our common Saviour, who is Lord of the Sabbath Day, address *a word of exhortation.*

1. Prize the Lord's Day.

The more that others despise and trample on it, love you it all the more. The louder the storm of blasphemy howls around you, sit the closer at the feet of Jesus. 'He must reign till he has put all enemies under his feet.' Diligently improve all holy time. It should be the busiest day of the seven; but only in the business of eternity. Avoid sin on that holy day. God's children should avoid sin every day, but most of all on the Lord's Day. It is a day of double cursing as well as of double blessing. The world will have to answer dreadfully for sins committed in holy time. Spend the Lord's Day in the Lord's presence. Spend it as a day in heaven. Spend much of it in praise and in works of mercy, as Jesus did.

2. Defend the Lord's Day.

Lift up a calm undaunted testimony against all the profanations of the Lord's Day. Use all your influence, whether as a statesman, a magistrate, a master, a father, or a friend, both publicly and privately, to defend the entire Lord's Day. This duty is laid upon you in the fourth commandment. Never see the Sabbath broken without reproving the breaker of it. Even worldly men, with all their pride and contempt for us, cannot endure to be convicted of Sabbath breaking. Always remember God and the Bible are on your side, and that you will soon see these men cursing their own sin and folly when too late. Let all God's children in Scotland lift up a united testimony especially against these three public profanations of the Lord's Day:

1. *The keeping open of Reading-Rooms.* In this town, and in all large towns of Scotland, I am told, you may find in the public reading-rooms many of our men of business turning over the newspapers and magazines at all hours of the Lord's Day; and, especially on Sabbath evenings, many of these places are filled like a little Church. Ah, guilty men! how plainly you show that you are on the broad road that leadeth to destruction. If you were a murderer or an adulterer, perhaps you would not dare to deny this. Do you not know, and all the sophistry of hell cannot disprove it, that the same God who said, 'Thou shalt not kill', said also, 'Remember the Sabbath Day to keep it holy'. The murderer who is dragged to the gibbet, and the polished Sabbath-breaker, are one in the sight of God.

2. *The keeping open Public-houses.* Public-houses are the curse of Scotland. I never see a sign, 'Licensed to sell spirits', without thinking that it is a license to ruin souls. They are the yawning avenues to poverty and rags in this life, and as another has said, 'the short cut to hell'. Is it to be tamely borne in this land of light and reformation that these pest-houses and dens of iniquity, these man-traps for precious souls, shall be open on the Sabbath? Nay, that they shall be

enriched and kept afloat by this unholy traffic, many of them declaring that they could not keep up their shop if it were not for the Sabbath market-day! Surely we may well say, 'Cursed is the gain made on that day.' Poor wretched men, do ye not know that every penny that rings upon your counter on that day will yet eat your flesh as it were fire, that every drop of liquid poison swallowed in your gas-lit palaces will only serve to kindle up the flame of 'the fire that is not quenched'?

3. *Sunday trains upon the Railway.* A majority of the Directors of the Edinburgh and Glasgow Railway have shown their determination, in a manner that has shocked all good men, to open the Railway on the Lord's Day. The sluices of infidelity have been opened at the same time, and floods of blasphemous tracts are pouring over the land, decrying the holy day of the blessed God, as if there was no eye in heaven, no King on Zion Hill, no day of reckoning.

Christian countrymen, awake! and filled with the same Spirit that delivered our country from the dark superstitions of Rome, let us beat back the incoming tide of infidelity and enmity to the Sabbath.

Guilty men! who, under Satan, are leading on the deep, dark phalanx of Sabbath-breakers, yours is a solemn position. You are robbers. You rob God of his holy day. You are murderers. You murder the souls of your servants. God said, 'Thou shalt not do any work, thou, nor thy servant'; but you compel your servants to break God's law, and to sell their souls for gain.

You are sinners against light. Your Bible and your Catechism, the words of godly parents, perhaps now in the Sabbath above, and the loud remonstrances of God-fearing men, are ringing in your ears, while you perpetrate this deed of shame, and glory in it.

You are traitors to your country. The law of your country declares that you should 'observe a holy rest all that day from your own words, works, and thoughts'; and yet you scout it as an antiquated superstition. Was it not Sabbath-breaking that made God cast away Israel? And yet you would bring the same curse on Scotland now. You are moral suicides, stabbing your own souls, proclaiming to the world that you are not the Lord's people, and hurrying on your souls to meet the Sabbath-breaker's doom.

In conclusion, I propose, for the calm consideration of all sober-minded men, the following serious questions:

1. Can you name one godly minister, of any denomination in all Scotland, who does not hold the duty of the entire sanctification of the Lord's Day?

2. Did you ever meet with a lively believer in any country under heaven, one who loved Christ, and lived a holy life, who did not delight in keeping holy to God the entire Lord's Day?

3. Is it wise to take the interpretation of God's will concerning the Lord's Day from 'men of the world', from infidels, scoffers, men of unholy lives, men who are sand-blind in all divine things, men who are the enemies of all righteousness, who quote Scripture freely, as Satan did, to deceive and betray?

4. If, in opposition to the uniform testimony of God's wisest and holiest servants, against the plain warnings of God's Word, against the very words of your catechism, learned beside your mother's knee, and against the voice of your outraged conscience, you join the ranks of the Sabbath-breakers, will not this be a sin against light, will it not lie heavy on your soul upon your death-bed, will it not meet you in the Judgement day?

Praying that these words of truth and soberness may be owned of God and carried home to your hearts with Divine power.

18th December, 1841.

8. Thy Spirit is good, lead me (Psalm 143:10)

For we are the circumcision, which worship God in the spirit, and rejoice in Christ Jesus, and have no confidence in the flesh. Though I might also have confidence in the flesh. If any other man thinketh that he hath whereof he might trust in the flesh, I more: (Phil. 3:3-4).

Teach me to do thy will; for thou *art* my God: thy spirit *is* good; lead me into the land of uprightness (Ps. 143:10).

Some children of God have this Word fulfilled in their experience, 'I will extend peace unto her as a river.' Their peace is calm, deep, constant. It is like the sleep of a little child. Some again there are whose peace doth more resemble a boat upon the sea, at one time lifted high on the swelling wave, again sinking into the very depths.

The peace which David had was of this last kind. In this psalm he was in the depths. The devil had seduced him into sin and darkness (see verse 3). But though a believer falls into the depths, he cannot rest there, he cries for two things:

1. *For new pardon* (verses 7 and 8), 'Hide not thy face'; 'Cause me to hear thy lovingkindness.'

2. *For new holiness*, 'Teach me'; 'Lead me'.

Three things: (1) The goodness of God's Spirit; (2) Show that that is a reason for the believer to cry, Lead me, or, Therefore he is a good guide; (3) How far will he guide?

1. The goodness of God's Spirit: 'Thy Spirit is good.'

1. Because he is God's Spirit

'Thy Spirit'. He is the Spirit that is one with the Father and with the Son. 'There are three persons in the Godhead.' Now everything that is good in the Father and the Son belongs to the Spirit also, for he is one with them. It often happens that three intimate friends are entirely of one mind in some matter; they walk out together and meet with something that moves their compassion. The same feeling flows through the heart of each but, ah, this is nothing like the oneness of Father, Son and Holy Spirit, they are really and truly one. The compassion which beats in the heart of the Father is the very same feeling, not similar, but the same feeling that beats in the heart of the Son and Holy Ghost. It is not like sympathy among friends which runs from one bottle to another, but it is like the pulse in the human body, the pulse that beats at the arm is the very same that beats at the heart. The love of the Father is the same love as that of the Son and Spirit, for Father, Son and Spirit are one God. I cannot explain to you how this is, I can only show you that so it is.

If you knew the feeling of one, you know the feeling of all. Do you read that God the Father so loved the world? Well, you may be sure the same love was in the hearts of Son and Spirit. Do you read of Christ's compassion on the multitude? Well, you may be sure that this is the very heart of Father and Holy Ghost. 'Have I been so long time with you and yet hast thou not seen me Philip? He that hath seen me hath seen the Father.' When you see Christ, he is the brightness of the Father's glory and the express image of his person. In him dwelt all the fullness of the Godhead bodily.

When the Father is good, then so is the Spirit. Is the Son good and gracious, then so is the Spirit.

Some people say, 'I have no fear of Christ. I think I could sit at his feet but I fear the Father.' How foolish this is. 'I and my Father are one.' Some again say, 'Ah, I remember how compassionate Christ was to sinners, but I fear the Holy Ghost is not so.' How foolish! He is the Spirit of Christ, essentially one with him. Everything that was in the heart of Christ is in the heart of the Spirit: the same infinite everlasting compassion. 'Thy Spirit is good.'

2. From his names

(a) The Oil of Gladness
Psalm 45:7: 'Thou lovest righteousness, and hatest wickedness: therefore God, thy God, hath anointed thee with the oil of gladness above thy fellows.'

The oil was fragrant, being made up of many sweet spices, 'of myrrh and sweet cinnamon and sweet calamus and cassia and oil olive'. Ah, so is the Spirit, he is fragrant oil to the soul. Oh, if you have ever been anointed you will say, 'Thy Spirit is good.'

The oil was put on Aaron and his sons but not on a stranger. It was too precious to be wasted. So is the good Spirit.

He is the oil of gladness. Oil was used at feasts. So when the soul is feasting upon Christ, satisfied with his goodness, that holy oil of gladness is formed upon the soul. Dear brethren, do not live without this good Spirit.

(b) The Dew
'I will be as the dew unto Israel.' What is more lovely than the dew? How sweet and refreshing is the dew to the thirsty ground. Every green thing is revived by it. It comes when the earth is calm and still, it comes regularly, silently, unseen. Such is the Spirit of God. He comes on the soul when the soul is brought to rest in Christ. He comes silently on feet unseen and yet receives and refreshes the whole soul. Oh, how good a Spirit must he be who is like the dew unto Israel.

(c) The Wind: 'Awake, oh, north wind; and come, thou south' (Song 4:16), such is the Spirit of God.
First, the wind blows with keen and biting blast, stiffening the twigs with frost and breaking them in pieces. Then does it move in

the gentle summer gale, soft and balmy, breathing on flower and tree, making the green leaves to burst out and the blossoms to smile on the fruit trees. Such is the good Spirit, keen and awakening, when he convinces of sin. Balmy and comforting when he leads to Christ. Surely, thy Spirit is good.

(d) Comforter

Ah, this is his truest and sweetest name and it shows he is altogether good. Oh, my dear friends, I fear we have little interest in Jesus Christ if this name, the Comforter, does not fill our soul with unspeakable joy. He is called the Comforter:

Because it is he who leads the soul to a saving close with Christ, to rest upon him with a calm, childlike repose.

Because it is he who restores the soul, bringing us back to comfort and peace when we have lost it.

Thus Edwards, that holy one, says, 'Those words, "The Comforter," seemed to me, as it were, immensely great enough to fill heaven and earth.'

Have you ever been taught by the Spirit? Brought to Christ and comforted? Have you been lifted up by him into the presence of God, above the cares and sorrows of this world? Ah, then say you, 'Thy Spirit is good.' Most know it not. Ah, my friends, many of you think it comfort to have a nice home and health and troops of friends and money enough to last. But no, this is not true comfort. If the Spirit does not dwell within you, you have not a drop of true comfort in your lot and, ah, what will the end be of you that does not obey the gospel? There is no comfort in hell.

3. Good from what he does for the soul

Believer, what has he done for your soul?

(a) He awakened you

You were easy and happy in your sins, thinking that all was well with you when you were just perishing. The Spirit came uninvited by you, he fixed an arrow of conviction in your heart, you struggled but could not pull it out. He convinced you of sin.

What more has he done for you?

(b) He led me to Christ

I was going fast to hell, seeking rest and finding none. He took me to the cross of Christ and showed me the great surety and with that blood healed all my wounds.

What more?

(c) He dwells in me

The water that Christ hath given me is within me a well of living water springing up into everlasting life. Dear brethren, do you know this? How often he must be grieved. Just think if the Spirit of God dwells in you, how many polluting thoughts do you every day make to pass close beside him? Out of the very heart where he dwells, and yet he abides for ever. Often grieved he is driven away, only to return. Like the dove, when frightened from its nest, flies away only to return again. What a long-suffering Spirit he is! Let to your soul that this is true, 'Thy Spirit is good.'

2. Since the Spirit is good we should say, 'Lead me.'

1. A soul brought to Christ

That soul needs to be led. When a young believer comes first to know the Lord, he thinks, 'Oh, I shall be able now to run in the way of his commandments.' He is often ashamed to find that he is still weak and foolish, he is a child and needs to be taken by the hand. He feels blind, he needs to be led, he cries out, 'Lead me!'

A word to some: some of you are disheartened because you feel so much need of help. 'I am like a helpless child,' one cries. 'I am like a sheep that needs to be carried,' another cries. 'I am like a blind man that needs to be led,' a third cries. Do not be downcast. This is the very state of God's children. Teach me to do thy will. Uphold me by thy free Spirit. Lead me to the land of Uprightness. The Psalms are filled with cries for help.

A word to some who do not feel they need leading. Some feel no fear in the world. Some go boldly into places of temptation, you do not feel blind and helpless. Some of you began this day without seeking his leading Spirit. Ah, you have not the spot of God's children. You are none of his.

2. The Spirit is a good guide

This is the very argument. Since the Spirit is so good he will be able and willing to lead me. If you are walking in a hilly country it is of great consequence to have a good guide:

a. Wise: he that knows every track and footpath; knows every rock and precipice; every refreshing fountain. He knows all things.

b. Kind: one who will consider how you can walk, who will patiently sit by you when you are weary, hold you up when you are falling. Ah, such is the Holy Spirit. He is a wise and tender guide, infinitely tender and compassionate, even as Christ was.

c. He is within the soul: all other guides are without but he dwelleth in you and shall be with you. If a Christian friend, one more advanced in grace than yourself, were always to stay in the house with you, how often you would consult him, how much you would lean upon his advice. Oh, foolish and slow of heart to believe. There is a surer guide, far nearer, within you. Oh, how much unbelief there is in every heart. How much readier you are to believe a friend on earth, flesh and blood and bones, than the indwelling Friend whom no man hath seen or can see. Oh, how little difference between us and the world. They receive him not because they see him not.

Awake dear friends: lean on him the whole weight of your sanctification. Trust to his Word, go forward trusting in him.

Pray to him. There is no trust in the heart if no prayer in the heart, if no prayer on the lips. Your soul does not lean on him if your knee does not bend to him. He will be enquired of. Pray without ceasing, be instant in prayer. Say, 'Thy Spirit is good, lead me.'

3. How far will he guide the soul? 'Into the land of Uprightness.'

1. He will lead us to the end

There never comes a time in the life of a believer when he can do without having God. He is as helpless the last day of his life as the first. In truth, the true growth in grace is to grow in a sense of our weakness and to rest all on him.

(a) The Shepherd carried the sheep that he found all the way to home.

(b) God promises: 'Even to your old age am I he and even to hoar hairs will I carry you. I have made and I will bear. Even I will carry and will deliver you.' When carrying a stone to a building it needs to

be carried as much at the end of the way as at the beginning. Dear friends, remember the promise, 'He shall abide with you for ever.' Believe it and plead it. 'Lead me into the land of Uprightness.'

2. He will lead us into heaven

There are many bright lands in this fallen world. There is India with its cinnamon groves and palmy plains. There are the Islands of the South Sea, those gems of the ocean guarded by coral strands. There are scenes which seem almost unaffected by the fall, where spring and summer always reign, but where is the land of Uprightness? Ah, it is not here. Here sin reigns and the more lovely the land the darker the sin. The fairest parishes of Scotland are withered and desolate. But there is a land where the inhabitants are all righteous; oh, what a glorious land it must be. There is no lying there, no swearing, no drunkenness, no pride, no luxury, no lust, the land of Uprightness.

Learn: To be led by the Spirit or you will never end there. If any man have not the Spirit of Christ he is none of his.

Learn: To pray for that land and to pray, 'Lead me into the land of [uprightness].' When sea-sick persons arrive on shore, in a moment they are well. So shall it be.

9. Fast day Sermon (Isaiah 22:12-14)

And in that day did the Lord GOD of hosts call to weeping, and to mourning, and to baldness, and to girding with sackcloth: And behold, joy and gladness, slaying oxen, and killing sheep, eating flesh, and drinking wine: let us eat and drink; for to morrow we shall die. And it was revealed in mine ears by the LORD of hosts, Surely this iniquity shall not be purged from you till ye die, saith the Lord GOD of hosts.

1. There are times when God calls to weeping

1. Times of public calamity as this described in verse 5 of this chapter.
2. Times of public sin calling down the anger of God.

2. Sinful man in such times betake themselves to carnal mirth

3. This is a sin unpardonable. It is resisting the strongest means of grace. If affliction opens not the heart, nothing will.

1. The day here spoken of: a day of calamity, partly threatened and partly executed.

2. The duty suitable for such a time: weeping, humbling ourselves before God.

3. Who calls thereto the Lord God: it is not the cry of ministers, prophets, but of God himself.

4. How natural hearts hear this call: behold they cast contempt on all God's threatenings, they are at ease in Zion.

5. God's awful determination: never to pardon it.

a) Observe the manner, 'it was revealed in mine ear.' God does not proclaim his judgements. His most awful judgements are secret, unheard, unseen, like the blasting mildew; like the secret oncoming of disease.

b) The maker of it. An unpardonable sin. Many ask, what is the unpardonable sin? Here it is.

Doctrine: In time of threatened calamity God calls to humbling of ourselves before God. There are times when God calls.

1. When we are under the stroke of God's hand

So it was with Jerusalem at this time and you see God explained his own providence. So with Nehemiah, when he heard of the ruined state of Jerusalem (Neh. 1:1-4). So David, for the death of Saul and Jonathan (2 Sam. 1). It was not for this reason that this day has been set apart. Our church has never been in a more prosperous condition for two years. The pestilence has been mended from our shores. God has smiled upon the labours of the farmers. Yet we are under some strokes of God's hand.

This town in special manner has been veiled by commercial distress. Poverty is one of the secret curses that God sends. It lies heavy on us. Even for that, it becomes us to mourn and lie in the dust. It has been a rejection of our fast, that our people are poor and cannot afford a day from their work. I answer that very penalty is a call to set apart a season for humbling – and God may lift away the stroke. To speak plainly, dear friends, I have no confidence in poor laws or any change in our laws benefiting the poor, as long as we lie under God's displeasure.

To families in affliction. Afflicting time is humbling time. God calls you to consider your ways. Oh if you will not listen in a time of trouble, when will you listen? God may say, 'I will never forgive you.'

2. When we are under threatenings of God

So it was with Nineveh (Jonah 3). Yet forty days. Oh the mercy of God. He would not destroy them without forty days warning.

So with Ahab (1 Kings 21:27).

So with David (2 Sam. 12:15,16), when God threatened to take away his child.

It is for this reason God calls you this day to weeping and mourning.

You know the danger with which our church is threatened. We have declared that it is a fundamental law of our church that no pastor be intended on any parish contrary to the Christian people. For since 1834 the civil courts have commended us to ordain in the face of this resolution. They have even forbidden us to preach the gospel within a certain district of our country. We have laid our wrongs before the legislature of the country. Still no redress appears for us. How it will end no one can tell. The two dangers are these:

1. That the health of some may faint in the struggle, that they may cease to contend for the crown.

2. That the government may declare that it shall be the law of the land that pastors be dismissed. In this case there may be, as there was over in England, multitudes of the best ministers set adrift. You may lose your pastor in a single day. In Edinburgh, out of her thirty-four ministers, I suppose not more than six would remain. In Glasgow out of forty, I suppose not so many as six. In your own town, I suppose no more than three. To many I know this appears no calamity, but in the light of eternity it would be a heavy stroke on Scotland. I know that the sensual and political ministers and lovers of this world would like to see the clear riddance of our faithful ministers.

God is calling you to humble yourselves before the threatened stroke and then maybe he will repent of the evil and do it not.

Dear friends, I do call upon you to lie low before God, maybe he will repent him of the evil.

3. When under sin

We have the case of Israel (1 Sam. 12:6).

We have the blessing on the men that sigh and cry (Ezek. 9:4).

We have God's command (James 4:8).

1. Sins of Christians

1. *Great neglect of holiness.* God hath chosen us to be holy. Christ gave himself for our sins that he might redeem us from this present evil world. Yet it is to be feared there is much more enjoyment than holiness, much more taking pleasure in meetings and sermons than in studying a holy calling.

(a) Neglect of secret communion with God.

(b) Spiritual pride, or

(c) Shame of the gospel. Concealing the cross. When the Roman Catholic priests went to China, it is said they began by converting a great many things, so that they became more Chinese than the Chinese Christians; so with many. By reason of this the land mourns.

(d) So little of making it the first thing to get on in the divine life.

2. Great neglect of others

(a) In our own town, I suppose there are at the least 15,000 still living in practical heathenism without having a pastor to look after them. I bless God that there are two new churches nearly ready to be opened and trust all God's children will pray that we may get pastors after God's own heart. Still, what are these among so many? I do wonder that Christians who have money can live at ease and see these multitudes going down. It is a crying sin.

(b) Newspaper, the Press. The newspaper is one of the most extraordinary channels, either of good or evil. Those of you who know the state of the press in Scotland know that it is, at present, one of Satan's prime channels of diffusing poison. Is there a scheme of Popery to be set afoot? The Press will defend it. Is there a scheme of Christian philanthropy? The Press will besmear it with slanders. Is there a faithful servant of Christ, labouring night and day to win souls? The Newspaper will join with Satan in spitting on him, and do unspeakable harm. Some Christian people will feast upon these sweet morsels and behave as those blood hounds.

Some Christian men proposed in this town to wrest this weapon from Satan's hand, to set agoing a newspaper that should plead Christ's cause. What speed did it come? There was not found Christian liberality to support it.

2. Sins Of World

Sabbath Breaking

1. How many profane it by idleness, lounging or wandering or sleeping? How many when I think that they cannot blush?

2. Day of business. Merchant summing up his accounts, writing letters, reading newspapers rather than [doing] works of mercy. Buying and selling. Ale houses are selling spirits on the Lord's day.

3. Day Of Pleasure. A day of showing dress. A day of meeting worldly or loose companions. Oh, young people, beware despising the Gospel in such a time as this. You have passed through a remarkable time. Then, there was a time when there was a solemn awe before you. Ah, I fear you have trampled it. Come, lie in the dust, else then it will not be forgiven.

7 May, 1840.

10. The Highway of the Redeemed (Isaiah 35:8-10)

And an highway shall be there, and a way, and it shall be called The way of holiness; the unclean shall not pass over it; but it *shall be* for those: the wayfaring men, though fools, shall not *err therein*. No lion shall be there, nor *any* ravenous beast shall go up thereon, it shall not be found there; but the redeemed shall walk *there*: And the ransomed of the LORD shall return, and come to Zion with songs and everlasting joy upon their heads: they shall obtain joy and gladness, and sorrow and sighing shall flee away.

It seems to be the universal testimony of Scripture that the Jews who are at this day scattered among all nations shall yet be brought back to their own land. Though they have been sifted among all nations as corn is sifted in a sieve, yet the least grain shall not fall to the earth. In the 50th chapter of Jeremiah we are told expressly that the days are coming when 'the children of Israel shall come, they and the children of Judah together, going and weeping they shall go to seek the LORD their God. They shall ask the way to Zion with their faces thitherward saying, "Come and let us join ourselves to the LORD in the perpetual covenant never to be forgotten." '

That passage plainly refers to the time when God shall pour out a spirit of anxiety and of earnestness upon the Jews, when they shall look to him whom they pierced and mourn; when they shall anxiously ask the way to their native Zion with their faces thitherward; when they shall say one to another, 'Come and let us join ourselves to the Lord, to our crucified Lord, so that we may be one with him in the perpetual covenant that is not to be forgotten.' Now, it appears to me that the passage before us is also spoken of God's ancient people, and that it just fits into that passage of Jeremiah.

The passage before us is spoken of these same Jews when the time of *their weeping is past*; when they *have found* the way to Zion; when *they have joined* themselves to Christ as his body in the gospel covenant; and where they are now advancing, the ransomed people of the Lord, toward their beloved Zion. The joy that is in their hearts tingles all nature with liveliness. The wilderness seems to blossom as the rose, and to rejoice with joy and singing. The glory of their native mountains of Lebanon and Carmel and Sharon seem to be imparted to every land through which they travel. The weak hands and feeble knees become strong for the journey, those who have been so long blind have their eyes opened, the deaf hear, the lame man leaps as an hart, and the tongue of those who have been dumb sings the praises of Jesus. The very desert that surrounds their native land appears fresh and verdant, grass and reeds and rushes, and there is, as it were, a highway opened up to them, a way for the redeemed alone to walk on, a plain and safe and joyful way, so that they come to Zion with songs and everlasting joy upon their heads.

Now, though we cannot but agree with those who understand these passages in their literal sense, as intimating a true and real return of the Jews to Jerusalem yet to be brought to pass (a return for which the house of Israel with all their blindness yet pray continually and for which providence seems in many ways to be opening the door), yet we do at the same time regard them as affording a true and accurate description of the way in which every awakened soul is brought nigh unto God. And just as a discerning traveller after having passed through a country is able to recognise in the map the very turnings and windings of the road by which he has travelled, so those of you who have been awakened by God and made justified and sanctified men, walking toward the heavenly Jerusalem, will be able to mark not only the very road by which you have been led, but the very road on which you are walking, in the Bible map of the believer's journey to Zion.

If, then, you regard the passage in Jeremiah as a description of the way in which God awakens the soul and leads it to close with Christ, you must regard this passage in Isaiah as a description of the way in which God leads the soul that has already joined itself to Christ in the perpetual covenant, leads it on to the heavenly Jerusalem. In the first passage accordingly, we have weeping, anxious asking, and resolving. In the second we have walking in holiness, in a plain path, in safety and with songs and everlasting joy.

Let us shortly consider this highway of the redeemed then as the way by which God leads all covenanted believers, who have joined themselves to the Lord, to the heavenly Jerusalem.

1. It is a way of holiness: 'And an highway shall be there and a way and it shall be called *the way of holiness*, the unclean shall not pass over it' (verse 8).

As long as the Jews remain scattered among the nations they remain an unholy people, given up as they are this day to all the vices of the natural heart, but especially guile and covetousness. But when God shall awaken them and bring them weeping and anxious when they join themselves to Christ, then shall they go toward Zion a holy company. As they have been remarkable among the nations in their hardness and unholiness, the way they will go upon shall be called the way of holiness. And so it is with every soul.

As long as a man is out of Christ he never can walk in the way of holiness; a Christless soul must be a vicious soul. I appeal to those of you who are wholly unawakened; who are living quite secure in the world; who never felt one throb, never shed one tear of anxiety for your soul; is your way a way of holiness? Alas, to what does your life bear witness? If I could lift the curtain and paint every one of your characters in its true colours, oh, what a scene of pollution would we not behold. It is true we would find every one of you taking a different road and excelling in one wise, another in another, but would not every one of the ways be away from God and from holiness? The path of the just is as the shining light that shineth more and more unto the perfect day. But your path is as darkness that grows deeper and deeper till it reaches the pitchy blackness of midnight.

A Christless soul can never be a holy soul. I appeal to those of you who have been awakened; who have gone weeping as you go to seek the Lord your God; who are this day asking the way to Zion with your faces thitherward, but who have never yet joined yourselves to the Lord in the perpetual covenant. I appeal to you, is your way a way of holiness? Alas, you know and feel it is not. Your anxiety has made you cast off your outward sins and flee perhaps from your sinful companions, but are you not just as far as ever from the way of holiness? Your heart is broken with terror and yet you are as much the slave of sin as ever. Ah, my friend, how do you not discover the secret? Though you have been made anxious you have never yet consented to join yourself to Christ. You are yet Christless, and a Christless soul must evermore be a sinful soul.

But when a man is brought not only to be anxious about his soul but truly to unite himself to Christ, to receive the Lord Jesus and become one with him, then the covenant itself ensures that he shall walk in the way of holiness. That man is no longer left to grovel amid the miry pollutions and the everyday passions of the sinful world, he is lifted as it were on to a highway, and that way is the way of holiness. It is true he is not taken out of the world and yet he is lifted above the world while he is in it. He sits with Christ in heavenly places. The Spirit enlarges his heart and he runs in the way of God's commandments. If any be in Christ Jesus he must become a new creature. Sin cannot reign in his mortal body. Sin cannot have the dominion over him. It is impossible it ever should. It is true we do not step into perfect holiness by believing in Jesus; imperfections remain in the most advanced believer, as clouds may be seen in the clearest sky. But still the difference between a soul in Christ and a soul out of Christ in respect of holiness is as great as the difference between light and darkness. Daylight is always daylight, however much clouds may obscure it, even from the first streaks of the eastern sky; and the holiness of a believer will always be manifest and always growing, unto the perfect day.

Oh, then what shall we say of you, those of you who have no holiness but who are daily growing more hardened and sinful? You, whose daily vices cry aloud to heaven? You are on a highway indeed but it is the broad way that leadeth to destruction. You have no love to Jesus; no walking in his steps. You may be anxious for your souls, you may be weeping as you go, you may be asking, but certain it is you are not yet joined to Christ. This only will I say, you are not yet redeemed, you are yet unsaved. You are yet within reach of hell.

2. The way of the redeemed is a plain and simple way: 'The wayfaring men, though fools, shall not err therein.'

When the Jews are first awakened by God it is said, 'they shall ask the way to Zion with their faces thitherward.' Now this plainly implies that they are in doubt and perplexity as to the road, for no one would ask the way if he were not in doubt about it. But when they really join themselves to Christ and become his redeemed, his covenanted people, how strangely is the case altered with them. All their perplexity as to the right way is gone, the highway is so plain that these wayfaring men, even of the simplest of them, cannot err therein. Just so it is with every converted soul.

As long as a man is out of Christ, the way to heaven is full of perplexities and contradictions. I appeal to all unawakened souls, does not the Bible appear full of things you cannot understand? At one time does it not cast contempt on all your good works and honesties and uprightness, and in another place demand them? Does not Paul say in one place that he wants to be found in the Judgement *not having his own righteousness* but Christ's, and yet does he not say that *without holiness no man shall see the Lord?* Oh, what a world of contradictions does this Bible contain to your mind. A Christless soul must evermore be a soul without spiritual understanding. I appeal to you, awakened souls, who have been made anxious, yet have never put on Christ, is not the Bible way of salvation quite incomprehensible to you? You cannot but be anxious, for you feel that your souls are in danger, but still how are you confused and puzzled about the way of salvation, by the imputed righteousness of Jesus. How often do you ask the questions, What is it to believe? What is it to join myself to Christ? How can I become one with him? Ah, how does this prove that a Christless soul must evermore be a darkened soul. The reason why you are puzzled is a heart reason: you are proud and self-righteous; you do not wish to despair of saving yourself; and therefore you have not a heart to rest on Christ alone.

But when a man is truly emptied of self-righteousness and puts on the Lord Jesus, oh, how plain is the whole way to heaven. A wayfaring man though a fool could not err in it.

1. The way of justification becomes plain to him. Having once tasted the blessedness of being reconciled unto God by imputed righteousness, his heart evermore chooses this way of standing accepted before God, and he abides in Christ even unto death.

2. The way of sanctification becomes plain to him because the Spirit works in him to will and do according to God's good pleasure. The unconverted are always in the dark as to what is sin and what is holiness; they put sweet for bitter and bitter for sweet – but not so the redeemed believer. It is all a plain way, for it is the way in which his heart leads him. Being loved much he loves much, and love is the fulfilling of the law. Love works no sin against God and no ill to his neighbour. A child that loves its mother is often an obedient child before it has much judgement. Affection guides it swiftly and surely to do those things which are pleasing in the eyes of its parent. And just so the believer, reconciled to his Father, loves and therefore easily obeys.

Love is the best decider of casuistry. It is like the needle pointing to the north. Men without a compass may guess which is north and which is south, sometimes right, sometimes wrong, but he that hath the needle can say where is north. So love always points to God and doth his will. The believer loves Jesus and therefore the way of holiness is a plain one to him. Ah, my friends, it needs not learning or deep wisdom to be saved; not many wise men, not many noble are called.

The poor cottage believer who through a life of four-score years scarcely travelled beyond her native parish, who possessed not the faculties that lifted the statesman to the world's admiration, whose learning was all comprised within the boards of her Bible; that poor believer, united to Jesus by a simple faith, found the way of holiness a plain path in which she could not err. The questions as to right and wrong, which puzzle and confound the politicians of this world, gave her not a moment's hesitation. She loved the Saviour and therefore heard a voice behind her, 'This is the way, walk in it'; and now she this day finds, while she stands perfect before the throne, that God's promise is true. The wayfaring man though a fool shall not err therein.

Ah, my friends, if you find yourself often at a loss, which way to go, whether to go with the world in this or whether to turn from them in that; if the way of duty be dark and confused; if you want [lack] the quick discernment of one who loves, then how plain is it that something is wrong. You are not abiding in Christ. You are not joined to him in the covenant, you are not led by the Spirit, you are none of his.

3. The way of the redeemed is a safe way: 'No lion shall be there.'
When God brought in the Jews into the land of promise, one part of
the covenant which God made with them was that, if they would
keep his statutes and do them, he would rid evil beasts out of the
land, for the banks of the Jordan were often infested by the lion and
other ravenous beasts of prey. And accordingly, when he brings back
his ransomed people to their own land he renews his promise, that no
lion shall be there nor any ravenous beast go up thereon. Or if these
words be understood figuratively, it may be understood of the restraint
which is to be laid upon Satan in these happy days when he is to be
bound up for a season from deceiving the nations. In whatever way
you may understand it, it is true also of the covenant believer in
Jesus. Of his heavenward walk of holiness it may truly be said that
no lion shall be there, neither shall any ravenous beast go up
thereupon. As long as men are out of Christ, their souls are exposed
to the fierce ravages of all enemies. It is so with the unawakened:
wild passions, like furious beasts amid the jungles of this world, and
every ravenous affection may seize upon them. And Satan, the great
lion, worketh in them, for they are the children of disobedience. Is it
not so, my friends, with you? And there is positively no crime,
however horrible, that he is not able to work in them to do.

Your experience, those of you who are unawakened. How many
strange and monstrous sins have you been hurried into which in your
days of comparative innocence you never dreamed it possible you
could have committed? How often do wild and ravenous passions
seize upon your soul and hurry you away to rashless gratification of
them, regardless of consequences like the way of brutes that perish?
Ah, my friends, how plain it is that Satan, that great lion, has you in
his embrace, and you are far away from the highway of the redeemed.

They are delivered from the ravages of all enemies, they are lifted
above the power both of Satan and of wicked men. You must not
understand me as if I meant that the believer in Jesus has no enemies.
On the contrary, I believe it is never till then that he finds out that he
hath enemies and these on every hand of him, without and within.
Then it is that his passions within appear like terrible lions, and the
world's temptations and frowns are both hateful and terrible, and
then Satan the great lion is for the first time felt to be an enemy too
much for flesh and blood.

But here is the wonderful fulfilment of the Word of God, that even when their enemies are most numerous and terrible, they are raised high above them all. Even when they go through the jungles, the very haunt of the lions and every ravenous beast, even then they are lifted on a highway above all their terror.

It is true they often hear the roaring of the great lion and that makes them cleave closer to Christ, their guide through the wilderness. And then they are safe and high above their enemy. It is true that Satan often desires them that he may sift them as wheat, but Christ prays for them that their faith fail not; and even though they fall like Peter, yet the Saviour's prayer prevails and soon they regain the highway.

It is true the world frowns and laughs at them; they try to frighten or they try to shake them, for all that will live godly must suffer persecution. But it is just as true that the covenant believer is lifted high above the outcry of this lower world. He walks on the highway above the wilderness and as long as he is kept walking there he needs fear no evil, for no lion is there, neither can any ravenous beast go up thereupon. Ah, my believing friends, this is the way on which you walk. Take courage then and go forward. No lion ever yet crossed the path of faith. It is when you leave the highway for the jungle that you fall among lions. Keep on, then, abiding in Christ till you come to the heavenly Jerusalem where your present safety shall be perfected, for they neither hurt nor destroy in all my holy mountain, saith the Lord.

4. And lastly, **The way of the redeemed is a way of joy and leads to joy**

When Israel dwelt in their own land, God ordained that all the males should come up to Jerusalem three times every year to the three grand festivals: The Passover; the Feast of Pentecost or First-Fruits; and the Feast of Tabernacles. On these occasions, especially in the last, they used to come up from the country in bands or caravans and as they approached Jerusalem they sung psalms and carried the branches of palm trees with great joy. The passage before us is plainly a reference to that joyous festival. As long as the Jews are scattered among the heathen they no more go up to Mount Zion with palm branches and their mouths crying 'Hosanna'. But when God brings back the captivity of his people, they shall return and come to Zion with songs and everlasting joy upon their heads, they shall obtain joy and gladness, and sorrow and crying shall flee away. (And just so it is with every soul.)

As long as you are unawakened, you have none of these songs nor this everlasting joy. You have your songs and your merriment and we never will deal so falsely with you as to say that there is no pleasure in sin. There is great pleasure in sin, as every sinner knows. If there were no pleasure in it you would soon give it up. But it hath its pains too – the pleasures of sin are but for a season and then the pleasures of sin end in the pains of hell.

Whatever thing it is your earthly mind takes joy in, it is a joy that death shall sweep away, that judgement shall turn into gall and wormwood or the worm that never dies. But the ransomed people of Christ come to Zion with songs and everlasting joy upon their heads.

1. With songs
It is an unfailing mark of the children of God that they love to sing the praises of him who hath called them out of darkness into marvellous light, and the nearer they approach to their heavenly Zion the more do they abound in praises and love to sing the new song which none but the redeemed can sing. How then can you be among the number of God's people if you can bear to sing the praises of men or of sin but have no habitual joy in singing praises to your God? From the uttermost part of the earth may be heard songs even of glory to the Righteous One, whether it be amid the snowy Alps, in the plains of Hindustan, or the icy wilderness of Greenland. The people of Jerusalem cannot but sing the praises of Jerusalem. Is it true then that the walls of your dwelling never echo the praises of your Redeemer? Whether sung in solitude or borne to heaven from kindred bosoms, how plain then that you are not walking on the highway of the redeemed.

2. With everlasting joy upon their heads
Christ's covenant people have all the sorrows that other men have. They weep over buried friends and ruined fortunes. Yea they have sorrows which other men have not, fightings without and fears within. And yet they have a joy which other men have not, all other joys are temporary fading joys. Alas, many of you feel deeply that the most innocent joys of the world cannot last. But the believer has everlasting joy upon his head. His sins are pardoned, that begins an everlasting

joy. His stony heart is taken out and a heart of flesh put in, that too begins a joy that shall never end.

He has a burden taken off his back and therefore his step is light and cheerful. He has the Spirit of God dwelling in him and walking with him, and therefore his feet are made like hind's feet, his heart is enlarged and runs in the way of God's commandments. These ways are ways of pleasantness and all his paths are peace till, his race being run, the highway ends in the new Jerusalem. He obtains joy and gladness, and sorrow and sighing flee away.

Ah, my friends, do you remember that man who said, 'Either this is not Christianity or we are not Christians.' Oh, if you know nothing of this joy, in the pardon of sin and the new heart, then you know nothing of the highway of the redeemed. And you shall know nothing of the heaven of the redeemed.

Preached in Larbert, 26 June 1836;
Preached in Dunipace, 3 July 1836;
Preached in St. Peter's

11. The Words and Ministry of Christ (Isaiah 50:4)

The Lord GOD hath given me the tongue of the learned, that I should know how to speak a word in season to *him that is* weary: he wakeneth morning by morning, he wakeneth mine ear to hear as the learned.

These words are plainly intended to be the words of our Lord and Saviour Jesus Christ. This is evident from verse 6: 'I gave my back to the smiters, and my cheeks to them that plucked off the hair: I hid not my face from shame and spitting.' These words were written 700 years before he came into the world and yet even then it was declared that

1. His speech would be soothing to all distressed consciences.

2. Even from of old it was the main part of the character of Christ that he should bind up the broken-hearted.

3. That he should bring glad tidings for those that are alarmed about their soul.

4. That his Word should be, 'The LORD God hath given me the tongue of the learned, that I should know how to speak a word in season to him that is weary.'

The good news which Christ brings is here called a word in season. A word in season is a suitable word, a word which just answers a person's need. A word of mirth in a time of sorrow is not a word in season. Jesting is not convenient then. As vinegar upon wounds so is he that singeth songs to a heavy heart. It does not agree. It is like the meeting of two discordant colours which do not match and which is painful to the eye. It is like the meeting of two discordant notes which do not make melody but which jar upon the ear. It is like the meeting of two opposite elements, as fire and water, which produces mess and commotion. Just such is an unseasonable word. 'But a word spoken in due season, behold how good is it!'

Now, Christ's words to weary souls are all seasonable words. His voice is the true melody to a heavy heart. When he says to the soul, 'Let there be light,' then no man can say, 'Let there be darkness.' When he says to the heart, 'Be of good cheer,' then no man can take away our joy. When he says, 'Peace be unto you,' then no man can take that peace away.

Doctrine: All weary souls may find seasonable relief in Christ.

1. Some souls are weary with the fears of God's wrath; these may find seasonable relief in Christ.

Most people are not weary about their souls. They are often weary with a long journey or with a hard day's work or they are weary of the quietness of a long Sabbath day. All this is a natural weariness, quite common among all natural men. But weariness from fear of God's wrath is a supernatural weariness. It is a work of God upon the heart. Most men know nothing of it. Most men have got the smiting of the natural conscience when they do anything openly wicked. Most men have got sudden dartings of terror about death and judgement and eternity in their sober moments.

But, oh, that is not to be weary of the wrath of God. When a man carries a great load a long way and finds that he cannot get rid of it, then he is weary. When a man travels far under a scorching sun and cannot find shelter from its burning heat, then he is weary. Just so when a man finds that the wrath of God is a burden lying on him too heavy to bear, when he finds that he is carrying it by night and by day without rest or intermission, then that soul becomes weary. When a man finds that the wrath of God is beating on his head, that he is walking and talking and working and sleeping all under that burning, scorching wrath, ah, then he is weary. Now hear the Word of Christ: 'The LORD God hath given me the tongue of the learned, that I should know how to speak a word in season to him that is weary.'

Observe:
1. That Christ has got *the tongue of the learned* to enable him to speak peace to weary souls. All the learning of man is quite in vain to speak peace to weary souls. All the learning of schools and colleges, all the learning of books, is quite in vain. But Christ has got the learning of heaven. 'He is the alpha and the omega.' 'In him are hid all the treasures of wisdom and knowledge.' He has got the tongue of the learned. Therefore you may be quite sure that his words will be wise and prudent. You may be quite sure that the way he proposes peace will be the wisest and best.

2. *God has given him that tongue.* It is the anger of God that weary sinners are afraid of, and yet look here, God has given Christ the tongue of the learned to speak a word in season to weary souls. How plain then that God does not want any sinner to perish. The same God that is gathering clouds of vengeance has provided the hiding place from the wind. The same God who says, 'Vengeance is mine, I will repay,' says that he has given Christ the tongue of the learned to get weary sinners to flee from the wrath to come. How plain that God has no pleasure in you dying, and if you do perish it is not because God would have you perish but because you will not be lured by the silver voice of the Saviour. 'Come unto me, all ye that labour and are heavy laden, and I will give you rest.'

I would speak a word to weary souls
Some of you have been made weary of the wrath of God. You have wandered long under the burden too heavy for you to bear – and how you are weary. You have tried to find a shelter for your soul, but all in vain, and now you are weary. Well then, here is good news for you. 'The LORD God hath given me the tongue of the learned, that I should know how to speak a word in season to him that is weary.'

Objection 1: I am too weary to come to Christ.
Answer: You cannot be too weary. True, you have wandered a long lifetime in sin. True, you have dishonoured Christ by seeking other

saviours. But are you not all the more weary? If you are indeed quite wearied out with sin, if you are quite wearied out with your vain attempts to be your own saviour, this is the very reason why you should sit at the feet of Christ and learn of him. His Word is, 'Come unto me, all ye that labour.'

Objection 2: I have done all I could to flee from wrath and yet I am weary.

Answer: Have you fled to Christ? It is Christ only who has got the tongue of the learned. It is not the minister. It is not the Bible. It is the Saviour himself who speaks peace to weary souls.

Some distressed souls run to the minister and run to the Bible to find peace and when they do not find it they are disappointed and blame God as if he dealt badly by them. Now, it is quite right to make the most diligent use of means – ministers and Bible and Christian friends; but then you must fix your eye on Christ through them all. Remember he only can speak peace to a weary soul. Do not stop at the feet of a creature then, but sit like many at the feet of Christ.

I would speak a word to souls that were never weary with the wrath of God

You never felt that weariness about your soul, how plain then that you have never fled from the wrath to come. A work of grace has never been begun in your soul. Mary was weary and she sat down at the feet of Jesus. The jailer was trembling and weary and he listened joyfully to the tongue of the Saviour. The Ethiopian was weary and the word of Jesus was a word in season to his soul. But you were never weary, therefore you have never come to Christ.

Alas, poor souls, how weary will you be throughout eternity. Dear souls, let me carry your thoughts one hundred years forward. This controversy between me and you will then be at an end, and doubtless many who are this day hearing me quite at their ease will then be weary with feeling the wrath of God. Oh, when will this weary tossing have an end? Oh, when will this gnawing worm be done? Oh, when will this outer darkness pass away? How weary will you be of your pains! 'Oh, for a word in season now!' But no, there is no Saviour in hell. There are no [faithful] ministers there. No Bibles there. There is not one word to the weary there.

2. Some souls are weary with struggling against sin, these may find seasonable relief in Christ.

Most people have no weariness about sin because they do not struggle against it, they are willing captives.

1. I have heard of a man being so wretched and poor in this world as to commit a crime in order that he might be transported. Now, while they are loading such a man with irons and carrying him off to prison or carrying on board of ship, he does not feel the galling load of his chains, he does not feel weary. Why? Because he makes no resistance, he does it with all his heart, he is a willing captive. But put a burning desire of being free into his heart and there he is led captive against his will, then you will see how he will struggle and groan under his galling bonds. That is the man that is weary.

2. When a man is swimming down a river he is carried down by the current. It is easy to swim a great distance that way without the least weariness or fatigue. But when a man turns and tries to breast the current, when he struggles hard and makes no advance, then he is weary.

Now most people are willing captives, led captive by Satan at his will. They make no resistance. They go with all their heart, therefore they are not weary. Most people are swimming down the current, going with the world, walking according to the course of this world, therefore they feel no weariness.

But when God brings a soul to Christ, then that soul desires to be free from all sin, he desires to swim against the current of sin, he struggles hard and is weary. He tries to pray but his heart is like a stone, it is heavy and tending downwards. He tries to run but his heart is like a load of lead, he struggles hard to get rid of it. He makes vows and promises at the Sacrament table. But alas, a few weeks cannot pass till he sees all forgotten and broken. He is like one wrestling with a man stronger than himself, he cannot overcome him. He feels condemned to perpetual warfare and struggling and perhaps begins to repent of being a Christian. He is a weary soul indeed. Now hear the Word of Christ: 'The Lord God hath given me the tongue of the learned, that I should know how to speak a word in season to him that is weary.'

(a) Observe, Christ has the tongue of the learned. All the learning of man is wholly vain to give relief to this weary soul. Some would tell

him of the beauty of virtue, of its advantage and respectability. Some will tell him prudent maxims and worldly considerations. But these will not comfort the soul that is weary of a sinful heart. Christ has divine wisdom so that you may be quite sure his plan of holiness will be a sufficient one.

(b) God gave him this tongue. God does not wish any to live in sin. This is the will of God even your sanctification. No weary soul can blame God then; he wants you to come to Christ, that you walk in pleasantness and peace.

I would speak a word to the weary with sin
Are you weary struggling with a wicked heart?

1. Be of good cheer, Christ speaks this word to you, 'Arise, the Master calleth thee.'
Go to him and say, like little Samuel, 'Speak, Lord, for thy servant heareth.' Go and ask him if he hath nothing for thy case and he will tell you that his grace is sufficient for you, that his strength is perfected in weakness.

2. Be sure you go to Christ
Some souls when weary with sin go to their own vows and resolutions and make a Christ of them. Some go to the good advice of men and make Christ of them. Go you to Christ! You will be weary enough till you go to him. Never may you find rest till then. And he will lead you in the sweet paths of righteousness for the sake of his name (abide in me and I in you, so shall ye bear much fruit). He will tell you of his Holy Spirit which he gives abundantly to them that ask him; he will say: 'The LORD God hath given me the tongue of the learned, that I should know how to speak a word in season to him that is weary.'

I would speak a word to those that never were weary with sin
How plain it is that you must be a willing captive. You are in chains but you go with all your heart. You are swimming upon the top of the tide. You are walking according to the course of this world. Alas, poor souls, sinning is an easy work here, but, oh, it will be weary work in hell. When that sentence is once passed on you – 'He that is unjust let him be unjust still; he that is filthy let him be filthy still' – oh, how weary will your sinning make you.

When the desire of drinking remains but there is no drink given –
no, not a drop of water to cool the tongue – oh, what a hell there will
be in that thirst. When the lust of sloth remains, but no beds of ease
to lie on, no sleep for the eyelids, what a hell that will be. You will be
weary then, poor souls, if you will not be weary now. Who among us
shall dwell with the devouring flame, who among us shall dwell with
everlasting burnings?

3. Some souls are weary without the light of God's countenance. These may find seasonable relief in Christ.

This kind of weariness is quite unknown to unconverted souls.
They never felt the blessedness of God's smile and therefore they
know not what it is to lose that smile. A man who has been born
blind and never saw the light of the sun does not know and therefore
cannot feel his want. But a man who has enjoyed the light of the sun
for many years and the joyful sights of this green world, when that
man loses his eyesight he feels it sadly. Just so, the world are born
blind towards God, they never saw the light of his countenance, they
do not feel the loss. But a soul that has once been brought to see the
face of God reconciled, when that man loses his eye of faith and the
light of his Father's countenance, he feels it sadly. He gropes about
in the dark seeking some to lead him by the hand. He is weary indeed.
Many things cause this hiding of God's face:

1. A fall into open sin is one common cause of immediate darkness
upon the soul. A cloud comes between them and God, his prayer is
shut out. He cannot tune his voice to praise.

2. An idolatrous attachment to any of the creatures. Often through
mere carelessness the soul finds itself entwined by some earthly
attachment which engrosses the soul. God is a jealous God, he can
bear no rival. Darkness is sure to come.

3. Undue mixing with the world. Often the thoughtless Christian
is snared into worldly company where he does not mention the name
of Christ. Darkness comes down like a cloud.

4. Neglect of the means of grace. Often the soul becomes secure,
having had much peace and nearness to God, becomes high-minded,
despises means, grows slothful, will not rise when Jesus knocks.
Darkness comes.

Now, even the wisest believers are confounded when they find
themselves in this thick darkness. After the dazzling light of God's

countenance they feel quite dazzled and bewildered. They begin to sink in deep mire and often plunge at random to deliver themselves till they find the [tongue] the worse and they sit down weary. Oh, that it was with me as in months past. Was I ever a believer? Or was it all delusion?

Oh, it is a sad case, to water the church with the tears, to rise at midnight but not to praise God; to rise, to work, to sleep, to wake, still under the hidings of God's countenance. Oh, how weary the soul becomes. Now hear the word of Christ: 'The LORD God hath given me the tongue of the learned, that I should know how to speak a word in season to him that is weary.'

I would speak to souls that are weary

1. Do not go to the creatures for rest.
You are so helpless, you are very apt to depend upon men or upon books. You go from one to another seeking rest and finding none. Now, it is quite right to make use of means, for God is the God of means, but do not make a Christ of them. It is Christ who has the tongue of the learned. Oh, how unable often is the most experienced man of God to give rest or light to a weary soul. But Christ is quite able.

2. Go then to Christ.
His voice is like the sound of many waters. His mouth is so sweet. Grace is poured into his lips. He hath got the tongue of the learned. Go and sit at his feet like Mary; he will give you beauty for ashes, the oil of joy for mourning and the garment of praise for the spirit of heaviness.

God has two ends in view in letting you fall into darkness:
(a) *To teach you that you have no power in yourself to walk in holiness.*
   (b) *To teach you that you have no power in yourself to come back to Christ.*

Feel helpless then, feel at the mercy of a Sovereign God, feel that you cannot come to Christ when you like. Lie helpless at his feet. It is his usual way to come just when you are helpless. When you are quite emptied of self-dependence, then he comes in, even through the shut door, and says, 'Peace be unto you.'

When he speaks peace, none can speak trouble. And just as the sunshine is sweeter and brighter after thunderstorms, so will you find the sunshine of your Father's face sweeter and brighter because

it was hidden so long. Just as Christ rose from the darkness of the
sepulchre into the fullness of joy in his Father's presence and felt a
gladness which he never felt before, so when you come once more
from darkness into the light of God's favour, you will have a new joy
that will repay you for many nights of weeping. You will have a new
foretaste of the sweet surprises of the heavenly glory.

In St. Peter's, 1837
In Dunipace, May 1837

12. Divine Restoration (Ezekiel 36:27)

And I will put my Spirit within you, and cause you to walk in my statutes,
and ye shall keep my judgments, and do *them.*

These words do, first of all, apply to ancient Israel. They are, at
present, of all nations the most hard-hearted and far from righteousness. But the time is fast approaching when God will turn them
and they shall be turned. He will not do it for their sakes but for his
own holy name's sake. To show that his power can reach the hardest
heart and that his grace can stoop even to the murderers of his Son.
He will yet restore them to their own land and wholly change their
nature. Oh, it will be a lovely sight to see them thus rejoicing over
judgements; to see the people that crucified the Lord of glory leaning
on the Beloved, and having his Spirit in them.

These words do also apply to us, for this is the very change which
is wrought in every soul that closes with Christ. Except this work be
done in you, you shall never see the kingdom of God. It was here that
Nicodemus, that leader in Israel, would have learned what it was to
be born again. It is here that you may learn what that great [work] is
which is more wonderful than the making of a world.

1. It is the giving of a new heart and new spirit

1. The natural heart of every man is an old heart.
1. It is as old as Adam. The heart that is in every natural bosom now
is the very same heart that was in the bosom of father Adam. The
carnal mind is enmity against God. He does not say one carnal mind
but *the* carnal mind. If you go to the topmost bough of a lofty tree
and break off the topmost twig you will find it has the very same sap

as the root of the tree. Just so is it in man. The carnal mind that is in the child born but yesterday is the same that was in Adam. The root and father of us is an old heart.

2. It is as old as the man. However many changes a man may pass through in his life and however old a man may grow, still as long as he remains out of Christ, his old nature remains. When a child, he went astray from the womb speaking lies and he will go astray speaking lies to the grave. Foolishness was bound up in his heart when a child and the same foolishness is there when he is a grey-headed man. Many changes take place in a man. When a boy he learns to read, this opens up a new world to him. He goes out into the world or perhaps goes abroad a voyage or two. This changes the scene and he comes back a different man. The scene is changed a third time when he settles in the world. Again, cares and afflictions come over him and his brow is furrowed with many wrinkles. One change more. His head is covered with snowy hairs, his back is bent with age, he leans upon a staff. Now, here are many changes mentioned; there are many more. But if he hath never been brought to Christ he hath the same heart still, same as when he was a child. He has an old heart. It is the same with a tree. When young, it is but a sapling and bends to every breeze; it changes, grows up and spreads out its boughs. Again, it becomes a fruit bearing tree. Again, it is stripped and bares a gnarled and aged trunk. Still, it is the same tree that ever it was. It is of the very same nature. The sap is the very same.

Question: What does God do for a man when he brings him to Christ?
Answer: He gives him a new heart: 'A new heart also will I give you, and a new spirit will I put within you' (verse 26).

1. *Learn:* It is not a change upon the old nature that God promises to give. It is a new heart altogether. Oh, there is divine wisdom in this. It is quite possible to produce many changes on a tree without ever changing its nature. You may plant it in a better soil, you may warm the roots. You may apply medicines to the bark. You may very well improve the tree but it is plain you will never change its nature. In order to make it a new tree you must cut it off from the old root altogether and graft it into another tree of a different nature. And then, when the sap of that better tree flows into it, it will be another tree altogether; that is giving a new nature to it. Just so, my friends, it

is quite possible to produce great changes in you without ever changing your nature. You are changing every day, but, oh, are you made new? Have you been cut quite away from the old tree and grafted into a new tree? Have you had this word fulfilled in you, 'A new heart will I give unto you'?

I do not ask if you have been made more sober, more quiet and orderly in keeping the Sabbath, more regular in the house of God. But I ask, have you got a new heart? In Christ Jesus, neither circumcision availeth anything nor uncircumcision. Except a man be born again he cannot see the kingdom of God. My dear friends, it makes me tremble to think that many among you are turning more quiet and attentive to ordinances. I will tell you what I fear. I fear that that is all, that you are made better but not [made] Christians. Oh, do not rest short of the new birth. Remember – decent, worldly people will perish as well as drunkards. They will be bound in the same bundle. Oh, cry for a new heart.

2. Learn who can do it. 'I will give ... I will put.' It is the Lord. Other changes are natural. When children are brought to school it is quite natural that they should grow quiet and orderly. When you hear the Word preached every Sabbath day it is quite natural you should grow more serious and attentive. All this is the work of nature. But only God can give the new heart, for it is a supernatural work. God keeps it in his own hand. Oh, seek it from him. Oh, do not die without it. There are some dropping away from among you every day. Will none of you cry for a new heart?

2. A tender heart: 'I will take out.'

1. The natural heart is a stony heart.
(1) It tends to the earth like a stone. Throw a stone ever so high into the air, yet it will fall to the ground. Yea, the higher you throw it, it will fall down with the greater force. So is it with the natural heart. If you try to lift up a natural heart in thoughts of Christ and of God, it falls down like a stone. He has no heart for these things. Yea, the higher and sweeter the truth be, the soul shall with all the greater force fall down to the dust. As a millstone sinks to the bottom of the sea, so will a natural heart sink in hell, to the utmost distance from God and Christ. Oh, take heed, unconverted souls, there is that in your bosom which, in its nature, is enough to sink you at any moment to the lowest hell.

(2) It is hard. If you speak to a stone it does not hear. If you beseech it it makes no impression. If you tell it of wrath it weeps not. If you tell it of Christ it bleeds not. It is a stone. What more would you expect from a stone? Just such is the natural heart. It is a stony heart.

For more than a year I have stood here every Sabbath day and showed you out of the Scriptures that as many of you as are out of Christ are under the wrath and curse of God. Now, tell me, how many of you have trembled? Now, why have you not trembled? Ah, because you have a stone instead of a heart. Again, I have stood here every Sabbath day and told you of the love of Jesus toward hell-deserving sinners. Now tell me, how many have had their hearts drawn to Christ? Which of you have said, 'My Beloved is mine'? Ah, why is this? Because you have a stone instead of a heart. We have piped unto you and you have not danced. We have sung dirges to you and you have not lamented.

(3) It is hard even when broken. When you break a stone with a hammer, it is still as hard as ever, every fragment is a little stone. So is it with the natural heart.

1. Often a natural heart is broken under afflictions. Stroke after stroke comes upon the proud heart. It is broken to pieces. It is bruised to powder. The heart is bowed like a bullrush. Still, it may be as hard as ever. The sorrow of the world worketh death. Oh, it is a fearful thing to see a broken heart still a stony heart. Is this not the way with some of you? God has broken you with his hammer and you are as proud as ever! Ah, surely there is a sad day waiting you.

2. Often a natural heart is broken under conviction of sin. It is broken to pieces under the tremors of an accusing conscience. The mouth is stopped and he feels quiet before God. Yet the heart is as hard as ever. It is unaltered by the love of God. It does not flow down at the sight of love. The heart is as proud as ever. It will not submit to the righteousness of God, it remains unbelieving and stony. 'Though thou dash me in pieces, yet I will not bend.' This is an awful sight, to see a guilty awakened being not subdued by the love of Jesus. Is this not the case with some of you? You are anxious for your soul and tremble at the Word, yet you will not come to Christ that you may have life. Oh, pray for a melted as well as a broken heart. Lord, thou hast broken my heart by thy Law, now melt it by revealing thy love!

Question: What does God say he will do for a man in Christ?
Answer: 'I will take the stony heart out of your flesh and give you an heart of flesh.' Whenever God brings a soul to Christ he gives him a tender heart, tender in three ways:

1. It melts at the view of Christ

God leads the soul to Calvary and points to the bleeding Cross, to the Son of God that hung thereon. He shows the love that provided such a Saviour, the love that wounds. The heart melts at the sight. Woe is me that ever sinned against so excellent a Saviour, so loving a God. 'Then shall ye remember your own evil ways' (verse 31). Oh, it is sweet to have a heart of flesh that melts at the remembrance of sin.

It melts into love at the sight of Christ, like the poor woman which stood behind Christ's feet weeping. Her head was waters and her eyes a fountain of tears. The stony heart flowed down at his presence. Like Mary at the feet of Jesus, the heart of flesh loves to be ever at his feet. My dear friends, have you got this heart of flesh? Does it flow down at the name of Jesus? Oh, cultivate a tender heart, from nothing so much as a stony heart. Plead his promise, 'I will give....' Remember he must give it day by day. Plead again and again.

2. It melts at the view of a lost world

A stony heart is quite unconcerned about the perishing world. Am I my brother's keeper? That is the voice of the stony heart. It can look on the thousands without a shepherd in all our towns and yet not bleed nor move. It can look on our little children training up in ignorance and sin and yet not come to their help. It can hear of scattered Israel and millions of perishing Gentiles and hug its darling money closer to its breast than ever. Oh, how loathsome is a stony heart!

But God can change it. I will take away the stony heart and put in a heart of flesh. Happy, happy Christian. Jesus takes the heart out of his own bosom and puts it in your bosom. He opens his vein and lets his own blood flow into your veins. He gives you that same gentle, tender, dovelike, lamblike heart that is in his own bosom.

Question: Have you got this tender heart? Jesus pitied the multitudes, do you? He was grieved when he saw the hardness of their hearts, are you? He was angry when little children were forbidden to come to him, are you? He gave to every one that asked of him, do you? He had pity on the wicked and undeserving, have you? He wept over

Jerusalem, do you? Oh, happy are ye if you have his tender heart, for by this you know that you know him by his Spirit which he hath given you.

3. It melts with love to Christians

A stony heart has a real aversion to Christians. He can bear them if they will speak and act like the world, but whenever they act as Christians indeed, he abhors them. But when in Christ God gives a heart of flesh, it melts with love to Christians. By this all men may know that you are his disciples if ye have love one to another. We know that we are passed from death to life because we love the brethren. If you have not this mark you are yet unborn again, you have yet a stone in place of a heart.

3. My Spirit

1. By nature we have got the spirit of the devil. He is called the prince of the power of the air, and we know he works in the children of disobedience. Every natural heart is acted on by the devil.

1. This is plain in the pride of natural hearts. It was pride that hurled the devil out of heaven. God resisteth the proud. Yet every natural heart is full of pride.

2. In enmity to God. The devil is the great enemy of God and the natural heart is in his image as this, the carnal mind is enmity against God.

3. In love of lies. The devil was a liar from the beginning, he is the father of lies. Yet every natural heart goes astray from the womb speaking lies.

4. In leading others into sin. This is the chief feature in the devil's character, such also is the natural heart. Oh, what a vile devilish spirit is in every unconverted soul.

Question: What does God say he will do for this.
Answer: 'I will put my Spirit within you.'

Oh, what a miracle of love there is here to the soul that is in Christ. I would not have believed it, had the words not been in the Bible. This is more than the eye hath seen or ear heard, more than hath entered into the heart to conceive.

1. If God had said, 'I will send a good angel to you, the angel that ministered to Jesus in his agony; I will send Michael, that stands at

my right hand to be your Mentor, your counsellor, your friend', oh, this would have been good and gracious. But says he, 'I will send my Spirit, the Holy Ghost, the Comforter, equal with me, one with me, my Spirit.' Think on the words, dear Christians, till your hearts glow.

2. Again, if God had said, 'I will send my Spirit now and then to visit you, to enter under your roof, to shine upon the Bible, to be a voice behind thee, to be a shield around thee, to be a river to thee to drink out of', oh, this would have been worthy of our God to give. But says he, 'I will put my Spirit within you.' 'Lord, I am not worthy that thou shouldest enter under my roof,' saith the soul. 'I will come into thy bosom,' saith God. 'I will dwell in them and walk in them.'

Question. Have you received this Spirit to dwell within you? Then learn these things.

1. Learn to hold intimate communion with God. The Spirit of God will continually be lifting the heart to sweet adoring thoughts of God. Through Jesus we have access by one Spirit unto the Father. The Spirit is one with the Father and Son and wherever he dwells he will be lifting himself toward God. If you are the temple of the Holy Ghost, then what sweet fellowship you will have with the Father and Son. Oh, what adoring looks at Jesus will not the Spirit make you cast.

2. Learn to make every want known to him. If you had a dear Christian friend living in the same house with you, how often you would be asking him the meaning of the Bible; how often you would be asking him for counsel in difficult emergencies; for comfort in dark, distressing moments.

Well, then, if God has put his Spirit within you, here is a friend more than all the earth can give and, oh, he is within you. He is the Spirit of truth, ask him for light. He is the Comforter, ask for comfort. Unbosom everything to this indwelling Friend.

3. Learn to obey all the commandments. 'I will cause them to walk.' If the Holy Spirit dwells in you, he will lead you into all holy obedience. Oh, it is sweet to be thus constrained to the blessed service of God. I do not say you ought to be holy, but I say you must be holy as he that dwelleth in you is holy.

Question. Perfect? If the branch were fully in the vine and the sap were fully in the branch, then there would be perfect leaves and fruit. But imperfect faith makes imperfect obedience. Oh, believe more and you will love more and obey more. Dear Christians, how sweet a thing is holiness, when the Holy Spirit dwelleth in you. Let this be your cry, 'Enlarge my heart and I shall run in the way of thy commandments.'

13. The Love and Leading of God (Hosea 2:14)

Therefore, behold, I will allure her, and bring her into the wilderness, and speak comfortably unto her.

It has often been remarked that of all the prophets Hosea was most really a Jew. Isaiah, Jeremiah and Ezekiel often wander into other countries and tell the fate of Moab and Egypt and Babylon. Daniel also ranges over all countries and kingdoms. But Hosea clings to his beloved Israel. His harp was tuned for Israel and he seems to have had no heart for any other theme. The sins of Israel call forth his vehement indignation. Their miseries call forth his tenderest compassion. The great love of God to them he describes in strains of softest tenderness, their coming glory in strains of most exhilarating gladness.

This passage before us is one of those where, in the name of Jehovah, he pours out the strains of the most loving tenderness. It declares the manner in which God will save Israel. It is also full of very precious instructions for your souls and mine.

1. God will bring them into a wilderness
This is the way in which God began their salvation before. He led them forty years in a howling wilderness, Deuteronomy 8, 'thou shalt remember.' This is the way in which God will deal with them again, read Ezekiel 20:35, 'I will bring you into the wilderness', and again in Jeremiah 30:6,7.

It is interesting to observe that God is doing this with the Jews in many places and especially in their own land. Whenever Jews have much trade and business in the world, they are quite careless about their souls. We found in Marseilles, in Lebanon and in Hamburg that the chief trade of the place is in the hands of the Jews and they are very wealthy. What is the effect? They despise all divine things. They care not to hear of Messiah or to return to their own land. They love the fleshpots of Egypt and eat bread to the full. Dear friends, there is no greater hindrance to the gospel than riches. It is easier for a camel to go through the eye of a needle than for a rich man to enter into the kingdom of God.

In their own land they are in a wilderness indeed. They are *often* wronged and cheated by the Turks. The week before we arrived in Jerusalem a Jew had been beaten to death by order of the Governor. *They are in great poverty.* Almost all the Jews in Palestine are supported by money gathered in all the synagogues of Europe. They are quarrellers; unable to hurt Gentiles, they wrong and hurt one another. They suffer the ravages of the plague. For two years the plague has been wholly out of the holy city. When we were there, about five died every day and most of these Jews. Their look is peculiarly wretched in Jerusalem, the city where David dwelt. Here is the gold become dim and the most fine gold changed. The precious sons of Zion comparable to fine gold, how are they esteemed as brethren, the work of the hands of the potter.

In places we found them in constant terror of the Bedouin Arabs. They had buried all their best clothes and valuables underground. Every night two soldiers and ten Jews kept watch, walking round to give alarm if the enemy appeared. When we looked upon their haggard, afflicted faces, the words of Moses came up to mind, 'I will send a faintness into their hearts.... and the sound of a shaken leaf shall chase them.... and they shall fall when none pursueth' (Lev. 26:36).

But the deepest affliction often is that they do not know the way of forgiveness and many of them are restless and unhappy. One evening in Jerusalem I went to see the remains of the old wall of the outer court of the Temple. A lonely Jew was sitting on the ground deeply engaged in prayer. His face was so pale and his look so dejected that I did not like to disturb him. At last I asked him if he thought this a better place to pray than his home. He said no. I asked what he was reading and he showed me, the 22nd Psalm, 'My God....' I read it over before him till I came to the verse, 'they pierced my hands and my feet.' He said that this was David, I tried to show him that it was Messiah who was pierced for us. He only shook his head. He acknowledged that he did not know the way of forgiveness. And one young Jew in Jaffett said, when we pressed him about forgiveness, 'I was forgiven all my sins when I had taken four steps in this holy land.' So the Talmud teaches them.

Now, then, is the time for carrying the gospel to them. When Manasseh was in affliction, the Spirit touched his heart and he humbled himself greatly before the God of his fathers and prayed unto him and was entreated of him. So will it be with Israel in their affliction. Let us be up and doing to carry to them the glad tidings of eternal life, and the Lord be with us.

This is the first work of the Spirit in bringing a soul to Christ. He leads him into the wilderness. As long as sinners are in the whirl of business and of everyday society, the gospel falls among thorns, it is choked as soon as sown. But when God determines to save a soul, he takes him by the hand and leads him apart from the crowd. Sometimes this is done by sickness or some awful bereavement. God makes the man's gourd to wither and then all this world is a wilderness to him. Sometimes he does it by the arrow of conviction. Just as the deer, when it is wounded, retires from the herd which bound careless by and seeks the solitude of some shady wood, so does an awakened soul retire from the world. He is alone with God. Before he compared himself with others, now with God. If any of you are thus dealt with, remember it is the beginnings of a work of grace in your heart. Quench not the Spirit.

In the same way, God awakens backsliders. When Jonah flew, God raised the winds and waves against him; so some of you have said, 'I wish to go after my lovers', and God has chastened you sore. Do not wonder, it is done in love. In very faithfulness he has afflicted you.

2. Allures and speaks comfortably
Luther upon this passage says, 'The gospel is the true alluring speech that draws the heart of man.' And he might have added that God himself is he who draws the soul by this alluring speech, 'I will.' There is no other speech that is fitted to an awakened soul. It is the very medicine for a sin-drunken soul. It is the plaster fitted for the mould. And there is none other but God who can apply it to the soul.

You will be glad to know that in more cases than one we found the gospel alluring speech to the Jews. In one case in France particularly we found a person of education who was most deeply interested in his brethren and in the fate of his own soul. Whenever we entered upon controversy he was animated and full of argument but when we allured him and spoke to his heart, when we showed him his lost condition and the salvation grounded in the blood of

Jesus, he had not a word to say, his tongue faltered, his lips quivered and his hands could not conceal the big drops that fell from his overflowing eyes.

In Sychar

We found one Samaritan who was truly anxious about his soul. We do not know from where he had been instructed but he knew something of his sin and misery and the gospel was an alluring speech to him.

In Tyre

We met with one young man who was deeply interested. We showed him the dry bones, he was immediately struck with it. He afterwards met us and turned up the passage about the spies.

In Jaffe

We met several. On the last day of our stay, first one came in and then another, asking for the New Testament and anxious to hear the alluring sound of the gospel. There were six altogether and one confessed that he had long felt that Christ was true.

In Germany

We met with many who have been allured and rejoice in Christ Jesus. *A word to anxious souls among you.* Dear souls, nobody deserves the words, 'I will allure.' It is a work of God. Now, there are many false comforters gone out in the world. There are other ways of relieving the voice of conviction besides the blood of Jesus. One anxious soul went to Young, the author of the *Light Thoughts*, asking, 'What shall I do to be saved?' 'Go more into the world,' was his reply, 'and you will soon lose these dismal thoughts.'

Dear souls, take heed and do not follow this blasphemous advice. Oh, it is easy to drown conviction and to sear the conscience. The world cannot give you true comfort. Its praise and its admiration, its pleasures and merriment cannot blot out one sin. It cannot give you lasting comfort, for the world passeth away and the lust thereof.

But some look to ministers for health and cure. Oh, I have seen a soul go from mountain to hill seeking rest. I have seen a soul wander from sacrament to sacrament, from one good book to another, from one minister to another, seeking rest and finding none. Look again to the words, 'I will allure.' It is God you must go to. In vain is salvation hoped for from the hills and from the multitude of mountains. In vain you seek in the pitcher what is only to be found in the fountain. He that wounds must cure. He that brings you into the wilderness alone can speak to your heart. He that stilled the waves of the Sea of Galilee alone can calm your troubled bosom saying, 'Peace, be still.'

3. Vineyards

These words plainly refer to the temporal restoration of the Jews to their own land. Just as before when they came out of Egypt he divided to them the land by the hands of Joshua; just as the Valley of Achor where they were troubled by the sin of Achan became a door of hope; just as Moses and the children of Israel sang praise to God at the Red Sea; so shall the Jews once more be delivered from all their captivities and be brought to plant vineyards in their own land.

I know well that many good people are afraid to understand all these things literally and dare not believe in the real restoration of Israel. And still I cannot but think that if you will prayerfully consider the matter, you will come to see that all these things are truly promised. Their punishment has been literally fulfilled and so will their restoration be. In going over that wonderful land, you see at every step the Word of God literally fulfilled. One of our first walks was to Mount Zion. It is ploughed like a field – we walked in a field of barley growing on the top. Jerusalem has become heaps.....

Isaiah 24: *Few men left*. This is true to the letter. The country might support 15 million and yet some reckon only 80,000, some 200,000, and of these the great majority are women and children.

The new wine mourneth, the vine languisheth. In some spots, the vine is still cultivated, in Hebron and near Jaffett. Still in general the land is stripped of its vines. The vines have withered away.

All the merry-hearted do sigh. The only instrument of music we heard in the land was that of the shepherd's pipe, most melancholy music. We heard it twice but both were strangers, the one an Arab, the other an Egyptian.

Now, if all these be fulfilled to the letter, who can doubt but the promises of future mercy shall be as literally fulfilled: 'For I will take you from among the heathen...' (Ezekiel 36:24); 'Old men' (Zech. 8:4). 'I will give her her vineyards.'

Dear friends, I know you will greatly straiten your own souls if ye refuse to believe these things. All Scripture is profitable. And if ye pass these things by, and do not understand them as God intends you should, you are robbing your soul of soul peace, of soul joy and of soul glory. You will lose something through eternity.

Dear believers, who also love Israel, pray for the day of Jacob's gladness, for it will be a day of your Redeemer's glory. I remember David Brainerd used to say that he loved to see souls saved, not so much for the sake of the souls that were saved, as for the joy and glory that it gave to the Lord Jesus. Oh, if you had his intense love to Christ and desire for his honour, you too would desire above all things, that Jerusalem may become a diadem in the hand of our God.

4. Call me Ishi

The meaning of this touching declaration is that the Jews shall be brought to see the love of God so fully, to cleave to Christ so heartily, that they shall joyfully enter into a tender covenant engagement to be the Lord's, calling him 'Ishi' and no more 'Baali'. At present, the Jews everywhere look on God as a Baal or Lord, they look on him as an almighty, all-sovereign God. They acknowledge his power, they feel his vengeance. But their eyes are quite shut to the love of God. But when God pours out his Spirit he will reveal all that is in the deep heart of God.

December, 1839

14. The Danger of Complacency (Amos 6:1)

WOE to *them that are* at ease in Zion

The question we naturally ask on reading these words is, of whom speaketh the prophet thus? To this I answer:

1. *He is speaking* not of those who are out of Zion but of some who are in Zion. Now Zion in the Old Testament is frequently taken to represent the visible church, so that the men here spoken of are persons within the pale of the visible church. There are many woes in the Bible written out against those who are out of Zion. 'Pour out thy fury upon the heathen that know not God and upon the families that call on thy name.'

There is an awful day coming for those men who keep away from the house of God, who break his holy Sabbath profaning the day by idleness, who thus pour open contempt upon God and upon his Son Jesus Christ. But the woe here written is none of these. It is addressed to some who are in Zion; to some who are now in the midst of us; to some who sat down with us last Sabbath day at the same Lord's Table; to some who sing the same psalms and stand up at the same prayers with us. Oh that you would everyone enquire, 'Lord, is it I?'

2. He is speaking of those who are at ease in Zion
He is not speaking of those who have been made anxious about their souls and who often enquire, 'What must we do to be saved?', neither of those who have been brought to happy peace and rest in believing, but of those who are at ease in Zion.

(1) They are men who never trembled for their own soul, they put off the evil day. They have lived under the lively preaching of the Word and have often been bid to flee from the wrath to come, yet they never went away beating on their breasts. They never were moved to feel the dreadfulness of being out of Christ. Oh brethren, I much fear this is the way with most. You are at ease in Zion.

(2) They are men who never trembled for the souls of others. 'They are not grieved for the affliction of Joseph.' All gracious souls are anxious about perishing sinners. 'Rivers of water run down mine eyes because they keep not thy law.' Search and see, dear brethren, if you never had an anxious thought about the souls of others, then you are the very persons here spoken of, them that are at ease in Zion.

(3) Observe he does not say, Woe to them that are profligate sinners in Zion; Woe to drunkards in Zion; Woe to sinners in Zion; Woe to unclean persons in Zion. No, he says, 'Woe to them that are at ease in Zion.' There is many a heavy woe upon the head of those open sinners who live in Zion. But this is not one of them; this is a woe upon the head of those who are at ease, unawakened, cosy, unconverted souls. Those who never trembled for their soul; never wept for their soul; never fled from the wrath to come and who yet sit down among the children of God.

Of if any of you feel that this is your case, would that God would give you an ear to hear the Word of him that cannot lie. Woe to them that are at ease in Zion. In what ways I shall show briefly:

1. Woe to them that are at ease in Zion because these men are much harder to be awakened and converted than other men.

When the Word of God is brought with freshness and power upon the minds of wicked men who never heard it before, there is much greater likelihood, humanly speaking, that it will make [more] impression upon their minds than upon the minds of those who have slumbered under the preaching of the Word for years. When the Word of God has been carried by faithful men into savage countries, where the inhabitants have lived in open violation of every command of God; or when it has been carried into the howling waste of moral darkness and pollution which exists in the crowded lanes of our large cities, the Word has in many instances been accompanied with a power which is quite unknown in our well-watered congregations. There are two reasons why it is so:

(1) Those men who have lived in open violation of God's law, on the walls of Jericho as it were, are much more easily convinced of sin. When the Word says, *'cursed is everyone'*, they cry out, 'Ah, we have never obeyed any of the things written in the Book of the law that we were to do.' When the Word says, the wages of sin is death, they cry out, 'Ah then, this is our wages.' Like the Samaritan woman they find that this Book tells them all the sin that ever they did. Their mouth becomes shut and they stand quietly before God. They beat upon their breasts and will not be comforted.

(2) The gospel message comes with much greater freshness upon them. The love of God to men because they are sinners is all strange and new to them. Even though they have not been convinced of sin before, the very exhibition of the love of Jesus in giving himself for guilty men, that itself awakened conviction of sin. What did Jesus leave the bosom of the Father for? That he might become a curse for us. And did God the Father whet the glittering sword of justice against the man that was his fellow? Then I must be under a curse. That whetted sword must be suspended over me. And if they have been convinced of sin already, oh, with what erect ears does the sin-sunken savage hear of Immanuel – Jesus, a Saviour ready to save his people from their sins. If he be indeed under the teaching of God, he feels drawn to Christ by an irresistible longing and cries, 'Lord, I believe, help thou mine unbelief.' Oh, how hard it is to convince you of sin. Now my friends, how very different is the condition of every unconverted man before me:

i) How hard it is to convince you of sin. You have lived in Zion, in the very midst of the people of God and under all the restraints of a Christian land, so that the very atmosphere you breathe has made you outwardly conform to what may be called outside, Christianity.

It may be that you have been brought up by religious parents or at least by parents who kept you from gross sin, and you have thus grown up decent and civil. You have a certain respect for the Bible and the house of God. You join in all the ordinances and ceremonies which they enjoin, and though you know, well or may easily know if you wish, that you have never been converted by God; that you have no true relish for holy things as the people of God have, yet the argument is almost irresistible: If I be so like God's people outwardly, surely I am also like them inwardly. Ah, how hard it is to convince you of sin, how hard to make you beat on your breast and say, 'God, be merciful to me a sinner.'

ii) How little freshness or power the gospel has on your mind. You have heard of the love of Jesus since you were a child, you have learned it in catechising and read it in schoolbooks. You have heard it from teachers and ministers. Oh, how many summons have many of you heard, setting forth Christ's love to sinners? How many sacraments have you seen showing forth that dying love still more plainly? Oh then, if you are unconverted, how must not the Word fall upon your ear like an accustomed sound.

It is said that those who live close by a waterfall get so habituated to the roaring of the waters that they at last altogether forget the noise that is so constantly in their ears. It is said that soldiers in a field of battle get so accustomed to the roar of the cannon that they are at last not in the least startled by the loudest firing though it be ever so close to them. And ah, is it not so with you? You have heard the roaring of the waters of the gospel. You have heard the roaring of the gospel's cannon-fire. Now do you not hear? It is like any other noise to you and you can lay down your head and sleep. Woe indeed to them that are at ease in Zion. Woe indeed, for it is most likely you will walk through life till you find yourself in hell. If you were publicans and harlots, there would be some hope of awakening you. But woe to you who are at ease in Zion, for the publicans and harlots do enter into heaven before you.

2. Woe to them that are at ease in Zion, because they are provoking the Spirit of God in a high degree to have done striving with them.

It seems plainly to be the doctrine of the Bible that the Spirit of God never acts upon the human heart except through the Word as an instrument. No doubt the Spirit could convert all hearts by his own almighty power without any instrument, but he has plainly told us that he will not. In the gospel economy, God has seen fit always to convert or sanctify the heart *through or by means of* the Truth and never without the Truth. And as we know the Spirit is a loving Spirit, not willing that any should perish but that all should come unto Christ and live. We cannot doubt that wherever the Word of God is faithfully presented, there the Spirit is present to carry it home to all anxious hearts. It is he that thrusts convictions into hard, stony hearts. It is he that opens ducts of the eye and makes the tear flow down the sin-worn cheeks. And here we learn that those who sit unmoved under the faithful preaching of the Word are striving against the mighty Spirit of God.

But it is also a great Bible truth that the Spirit will not always strive with men; that though he wait long, he will not wait always, that he is grieved by being resisted. When Ephraim is joined to his idols then the Spirit says, 'Let him alone.' How plainly then are those who are at ease in Zion unconverted whilst daily listening to the Word, grieving and striving and provoking the Spirit of God. Ah, it is fearful to think how the unconverted among you are kicking against the pricks. How you are day after day insulting God. My friends, the ordinances of God are no common things, the Spirit of God is in them of a truth, and if you have wearied of them and turned from them with loathing, you have not insulted man but God. You have read your Bible it may be, day after day, and are yet unconverted. Well, this is one continued resistance to the Spirit of God. You have sat under the preaching of the Word, Sabbath after Sabbath, and are yet unconverted. Here again is a long, dark line of striving against God. You have dared to sit even at the Lord's Supper and eaten of that bread and drunk of that cup, and this has been the crowning of your resistance to the Spirit of God.

Oh, do you not tremble lest the Spirit may have withdrawn from you and if so, farewell conversion, farewell salvation. You may sit under the Word till you die; you may partake of every sacrament; but if the Spirit be away, alas the efficacy of all is gone. You may have seen a rotten tree standing on the bank of some placid river, bending its withered branches till they dipped in the clean stream and turning its withered roots till they bathed in the passing waters, but all in vain. No drop of moisture could that sapless tree drink up to re-adorn its leafless branches. The principle of vegetation is gone, never to be revived. Just so may you be left planted close by the gospel stream; you may sit under the liveliest ministry, your roots may dip into the waters of salvation flowing abundantly past you; you may see hundreds flourishing on every hand of you in all the freeness of vital Godliness, but you are let alone by the Spirit of God. And like a withered tree, a monument to all who are at ease in Zion, waiting only to be cut up for the burning.

3. Woe to them that are at ease in Zion for they shall meet a heavier damnation than others.

The prophet plainly shows this in the passage before us where he says, 'Therefore, now shall they go captive with the first that go captive?' And it is plain that it will be so both judicially and naturally.

(1) Judicially or by the express appointment of God. It is expressly provided by God that to whomsoever much is given, of him shall much be required. These were dreadful words which Jesus, the gentle Saviour, spoke when he upbraided the cities wherein most of his mighty works were done, because they repented not: 'Woe unto thee Chorazin! woe unto thee Bethsaida! for if the mighty works, which were done in you, had been done in Tyre and Sidon, they would have repented long ago in sackcloth and ashes. But I say unto you, it shall be more tolerable for Tyre and Sidon at the day of judgement, than for you. And thou, Capernaum, which art exalted unto heaven, shalt be brought down to hell: for if the mighty works, which have been done in thee, had been done in Sodom, it would have remained until this day. But I say unto you, That it shall be more tolerable for the land of Sodom in the day of judgement, than for thee' (Matt. 11:21-24).

In like manner, brethren, those of you who have had most of the godliest ministers; those of you who have heard most of the faithful showing forth of Jesus; those of you who have seen oftenest the broken bread and poured-out wine, and are yet unconverted, shall meet the heavier damnation. You that were exalted as it were to heaven last Sabbath handling the emblems of Christ's dying love, and are yet unconverted, shall be thrust down far deeper into hell.

(2) It shall be so naturally or in the nature of things.

(i) It will greatly aggravate your hell to look back on the many opportunities you had of turning to God. If you had been a heathen without an offer of mercy, you would have had no greater torment than the fallen angels who never had the offer of a Saviour. But when Jesus has been offered you from youth to old age; when the Word of Life has been always sounding in your ears; when godly friends and ministers have besought you and prayed for you; when the Spirit himself has been so often at your heart; when the grieving, resisting and quenching the Spirit has been all your own act and deed, oh, who can tell the mountains of agony that shall be heaped upon your soul, sinking you deeper and deeper into the torments of eternal flame, when the one hateful thought comes across you, that you are the murderer of your own soul?

(ii) How will it aggravate your hell, when your false hopes are all blasted! You thought to buy heaven by a little bodily exercise; by hearing sermons; saying of prayers; and partaking of sacraments. You thought your outward decency and your ability to talk about good things now and then would assure you a portion in an eternal world.

(iii) How will your hell be aggravated by shame and everlasting contempt! There is not a stronger feeling in the human breast than shame, and here we find in Christ's sufferings that is set next to the agony of the cross: he endured the cross, despising the shame. And the Bible plainly shows that God will make fearful use of that feeling in the day of retribution when *some shall rise to shame....*

Oh, how many of you, my friends, keep up a profession of godliness just to avoid shame and contempt? How many of you may have sat down at the communion table just to keep up appearances, though you know you are unconverted? Think, then, what everlasting blushes shall cover your faces, when your hollow-hearted hypocrisy is made known to men and angels. Where will you hide your faces in that day, when Christ shall lift off the mask and show you to your friends and neighbours as you really are?

The higher that a stone is thrown into the air, it will come down with the greater force. So you, the higher you were raised up by these false hopes, the deeper you will sink in hell. Oh, what will it avail you in that day, that you have sat so often among God's people, yea, that you have been always taken for God's people? Awaken then ere it be too late. No more deceive yourselves by thinking that to be in Zion is to be a child of God. Many shall say to Christ in that day, 'Lord, Lord, have we not sat among thy people and heard thy ministers and eaten thy sacrament?' But Christ will say to them, 'I never knew you; depart from me, all ye that work iniquity.'

Larbert 15 May 1836
Dunipace 22 May 1836
St. Peter's 1837.

15. The Wonder of Conversion (Zechariah 3:1,2)

AND he shewed me Joshua the high priest standing before the angel of the LORD, and Satan standing at his right hand to resist him. And the LORD said unto Satan, The LORD rebuke thee, O Satan; even the LORD that hath chosen Jerusalem rebuke thee: is not this a brand plucked out of the fire?

The conversion of a soul is the most wonderful event in the history of the world. Although the most of men do not care about it or would laugh at such a thing, yet it is far more wonderful than a thousand battles and sieges. The history of the conversion of every soul is the history of the world. It may be looked upon from many points of view:

1. The world can see the change
They see one of themselves, a gay, thoughtless youth, or wicked abandoned woman, stricken as with a sharp arrow. They begin to weep and pray over their Bible. Again a word of light and mercy falls on their ear, they call on the name of Jesus and rejoice believing. Their face is altered, their ways, their speech, their companions all are changed. The world say souls like this have become religious, have become saints, or mad about religion.

2. God's people can see deeper than this
They see that the Spirit has been poured out upon the heart, that the Holy Spirit has both softened the heart and pressed the Word home with power. They see that a poor prodigal has been brought from the far country, from the husks, to wear the best robe and to be embraced by the Father's arms.

3. Another view still

A contest between the Saviour and Satan. This world is a great battlefield, 'I will put enmity between thy seed and her seed.' The whole world lies in the Wicked One. He is the god of this world. He keeps unconverted souls asleep in his palace, he lulls them with softest music and binds them with silken cords of pleasure. But ever and anon Jesus plucks a brand out of the burning, and then a fierce contest begins for that soul. This is brought before us here.

1. Satan resists every awakened soul

Verse 1: 'He showed me Joshua the high priest standing before the angel of the LORD, and Satan standing at his right hand to resist him.' This was a vision which Zechariah saw. Joshua evidently represented the Jewish nation or rather those who were saved among the Jewish people at that day. God thus set before them for their comfort and encouragement the way in which they were delivered. This describes the way with every saved sinner.

As long as you are unconverted Satan does not resist you. He leads you captive at his will. When the strong man keepeth the house his goods are at peace. Satan lulls the soul into serenity – crying, peace, peace, when there is no peace. He puffs you up with pride and a vain conceit of your knowledge or character. He binds you down with some creature attachment, some idol or some darling lust. He keeps you far from a rousing ministry or makes you harden your heart against it.

Many of you are in this state – sleeping under Satan's lullaby. But the moment Christ awakens the same to flee from the wrath to come, Satan stands at your right hand to resist you. I have no doubt this is the case with some here present. His resistance is two-fold:

1. He accuses you to God

In ancient courts of justice, the accuser was always placed at the right hand (Ps. 109:6). This is alluded to here. This is one great part of Satan's work, he is 'the accuser of the brethren who accuses them before our God day and night' (Rev. 12:10). He begins this work at the very first spark of grace being put into the soul. When a sinner is awakened and goes trembling before God to seek an interest in Christ, Satan stands at his right hand to resist him. Satan pleads against the soul.

(a) He recounts the life they have led. How their heart is deceitful

above all things and desperately wicked. How they have lived in such and such sins, in spite of light and warning. That soul is too black to be washed, too wicked to be changed.

(b) He accuses them of unbelief. That soul has heard the gospel and despised it, has crucified Christ afresh and put him to an open shame, has grieved and quenched the Holy Spirit.

(c) He accuses them of drawing back. Even when under convictions they have gone back to sin again.

2. Satan pleads in the sinner's conscience

(a) He says you have sinned too much. Sins like yours were never pardoned. Your case is a singular one. You have sinned against light and knowledge. You have sinned against your convictions. Your sins are like mountains. How dare you come to a holy Saviour?

(b) He says you are too late. If you had come to Christ in youth, there would have been hope, for they that seek Christ early shall find him. If you had come the first time you heard the gospel preached, but you have been resisting the Spirit of God and he will not always strive and you are too late.

(c) Sometimes he takes another plan, and fills you with horrid lusts and blasphemies when you are on your knees. You are earnestly engaged in seeking after Christ, but he blows the fire of your lusts so that they begin to rage within you. There is a fearful storm in your heart and you hardly dare to pray.

Learn: What a solemn situation an awakened sinner is in. I doubt not some of you are in this very situation. You are standing before Christ the great Angel of the Covenant, you are seeking him day and night but then Satan stands at your right hand, accusing you day and night. You are within reach of the Saviour and he has laid his hand upon you. Do not rest in this condition. You are not yet saved. Many persons are discouraged and draw back and lose their love. Press you forward!

Learn that it is Satan that is resisting you. Christ is drawing you. God is inviting you. All God's children are helping you. It is only Satan and your wicked heart that are against your salvation. Whenever anyone says you have sinned too much, or you are too late, or better to go back to your old sins, remember this is Satan resisting you. All the resistance is on the devil's part. Jesus never will resist you, 'him that cometh unto me I will in no wise cast out'.

2. Christ's defence of the awakened soul

'If any man sin we have an advocate with the Father, Jesus Christ the righteous.' He is the great advocate and intercessor who pleads the cause of his own before the Father. And he does this before their conversion as well as after. If Jesus did not carry on the work of grace in the awakened bosom and rebuke Satan, the work would stop and no sinner would be saved. But Jesus stands up for the soul and gives more grace and carries the soul through.

1. Christ pleads the free election of God

'The Lord that hath chosen Jerusalem rebuke thee.' Jerusalem was one of the wickedest cities that ever was, they sinned against the light of prophets, apostles and the Son of God himself and yet the Lord chose Jerusalem. He often chooses the vilest to the praises of the glory of his grace.

Now, Jesus answers Satan, 'If God chooses the worst of sinners, who can hinder him? "I will have mercy on whom I will have mercy." Granting what you say that that soul has sinned infinitely so that no case is like it, yet still, the Lord that chose Jerusalem can choose that soul if he pleases.'

Oh brethren, here is good news to the vilest. Here is an answer to all Satan's accusations. The Lord chose Jerusalem and may choose me. He is an electing God. He will have mercy on whom he will have mercy. He is not bound to the rules of man. He often takes the most unlikely. Strange brethren, the very doctrine of election that so often beclouds the minds of sinners is the most cheering of all. God may choose whom he pleases; and if he chooses them, all the powers of hell will not prevent their being brought to Christ and to glory.

2. Christ pleads that the soul is plucked out of the fire

a. Natural men are brands in the fire

1. They are condemned to the fire, 'For as many as are of the works of the law are under the curse as it is written, Cursed is everyone that continueth not in all things which are written in the book of the law to do them.' 'He that believeth not is condemned already because he believeth not on the name of the only begotten Son of God.' Every natural man is like a piece of wood heaped on the fire; though the fire has not yet reached him, it is coming nearer every day. Whosoever

was not found written in the Lamb's book of life was cast into the lake of fire.

2. Sometimes they have the beginnings of the fire in this life. As the godly have a foretaste of heaven so the wicked have a foretaste of hell. Wicked men have awful sinkings of heart, accusations, gnawings of remorse, flashes and pangs of terror which are the beginnings of hell. They have also hot, burning lusts that burn and burn and will not be satisfied. These are sparks from hell.

b. Jesus plucks out of the fire

A soul brought to Christ is a brand plucked out of the fire. All accusations are vain when we are in Christ's hand. When Christ draws a soul to himself he puts his own hand upon it and draws it to himself and then grafts it into the true vine. Now, a soul awakened by Christ is plucked out of the fire.

Here we may ask the question: Is every awakened person brought to Christ? I answer, 'No.' Alas, how many in this congregation seemed at one time brands plucked out of the fire, but they fell back again into the fire. But every one whom Jesus plucks out of the fire he will bring to himself and keep out of the fire. Do not rest, beloved, till you know that Christ has plucked you out of the fire. Do not rest in mere convictions, anxieties, tears, etc, rest only in Jesus. Come unto me and I will give you rest.

Here is the complete answer to all Satan's accusations. And we are infinitely vile and worthy of the everlasting fire. But are we not brands plucked out of the fire? He has done it and who can say he does wrong? He sent from above, he took me, he drew me.

This congregation is made up of these two: (1) Brands in the fire, and (2) Brands plucked out of the fire. Have you never experienced a work of grace in your soul, never been convinced of sin nor drawn to Jesus? Then you are a brand in the fire. But there is one able to pluck you out. Oh brands, cry upon him. He alone is able and the time is short. Soon, soon you will be in the fire of hell out of which no hand can pluck you. See Psalm 116 and Psalm 18.

Lord Jesus, help!

16. Types of Jesus:

Type 1. Jacob's Ladder (Genesis 28:19)

And he called the name of that place Beth-el: but the name of that city *was called* Luz at the first.

1. The circumstances
1. Jacob seemed to come by chance to Bethel. He set out from Beersheba with his staff in his hand. He passed Hebron – Bethlehem – Salem – Moriah, where his father had been. When the sun was going down he stopped. This was the spot where God was to bless him.

So Zaccheus was guided up the tree by curiosity.

So the Samaritan woman to the well.

Happy if this Sabbath school were made a Bethel to you.

2. Jacob was in distress
No tent, no house, no covering, no bed, a stone for his pillow. It would be very dark, wild beasts howling round. *His mind* too would be uneasy. He had sinned in lying to gain the blessing. He fled from his brother's anger. He was parting from home, father, mother, etc.

Still God helped him there.

God came to John in Patmos – when a slave.

He came to Jacob at Bethel.

So he comes to many still.

Seek spiritual mercy when you are in want of temporal comforts. When you have a hard pillow, seek a sight of the ladder.

2. The vision
A ladder and angels on it. God above it. This represented Christ.

1. Because Christ is the way (John 14. John 1:51).
a. It was *set on earth*. Christ is very near you, not out of reach but touching the ground. Have you stepped upon it?

b. *Reached to heaven*. Christ teaches all the way. A complete Saviour. How high are you up?

c. It *leads* to God. The Lord was above. By Christ you may come into his favour, his presence.

2. Angels come to us by Christ (Heb. 1:14)

Away from Christ the devils alone are near you. Satan enters into you and leads you captive at his will. But when you lie at the foot of this sweet ladder, then angels come down to minister to you (91st Psalm). Would you not like to have holy angels coming down to visit you, to hold you up, and carry you to Abraham's bosom?

3. The promises

1. To the church: 'as the dust.'

Everyone that is saved longs that Christ may have a crown full of jewels.

2. To himself.

I am with thee – keep thee – bring thee – not leave thee.

Jesus will be with every soul he saves to the end.

2 September 1841

Type 2: The Burning Bush (Exodus 3:1-6).

Now Moses kept the flock of Jethro his father in law, the priest of Midian: and he led the flock to the backside of the desert, and came to the mountain of God, *even* to Horeb. And the angel of the LORD appeared unto him in a flame of fire out of the midst of a bush: and he looked, and, behold, the bush burned with fire, and the bush *was* not consumed. And Moses said, I will now turn aside, and see this great sight, why the bush is not burnt. And when the LORD saw that he turned aside to see, God called unto him out of the midst of the bush, and said, Moses, Moses. And he said, Here *am* I. And he said, Draw not nigh hither: put off thy shoes from off thy feet, for the place whereon thou standest *is* holy ground. Moreover he said, I *am* the God of thy father, the God of Abraham, the God of Isaac, and the God of Jacob. And Moses hid his face; for he was afraid to look upon God.

1. The Condition of Moses

1. He had refused to be called the son of Pharaoh's daughter

He had left all for Christ. He had left one who was like a mother to him, treasures, honours, all for Christ. It was then Christ revealed himself to him, in the burning bush. If we leave anything for Christ he gives a hundredfold more (Matt. 19:29).

2. A stranger in a strange land (see Exodus 2:22, also 15).
He was lonely and desolate. Often when God's people are at a low
ebb, Jesus comes. Malachi 4: 'Unto you that fear my name...' See
John 20.19.

2. What he saw
1. A bush. Isaiah 9, a *rod.* John, a *tender* plant. *Branch* (Jer. 23:5;
Zech. 3:8; 6:12). Plant of renown (Ezek. 34:29). Rose (Song 2:1).
His lovely human nature.

2. *Burning.* God's anger like fire (Deut. 4:24; Dan. 7:10; Ps. 18:8;
Heb. 12:29). Paschal lamb. How dreadful for a sinner to fall into his
hands.

3. *Not consumed.* Christ ever liveth.

3. What Moses did
1. Turned aside. Psalm 3:2. Holy curiosity.

2. Must take off his shoe and hide his face.
In coming to Christ we condemn ourselves and cast away our own
righteousness and part with our sins.

Type 3. The Pillar Cloud (Exodus 13:20-22)

And they took their journey from Succoth, and encamped in Etham, in the
edge of the wilderness. And the LORD went before them by day in a pillar of
a cloud, to lead them the way; and by night in a pillar of fire, to give them
light; to go by day and night: He took not away the pillar of the cloud by
day, nor the pillar of fire by night, *from* before the people.

1. Where this cloud came to them
When they came to the edge of the wilderness. They were fleeing out
of Egypt, a vast wilderness before them, without shelter, without
defence. The pillar cloud rose up before them. So it is with the soul
awakened to flee. Christ rises up before the soul and says, 'Come
unto me and I will give you rest.'

2. What was the cloud to them

1. A shade. 1 Corinthians 10:1,2: All baptised in the cloud. Perhaps
the cloud gave refreshing dews, at all events it gave a vast shadow,

the shadow of the cloud. Psalm 121:5: The LORD is thy shade. Have you fled to the pillar cloud for rest. Is the LORD Jesus your shade?

2. A light. Exodus 13:21, to give them light. In the dark nights in the howling wilderness, this tall pillar of fire gave them light. So Christ is the light of sinners (John 8:12). Make use of the light while ye have it. Is Christ your light? Many love the darkness rather.

3. A guide. Exodus 13:21, 40:34, Numbers 9:15, 10:34. They did not know where to go in the vast wilderness, or what were the best times. The cloud directed them in both. When it rose they moved forward, when it rested they rested, however long a time. It went before them to show them where to go. All this represents the Lord Jesus. He is an Almighty, all-wise, all-tender guide to all that have fled to him. He himself went through the wilderness and through death as a forerunner. Now he is guiding his own like a shepherd. Do you follow Jesus? Is he leading you?

4. A Defence. Exodus 14:19. The Israelites were marching through the sea, hotly pursued by Pharaoh and all his cavalry. The pillar cloud removed and came between so that the Egyptians could not find them all that night. It was dark to the one and light to the other. Christ is the same defence still to all that trust in him. He will come between you and your enemies.

Type 4. The Brazen Serpent (Numbers 21:1-9)

And when king Arad the Canaanite, which dwelt in the south, heard tell that Israel came by the way of the spies; then he fought against Israel, and took some of them prisoners. And Israel vowed a vow unto the LORD, and said, If thou wilt indeed deliver this people into my hand, then I will utterly destroy their cities. And the LORD hearkened to the voice of Israel, and delivered up the Canaanites; and they utterly destroyed them and their cities: and he called the name of the place Hormah. And they journeyed from mount Hor by the way of the Red sea, to compass the land of Edom: and the soul of the people was much discouraged because of the way. And the people spake against God, and against Moses, Wherefore have ye brought us up out of Egypt to die in the wilderness? for there is no bread, neither is there any water; and our soul loatheth this light bread. And the LORD sent fiery serpents among the people, and they bit the people; and much people of Israel died. Therefore the people came to Moses, and said, We have sinned, for we have spoken against the LORD, and against thee; pray unto the LORD, that he take away the serpents from us. And Moses prayed for the people. And the LORD said unto Moses, Make thee a fiery serpent, and set it upon a pole: and it shall come to pass, that every one that is bitten, when he looketh upon it, shall live. And Moses made a serpent of brass, and put it upon a pole, and it came to pass, that if a serpent had bitten any man, when he beheld the serpent of brass, he lived. See also John 3:14,15.

1. The lifting up of Christ

1. The serpent was lifted up as a pole between heaven and earth. So was Christ on the cross. He was lifted up as if he belonged to neither though he was Lord and maker of both.

2. It was a dead serpent that was lifted up. A most unlikely means of giving healing. So it was a dead Saviour that was lifted on the cross.

3. It was in the wilderness. Where no other remedy could be had, no other refuge. So Christ came when there was no eye to pity. He was lifted up in the wilderness.

4. The sight of all Israel. In midst of the camp. So Jesus was crucified before all Israel assembled at the Passover and is to be preached to every creature under heaven.

5. Moses the lawgiver held up the serpent. So it was the curse of the law that nailed Christ to the tree. The law holds up Christ as the end of the law for Righteousness.

6. It must be done. The serpent must be lifted up or the people would die. So Christ must be lifted up or sinners perish.

2. The believing on him

1. A look to the brazen serpent healed. They did not need to touch it, nor to kiss it, but only to look. From the utmost part of the camp they might look and be healed. So you do not need to touch Christ or to see him with the bodily eye, but only *believe*.

2. All were bid to look and whoever looked lived. So all are bid to believe and whoever believes is saved. Whosoever.... old or young, rich or poor, sins many or few.

3. A look gave health, looking to Christ gives more. Deliverance from hell, peace with God, the Holy Spirit and eternal glory.

Type 5. Cain and Abel (Genesis 4:1-15)

And Adam knew Eve his wife; and she conceived, and bare Cain, and said, I have gotten a man from the LORD. And she again bare his brother Abel. And Abel was a keeper of sheep, but Cain was a tiller of the ground. And in process of time it came to pass, that Cain brought of the fruit of the ground an offering unto the LORD. And Abel, he also brought of the firstlings of his flock and of the fat thereof. And the LORD had respect unto Abel and to his offering: But unto Cain and to his offering he had not respect. And Cain was very wroth, and his countenance fell. And the LORD said unto Cain, Why art thou wroth? and why is thy countenance fallen? If thou doest well, shalt thou not be accepted? and if thou doest not well, sin lieth at the door. And unto thee shall be his desire, and thou shalt rule over him. And Cain talked with Abel his brother: and it came to pass, when they were in the field, that Cain rose up against Abel his brother, and slew him. And the LORD said unto Cain, Where is Abel thy brother? And he said, I know not: Am I my brother's keeper? And he said, What hast thou done? the voice of thy brother's blood crieth unto me from the ground. And now art thou cursed from the earth, which hath opened her mouth to receive thy brother's blood from thy hand; When thou tillest the ground, it shall not henceforth yield unto thee her strength; a fugitive and a vagabond shalt thou be in the earth. And Cain said unto the LORD, My punishment is greater than I can bear. Behold, thou hast driven me out this day from the face of the earth; and from thy face shall I be hid; and I shall be a fugitive and a vagabond in the earth; and it shall come to pass, that every one that findeth me shall slay me. And the LORD said unto him, Therefore whosoever slayeth Cain, vengeance shall be taken on him sevenfold. And the LORD set a mark upon Cain, lest any finding him should kill him. (See also Hebrews 11:4.)

1. The sacrifice

1. Their occupations: Abel was a keeper of sheep. Cain tilled the ground. Perhaps Abel chose this employment because he loved Jesus, and loved to tend lambs and sheep which represented Christ. It is good to choose an employment that will not drive Christ out of your mind.

2. The time: 'At the end of days'. Probably on the seventh day. See how ancient the Sabbath is, even from the beginning of the world.

3. (a) Cain brought of the fruit of the ground, some barley, or some figs, or grapes, and laid them upon God's altar.

(b) Why he did not feel his sins. He did not feel the veil that separated between him and God. He did not know that he was under God's anger and that God would not accept of these things at his hands. So many children go to pray to God like Cain. You do not feel your sins and that your praises and prayers are sinful in his sight.

He did not feel his need of Christ, he did not feel that he needed one to die for him and carry his sins away. He did not believe that Christ was the way and that he must go through the veil.

(c) *The Result*: God did not accept him or his offering. God did not burn up his gifts – no fire, no smoke. There they remained. No smile on the heart of Cain, no token for good. God did not accept him. This is the fate of all who go to God without Christ.

2. Abel brought a lamb

1. What a lamb, like Jesus. A harmless creature, very gentle and tame, so was Jesus – Hebrews 7: Holy, harmless, undefiled; 2 Corinthians 5: He knew no sin; 1 Peter 2:22, did no sin; his fleece very white. Such is the righteousness of Jesus.

A firstling. It was a lamb in its prime or the firstborn. So Jesus was the only begotten of the Father, and he was in his prime.

Of the fattest. The best in all his flock. So was Jesus.

One for his brother too (v.7).

2. *Why a lamb.* Hebrews 11:4: *By faith*. He felt his sins and his need of Jesus. He felt everything he would offer to God would be polluted. He believed that God had promised to send his Son to die. He closed with Christ as his own, laying his hand on the head of the lamb, and when he saw the red blood gushing he saw the way in which his own sins would be carried away. Exhort the children to come to God in Abel's way. Come, laying your hand on the lamb. Come, looking at the blood of the lamb. He being dead yet speaketh.

3. *God accepted both Abel and his offering.*
God made him accepted in the beloved. God accepted Abel. He pardoned him, adopted him, sanctified and took him to glory. He loved him freely. He embraced him and never parted from him. *His offerings*. All his praise. All his prayers were pleasing in God's sight. When you come to God by Jesus, both you and your gift are accepted.

God bends his ear to their requests. He comes to hear their praise.

Type 6. The Burnt Offering (Leviticus 1:1-10)

And the LORD called unto Moses, and spake unto him out of the tabernacle of the congregation, saying, Speak unto the children of Israel, and say unto them, If any man of you bring an offering unto the LORD, ye shall bring your offering of the cattle, even of the herd, and of the flock. If his offering be a burnt sacrifice of the herd, let him offer a male without blemish: he shall offer it of his own voluntary will at the door of the tabernacle of the congregation before the LORD. And he shall put his hand upon the head of the burnt offering; and it shall be accepted for him to make atonement for him. And he shall kill the bullock before the LORD: and the priests, Aaron's sons, shall bring the blood, and sprinkle the blood round about upon the altar that is by the door of the tabernacle of the congregation. And he shall flay the burnt offering, and cut it into his pieces. And the sons of Aaron the priest shall put fire upon the altar, and lay the wood in order upon the fire:

And the priests, Aaron's sons, shall lay the parts, the head, and the fat, in order upon the wood that is on the fire which is upon the altar: But his inwards and his legs shall he wash in water: and the priest shall burn all on the altar, to be a burnt sacrifice, an offering made by fire, of a sweet savour unto the LORD. And if his offering be of the flocks, namely, of the sheep, or of the goats, for a burnt sacrifice; he shall bring it a male without blemish.

1. The sacrifice

1. Rich and poor could equally come

The very rich man brought a bullock (v.3), the poorer brought a sheep or goat (v.10), the poorest, two turtle doves or two young pigeons (v.14). Joseph and Mary were very poor and they brought the last (Luke 2:24). Rich and poor are equally welcome to Jesus Christ. The richest need to go and the poorest are free to go. Nobody can keep you from Christ because you are poor. Lazarus was very poor, a beggar covered with sores, yet he came to Jesus. Bad clothes should not keep you from church, nor from Christ.

2. The animals

(1) A bullock to represent Christ in his thought and majesty. He was the only begotten Son of God. The Lion of the tribe of Judah.

(2) A sheep to represent his meekness (Isa. 53). He is led as a lamb to the slaughter, Behold the Lamb of God (John 1:29).

(3) A turtle dove or pigeon to show his dove-like Spirit. The Holy Spirit came down like a dove (Luke 3:22). Christ calls his believing

people, O my dove (Song. 2:14). He calls Israel, thy turtle dove (Ps. 74:19), because in the image of Christ. For the same reason, in Israel they brought a dove.

3. A male without blemish - Representing Christ:
(1) *He was a man in his prime.*
  (2) *He was without blemish.* Such a sacrifice became us. If he had sin he must have died for his own sin.

2. The sinner's part

1. He brought it of his own voluntary will
No man forced him to do it, he came willingly and freely. How one thing here is unlike the gospel – the man provided his own bullock or lamb or doves – but we do not provide Christ, Christ gave himself. But the other is exact, we must come willingly to Christ. True, God makes all willing who come (Ps. 110), but they never come but willingly. If once you saw Christ you would run willingly to him. No one would force all your heart to hear of Jesus.

2. He brought it to the door
No further. He dared not lest he should die. The priest must stand between him and God. So now, sinner, you cannot go to God but by the High Priest.

3. He put his hand on its head
This implied confession. 1 John 1:9: if we confess our sins.... It implied appropriation. This is my lamb, my sin bearer. Come thus to Christ, laying your sins on his head.

4. He killed
On the Day of Atonement the high priest killed the bullock or goat. Here the sinner himself killed the animal. Both are true. Christ offered himself yet we slew him. Our sins bound him, nailed him, crucified him, weighed down his head, broke his heart.

5. He flayed (v.6)
The cutting in pieces showed the agonies of the Lord Jesus as in Psalm 22. It pleased the Father to bruise him. The flaying is a laying hold of his righteousness. Genesis 3:21, God made coats of skins.
  Put ye on the Lord Jesus (Rom. 13:14).

Nothing in my hand I bring
Simply to thy cross I cling
Naked come to thee for dress
Helpless look to thee for grace
Foul I to the fountain fly
Wash me Saviour or I die.

3. The Priest's part
Representing the work of Christ in offering up himself.

A. He sprinkled the blood, verse 5, round about upon the altar, so verses 11 and 15, the blood shall be wrung out at the side of the altar. It was an animal without blemish and yet its blood was poured out and came running out. So Christ was without blemish and yet he poured out his blood. Isaiah 53: 12: 'He hath poured out his soul unto death.' They crowned him with thorns which made the blood flow, they pierced his hands and feet, a soldier pierced his side and there came out blood and water. All this was the sprinkling and wringing out of the blood. Why did Christ need to pour out his blood?

1. To show God's anger against sin
The casting of the rebel angels into hell was not such a sign of God's hatred against sin as the shedding of the blood of the Son of God. Oh, think what an evil thing sin is when God will not forgive it without making his Son shed his precious blood for it. If you want to see the evil of sin, go to Calvary and see the good flowing out from the holy dove of God.

2. To show God's truth
God had said to Adam, 'Thou shalt surely die.' Now, when Jesus undertook to stand in our place he had need to die in our room and therefore he tasted death. Isaiah 63:3: 'I have trodden the winepress alone' – that awful day will come when Christ shall wash his feet in the blood of the wicked. It is as sure as the pouring out of his own blood.

3. To obey his Father
John 10:18, 'This commandment' – Jesus was obedient unto death. It was the highest point of his obedience.

Question: have you come to the blood of sprinkling? Hebrews 12.

'The blood of Jesus Christ his Son cleanseth us from all sin' (1 John 1:7).

Then you can sing, 'Unto him that loved us...' (Rev. 1:5).

Nothing else can blot out your sins but that blood. Without the shedding of blood there is no remission of sin.

B. He arranged the wood and the sacrifice (vv.7,8)

'He shall lay the wood in order upon the fire.'
'He shall lay the parts, the head, and fat, in order upon the wood.'

If the sacrifice had not been rightly arranged it would not have burned. He needed to lay the pieces of wood regularly and then to lay the parts of the sacrifice all out in pieces regularly upon the wood. This describes the calmness and forethought with which Christ offered up himself. It was like the priest arranging the wood and sacrifice.

1. *He calmly foretold* all that was to happen to him (Matt. 16:21; 20:17, 18). Eleven different facts. This was like laying the wood on the altar.

2. *He calmly went forward.* Isaiah 50:7, I set my face like a flint. Luke 9:51, He steadfastly set his face to go to Jerusalem. Mark 10:32,33, Jesus went before them and they were amazed.

3. *He calmly gave himself up to death.* John 18:4, Jesus therefore, knowing all things that should come upon him, went forth. Verse 11, the cup which my Father hath given me, shall I not drink it?

He was silent under every accusation. He answered not a word. He did not come down from the cross. All this was the calm and tranquil arranging of the sacrifice by the high priest. He through the eternal Spirit offered himself.

Learn: the amazing love of Christ to sinners. He not only undertook but went through with his great work. Calmly and fully. No man asked him to come and die. The world were not asking him, they denied and despised him, and yet he loved them. Strange love. You need not fear to come to him. He will in no wise cast you out for all you have done.

C. He burned all

The whole animal was consumed, went up in smoke and flame, nothing remained, therefore called a whole burnt offering.

1. The fire showed the wrath of God. So in the burning bush (Exod. 3:2). And on Sinai (Exod. 19:18), the Lord descended in fire. His eyes are like fire (Rev 1:14); Daniel 7:9, his throne a fiery flame, his wheels as burning fire. A fiery stream issued and came forth from before him. Hebrews 12:29, our God is a consuming fire. As fire is to wood so is God to a naked, unpardoned sinner.

2. The fire burned all; so Christ was consumed *body and soul* in the wrath of God. So will unpardoned sinners be, both body and soul will be burned in hell. Isaiah 33:14, who among us. Mark 9:44, The worm dieth not in the fire. Matthew 25:41, everlasting fire.

3. Sweet savour; God was well pleased with the believing sinner. God's justice is satisfied, he is well pleased for Christ's righteousness sake. If you are surrounded with the smoke of the lamb, then God will rest over you in his love.

Type 7. The Passover (Exodus 12:1-11)

And the LORD spake unto Moses and Aaron in the land of Egypt, saying, This month shall be unto you the beginning of months: it shall be the first month of the year to you. Speak ye unto all the congregation of Israel, saying, In the tenth day of this month they shall take to them every man a lamb, according to the house of their fathers, a lamb for an house: And if the household be too little for the lamb, let him and his neighbour next unto his house take it according to the number of the souls; every man according to his eating shall make your count for the lamb. Your lamb shall be without blemish, a male of the first year: ye shall take it out from the sheep, or from the goats: And ye shall keep it up until the fourteenth day of the same month: and the whole assembly of the congregation of Israel shall kill it in the evening. And they shall take of the blood, and strike it on the two side posts and on the upper doorpost of the houses, wherein they shall eat it. And they shall eat the flesh in that night, roast with fire, and unleavened bread; and with bitter herbs they shall eat it. Eat not of it raw, nor sodden at all with water, but roast with fire; his head with his legs, and with the purtenance thereof. And ye shall let nothing of it remain until the morning; and that which remaineth of it until the morning ye shall burn with fire. And thus shall ye eat it; with your loins girded, your shoes on your feet, and your staff in your hand; and ye shall eat it in haste: it is the LORD's Passover.

1. The lamb

1. *Chosen out of the flock* (v.3). As 10th day. So Christ was chosen beforehand to suffer. Chosen by the Father (Isa. 42:1): Behold my servant, whom I uphold; mine elect; v.6. I, the LORD, have called thee; Job 33:24: I have found a ransom.

2. *A lamb* to show the meekness and gentleness of Christ. Name he gets in Revelation, a lamb as it had been slain (Rev. 5).

3. *Without blemish.* So Christ: 1 Peter 1:19, 'a lamb without blemish;' 2:22: no sin. Such a high priest became us (Heb. 7:26). If not he must have died for his own sin.

4. *A male of the first year* to represent mankind in his prime. Christ was thirty-four years of age, that he might render full obedience, magnifying God's law and making it honourable.

2. The killing

1. Before all Israel
To show the public death of Christ. He suffered without the gates in the presence of all Israel assembled at the feast of the Passover (John 19:20). Calvary was nigh to the city. So the brazen serpent was lifted up in the sight of all Israel. So Christ is lifted up now in the preached gospel in the sight of all his believing people.

2. *The time:* 'between the evenings'. The evening began at three o'clock but sunset was the natural evening. Between three and sunset the Passover lamb was slain. At the same hour Jesus died (Mark 15:25, 34). He was nailed to the cross at nine o'clock in the morning (the third hour).

At twelve o'clock the darkness came on till three o'clock. At three o'clock the darkness was at its height, Jesus cried, Eloi..... Then it vanished, he cried, Father, into thy hand.... and gave up the ghost. *Between the evenings.*

3. The sprinkling of the blood (vv.7,22)

1. *The blood must be applied.* Take a bunch of hyssop and dip it in the blood. In vain Christ has died for you if you are not sprinkled with his blood. Purge me with hyssop.

2. *Sprinkle their whole houses*. The lintel and two side posts. It is not enough that all in your house are saved, try and get the souls of all.

3. *None were to come out (v.22)*. We must abide in Christ. Not enough to believe this. Abide under court of the blood.

4. Eating

1. *In what state?* Roast, not raw, not boiled, not a bone broken, but roasted whole. To show the entire sufferings of Christ. Not a bone of him was broken and yet he was consumed whole by the wrath of God. It is Christ crucified we must feed on.

2. *With what?*
a) *Unleavened bread*. Deuteronomy 16:4, there shall be no leaven seen with thee. 1 Corinthians 5:8, 'Sincerity and truth', without any guile. Come simply to Christ out of a sense of need, then you will find him sweet indeed.

b) *Bitter herbs,* the dish (Matt. 26:23); Bitter remembrance of sin (Ezek. 16:63).

3. *In haste (v.11)*
Like a traveller, loins, shoes, staff. To show that those who feed on Christ are pilgrims and strangers, this world is not our home. We have been chosen out of it. We seek a better country. Jesus said, 'I go to prepare a place for you.'

In haste. The time is short. We are in an enemy land. Make haste to be saved. Feed on Christ.

Type 8. The Day of Atonement (Leviticus 16:1-10)

And the LORD spake unto Moses after the death of the two sons of Aaron, when they offered before the LORD, and died; And the LORD said unto Moses, Speak unto Aaron thy brother, that he come not at all times into the holy place within the vail before the mercy seat, which is upon the ark; that he die not: for I will appear in the cloud upon the mercy seat. Thus shall Aaron come into the holy place: with a young bullock for a sin offering, and a ram for a burnt offering. He shall put on the holy linen coat, and he shall have the linen breeches upon his flesh, and shall be girded with a linen girdle, and with the linen mitre shall he be attired: these are holy garments; therefore shall he wash his flesh in water, and so put them on. And he shall take of the congregation of the children of Israel two kids of the goats for a sin offering, and one ram for a burnt offering. And Aaron shall offer his bullock of the sin offering, which is for himself, and make an atonement for himself, and for his house. And he shall take the two goats, and present them before the LORD at the door of the tabernacle of the congregation. And Aaron shall cast lots upon the two goats; one lot for the LORD, and the other lot for the scapegoat. And Aaron shall bring the goat upon which the LORD's lot fell, and offer him for a sin offering. But the goat, on which the lot fell to be the scapegoat, shall be presented alive before the LORD, to make an atonement with him, and to let him go for a scapegoat into the wilderness.

1. The dress of the high priest (v.4)
He shall put on the holy linen coat. On other days he wore the garments of great splendour and beauty.

1. The holy linen coat and, above that, the robe of the Ephod all of blue with golden bells and pomegranates.

2. Above that the Ephod of blue and purple and scarlet and fine twined linen, upon which was the breastplate and jewels. But now he put on only the holy linen coat, white and pure, but without any splendour or glory in it.

a) He went up to the brazen laver and washed himself in water.

b) Then he put on the holy linen coat.

This sets full to Jesus taking upon him a holy human body and soul. In himself he was God over all. He was rich. He was the creator and upholder of all things. Had he come in all his divine majesty and glory, what eye could have looked upon him? But he laid that aside (Phil. 2). He being in the form of God.... His body is holy and pure like the linen garments. This is the raiment he offers to sinners, (Rev. 3:18), and in which the Lamb's wife will be arrayed at last (Rev. 19:8).

2. He killed a bullock for himself
Aaron was a sinful man like us. He made the golden calf (Exod. 32). He murmured against Moses (Num. 12), and spoke unadvisedly with his lips (20:24). And therefore before he would be a complete type of Jesus he needed his own sins to be taken away. The bullock represented Jesus, the sweet incense also represented his sweet work, sweet-smelling before God. He took the incense and that blood together and went in within the veil, sprinkling the blood seven times on the golden pavement. This is the only way in which sinners can

come in to the holiest of all. You must stand on blood, be sprinkled with blood and surrounded with a cloud of incense. In this way the guiltiest may come in before God.

3. He killed the goat for the people

1. *The goat was chosen by lot (v.8)*. Proverbs 16:33: 'the lot is cast into the lap; but the whole disposing thereof is of the LORD.' So Christ was chosen by the Father to his work which was for him to do.

2. *He killed it (v.15)*. Aaron was a type of Jesus, so was the goat. This therefore showed Jesus offering himself. He through the eternal Spirit offered himself. I lay it down of myself. This shows the love of Christ to sinners. He gave himself for us.

3. *He carried in the blood (v.15)*. This is the way Jesus did with his own blood (Heb. 9:12, 24). He is entered within the veil i.e. into heaven, there he appears for us. A lamb as it had been slain. The marks of his wounds ever seen upon him. This is what gives boldness to believers. Have you chosen Christ? Then you may enter along with him into the holiest. You cannot be condemned for Christ has died, yea rather is risen, who is even at the right hand of God for us.

4. He came out and sprinkled the blood (v.18).
This is what Jesus is doing now, applying the blood he shed to the souls of sinners. Stretch out your guilty souls to him.

Type 9. Scapegoat (Leviticus 16:5-10)

And he shall take of the congregation of the children of Israel two kids of the goats for a sin offering, and one ram for a burnt offering. And Aaron shall offer his bullock of the sin offering, which is for himself, and make an atonement for himself, and for his house. And he shall take the two goats, and present them before the LORD at the door of the tabernacle of the congregation. And Aaron shall cast lots upon the two goats; one lot for the LORD, and the other lot for the scapegoat. And Aaron shall bring the goat upon which the LORD's lot fell, and offer him for a sin offering. But the goat, on which the lot fell to be the scapegoat, shall be presented alive before the LORD, to make an atonement with him, and to let him go for a scapegoat into the wilderness.

1. The choosing of the goat

a) *The congregation brought two goats (v.5).* So Christ was taken from among men. The Jews and Gentiles both delivered him to be crucified.

b) *The two were presented before the Lord (v.7).* So Christ presented himself to bear the sins of many. Luke 9:51: He steadfastly set his face to go to Jerusalem. John 18:11: The cup.

c) *Aaron cast lots.* So Christ was chosen by the Father. Behold, mine elect.

2. The laying on of sins

a) *The goat had no sins.* No more had Christ. It was not his own sins he groaned under.

b) *Aaron laid both his hands on the head.* So Christ laid our sins upon himself. Isaiah 53:6: the Lord laid on him *all the sins of Israel.* Christ bears all the sins of all that are laid upon him. It mattered not what kind of sin, or how many etc. This explains his cry (Ps. 38:4). Have you laid your sins upon him?

3. The carrying away

Christ not only took our sins upon him but carried them away from us. The fit man represented Christ, the goat also. None was fit but Christ for this amazing work. The sins Christ carries away can never return. They are cast behind his back, into the depth of the sea; they shall not ever be mentioned, they shall be sought for and not found.

Type 10. The Red Heifer (Numbers 19:1-10)

And the LORD spake unto Moses and unto Aaron, saying, This is the ordinance of the law which the LORD hath commanded, saying, Speak unto the children of Israel, that they bring thee a red heifer without spot, wherein is no blemish, and upon which never came yoke: And ye shall give her unto Eleazar the priest, that he may bring her forth without the camp, and one shall slay her before his face: And Eleazar the priest shall take of her blood with his finger, and sprinkle of her blood directly before the tabernacle of the congregation seven times: And one shall burn the heifer in his sight; her skin, and her flesh, and her blood, with her dung, shall he burn: And the priest shall take cedar wood, and hyssop, and scarlet, and cast it into the midst of the burning of the heifer. Then the priest shall wash his clothes, and he shall bathe his flesh in water, and afterward he shall come into the camp, and the priest shall be unclean until the even. And he that burneth her shall wash his clothes in water, and bathe his flesh in water, and shall be unclean until the even. And a man that is clean shall gather up the ashes of the heifer, and lay them up without the camp in a clean place, and it shall be kept for the congregation of the children of Israel for a water of separation: it is a purification for sin. And he that gathereth the ashes of the heifer shall wash his clothes, and be unclean until the even: and it shall be unto the children of Israel, and unto the stranger that sojourneth among them, for a statute for ever. See also Hebrews 9:13.

1. The animal

1. *A red heifer*
a) *A very rare colour* to typify the *only begotten* Son of God, the pearl of great price.

b) *To typify the scarlet sins* with which Christ was covered, not his own but ours. Also to typify the spotless purity of Christ. Both his divinity and manhood were sinless. He knew no sin, he did no sin, he was the lamb without blemish and without spot.

2. *No yoke*
a) *That Christ had never borne the yoke of sin.* This is a heavy yoke upon the neck, but Christ never wore that yoke.

b) *That he came willingly to suffer.* John 10. No man taketh my life from me. Here is the love of Christ that passeth knowledge that he came freely and died for sinners.

2. The place (v.3)

The priest led her out of the camp. It was looked upon as covered with sin, as unfit to remain in the camp of God, where God dwelt and his people. So Christ went forth of the city of Jerusalem. He suffered without the gate (Heb. 13:12; John 19:17). On him were laid the iniquities of us all.

1. *Learn the evil of sin.* It cannot be borne in the camp of God, even when laid on his dear Son.

2. *Learn to bear his reproach.* If you will be saved by Christ you must bear his reproach (Heb. 13:13). You must take up your cross and follow him.

3. The death and burning

1. *Death.*
One shall slay her before his face. Anyone, to show how Christ was crucified by wicked hands and yet before his face, to show that the priest consented. So Christ consented to his own death.

2. *The sprinkling (v.4)*
The priest sprinkled the blood before the tabernacle, to show that Christ would pour out his blood and show it to his Father.

3. *The burning (v.5)*
Skin, flesh, blood, dung – all was burnt to show the emptiness of Christ's sufferings. He was consumed for us. This shows what is due to sin. What Christ suffered for us!

Type 11. The Enemies of Joseph (Genesis 37)

1. Their plotting

1. *They conspired against him.* Ye shall be hated of all men.

2. *Called him names*. This dreamer. God gave him his dreams. They should have loved him for them.

3. *Lie.* One sin leads to another. He that keeps the whole law and yet offends in one.

2. The execution.

1. *Stripped him of coat*. Mark of their father's peculiar love. It is this that makes the world hate us.

2. *Sat down to eat bread*. Psalm 14:4, dead conscience or they would not have eaten bread.

3. *Judah.* Covetous. What profit? Sold him for twenty pieces of silver, so Judas.

3. The news

1. *Reuben, the saviour.* He had not acted a manly enough part. Quit you like men!

2. *The lie,* not in words but in fact. A lie is the wish to deceive.

3. *Jacob's sorrow* (35). He had idolised Joseph, now his idol is taken away. God cannot bear idols. He could have said, 'Now I will live more to God than I have ever done'.

17 February, 1842

Type 12. Joseph's Prosperity (Genesis 39)

1. The Lord was with him. Sold as a slave, no friend, he had his God.

2. Found grace in eyes of Potiphar. If a man's ways please the Lord. The world hates a child of God but God is able often to overrule that. God gave Joseph grace in the eyes of the Egyptians.

3. The Egyptian blessed for Joseph's sake. Happy house that has a Joseph. God loves it, Jesus visits it. Angels.

His trial

1. Great wickedness. Most men look on it as small.

2. Against God. How shall I? What has not God done for me? Shall I pierce the bosom that has redeemed me?

3. Would not be with her. The youthful lusts. Do not be familiar with sin. Keep far from the door.

The result

1. The lady's wickedness. She sought revenge. One sin leads to another.

2. The master's love soon gone. His wrath was kindled.

3. The Lord with him still. God has not promised to keep us out of prison but to be with us there.

Type 13. Joseph's Faithfulness (Genesis 39:22ff.)

The keeper of the prison looked not to any thing that was under his hand; because the LORD was with him, and that which he did, the LORD made it to prosper.

1. All under his hand

New prisoners committed to his care. God's children should be faithful, dutiful servants – (we should be able to depend upon their honesty) – keeping their word and fulfilling their work.

2. Joseph's tender compassion (Gen. 40:7)

'Why look ye so sadly?' A rough jailer would not have minded but Joseph was full of compassion. Remember those in bonds. Weep with those that weep.

3. Joseph would lead men to God (40:8)
'Do not interpretations belong to God?' Like Daniel he did not want the praise.

4. Joseph's wisdom
Interpreting the dreams.

5. His modest desires
He does not blame his brothers, 'I was stolen.' Nor his master's wife, 'I have done nothing.' 'Think on me', 'bring me out of this house'.

6. Joseph did not rely on men
The butler forgot him (Gen. 40:23).

Joseph's love to his brethren (Gen. 45)
When he saw their perplexity he did not refrain himself, he wept aloud. I am Joseph, your brother. Where grace reigns in the heart it refines and enlivens the natural feelings. In this he was a type of Christ who revealed himself to sinners in their extremity saying, I am Jesus your brother.

a. Joseph sees the hand of God
'God did send me' (v.5). 'God sent me before you' (v.7). 'Not you, but God' (v.8). The world sees God's hand in nothing but those who are like Joseph see it in everything, even in sins done against them. The world are but the rod.

b. Joseph's honour of his father
'Haste ye, and go up to my father' (vv.9, 13). Some would have been ashamed of their old father, not so Joseph. Not so a true believer.

c. Even the world are pleased
Who is it that will harm you?

d. All works for good
Jacob who had said, 'All against me', now said, 'It is enough' (v.28).

Type 14. The Anointing of David (1 Samuel 15–16)

1. Samuel at Ramah

Then Samuel went to Ramah; and Saul went up to his house to Gibeah of Saul. And Samuel came no more to see Saul until the day of his death: nevertheless Samuel mourned for Saul: and the LORD repented that he had made Saul king over Israel (1 Samuel 15:34,35).

a) Saul had turned out a wicked king and Samuel would not go to see him yet he mourned for him. Good men hate sin and cannot countenance it, yet mourn for the sinner.

b) I have rejected him. I have provided me a king. God casts down kings and sets up kings. Good kings come from God. You should see his hand in all public events.

c) Samuel's difficulty. How can I go? Unbelief remains even in Samuel's bosom but God relieves him, shows him how to cover this design. God is able to deliver his own in difficult duties.

2. Visit to Bethlehem

And the LORD said unto Samuel, How long wilt thou mourn for Saul, seeing I have rejected him from reigning over Israel? fill thine horn with oil, and go; I will send thee to Jesse the Beth-lehemite: for I have provided me a king among his sons. And Samuel said, How can I go? if Saul hear it, he will kill me. And the LORD said, Take an heifer with thee, and say, I am come to sacrifice to the LORD. And call Jesse to the sacrifice, and I will shew thee what thou shalt do: and thou shalt anoint unto me him whom I name unto thee. And Samuel did that which the LORD spake, and came to Beth-lehem. And the elders of the town trembled at his coming, and said, Comest thou peaceably? And he said, Peaceably: I am come to sacrifice unto the LORD: sanctify yourselves, and come with me to the sacrifice. And he sanctified Jesse and his sons, and called them to the sacrifice (1 Sam. 16:1-5).

Ramah is six miles north of Jerusalem, Bethlehem six miles south. The aged prophet proceeded down the deep valleys.

a) The elders trembled
They knew he was God's prophet, that he went on God's errands and that none of his words fell to the ground. They knew they were guilty

and deserved vengeance and they trembled, and said, 'Comest thou peaceably?'

In the same way Jerusalem was troubled when Christ was born (Matt. 2:3). And Peter said, 'Depart from me' (Luke 5:8). This proceeds from unbelief.

b) He pacifieth them
Peaceably. I came to sacrifice. God's messengers are messengers of peace. We are not sent to carry wrath but to lead men to Christ.

c) Preparation
Sanctify yourselves. He sanctified Jesse and his sons. It is right to prepare to meet with God on solemn days. On Saturday evenings to prepare for the Sabbath.

3. The Anointing

And it came to pass, when they were come, that he looked on Eliab, and said, Surely the LORD's anointed is before him. But the LORD said unto Samuel, Look not on his countenance, or on the height of his stature; because I have refused him: for *the LORD seeth* not as man seeth; for man looketh on the outward appearance, but the LORD looketh on the heart. Then Jesse called Abinadab, and made him pass before Samuel. And he said, Neither hath the LORD chosen this. Then Jesse made Shammah to pass by. And he said, Neither hath the LORD chosen this. Again, Jesse made seven of his sons to pass before Samuel. And Samuel said unto Jesse, The LORD hath not chosen these. And Samuel said unto Jesse, Are here all *thy* children? And he said, There remaineth yet the youngest, and, behold, he keepeth the sheep. And Samuel said unto Jesse, Send and fetch him: for we will not sit down till he come hither. And he sent, and brought him in. Now he was ruddy, and withal of a beautiful countenance, and goodly to look to. And the LORD said, Arise, anoint him: for this is he. Then Samuel took the horn of oil, and anointed him in the midst of his brethren: and the Spirit of the LORD came upon David from that day forward. So Samuel rose up, and went to Ramah (1 Samuel 16:6-13).

a) Samuel's mistake
Eliab came in, like a king, tall and of a noble countenance. Samuel said, 'Surely the Lord's anointed is before me.' But God showed him his error and so with the other five of the sons (1 Chron. 2:13). We must not judge by outward appearance. We are easily mistaken in our judgement of others.

b) *Samuel's obedience*

'We will not sit down till he be come hither.' When David came in, a Shepherd lad, about twenty, Samuel might have said, 'How shall this stripling be king?' No. God said, 'Arise, anoint him for this is he.' So Samuel did it. We must believe God in spite of appearances.

4. The Effect

The Spirit of the Lord came upon David from that day. The sovereignty of God, he chose the youngest and least concerned. The suddenness of grace – *from that day*. In how short a time God can give grace. One day among his sheep, the next anointed of God.

Type 15. The Arming of David (1 Samuel 17:38-58)

And Saul armed David with his armour, and he put an helmet of brass upon his head; also he armed him with a coat of mail. And David girded his sword upon his armour, and he assayed to go; for he had not proved *it*. And David said unto Saul, I cannot go with these; for I have not proved *them*. And David put them off him. And he took his staff in his hand, and chose him five smooth stones out of the brook, and put them in a shepherd's bag which he had, even in a scrip; and his sling was in his hand: and he drew near to the Philistine. And the Philistine came on and drew near unto David; and the man that bare the shield *went* before him. And when the Philistine looked about, and saw David, he disdained him: for he was but a youth, and ruddy, and of a fair countenance. And the Philistine said unto David, Am I a dog, that thou comest to me with staves? And the Philistine cursed David by his gods. And the Philistine said to David, Come to me, and I will give thy flesh unto the fowls of the air, and to the beasts of the field. Then said David to the Philistine, Thou comest to me with a sword, and with a spear, and with a shield: but I come to thee in the name of the LORD of hosts, the God of the armies of Israel, whom thou hast defied. This day will the LORD deliver thee into mine hand; and I will smite thee, and take thine head from thee; and I will give the carcases of the host of the Philistines this day unto the fowls of the air, and to the wild beasts of the earth; that all the earth may know that there is a God in Israel. And all this assembly shall know that the LORD saveth not with sword and spear: for the battle *is* the LORD's, and he will give you into our hands. And it came to pass, when the Philistine arose, and came and drew nigh to meet David, that David hasted, and ran toward the army to meet the Philistine. And David put his hand in his bag, and took thence a stone, and slang *it*, and smote the Philistine in his forehead, that the stone sunk into his forehead; and he fell upon his face to the earth. So David prevailed over the Philistine with a sling and with a stone, and smote the Philistine, and slew him; but there was no sword in the hand of David. Therefore David ran, and stood upon the Philistine, and took his sword, and drew it out of the sheath thereof, and slew him, and cut off his head therewith. And when the Philistines saw their champion was dead, they fled. And the men of Israel and of Judah arose, and shouted, and pursued the Philistines, until thou come to the valley, and to the gates of Ekron. And the wounded of the Philistines fell down by the way to Shaaraim, even unto Gath, and unto Ekron. And the children of Israel returned from chasing after the Philistines, and they spoiled their tents. And David took the head of the Philistine, and brought it to Jerusalem; but he put his armour in his tent. And when Saul saw David go forth against the Philistine, he said unto Abner, the captain of the host, Abner, whose son *is* this youth? And Abner said, *As* thy soul liveth, O king, I cannot tell. And the king said, Enquire thou whose son the stripling *is*. And as David returned from the slaughter of the Philistine, Abner took him, and brought him before Saul with the head of the Philistine in his hand. And Saul said to him, Whose son *art* thou, *thou* young man? And David answered, I *am* the son of thy servant Jesse the Beth-lehemite.

a) Saul armed David with his armour (v.38). A brazen helmet, a coat of mail and a sword. The ruddy boy was almost overwhelmed for he had never worn it before. He was accustomed to walking free on his native mountains.

This is like the young believers going to fight Satan. He puts on the world's armour, promises, vows, resolutions in his own strength, all like clumsy armour, not God's. Put ye on the whole armour of God.

b) 'I cannot go with these'. He felt them an incumbence instead of a defence. So the true child of God cannot fight in the world's armour.

c) His staff, his sling and his bag and chose five smooth pebbles from the brook. These were small things to fight the giant with but David believed in God – who is able to work by small things, not by might.....(Zech. 4). A small word is enough for conversion or to deliver from temptation.

The Words
a. Am I a dog? The Philistine despised David's weapons.

   b. Cursed him by his gods. It is no sign of a good cause to curse; idolaters are always cursers.

c. Come and I will give. No reference to God, as if there were no God.

 a) David's trust: I come unto thee in the name....

 b) He seeketh God's glory, not his own.

"that all the earth may know",

"all this assembly shall know".

The battle

a. David ran to meet him. What courage faith gives. He did not run away but ran to meet him. If God be for us, who can be against us?

 b. He slang the stone and it struck. God anointed the stone. Had that stone failed, all had failed. God directs the smallest things.

 c. David's modesty. I am the son of thy servant Jesse.

Type 16. David at the Court of Saul (1 Samuel 18:1-16)

And it came to pass, when he had made an end of speaking unto Saul, that the soul of Jonathan was knit with the soul of David, and Jonathan loved him as his own soul. And Saul took him that day, and would let him go no more home to his father's house. Then Jonathan and David made a covenant, because he loved him as his own soul. And Jonathan stripped himself of the robe that was upon him, and gave it to David, and his garments, even to his sword, and to his bow, and to his girdle. And David went out whithersoever Saul sent him, *and* behaved himself wisely: and Saul set him over the men of war; and he was accepted in the sight of all the people, and also in the sight of Saul's servants. And it came to pass as they came, when David was returned from the slaughter of the Philistine, that the women came out of all cities of Israel, singing and dancing, to meet king Saul, with tabrets, with joy, and with instruments of musick. And the women answered *one another as* they played, and said, Saul hath slain his thousands, and David his ten thousands. And Saul was very wroth, and the saying displeased him; and he said, They have ascribed unto David ten thousands, and to me they have ascribed *but* thousands: and *what* can he have more but the kingdom? And Saul eyed David from that day and forward. And it came to pass on the morrow, that the evil spirit from God came upon Saul, and he prophesied in the midst of the house: and David played with his hand, as at other times: and *there was* a javelin in Saul's hand. And Saul cast the javelin; for he said, I will smite David even to the wall *with it.* And David avoided out of his presence twice. And Saul was afraid of David, because the LORD was with him, and was departed from Saul. Therefore Saul removed him from him, and made him his captain over a thousand; and he went out and came in before the people. And David behaved himself wisely in all his ways; and the LORD *was* with him. Wherefore when Saul saw that he behaved himself very wisely, he was afraid of him. But all Israel and Judah loved David, because he went out and came in before them.

1. Jonathan's love to David

v.1: The soul of Jonathan was knit with the soul of David and he loved him as his own soul. Jonathan was not jealous of David's having conquered the Philistine. He was not jealous of his coming into his father's house and being greater than himself. He loved him as his own soul. He was a lover of good men. Grace knits souls together.

v.3: He made a covenant with him. An agreement that they would love one another, to make it perpetual. The love of saints is forever.

Jonathan clothed him. David was clothed like a shepherd, Jonathan like a prince. Yet he did not disdain him, Jonathan gave him his own garments. So the Lord Jesus clothes us with his white raiment.

2. David's Prosperity

1. All loved him
Even Saul's servants, though he was set over the men of war. They did not envy him, he walked so wisely.

2. The women sang his praise
vv.6,7: Saul hath slain his thousands and David his tens of thousands.

3. Yet David behaved wisely.
And the Lord was with him. Difficult to bear prosperity, yet David was upheld in it.

3. Saul's hatred

1. He was angry at the song. Although it was true, yet he was angry. Jealousy is cruel as the grave. He eyed him.

2. The evil spirit came upon him. Neither give place to the devil.

3. Cast javelin, Hatred begets murder.

4. Yet God preserved David. The Lord knows how to deliver the godly.

Type 17. David's Deliverances (1 Samuel 19)

His Danger. Saul (v.1) spake to Jonathan and his servants that they should kill David but God delivered him.

1. By Jonathan's intercession
a) He made David hide himself using all proper precautions.
    b) His defence of David
    1. He hath not sinned against thee. David was innocent, his blood innocent blood.
    2. He had done good, put his life in his hand.
    3. God was evidently smiling on his labours.
    It is right to defend the innocent. God blesses the use of such means even when apparently hopeless, 'Saul sware ... he shall not be slain.'

2. By Providence
David obtained a new victory but Saul was only the more enraged. The more God's children prosper the more they are hated. David played on the harp. He was of a forgiving heart. Saul cast the javelin and he slipped away. God knows how to deliver the godly.

3. By Michal – his wife
The snare. He sent messengers to the house to lie all night and kill him in the morning. Michal's plan (v.11), 'If thou save not thy life tonight' – this may be said to awakened souls. Verse 12: She let him through a window.
    Michal's lie. She hid an image in the bed and said he is sick (v.14) and when Saul blamed her she said, 'Let me go' (v.17).
    From 2 Samuel 6:20 we learn that Michal was not a good woman. It is not right to lie even to save life, but God made use of her sin to save his beloved David.

4. By his Spirit
David fled to Ramah to Samuel and joined the school of the prophets. Saul sent messengers but the Spirit came upon them and they joined the band of young prophets again. Last of all he went himself, burning with anger to kill David with his own hand (v.22). But the Spirit of God came on him too and he joined the prophets. If God be for us who can be against us.

Type 18. The Kingdom given to David (1 Samuel 28)

1. Saul's Distress

1. Samuel was dead. Samuel had been a faithful monitor to Saul. God took him away in anger (v.3). Ministers are often removed in anger.

2. The Philistines gathered against him. Pitched in Shunem in the very heart of the country. God can bring adversaries against us. He has armies in his hand, 'Saul was afraid and his heart greatly trembled.'

3. God did not answer him. He went to pray but no answer came. It is a fearful sign when we have no answers to our prayers.

2. Saul's application to the woman at Endor

1. He disguised himself.

2. The woman was one who pretended to divine. Sometimes God seems to have permitted them to use supernatural power. When a man leaves God he betakes himself to the devil.

3. She brings up Samuel. God permitted this.

3. The conference with Samuel

1. Saul's application. 'I am distressed'. When Samuel was alive, Saul would not listen to his directions but now that he was dead he wanted guidance. So with many.

2. Samuel's answer.
a. *'The LORD is departed from thee and is become thine enemy'.* When we sin against the Spirit of God he leaves and becomes our enemy (Isa. 63:10).

b. *The Kingdom given to David.*

c. *His sin.* 'Thou obeyest not' (v.18). A single sin is often the turning point of a man's downward career.

d. *The destruction of himself and his army.* 'Tomorrow shalt thou and thy sons be with me.' Men always think if one were to come from the dead they would believe. Here one came from the dead and Saul is no better.

Type 19. The Ark to Mount Zion (1 Samuel 13)

1. The first act of David's government is a recognition of God. So it should be of all government, of all families. Psalm 132:1-5 shows David's determination. We ought not to rest till Christ has a place in our family, till God's Ark is there.

2. Uzzah's error
(a) The first error was carrying the Ark in a cart (2 Sam. 6:3). This they had learned from the Philistines, it was contrary to God's law (Num. 4:15). *The Kohathites* were to carry the Ark upon their shoulders. The *Gershonites* to carry the curtains. *The Merarites* to carry the boards and pillars. The two latter were to carry their loads in wagons by oxen but the *Kohathites* were to bear upon their shoulders (Num. 7:7-9).

(b) The next error was Uzzah putting out his hand to touch the Ark (2 Sam. 6:6). He seems to have been a good man, else David would not have chosen him to drive the cart, but he did wrong, *contrary* to the law (Num. 4:20), which forbade even the priests to look when the Ark was covered. *Contrary* to the experiences of the men of Bethshemesh twenty years before (1 Sam. 6:19,20), God smote them for looking into the Ark.

Learn
1. That we should seek God after the due order
Some good men like Uzzah take up preaching at their own hand in times when iniquity abounds, when the Ark trembles. Now we must seek God after the due order.

2. God punishes even his children
Moses and Aaron sinned at Meribah in not believing God who said, 'Speak to the rock', whereas Moses struck it twice and called the people rebels, (Num. 20). He spake unadvisedly (Ps. 106:33). Therefore Aaron died on Mt. Hor (Num. 20) and Moses on Mt. Nebo, to the top of Pisgah (Deut. 34).

Eli honoured his sons more than God, he did not restrain them, therefore God punished him. The Ark was taken away from him, he died suddenly, no old man in his house, both his sons should die one day.

David also and *Jacob* afford remarkable examples. Also Lot. Psalm 89:30-34 explains this.

Luke 9:25: Suffer damage; this shows that a believer may sin, suffer eternal damage, lose something for eternity. If the righteous scarcely be saved, where shall the ungodly and sinners appear?

3. Obed Edom's blessing
The presence of God brings blessing. The presence of a Christian. What is death to one is life to another. In Philistia it carried disease and death, here life and blessing. So does the gospel. The word preached did not profit them.

Type 20. True Worship in God's Presence (1 Chronicles 15)

1. David now brings up the Ark after the due order
a) Carried by the Priests (vv.2-14)
   b) With music (16-24)
   c) David also joining (v.27)
   d) Michal despises him in her heart. He went home to bless his household (2 Sam. 6:20) but found nothing but opposition.

2. Its present state
Micah 3: ploughed. *Place of David's* sepulchre: Acts 2:29, Lamentations 5:18: 'The Mount desolate'.

Often literally referred to, especially in Psalms (e.g. 48:2 and 125:1). Often the place where God is acceptably worshipped because the Ark was there all the reign of David (see Pss. 65:1 and 84:7). The church of God: sometimes the place where Christ now is as king because David was king there (Ps. 2:6, Heb. 12:22 and Rev. 14:1). Sometimes for Jerusalem and the Jewish state (Pss. 51:18, 69:35 and 87:2,5).

17. Blessed are they who are not Offended in Christ (Matthew 11:1-15)

And it came to pass, when Jesus had made an end of commanding his twelve disciples, he departed thence to teach and to preach in their cities. Now when John had heard in the prison the works of Christ, he sent two of his disciples, And said unto him, Art thou he that should come, or do we look for another? Jesus answered and said unto them, Go and shew John again those things which ye do hear and see: The blind receive their sight, and the lame walk, the lepers are cleansed, and the deaf hear, the dead are raised up, and the poor have the gospel preached to them. And blessed is *he*, whosoever shall not be offended in me. And as they departed, Jesus began to say unto the multitudes concerning John, What went ye out into the wilderness to see? A reed shaken with the wind? But what went ye out for to see? A man clothed in soft raiment? behold, they that wear soft *clothing* are in kings' houses. But what went ye out for to see? A prophet? yea, I say unto you, and more than a prophet. For this is *he*, of whom it is written, Behold, I send my messenger before thy face, which shall prepare thy way before thee. Verily I say unto you, Among them that are born of women there hath not risen a greater than John the Baptist: notwithstanding he that is least in the kingdom of heaven is greater than he. And from the days of John the Baptist until now the kingdom of heaven suffereth violence, and the violent take it by force. For all the prophets and the law prophesied until John. And if ye will receive it, this is Elias, which was for to come. He that hath ears to hear, let him hear.

When a good man has been very earnest in his counsels and encouragements, persuading others to duty, there is a reaction of his own advice back upon himself and a new energy is thereby communicated to his own exertions. In the first verse of our passage accordingly, we see how completely our Lord partook of all that was sinless in our nature when we remark that it was just when he had finished commanding his disciples that he himself departed thence to teach and to preach in their cities. He thus showed his disciples that precepts and example went hand in hand in his ministry, and by his teaching as well as preaching showed how surely the evangelisation of the world is to be effected, not only by more solemn and lengthened discourse but also by homely and familiar intercourse. It seems also not unworthy of remark that the field he chose for his own labours was the cities of his disciples, their cities. He had bid them go to the cities of Israel and to go over them in haste for the time was to be short (10:23). But from this specifying of the scene of his own labours, whilst they were on their missionary tour to help the lost sheep of the house of Israel, I conclude that he would not send them to evangelise their native cities, knowing that ' a prophet hath no honour in his own country'. And (as he had just told them) 'that a man's foes would be those of his own household'. And accordingly that he himself would give his attention to them in their absence. His disciples were all Galilean, chiefly of Bethsaida and Capernaum, and this we find was the very district to which Christ directed his steps. Our Lord would thus teach us that in preaching the gospel, provided we do not flinch from duty or recede from principle, all natural advantages are to be made use of and all natural hindrances to be avoided.

From the evangelist Luke, who preserves the chronology of events which Matthew does not, we learn that, in the course of this teaching and preaching, our Lord came to a small city called Nain at the gate of which he restored alive the only son of a widow in her own presence and before all the mourners and loiterers about the gate. And it is said there came a fear on all and they glorified God saying that a great prophet is risen up among them and that God hath visited his people. And this rumour of him went forth throughout all Judea and throughout all the region round about. So far indeed did the rumour of the wonderful deed of the Saviour spread around, that we find it came even to the ears of John the Baptist as he lay in a dungeon of the lonely fortress of Macherus beyond the Dead Sea. The disciples of John, his faithful ministers who had followed him in his day of popularity and did not leave him in the hour of his loneliness when laid by from public life by the cruelty of a licentious despot and who were yet to bear his headless body to the grave, these disciples showed him all these things. Such was the occasion of the message to the Saviour, the facts and consequences of which occupy the remaining verses of our passage. 'John sent two of his disciples to Christ and said unto him, 'Art thou he that should come' (or rather, 'he that cometh') or do we look for another?'

Two modes of interpretation have been made use of to explain the object of this message of the Baptist. The first of these and most common is that which suppose that John sent these two disciples not for his own sake but for themselves. All his teaching was intended to lead men to the Saviour, but these two, unlike those other two disciples of whom John speaks who the first time that ever they heard their master say, 'Behold the Lamb of God', forsook their old master to follow and abide with him who was both their master and Lord, these two disciples are supposed to have been hard and impracticable, like Thomas slow to believe, or like Nathaniel prejudiced against any good thing coming out of Nazareth. To whom then could he send his doubting disciples but unto him who had the words of eternal life and who never cast out any that sincerely came to him? In support of this view it is well shown that the noble testimony we find John the Baptist giving to the Saviour at his entrance on his ministry and before he had done any miracle, makes it clearly impossible that John could now have changed his views concerning Jesus when, instead of the evidence of his Messiahship diminishing, it was increasing every day with every new miracle he wrought and every new doctrine he delivered. A strong confirmation of this view is to be found in another report which the disciples of the Baptist brought to their master about Christ which evidently shows that they bore no very good will to the Saviour (John 3:26): 'Rabbi, he that was with thee beyond Jordan, to whom thou bearest witness, behold the same baptiseth and all men come to him.' The believing and magnanimous answer of the Baptist, in which with prophetic eye he looked forward to his own decrease and believed that he who is from above is above all, shows that no jealousy of the fame of Jesus filled his breast and that he was the same faithful John as when he pointed to the Lamb of God on the stony banks of Jordan. And lastly, this view is confirmed by the briefly told but most interesting fact that the disciples of the Baptist were by this visit evidently reconciled to the Saviour, for in that bitter hour when they had performed the last sad rites to the mangled remains of their beloved master, it is said with pathetic simplicity, 'they went and told Jesus'.

The second mode of interpretation which has been advanced in order to account for this message of the Baptist by his two disciples is that it was not for their sake but for his own sake. Not that John had the least doubts as to the Messiahship or dignity of Jesus, such a supposition is necessarily excluded by the reasons I have already stated. But John, like the rest of the disciples, was greatly in the dark as to the true nature and object of Messiah's kingdom. A diligent student of the Old Testament prophets, this man of God looked forward with exalting hope to the setting up of the kingdom of God among men, making its nearness almost his only argument in pleading for repentance. Knowing himself, as he declared, to be the voice crying in the wilderness, Prepare ye the way of the Lord. The soul of this mighty Elijah was lifting itself up with holy expectation and so much the more as the day seemed to be drawing nigh. But suddenly, an arresting hand was laid upon his unwearied labours and he had to exchange the fresh breeze of the wilderness for the cold damp of the dungeon. Strange treatment this for the forerunner of the King of Kings! What is the Messiah engaged with that he should leave so helpless and neglected his faithful and able messenger? Has he too retired into obscurity and silence? Nay, for his disciples bring him news that all men make mention of the wonders done by his hand. All men confess that it was never so seen in Israel. The sick, the lame, the blind are healed and more than all, the widow's son at Nain hath been raised from the dead. The energetic mind of John, as he thought again and again over these things, comparing them with the clear and emphatic declarations of Isaiah, was puzzled and confounded. He knew well that it was said of Messiah, ' I will give thee for a covenant of the people, for a light of the Gentiles; to open the blind eyes....' And he saw that in Jesus this was fulfilled, but he read on, 'To open the blind eyes, to bring out the prisoners from prison and them that sit in darkness out of the prison-house.' Or again he turned to where it said of Messiah, 'The Spirit of the Lord God is upon me because the Lord hath anointed me to preach glad tidings to the meek. He hath sent me to bind up the broken-hearted.' And he could not but see here that very Jesus who gladdened the poor widow's heart at Nain. But he read on. 'To bind up the broken-hearted, to proclaim liberty to the captives and the opening of the prison to them that are bound.' And though his faith was not shaken yet there was incomprehensible mystery here which his active mind could not unravel and could not patiently rest under. In this mixed state of mind he determined on sending his two disciples with the message before us to the Saviour and the meaning of his question was simply this: if indeed all these miraculous signs of the Messiahship are done by thee, why not all that the prophets have foretold? If thou be the opener of the prison doors, why is thy servant, whose chief delight it was to bid men repent and hasten into thy kingdom, the inmate of a gloomy dungeon? Since thou art indeed Messiah, why not take thy great power and reign?

Very many things seem to favour this interpretation. First of all, the true rendering of verse 2 is when John had heard in prison the works, not of Christ but of *the* Christ, the Messiah. 'Works character- istic of Messiah' (Campbell). He sent two of his disciples to know what hindered, that all the works characteristic of Messiah were not done.

Again, this view is supported by the question proposed to Christ, Art thou he that cometh? A name of Messiah taken from the Psalms (118:26); Art thou indeed he of whom Isaiah and all the prophets spake and yet why are my prison-doors still barred?

Again, it is supported by this, that on the first supposition the indirect mode of putting the question is always inconsistent with the direct, manly bearing of John, who would rather have said plainly to his disciples, Go and satisfy yourselves that this is indeed the Christ. Whereas the indirectness contained in it, under the second supposition, is very natural in one who would be ashamed to acknowledge that he felt the pain of being bound in silence and gloom.

Again, it is supported by the reply of the Saviour which is directed not to the disciples but to John. He does not say, Look ye and consider ye and be no more unbelieving, but, Go your way and tell John. And further, the message which they are to bring to John seems much better suited for the Baptist than for the disciples. Had Christ's object been to soften the hearts of hard, unbelieving men, would he not have shown the power of his doctrine rather than the power of his miracles? Whereas if we understand the evidence designed for the Baptist, we can see at once the fullness and applicableness of these miracles, the way miracles of the Messiah reprove the murmuring of John. And indeed it is only when thus understood that verse 6 can have any clear significance: 'Blessed is he, whosoever shall not be offended (or scandalised) in me.' This was the very state of mind into which John was all but precipitating himself. And accordingly what a word in season was this to the fainting Baptist: 'Behold ye have seen with your eyes and now go tell John that I fulfil all the prophecies which a suffering Messiah can fulfil, and blessed are they who are not scandalised because the prophecies as to my triumphant kingdom and my coming in power are not yet fulfilled. Blessed is he to whom my cross is not a stumbling-block.'

And lastly, this view is confirmed by the Saviour's generous and honourable defence of John's character which immediately follows.

He saw that the spectators would evidently understand this message of John's as a slur upon his character, what they would think even if they did not say it. Is this the man who bade us repent for the kingdom was at hand? Is he now wavering in his opinion as to the Messiahship of Jesus, he who laid claim to visions and revelations concerning him? Christ knew that the uncharitable heart of man would cast up a thousand-such hard thoughts and speeches. And accordingly he shows that John was no waverer, no reed of the wilderness bending before any breeze, nor a king's flatterer clothed in purple and soft garments, but a prophet and more than a prophet, the last and the greatest of Old Testament prophets, the usherer-in of Messiah. And yet the least in his triumphant kingdom should be greater than he, so that John was right in looking forward to a time of greater glory and power.

Perhaps the most perfect interpretation of this whole passage, however, may be formed by a combination of these two views which I have stated at some length. It is not unlikely that the doubts expressed and reiterated by his disciples were the very immediate causes of the Baptist's impatience to have the mystery of Christ cleared up to him. So that the message to the Saviour was intended both to clear away their doubts and his own impatience.

Application
Of the very many lessons which might be learned from either view of the subject, one remark suggests itself to me from the last, that though Christ be not all to us which we expected him to be, yet blessed are we if we embrace him as he is. John was well nigh offended that Christ did not come as a deliverer to burst open his prison-doors. When first a man becomes seriously interested about his salvation and his views have been directed to Jesus the Saviour of sinners, the man may form many ideas out of his own fancy of all that the Saviour is to do for him, ideas which in experience he may never find realised, or at least not realised at the time he expected. To such a man the Saviour sendeth his message, 'Blessed is he who is not scandalised in me.' Should any of you take up with the notion that Christ is a Saviour not only from present sin and future suffering, but from present suffering also, it may be but a few months may pass over you until you shall be painfully awakened to see that affliction is, as it were, the daily bread of Christ's followers; that instead of being released from all suffering on this side of the grave, they enter into

life through great limitations. You may be tempted to murmur at this like John in his dungeon, more especially if, as in his case, you are laid by from a life of usefulness; and when the pleasure of the Lord seemed to be prospering in your hand. 'What!', you exclaim, 'Is it thus that Christ defends and saves them that put their trust in him? The wicked are flourishing like the green bay tree, 'there are no bands in their death, but their strength is firm', they are not in trouble as other men, neither are they plagued like other men, their eyes stand out with fatness, they have more than heart could wish. Behold these are the ungodly who prosper in the world; they increase in riches. But as for me, verily I have cleansed my heart in vain and washed my hands in innocency.' When such is thy meditation, do, afflicted believer, remember the Word of Christ, 'Blessed is he whosoever is not scandalised at me. It is true I am a Saviour from all suffering, but the way in which I save thee from present suffering is by making all things work together for thy good, not by taking away the cup of sorrow from thee but by taking out of it its real bitterness; not by taking away the cypress from thy brow but by extracting from it all the thorn; not by making death less sure and fearful a calamity, but by taking away the sting of death and the victory of the grave.' It is in heaven only that God himself wipes away 'all tears from the eyes'.

But a much more common and more pernicious error into which believers fall is that of fancying that when they sincerely come to Christ they shall be freed from all indwelling sin, even in this life. Christ is the Saviour of sinners and he who comes rightly to him must come to be saved not only from wrath, but from sin; not only from the curse of a broken law but from the power of indwelling corruption. And accordingly the sincere and genuine believer immediately on his receiving the free grace and peace of the gospel, the peace and joy of believing, looks up to Christ for the fulfilment of the precious promise, sin shall not have dominion over you, for ye are now no longer under a condemning law, a trembling enemy of God; but you are under a system of grace in which thou canst look up to God for upholding, renovating grace. There is not perhaps a more beautiful moral landscape in the universe than that of a soul first awakened to lay hold on the mercy of God in Christ and the immediate peace of the gospel, looking inwards upon its so long fostered affections for sin – which like ancient rivers have worn a deep channel into the heart; its periodic returns of passion hitherto irresistible and

overwhelming like the tides of the ocean; its perversity of temper
and of habit, crooked and stiff like the gnarled branches of a stunted
oak – and then turning the eye of faith away from the hideous spectacle
to Christ who hath redeemed from wrath and who therefore will (he
is pledged to it) redeem from sin. This is the faith that says to the
mountain, Be removed, and it is gone; and to the sycamore tree, Be
thou uprooted, and it is hurled into the sea.

And there cannot be imagined a more beautiful spectacle than a
soul with such a heart in view, yet looking confidently and cheerfully
away from it all to the fulfilled work and the promised work of the
Saviour, to the shed blood and the Spirit promised to be given. Now
though it be impossible for us to reckon too confidently on the
faithfulness of God's promises, and this is indeed the greatest of all
causes of the perdition of men, that we cannot get them persuaded to
reckon confidently upon the faithfulness of any one of God's
declarations, yet it is absolutely necessary that our confidence be
guided by a sound intelligence of what these declarations are, else
we may confide in what God hath not really promised. Accordingly
there is nothing more common than to see a man today a rejoicing
believer, glorying in the cross of Christ as the only way by which
lust is to be conquered and the old man, as it were, overcome, and
tomorrow overclouded with despondency and dismay, like John in
his dungeon. I thought that when I came to Christ I was to be delivered
from the chains of worldliness, my prison-doors were to be opened,
and I should walk forth in the liberty and light of the children of God.
Yet behold! I have got a glimpse of liberty, only to feel the pain of
imprisonment more. I have tasted peace for a moment, only to know
more true bitterness of enmity. I have known the forgiveness of sins,
only to make me groan more heavily under my sin that dwelleth in
me. Blessed (says the Saviour to all such), blessed is he that is not
scandalised at me, because I am not all he expected me to be, in a
day. The truth is, the Saviour hath not fallen from one tittle of his
promise; his promise is that sin shall never reign in the believer. He
never promised that it should not dwell in him, as a tormenting and
hateful guest. And is not thy present despondency a proof that the
promise hath been fulfilled in thee, the dominion of sin hath been
shaken to its basement? Lust no more holds a sceptre over a breast at
ease. The war of the inner and outer man is begun and there never
shall be peace again until thou art ushered into heaven on the shoulders

of the conquering Saviour. When the body hath crumbled into the grave and thy spirit ascended to thy God sprinkled (as it is in this hour) from all condemnation in the blood of Christ, then shall Christ's promise be fulfilled in its utmost and largest sense, for thou shalt be presented unto Christ without spot or wrinkle or any such thing.

But while this body is thy dwelling place it is best for thee daily to feel the movements of indwelling sin: that thou mayest not grow vain and boastful over thy fellowmen; that thou mayest daily see that free grace, given every day like the manna, alone maketh thee to differ; that thou mayest cry out in pain every day, Oh wretched man, who shall deliver me from the body of this death? And mayest daily return answer to thy soul, I thank God through Jesus Christ.

18. Sitting at the Feet of Jesus (Mark 5:15)

And they come to Jesus, and see him that was possessed with the devil, and had the legion, sitting, and clothed, and in his right mind: and they were afraid.

There can be no doubt that the miracles of Jesus had a deep spiritual meaning. When he opened the eyes of the blind it was intended to show how able he was to open the eyes of the understanding. When he said to the leper, 'I will, be thou clean', he showed how ready and able he is to create a clean heart in the sinner. When he called dead Lazarus from the tomb, he showed that he could raise dead souls. In like manner when he drove the unclean spirit out of this poor, wretched man, he wished to show you how ready and willing he is to deliver those of you who are led captive by Satan at his will.

1. The Sad Case

Let us look upon it as if we had been present and the Lord anoint our eyes to see our own condition painted there.

1. He comes out of the tombs (vv. 2-5)

And when he was come out of the ship, immediately there met him out of the tombs a man with an unclean spirit, Who had his dwelling among the tombs; and no man could bind him, no, not with chains: Because that he had been often bound with fetters and chains, and the chains had been plucked asunder by him, and the fetters broken in pieces: neither could any man tame him. And always, night and day, he was in the mountains, and in the tombs, crying, and cutting himself with stones.

On the eastern shore of the Lake of Galilee, there is a fine mountainous country and in the rocks are, to this day, many deep tombs cut by the hand of man. Among these did this poor, wretched man dwell night and day. He loved the solitude of the dead. The serpents that lurked in the caverns did not affright him. The noisome corruption of the putrefying bodies did not disgust him. This was his chosen dwelling. Striking emblem of the state of the unconverted soul. You dwell, as it were, among the tombs. The house of a Christless family is like the house of the dead.

The silence
There is no sound of prayer or praise ever heard there. The sweet name of Jesus is not breathed in your family. You dwell among the dead. Your bosom friends are the dead. The corruption of the grave is in your families. As the worms feed on the decaying body, so lusts greedily feed upon your souls.

You love the company of souls as dead as yourselves. You do not love the cheerful noise of God-fearing men. You love better the company of those whose souls are dead to God and to Christ and to eternity. You love the darkness of the tomb. You love the deeds of darkness. You love the darkness rather than the light of the sun of righteousness. You hate the light of the gospel. Men who like John, are a burning and shining light you cannot bear.

2. No man could bind or tame him
As the poor, possessed man drew near to Jesus, you might see in his eye a wild fierceness, that showed him to be untameable. His strong, brawny arms bore the mark of many a scar for they had often bound him with chains and fetters, but he plucked them asunder and broke them in pieces. And as he came wildly forward, the villagers shrank back, for they dared not pass that way.

This is but a feeble emblem of an unconverted soul. If we could look upon the unconverted as God does and as holy angels do, we would see the same frantic and untameable creature. Is there any here who has a proud heart? Who can tame you? Who can bind you? Who can make you stoop to the lovely self-denying services of love? Who can change you into the lamb-like spirit of Jesus?

Is there any here who has an adulterous eye? An eye full of adultery that cannot cease from sin? Who can bind it? Who can tame it? Who can make you pure in heart?

Is there any here who has a passionate or malicious tongue? The tongue can no man tame. It is an unruly evil, full of deadly poison.

Is there a lover of strong drink here? Who has yet learned how to tame you? Who can bind you from your favourite haunts? From your soul and body-destroying sin?

There are many fetters and chains put upon the unconverted.

(i) Parental authority. This is a sacred band, formed by God's own hand, 'Honour thy father and thy mother, that thy days may be long upon the land which the Lord thy God giveth thee.' For a while it seems to bind; the father's solemn word, the mother's affectionate look bind the wild heart, but soon it breaks loose and, like a torrent thawed by the break of spring, rushes on more fiercely because of the bands that are bound by it.

(ii) The ministry. This is another hand appointed by God and for a time it seems to prevail. The awful warning, such as you heard last Sabbath evening, restrains for a while the careless sinner. The love of Christ is like a pleasant song of one that hath a pleasant voice; for a time perhaps the world is forsaken, the dance and song are laid aside, the Bible and secret prayer are followed for a time, but soon the fierce nature of the ungodly soul rises like a flood, carrying all these bands away.

(iii) Love of character. This is yet another band. In our land, to be openly ungodly is not respectable, so that love of character restrains many of you from going deep into sin. There is a formal, hypocritical godliness among you which keeps many of you back from the open excesses of loose and reckless men. Many of you would not be seen as an open Sabbath-breaker or swearer or whoremonger, who in your hearts are guilty of all, just because you love the applause of men. And yet how easily when the wicked heart rises on its gigantic power, it breaks through this band also. Like Samson rising from Delilah's lap. No man can bind, no man tame an unconverted soul. Try it if you will – education, parental authority, the soft persuasives of wife and children – try them all to bind a drunkard, or to make a man love the Lord Jesus Christ, and you will see that none can bind or tame the Christless soul.

3. Cutting himself

Not only could you see the marks of chains and fetters on the brawny limbs, but many a bleeding scar upon his body. In his right hand he carried a stone sharpened like a knife and often he drove the sharp edge into his tender flesh, till the purple blood streamed down his reeking side. Strange madness, cruel to himself. So it is with every unconverted soul.

So it was with Paul when he was in the height of his rage against the lowly believers in Jesus, breathing out threatenings and slaughter against the disciples of the Lord, he was but cutting himself with stones. 'Saul, Saul, why persecutest thou me? It is hard for thee to kick against the pricks.'

So with Israel, 'O Israel, thou hast destroyed thyself; but in me is thine help' (Hosea 13:9).

So with every soul that sins against Jesus. 'He that sinneth against me wrongeth his own soul: all they that hate me love death' (Prov. 8:36).

Unregenerate men cut themselves with stones in two ways:

(a) In committing sin. Every sin is a new blow at their own soul. If any of you were to be taken to hell for an hour you would see that every one there is rewarded according to his works. All have sinned infinitely and therefore all suffer infinitely. But yet some suffer more than others. All have the worm that never dies but some have a deeper bite from its soul-withering tooth. All feel the fire that can never be quenched but some have a deeper wave of that dismal lake beating over them for ever. Every sin will have its own amount of suffering, so that every time you sin, it is destroying yourself. Every oath that proceeds from your lips is a new stab at your soul for eternity. Every look of lust that flames from your eye is a new stripe eternally for your guilty soul. If God be just and true, there will be a full weight of wrath for every sin.

(b) In despising Christ. 'He that sinneth against me wrongeth his own soul.' Every time that unregenerate man looks at Christ and despises him, he wrongs his own soul. In Christ there is a way of forgiveness open to the vilest of you all. He that findeth Christ findeth life and shall obtain favour of the Lord. But if you turn away from this fountain, what are you doing but destroying yourself? Cutting yourself with stones? Wronging your own soul?

2. The Power and Craft of the Devil

1. In the complete possession of this man
Verse 2, 'with an unclean spirit'; verse 9, 'What is thy name', and he answered, 'Legion, for we are many.' The intimations given us in the Bible concerning the devil and his angels are clear. If the Bible be true, there is a devil. It seems very evident that when the Lord Jesus walked on this world, Satan summoned all his legions to the field of battle. Just as Napoleon Bonaparte used to concentrate his forces upon a particular fortress, bringing his legions from the east and west to meet on a certain day upon a given spot. So does Satan, the craftiest of all generals, summon his legions to bear down upon the spot where Jesus is working.

So in the case of our Lord's temptations. Satan entrusted it to none of his angels but himself alone undertook the daring enterprise. So in the case of Mary Magdalene. Perhaps it was rumoured in hell that Mary was to be made a child of God and an heir of glory. Seven devils were immediately sent to fill her soul and keep possession of the palace and its goods. So in the case of this poor wretched man. No doubt Satan saw the Saviour crossing the lake. He saw him step on the shore and filled the unhappy bosom with a legion of evil spirits. My name is Legion, for we are many.

So it is still. Though Satan's chain has been shortened, yet how many of your minds does he blind lest the light of the glorious gospel of Christ should shine unto you. Into how many hearts does he enter, persuading you to betray with a kiss that lovely Lord Jesus? Yes! unconverted men, ye are my witnesses that *there is a devil!*

The poor, blinded wretch who stands up with God's Word in his hand to prove that there is no devil, is himself the clearest evidence of Satan's power. Wherever God seeks the conversion of a soul, Satan stands at the right hand to resist him. Every time of awakening is a time of deep Satanic agency. Every converted bosom is a scene of many a dark conflict.

2. In making the man averse to Jesus. 'What have I to do with thee.... I adjure thee by God, that thou torment me not' (v.7).

Jesus had everything to do with the poor soul. He loved him before the foundation of the world. The Father gave him to Christ before the world was. Christ had borne him upon his heart from all eternity.

Soon he was to bear his sins upon his own body. He was the Shepherd come to seek him. The Physician come to heal him. The Saviour come to pluck him from the burning. And yet the wretched man cries out, *Torment me not!*

Ah Satan, Satan, my heart trembles as I read. What a liar art thou. How amazing thy power to deceive. Are there none of you who have used the same words when Jesus came to you in the Bible, came to you in his ambassador, came to you in convictions? Have none of you cried out, What have I to do with thee, torment me not! I was visiting the other day and came to a locked door. What did that mean? *Torment me not, torment me not.* Ah, Satan is mighty still!

3. In making the whole country rise against Christ (vv. 12, 13, 17).

And all the devils besought him, saying, Send us into the swine, that we may enter into them. And forthwith Jesus gave them leave. And the unclean spirits went out, and entered into the swine: and the herd ran violently down a steep place into the sea, (they were about two thousand,) and were choked in the sea.

When one fortress is taken, it is customary for the besieged army to retire to a stronger. So did Satan here. The mighty Word of Jesus had dispossessed them from the wretched man and now they retire to defend the whole country against Christ. Their entering into the swine and harrying them into the sea was a stratagem to arouse the fears and anger of the Gadarenes against the Saviour of the world.

And they began to pray him to depart out of their coasts. O foolish Gadarenes, who hath bewitched you? Will not he that saves this wretched, guilty man be a precious Saviour to you? Will not he that gives this wretched creature a right mind give you the same? Ah Satan, this is thy work, 'they prayed him to depart out of their coasts'.

Ah, how often have I thought that the conversion of one soul would burn your hearts to seek Jesus too. But no! It is not so. You have prayed Jesus to depart and he has left you.

3. The new creature

If any man be in Christ Jesus he is a new creature. So it was here and so in every converted soul. His place, his clothes, his mind, his prayer, his life – all, all is new.

1. His place

'Sitting at the feet of Jesus'. Before he cried out, 'What have I to do with thee?' Now no place in all the world is so sweet to him as the feet of Jesus. This was Mary's place. She sat at Jesus' feet and heard his words. So this poor soul could listen for ever to that voice that had spoken peace to his guilty soul.

Ah, my friends, do you know what it is to sit at Jesus' feet and hear his Word? Ah, there is not a stranger sight in this world than to see a proud sinner brought to sit down low at Jesus' feet. It is there you will be, dear soul, if you are truly saved. No place for a saved soul like Jesus' feet. You will, as it were, lose sight of every other being and sit down at the feet of an unseen, once-crucified Jesus.

2. His clothing

Before, he wore no clothes, now he is 'clothed'. No more a naked savage, but decently covered, a humanised man at Jesus' feet. So with the sinner ransomed from Satan's grasp. No more art thou naked but covered with the robe of righteousness, the garment of salvation.

3. His right mind

Before he dwelt among the tombs, a frantic man, and from his eye the wild fire of frenzy glared and his strange gesture showed the maniac, near whom no villager would walk. But now his eye is calm, his heart at rest, his graceful lips speak only love, his bosom gently heaves while he looks upward on the face of his Deliverer. Oh tranquil soul, no longer the wild maniac but in his right mind.

So with the soul believing in Jesus. As long as you are far from Christ and far from God, you are out of your right mind. As long as you are unpardoned and yet happy, you are wrong in your mind. Ah, I know the devil tempts you to think that we are out of our right mind. They said of Jesus, 'He hath a devil and is mad, why hear ye him?' And no doubt you will say the same of us. But the reverse is true. It is you, it is you that are out of your right mind.

If you had been an hour in eternity, had you seen the misery of the lost or the blessedness of the saved for a single hour, you could not live as you do now. But you that have fled to Jesus you see everything truly now as God sees it. You see sin as it truly is, Christ as he truly is, eternity as it is. Go on bearing the reproaches of an unbelieving world and remember you are in your right mind. Once you were blind but now you see.

19. 'Go ye into all the world' (Mark 16:15)

And he said unto them, Go ye into all the world, and preach the gospel to every creature.

1. We should all help to send the gospel to the heathen because Christ commands it. There is something particularly sacred about a parting word:

i) When a father assembles his children round his dying bed and gives them the last affectionate counsels that ever they will hear from his lips, you may be quite sure that as long as they have hearts to feel, they will remember these dying words, or

ii) When a friend is going to a far distant shore to tarry for many a long year, when you accompany him to the ship and listen to his last affectionate advice, you say, as you return weeping to your solitary house, 'Well, I may forget much that he has told me, but his parting word I never will forget.'

iii) Now brethren, we have here the parting word of the Saviour. This was one of the last interviews that ever he had with his disciples. He was going on a long, long journey, far above all heavens into the presence of God himself. For the heavens must receive him till the restitution of all things. He was going to a far distant and far better country. He was going up to his Father and their Father, to his God and their God. But he would not without leaving a parting word behind him. And here it is, 'Go ye into all the world, and preach the gospel to every creature.'

Now if Jesus be your friend and your Saviour, you will keep all his commandments. He himself said, 'If ye love me keep my commandments.' If you have been saved by Christ and truly love him, then your heart will break within for the longing that it hath at all times for his judgements. You will not be perfect, far from it, but you will wish to be perfect even as your Father in heaven is perfect. More especially will you love to keep his dying commandment. As that night in which he was betrayed, he took bread and gave it to his disciples and said, 'This do in remembrance of me.' But most of all you will love to keep his parting commandment when he said, 'Go ye into all the world and preach the gospel to every creature.'

Thus it must have been with the disciples when the cloud had received him out of their sight, when they had gazed their last upon that face of love and kindliness which ever beamed with tenderness to all the world. As they descended now without Christ and passed the very garden where he had so often taught them, where he had so mysteriously agonised in blood, they would be saying to one another, 'Well, we may forget to do much that he told us, but this parting word we will never forget.'

Ah my friends, is it really so with you? The parting command of Christ, the one which should be deepest of all graven in your heart. Is it written there with the finger of the Spirit so deeply, so indelibly that all the power of hell cannot erase it? And have you this feeling constantly rising in your heart, 'Well, I may forget much that Christ has bid me do, but this parting word I never will forget'?

Alas, how many of you that know the Saviour must be conscious in your own breasts that you have never done anything heartily in obedience to this, the parting command of Christ. Look back over your life since you became a child of God, and answer to God and your own conscience whether you have kept this command of Christ, this parting word of the Saviour. Have you ever given anything to send the gospel to the heathen? Have you ever denied yourself the smallest gratification? Have you ever dined more sparingly, or laid aside some gaudy piece of dress, that you might have more to give to send the gospel to the heathen?

Tell me, did you ever kneel down and pray that this command of Christ might be obeyed, that all the world might know the glad tidings of a Saviour? I would not be surprised if the world care nothing about it, if they despise the command, if they keep their money to serve their own luxury and ease, if they exclude the heathen from their self-righteous prayer. But oh, believers, dare you forget the parting word of command, 'Go ye into all the world, and preach the gospel to every creature.'

2. Objection
Though this be the parting command of Christ, yet I do not see any good reason for it.

Answer: It is quite true that many men do not see any reason why we should go into all the world and preach the gospel to every creature. But even though we could see no reason for it, still Christ is wiser than we and we should obey him. A dying father might leave an unreasonable command with his children, and in this case perhaps it would be quite right to leave it without obeying it. But it cannot be so with Christ for he is the wisest of all. In him are hid all the treasures of wisdom and knowledge. And he is the best of all and therefore we may be quite sure that all his commands are wise and good, even though we cannot see the reason of them.

In the army it is wisely ordered that when the General Officer gives the word of command, no man is to stand and decide whether it be good and reasonable but every man is instantly to obey it. If any man were to stand and argue the matter, it is plain that every man would have his own opinion, no general movement would be made, and there would be an end to the discipline in the Army. The one thing which has given all its security to the armies of Europe and all other armies is that commands of the officer are not questioned but obeyed. The men do not stand to question whether it be reasonable and right, but they run to obey. And just in the same way with Christ, that great Captain who met Joshua on the plain of Jericho with a drawn sword in his hand. If we are his soldiers we must not stay to dispute but we must run to obey. 'I made haste and delayed not to keep thy commandments.'

Again, on board of ship it is wisely ordered that the Captain and the Captain alone shall have supreme command, that when he gives the word, no man is to stand and see whether it is a wise and prudent command, but every man must run and obey. It is to this fact the superiority of the British Navy over every other is principally owing. It is to this fact that the safety of many a ship from being wrecked and castaway is altogether owing.

We have been told of a vessel sailing in the Southern Seas when all was calm and not a cloud darkened the blue sky, it was a lovely summer evening. Every sail was spread to the gentle breeze and the oldest seaman on board had no sign of approaching danger, when suddenly the Captain bade not a moment be lost, but every inch of canvas be taken in. The seamen were surprised, they saw no reason for it, the oldest and wariest could not understand it, for sea and sky promised fair. But all ran to obey, not a moment was lost, every sail was gathered in; but they had hardly done when the wind rose to a hurricane, when the calm sea rose mountainous high and such a night came on as would inevitably have destroyed man had the sails been spread. The eye of the wary Captain had been watching the barometer and he knew from its sudden fall that an awful storm was at hand.

And that night proved to the men that it is good to obey a command even though they did not know the reason of it. Just so with us, brethren. Christ has said, 'Go ye into all the world, and preach the gospel to every creature.' It is the parting command of the Saviour that died for you. And however little you may see the reason for it, still obey it. He is your Captain. He is far wiser than you. If you would save your souls from shipwreck, trifle not with this parting word, 'Go ye....'.

3. Objection

If we were all to go over the world preaching the gospel, then no Christians would be left at home.

Answer: To this I answer that by many the command is obeyed in the Spirit and not in the letter. Even the first disciples did not all obey it in the letter, for whilst many of them were scattered abroad and went everywhere preaching the Word, still many remained in their own houses, many went back to their friends to tell them, 'what great things the Lord has done for them'.

When the General of an Army issues the command to besiege some strong garrison and to take it by all possible means, he never intends that every individual of the Army actually scale the walls and enter into the city. He knows well that many must remain behind to take care of the baggage. Some must cheer on their comrades by the sound of the pipe and drum. And many who are sick and wounded must remain far from the scene of action. Still every heart is engaged in the enterprise. Every hand is anxious to help forward the victory. Just so, brethren, when Christ says, 'Go ye into all the world, and preach the gospel to every creature,' he does not mean that every Christian must go. He knows that many must stay behind to take care of the church at home; that many must cheer on their brethren to the work of the unceasing cry of prayer; and that many too must stay behind because they are sick and wounded. But though every Christian must not go, still every Christian heart must be engaged in the enterprise. Every Christian tongue must plead in its behalf. Every Christian hand must do what it can to help forward the victory.

Again, when the Captain of a ship gives the command to spread every sail to the wind, he does not intend that every seaman is to go aloft. He knows well that many must remain below to handle the ropes on deck. He knows that many are unskilful and unable to climb to the top mast. Still every one must bear a hand, every hand and eye must be engaged in the business, every one must do something that the ship may be speeded onwards. Just so brethren, when Christ says, 'Go ye into all the world, and preach the gospel to every creature', he does not mean that all should actually go, he means that every one must bear a hand. That every heart and eye must be intent on the grand achievement, the conversion of the world.

There are many ways in which this command may be obeyed:

1. By many this command ought to be literally obeyed.
Brethren, there may be some here this day listening to the parting command of Christ, who should obey it literally. There may be some to whom God has given natural abilities and a saving knowledge of Christ and much likeness to Christ, in that one feature of compassion for a perishing world. And an open door in Providence. If there be one such here, go home and think if that Word of Christ be not spoken to you, 'Go ye into all the world, and preach the gospel to every creature.' Go and see if, like Paul, you be not converted for this very job that you may be God's witness to the ends of the earth. See if you cannot say, 'Eternity is laid upon me, yea woe is unto me if I preach not the gospel.'

I do not say that you will altogether ruin your soul if you do not obey that necessity, but I say that you will lose a great weight of eternal glory. You will be just saved and nothing more. You will be dark and dimly lit compared with them who have turned many to righteousness and shine as the stars for ever and ever.

2. All of you may obey this command by supplying the means of sending others.
There is not one child of God hearing me who can be exempted from obeying it in this way. Be you rich or be you poor, it is equally in your power to deny yourself that you may have something to give in the cause of Christ. My friends, the cause of charity or Christian love is quite misunderstood in our day. They have got the notion that if they give a little, if they give as much as their neighbours, if they give what they will never miss, that is Christian charity. My friends, that is not what Christ did, therefore it is not Christian charity. Christ did not give a little, he gave much. Christ did not give only as much as his neighbours, he gave more than all beside. Christ did not give what he would never miss – he gave himself for us.

Brethren, go you and do likewise. In this you must be a peculiar people, quite different from the world. The world copy from one another but you must copy only from Christ. You never will be a happy believer till you deny yourself that you may be able to give, for you never will be like Christ till then. He gave himself to hunger and thirst, to weariness, to the cursed death of the cross. And all for the sake of poor lost souls. And will you eat bread to the full and drink to the full and endure no pain, no privation for the sake of poor lost souls? And do you really think that you have got the mind that was in Christ? And do not say I bid you do a painful or a foolish thing. Christ left this Word to very poor fishermen. It is more blessed to give than it is to receive. Christ's cause is the best of all banks to lodge your savings in. Cast thy bread upon the water and it shall return after many days.

3. You can obey this command by helping others with your prayers. That Word of Christ is as full of meaning as ever, 'The harvest truly is plenteous but the labourers are few. Pray ye therefore the Lord of the harvest that he will send forth labourers into his harvest.' There is not one believer hearing me who can be exempted from obeying this command. It is much to be feared that in our day the duty of praying for the heathen is altogether neglected. I put to your own selves, do you make conscience of daily pleading with God on behalf of the world? And yet do you think yourself in the image of Christ? Is this the mind of him who wept over Jerusalem? It is said that Christ is not willing that any should perish but that all should come to the knowledge of the truth. And are you willing that the millions of India thence perish, and if not, will you not pray?

Little children who love the Saviour, perhaps you can do little in any other way. Yet when you kneel by your bedside, remember the poor children of India who pray to bloody idols that cannot save, and ask of God to send forth labourers into the harvest. Grown men who often enter through the rent veil, remember ye are priests unto God. Now a priest does not speak for himself only but for others also. Will you be selfish even in your prayers, even in the presence of God? Oh that you would wrestle with God and ye shall prevail. If ever India be converted, it will be in answer to prayer. 'Ask of me,' said the Father to the Son, 'and I will give thee the heathen.' Brethren, we are the body of Christ; let us ask the Father and he will give it to us.

St. Peter's, 5 March 1837

20. Strive ye to enter in (Luke 13:23-30)

Then said one unto him, Lord, are there few that be saved? And he said unto them, Strive to enter in at the strait gate: for many, I say unto you, will seek to enter in, and shall not be able. When once the master of the house is risen up, and hath shut to the door, and ye begin to stand without, and to knock at the door, saying, Lord, Lord, open unto us; and he shall answer and say unto you, I know you not whence ye are: Then shall ye begin to say, We have eaten and drunk in thy presence, and thou hast taught in our streets. But he shall say, I tell you, I know you not whence ye are; depart from me, all ye workers of iniquity. There shall be weeping and gnashing of teeth, when ye shall see Abraham, and Isaac, and Jacob, and all the prophets, in the kingdom of God, and you yourselves thrust out. And they shall come from the east, and from the west, and from the north, and from the south, and shall sit down in the kingdom of God. And, behold, there are last which shall be first; and there are first which shall be last.

Reasons for immediate entrance into Christ

1. The gate is strait
Christ gave this as a reason before in his Sermon on the Mount, 'Enter ye in at the strait gate, for strait is the gate....'

a. Not easy
A strait gate is one which you do not easily find! And when you have found it do not easily get through! So it is with Christ. It is not an easy thing to enter into Christ. All that have ever been brought to Christ will tell you that it is no easy thing, that God alone could have brought them through. Some think it is an easy thing to be saved; it is only to take a thought, to be a little sorry for sin, to shed a few tears, to say a few prayers. It will do well enough for an hour of sickness or an hour of death. Now, I tell you the gate is strait, and it is easier for a camel to go through the eye of a needle than for a rich man to enter into the kingdom of God. It is the most wonderful thing in the world to be brought through that strait gate. It is impossible with man, but with God all things are possible. Begin today then, do not put off. Few men ever enter in who are up in years. Strive to enter in at the strait gate.

b. Not many at a time

When a company of men come up to a very narrow gate they decide to enter one at a time. So it is in conversion, you must go in one by one. The gate of death is like it in this, no friend can go with you. They accompany you to the gate but then you must part company and enter alone. So in coming to Christ, it is a strait gate. You must believe alone. Friends often try to take you with them through the strait gate. Ministers try to draw you in, but you must enter alone. Oh strive to enter in then at the strait gate.

c. You cannot go with your proud, self-righteous notions.

You must be converted and become a little child. When a person clothed in large, wide, flowing garments comes to a very narrow gate they cannot get in, their clothing hinders them. So when a person is clothed with his own righteousness, he cannot enter in at the strait gate. Except ye be converted and become as little children, ye shall not enter into the kingdom of God. How far the most of you are from this. You were born with proud, self-righteous notions; these cleave to you and will not let you go. You must become little of stature. You must see yourself a vile, lost sinner and Christ a full, free Saviour, else you cannot enter in at the strait gate.

What hope is there in this? You have heard long and much of Christ and yourself and yet you are as proud and self-righteous as ever. Ah, I fear the most will never enter in at the strait gate.

2. The gate will soon be shut (v.25)

'When once the master of the house is risen up.' The gospel is here compared to a marriage feast which God has prepared, the gate is standing wide open, and the servants are sent to every creature saying, 'All things are ready'. But the time is near at hand when the master of the house will rise up and shut the door and no more shall enter in to the marriage.

a. So it was at the flood

The Ark stood with its door wide open for 120 years, inviting sinners to flee into it from the coming wrath. But when the set time was come, the master of the house rose up and shut the door. God shut Noah in and shut the rest of the world out.

b. So the refuge city
Its gates were open night and day that the manslayer might fly thither. But when the Saviour comes, the gate will be shut; no more sinners will find refuge.

c. So the sheepfold.
Christ says, 'I am the door. By me, if any man enter in he shall be saved and shall go in and out and find pasture.' When all the little flock are gathered in, then the chief shepherd shall appear and shut to the door.

Objection:
Some, I fear the door is shut already to me.
   Answer: No, not till the master is risen up. Christ is still sitting at the right hand of God. The door is still wide open. It was not till the day of the flood that the door of the Ark was shut. It is not till the day of Christ's rising up that the door of the kingdom will be shut. The door is wide to the wall. The veil is rent from the top to the bottom. Christ says, I am the door, not I was the door, by me if any man enter in. True, you have long refused the open door, you have long avoided the strait gate. Still, you are included in that word, Any man.
   But remember, it will soon be shut; the moment Christ rises up he will shut to the door and it will never be opened again. The moment Christ comes in the clouds of heaven, the door will be shut for ever. It will be shut all in a moment. Just as a snare comes upon a bird, as a thief comes upon a house, as travail comes upon a woman with child, so shall the rising up of the Saviour be. And the shutting to of the door, the sound of that shutting door, shall ring through a slumbering world.
   Remember it is open now. If any man enter in he shall be saved. But I cannot answer for its being open another day, another hour, another minute. Oh, strive to enter in at the strait gate.

3. All a sinner's anxieties will be vain when Christ comes
Many shall seek to enter in.... ye begin to stand without.

a) Many seek to enter into Christ now who are not able to enter in.
One came running to Jesus and kneeled down and said, 'Good Master, what good thing shall I do that I may inherit eternal life?' But the man went away sorrowful. The camel was not able to enter through

the needle's eye. So it is among you. Many run to Christ but go away sorrowful. Once a trembling woman was laid hands on by a merciful God and drawn out of Sodom; but she looked back and became a pillar of salt. There are many such among you. Many of you have had your deep impressions, your tears, your tremblings, and are this day a pillar of salt. Oh, begin again and strive to enter in.

b) True meaning of the words

There is a day coming when all Christless persons shall begin to seek, when many a prayerless, godless soul among you shall run and kneel and pray and tremble, saying, 'Lord, Lord, open unto me', but all in vain.

(i) Christless persons will be as earnest to get in at Christ's door in that day as Christ is earnest to get in at their door this day. You read of Christ in the Bible, that he is come to seek and to save that which was lost. He is the Good Shepherd seeking after the lost sheep. He is seeking to enter in to the sinner's heart. You read how he comes to their door and knocks, 'Behold I stand at the door and knock, if any man hears my voice and opens the door I will come in to him.' I have stood at the door; he stands without and knocks at sinners' doors. You read how he cries aloud and redoubles his arguments, 'Unto you, O men, I call,' and his word is, 'Turn ye, turn ye, why will ye die?'

Dear souls, this is the very picture of what you will be in that day. If you do not enter in before the door is shut then you will seek to enter in and shall not be able. As Christ knocked at your door, so you will stand without and knock at his door. As he cried aloud to you, so you to him, 'Lord, Lord, open unto us.' As loud and as long as he cried at you, will you cry at him. 'Then shall they call on me but I will not answer. They shall seek me early but shall not find me.'

(ii) Christless persons will be as anxious to get in at Christ's door as their godly friends and ministers are now anxious to bring Christ into their door. Some of you know that godly ministers and friends are seeking your salvation. They often stand without and knock again and say, 'Open unto us.' We teach you publicly and from house to house, warning every man and teaching every man, that we may present every man perfect in Christ Jesus. Some of you are troubled and annoyed when we come to beseech you to be reconciled unto God. Many of you try to be out of the way when the minister of Christ comes and yet you are the very persons that will seek Christ when the door is shut, crying, 'Lord, Lord, open unto us.'

My dear friends, stretch your eye forward a few years. Already I see it as if the day were come. The apprentice looks forward to the day when he shall begin business for himself. The merchant looks forward to the time when he shall retire upon his money. Look forward just a little further. He that shall come will come and will not tarry. And see what a different scene this parish will present.

There are many in it who are not in the house of God, who would not come the length of the street to hear the message of a Saviour. These will be up and seeking. Old grey-headed men and women among you that have grown old in Christlessness, whose knee is unused to bending in prayer; young men who hate the calls and invitations of the moment. You that love sin and pleasure more than God, who shut your ears from hearing the words of godly friends. You will be busy men in that day, what prayers and arguments you will use, 'Lord, Lord, open unto us. Thou hast taught in our streets, we have been at thy sacraments.' Then shall he answer, 'Depart from me, all ye that work iniquity.' 'Than shall they call and I will not answer. They shall seek me and shall not find me.'

Oh, will none of you antidote that anxiety? Oh, strive to enter in at the strait gate. It is but a little while and all this shall be as I have said. Oh, begin now. May God awaken some of you to begin today. 'Turn ye, turn ye, why will ye die?' You will be miserable when you see others in the kingdom and yourselves without, 'There shall be...' (v.28).

Many things make up the misery of hell:

a. Bodily torment, their worm dieth not and their fire is not quenched.

b. Darkness, blackness and darkness for ever, like the Egyptian darkness when none rose up from his place for three days.

c. The absence of God. God will withdraw his comfortable presence from them. There will be no comfort there.

d. There is another element, *they shall weep and gnash their teeth when they see Abram.* The sight of so many, once sinners like themselves, of the same nature under the same curse, all entered in by the door, washed, justified, sanctified, glorified, the very sight will make them gnash their teeth in rage and misery.

(i) You will see patriarchs and prophets there, Abram, etc. They had few advantages compared with you. Christ was made known to

them only in types and shadows and yet they saw his day and were glad. And not one of them shall be wanting in that day. They are in the kingdom of God and you thrust out.

(ii) You will see men of every climate there. Many shall come from the east, from Hindustan and China, the fruit of the wandering missionary. Many from the West, Brainerd's holy Indians. From the North, Greenlanders, meek and lowly in heart. From the South, islanders of the South Seas. Men of every country and kindred and people and tongue. A great company. They had few advantages, you had the Bible and ministers from your infancy. Yet they are sitting in the kingdom of God and you yourself thrust out.

(iii) Many last first, and first last. You will see some you reckoned the least of the human race: the harlot Rahab; the thief that died with Christ upon the cross; Mary Magdalene; the woman taken in adultery; the beggar Lazarus in Abraham's bosom. A ransomed company, washed in Christ's blood, as white as snow, as white as wool. All filled with Christ's Spirit, holy and happy, with glorified bodies, wearing crowns and golden harps singing, 'Worthy is the Lamb that was slain. Thou hast washed us from our sins in thy blood and made us to our God, kings and priests and we shall reign with thee.'

Word to moral, worldly men

You know some poor despised Christian who once lived a wicked life in the world. Once he was a blasphemer, a persecutor and injurious. Come like the woman that washed Christ's feet which previously was a sinner, a strange change has come over that soul. The Bible and the house of prayer are now his favourites. No more the haunts of pleasure and of sin, and yet you despise them. You say, well if that person turns religious we may all hope for mercy. You despise their words and ways. You say it is hypocrisy.

Ah, stay a moment. Think what this place says, that you will one day see that soul in glory and yourself thrust out. God with them. Cast in your lot with them, follow their faith if you would be happy. Oh, strive to enter in, let it not be a bitter day to see the publicans and harlots entering into heaven before you.

Objection

Some awakened soul may say, 'I am the least in the world to be saved. No hope for me.'

Answer: There is hope, for many that are last shall be first and the first last. Oh, strive to enter in at the strait gate.

I have often wondered to observe how little curiosity worldly men have about eternal things. The smallest worldly thing takes up their attention and affords matter for enquiry and discourse. Pleased with a rattle. Tickled with a straw. Some accident mentioned in the newspaper. A piece of dress or the flavour of a little wine afford matter for plain remark. Although they are like a passing cloud, whilst the enduring realities of an eternal world, of heaven and hell and God and Christ, are unthought upon. How few even think of asking such a question as that man does, 'Are there few that be saved?' Again it is still more sad to find some men who will ask questions about eternal things but who have no personal works of grace upon their own souls. How many are there among yourselves, who read good books and ask good questions, yet who have not personally entered in at the strait gate? Such a one was the man before us. How touching the answer of the Saviour.

Strive ye to enter in
Oh, my dear friends, salvation is not a thing of curiosity. It is not mere knowledge or curiosity that will save you, but a personal entering in at the strait gate. With the heart man believeth unto righteousness and with the mouth confession is made unto salvation.

St. Peter's, 9 December 1838

21. The Lost Sheep and Piece of Money (Luke 15:1-10)

Then drew near unto him all the publicans and sinners for to hear him. And the Pharisees and scribes murmured, saying, This man receiveth sinners, and eateth with them. And he spake this parable unto them, saying, What man of you, having an hundred sheep, if he lose one of them, doth not leave the ninety and nine in the wilderness, and go after that which is lost, until he find it? And when he hath found it, he layeth it on his shoulders, rejoicing. And when he cometh home, he calleth together his friends and neighbours, saying unto them, Rejoice with me; for I have found my sheep which was lost. I say unto you, that likewise joy shall be in heaven over one sinner that repenteth, more than over ninety and nine just persons, which need no repentance. Either what woman having ten pieces of silver, if she lose one piece, doth not light a candle, and sweep the house, and seek diligently till she find it? And when she hath found it, she calleth her friends and her neighbours together, saying, Rejoice with me; for I have found the piece which I had lost. Likewise, I say unto you, there is joy in the presence of the angels of God over one sinner that repenteth.

In order to see the full force and beauty of these parables, it is necessary that we know in whose hearing they were related; what occasion drew them forth; and what end our Lord had in view in relating them.

In the preceding chapter we are told that Jesus went into the house of one of the chief Pharisees on the Sabbath day to partake of his Sabbath meal. There seems indeed to have been an invited company of lawyers and Pharisees who were ever on the watch to entangle him in his speech or deride his behaviour. Leaving this house accompanied, it is probable, by many of those who had been at meat with him, multitudes of the lower classes, publicans and sinners to entertain whom would have been a stain upon the character of any Pharisee, seem to have gathered around him (14:25). To these as being more likely to value his rich offers of mercy he now directed his discourse. So that in the beginning of our passage (15:1), we find that these men who were the very outcasts of society were gradually pressing nearer and nearer to him, being far more deeply interested in his words than the supercilious Pharisees. These moments of increasing attention on the part of the crowd drew forth the murmurs of the Pharisees who were indignant that men of openly depraved moral character should find more interest in the words and a warmer reception in the manner of a professed teacher come from God than they themselves did. 'The Pharisees and Scribes murmured saying, This man receiveth sinners and eateth with them.' If this man were the holy being he professes to be, would he not associate with those who are like-minded with himself? What interest could a heavenly mind take in these depraved outcasts? And yet has not 'this man' left our society for that of such men?

Such was the objection of these self-righteous Pharisees and such was the occasion which drew forth the following parables. In refuting this objection, which he does in his own most peculiar and most powerful manner, not by meeting it with direct argument but by leading the mind to decide against it in a parallel case, our blessed Lord had evidently two purposes in view, because he was speaking for the sake of two classes of hearers. The sword of the Spirit is said to be two-edged; we shall find that it was eminently so on this occasion. His first object was to reprove the self-righteousness of the Pharisees. And his second object was to encourage the very chief of sinners who might be listening to him. To convince the proud and to animate the humble was the two-fold object he had in view. It remains to be seen how admirably gifted the parables were for both ends.

Christ seems at this time not to have been in the city of Jerusalem but probably in Bethany or Bethphage where rural and domestic images would be best appreciated. While at the same time the universality of these ideas ensured them an intelligent reception everywhere not only in Judea but over all the world. It is also interesting to remark that the first of these parables, that of the lost sheep, seems evidently to have been a favourite one of our Lord's. So we find him repeating it on another occasion and for a different purpose (see Matthew 18). It is the sign of a good householder that he brings out of his treasure things old as well as new.

He begins both the parables in the manner which is well known to be the best for arresting the attention and especially for carrying conviction to a crowd of objectors, namely by pointed interrogation. 'What man of you, having an hundred sheep, if he lose one of them, doth not leave the ninety and nine in the wilderness and go after that which is gone astray until he find it?' 'Either what woman having ten pieces of silver, if she lose one piece, doth not light a candle and sweep the house, and seek diligently till she find it?' Is there one of you who would not do this? Is not this just what everybody does? Is this not a faithful picture of human nature? And would you not esteem that man as a very senseless and careless shepherd of the flock, and that housewife a very stupid and improvident one, who should not act in this very way?

It appears to me that though Christ makes no reference to this part of the story in the application of the parables, he nevertheless intended this to be his first ground of defence against the objection of the Pharisees and of encouragement to the publicans and sinners. Let us see then how well-suited this part of the parable was to give reproof to the self-righteous and cheering intelligence to the sinner.

It is the lost sheep that the shepherd goes after with so much trouble and fatigue, not the sheep that never went astray. Nor is it a sheep that has been carried out from the fold and left bleeding and torn upon the mountains, making the valleys resound with its sad bleatings, mourning over its desolate condition, so far from the shepherd's shelter and the shepherd's care. We are told nothing more than that it is a lost sheep, wandered to such a distance from 'the green pastures and the still waters', that it is bewildered and lost. But the more dangerous the condition of the sheep, so much the more anxious is the shepherd. Everything must be risked rather than certainly lose one sheep of his hundred. He leaves the ninety and nine in the wilderness and pursues the bewildered sheep. In like manner it is the lost piece of money that raises all the good woman's anxiety. All her comfort in the nine other pieces is destroyed till she have found the tenth which is lost. Therefore she lights the lamp and sweeps the house and searches diligently till she find it.

Just so is it with the Saviour. He comes to seek and save that which was lost. The unfallen families in heaven seem as it were for a time to be forgotten and left behind whilst the Son steps down from the throne of the Universe, leaving the bosom of the Father and descends to this remote corner of his dominion where dwell so many who are lost. A world whose inhabitants like lost sheep have gone astray, turning every one to his own way. The unquenchable love of compassion burns in his bosom while he becomes 'a man of sorrows and acquainted with grief.' A love stronger than death, for it moved him to give up his life. The Good Shepherd gave his life for the sheep. It is on a principle which finds its responsive echo in the human heart that the Saviour has come down to the earth at all. Had he been in quest of the society of righteous spirits, why should he leave the mansions of glory, where ten thousand righteous angels were his ministers? When you see the shepherd far separated from his flock, in pain and weariness clambering the mountains, in haste and anxiety, penetrating far into the wilderness, need you ask whether he is in search of ease and pleasure or of the sheep that was lost? And just so when we find the Saviour in the villages of Judea, in weariness and painfulness, going from city to city, need you ask whether he comes to seek repose and satisfaction in the companionship of mortals or to seek and save that which was lost?

Such is the picture by which our Saviour points out the reason of his coming to the world. And since it was obviously intended as a two-edged weapon, let us attempt to see it in both ways:

1. For the sake of those who partake with the Pharisees in their self-righteousness and

2. For those who partake with the publicans in their earnest seeking of the Saviour.

1. If Christ came to seek and save the lost, the salvation of the gospel is not for righteous men. If you have a righteousness of your own, you have no need of Christ's. If you are whole, you need not the physician. If there is no wrath resting upon you, then you have no need of the shelter of the Redeemer's wings.

And yet should not this consideration forbid you to sit down perfectly at ease, that the Bible describes every one of us as sinners? 'We all like lost sheep have gone astray'; 'There is none righteous, no not one'. Consider if it may not be possible that you are so very much lost, so utterly bewildered that you do not so much as know that you are lost. Suppose the sheep to wander over the hills and through the valleys, to cross the scanty brooks and penetrate the thorny moors, till it gets into the pastures of the wilderness for the still waters and green pastures and begins to relish the dry reeds of the desert. Is the sheep the less a lost sheep that it now forgets its loss, that it has a happiness in the howling waste which it would not exchange for the richest pastureland and the shepherd's tenderest care?

In like manner, is that soul among you any the less a lost soul that it is so far gone from God and godliness as to have lost all relish for them? You have wandered over the mountains of vanity and across the scanty brooks of worldly pleasure and through the thorny moors of worldly cares and anxieties and now you are quite happy with the miserable pasturage of a perishing world. You feel no loss, no anxiety about eternal things. With your decencies and your worldly friends and pleasing occupations your whole love is engrossed. And if by chance your eye is arrested by the more than mortal figure of the Saviour bearing his message of salvation to every door, it is only to wonder how a messenger from heaven should condescend to the meanest and the most depraved. Ah miserable man, is it not the sorest of all maladies when the pulse is high and the cheek is flushed and the fever rages in the brain so that the patient tells you he is well? Is it not the most fearful of all madness when the crazy man will tell you frankly that he is wise? And oh, then, is it not the sorest spiritual malady of all when the spiritually sick man says, I am well and need no physician; the balm of Gilead is not for me? How sad is it, yet how frequent a case, for the minister of peace to stop some wandering, benighted man in the broad road of worldliness and tell him of a Saviour. The worldly man will answer in thought and look if not in word, What is all this to me? He knows not he is lost and therefore cares not to be found. If the lost sheep knew its danger, the rocks and valleys would resound to its bleatings of distress and it would flee to some refuge from the wild beasts of the wilderness.

If you knew your danger, your cry of distress would ascend incessantly to heaven and you would anxiously beseech your godly friends and ministers to tell you again and again of the way of salvation. But if you know not you are lost, how can you ever know the value of the Saviour of the lost? And if you know not the value of a Saviour, how can you ever be saved? Sin and wrath are abiding on you, yet you know it not. You are wandering on the edge of a precipice, yet careless and singing as you go. You are sick, yea dying, yet you say, We are well. If then all other arguments fail, ought not this one to arouse you, that Christ's salvation is put past you? If you are as you think you are, it is not even addressed to you. And then there is no other name given under heaven among men whereby you can be saved.

But secondly, if Christ came as a shepherd to seek the lost sheep, then the man who feels himself a sinner may well embrace Christ as a Saviour. 'Come unto me all ye that are weary and heavy-laden,' said our Lord, 'and I will give you rest.' Suppose then a man to be convinced by the Spirit of God of the sinfulness of his long life. He may have many palpable sins known to all the world, or his sins may have been all contrived and consummated within the dark chamber of his own ungodly heart. Whatever they be, let them be seen by him in the light of heaven, so that he loathes himself in dust and ashes. 'Against thee, thee only have I sinned', is his passionate exclamation. The vengeance of him who can by no means clear the guilty seems not only terrible and sure but just. Where shall he flee for peace? What shall he do to be saved? To such a man how interesting should be the story which tells how the Saviour is come for the lost. And yet why is it that any who are brought thus far should stop there, should refuse to take the righteousness of God and the peace of God which are so freely offered? Why is it there are so many walking in darkness and seeing no light, ever crying after the Saviour and yet never embracing him? Pressing through the crowd of proud and worldly men, as it were, into the very presence of Christ and yet not receiving that light and peace and purity which he came to give?

The only reason that can be given is that you do not believe Christ when he says that he came for the lost. You will not be persuaded to cast all your care upon him who declares he has cared for you. You think perhaps that you must have some other qualifications before you are permitted to rest on the words of the Saviour. And what is this but saying that Christ did not come for those who are in themselves utterly lost. And yet no reasonable man can account for so strange an event as the Saviour's presence in the world except upon the principle that he came for such as you, any more than you could account for the presence of the shepherd in the wilderness far away from his flock except upon the principle that he came in search of some wandering sheep. If the sheep could by any possibility find its way back, the shepherd would never have gone a step from the sheepfolds. If you could do anything to save yourself, Christ never would have trod this earth in the form of humanity. Let then the appearance of a listening Saviour in the world, an event so strange and upon any principle so unaccountable, dispel every unbelieving doubt, every suspicious dread of your offended God. It is indeed against God you have been sinning, the highest and holiest, and more than all, the kindest and tenderest of beings. Nay, it is against that beseeching Saviour you have been sinning, refusing him your confidence, despising all his anxiety and all his bleeding love. But you have not been more zealous in inquiring how you might get away from the very idea of God than he has been zealous to hedge up your godless way by threatenings and providences; and thus to drive or draw you to himself. Even now he stands stretching out his hands all the day long: 'whoso findeth me findeth life and shall obtain favour of the Lord'. Should not such an exhibition of Christ as this have you to take his salvation as it is offered? Come not although you are sinners but *because* you are sinners: for his name is the Saviour of sinners, even the chief.

The second part of the parable which our Lord seems to have regarded as the most forcible and important is told in these words:

'And when he hath found it, he layeth it on his shoulders, rejoicing. And when he cometh home, he calleth together his friends and neighbours, saying unto them, Rejoice with me; for I have found my sheep which was lost. I say unto you, that likewise joy shall be in heaven over one sinner that repenteth, more than over ninety and nine just persons, which need no repentance'.

'And when she hath found it, she calleth her friends and her neighbours together, saying, Rejoice with me; for I have found the piece which I had lost. Likewise, I say unto you, there is joy in the presence of the angels of God over one sinner that repenteth'.

Christ here passes from the argument drawn from his own singular compassion and anxious labours on behalf of the lost, to the argument drawn from the fact that angels partake, nay that God the Father upon the throne partakes, in his joy when he brings back such one lost sheep to the fold. Here alas his argument is drawn from human nature. There is no reason why the interrogation should end with the fourth and eighth verses. Indeed it is evident that our Lord still appeals to the common sense and observation of his audience, 'Which of you has not seen all this done again and again?' The only observation in the way of interpretation which is necessary in so simple and beautiful a narrative, is that there is evidently a difference between the rendition of the one parable and that of the other, which I cannot but think full of meaning.

In the first we are told, 'Joy shall be in heaven', a phrase which as it occurs in the Lord's Prayer, cannot but be understood of the angels, the creature inhabitants of heaven. Whereas in the second we are told that there is joy in the presence of the angels of God, which can hardly be otherwise understood than that he who so loved the world as to give his Son, he who hath no pleasure in the death of the wicked but rather that they should turn and live, rejoices on the throne of heaven over every recovered wanderer and fills with new ecstasies the myriads of attending angels.

Nor is it unworthy of notice that in the first, the joy is said to be future, 'joy shall be', whereas in the second it is said to be present joy which God takes of the repenting sinners. No sooner is there the movement of the penitent heart towards God, than there is joy in God. Jehovah smiles! And all the adoring thousands, whose blessedness it is to live in the very light of his countenance and to reflect back his image, cannot but participate in this beatific joy. If a confirmatory proof was required of the correctness of this interpretation, it is to be found in that passage of Matthew before alluded to, where Christ again makes use of the parable of the lost sheep, and where it is curious to observe that the interest of angels and of the

Father in the saints is also added to the interest which the Son himself takes (Matthew 18).

Again we attempt to use the two-edged weapon of the Saviour:
1. For the sake of those who are at ease and
2. For the sake of those who are ill at ease in Zion.

1. If there be joy in God and among the holy angels only over repenting sinners, there can be no joy over self-righteous men. We have already seen who they are who are the objects of the Redeemer's coming and what a man must find himself to be before he can know the true value of his coming, a lost and helpless sinner. I now proceed to show who they are that excite the sympathy of heaven's sinless inhabitants, nay of God himself. They are repenting sinners, sinners redeemed by grace, found and brought back by the Saviour. When the shepherd found the sheep he laid it on his shoulder rejoicing. He knew well that such a sheep could never find its way through all the entanglements of the wilderness and therefore he carried it. And so does the Redeemer. It is not enough that he converts the soul, he also sacrifices. He knows well the choking briars and tangled thickets that enclose the murderer. He knows the power of old habits, of old temptations and of old sins, and therefore he not only says, 'My blood is sufficient for thee', and thus whispers peace, but he adds, 'My grace is sufficient for thee', and thus infuses purity. Often struggling, often uneasy and restless, still is the sheep borne heavenwards by the good Shepherd of the sheep, who long before was prophesied of as 'gathering the lambs with his arm and carrying them in his bosom'. Over such it is that all heaven rings Jubilee, redeemed by grace, sanctified by grace, noble trophies of the Redeemer's Victory! All heaven sees of the travail of his soul and is satisfied. But what joy shall you cause in heaven? You who because you know not that you are sinners, know not the value of a Saviour, or a Sanctifier. How is the Redeemer's travail magnified in you, who have never known the value of his righteousness? Or how is his sanctifying grace made honourable in you, who have never known that you needed its power?

How fearful a situation is that of a self-righteous man? Instead of angels rejoicing over his salvation, supposing it possible for him to be saved in his self-righteousness, these sinless beings, who delight to honour the Son even as they honour the Father, would behold that man proudly entering the mansions of glory with a thrill of horror, for here would be a fearful evidence of the Saviour dishonoured, of Christ having died in vain. Instead of there being joy in the presence of the angels of God over the return of this self-converted, self-renovated man, these very angels of the presence would hide their faces from the fearful darkness of Jehovah's frown. Nor is there aught marvellous in this. For what greater insult could be imagined to be offered to the God and Father of our Lord and Saviour Jesus Christ than thus to pass through the gates of Paradise proclaiming the uselessness of the blood of Christ to justify and of the Spirit of Christ to sanctify?

Oh then, if the very idea of a self-righteous man standing in peace in the presence of God then be impious and horrible, how is it that he can stand in peace in the presence of God now? Oh, if your entrance into the heavenly Jerusalem, among that innumerable company of angels and before God the Judge of all and Jesus the Mediator of the New Covenant, would move with horror that vast and holy assembly, how is it you can look in upon yourself and yet remain unmoved? Saying peace, peace when there is no peace. Oh, how is it that we can look upon you steeped in the slumber of your imagined righteousness, smiling like a dreaming man amid all the cares and pleasures of this world's society and not attempt to bid you awake? Arise that Christ may give you light.

The angels would not rejoice but weep over you, even as Christ did over self-righteous Jerusalem because she would not attend to the things that belonged to her peace. And shall we be unmoved? Shall we not take up the warning of the prophet and say, 'Woe to them that are at ease in Zion'? I beseech you to listen to the Saviour's voice, 'Because thou sayest I am rich and increased with goods and have need of nothing; and knoweth not that thou art wretched and miserable and poor and blind and naked. I counsel thee to buy of me gold tried in the fire that thou mayest be rich; and white raiment that thou mayest be clothed and that the shame of thy nakedness do not appear; and anoint thine eyes with eye salve that thou mayest see.'

But secondly, if there be joy in God and among the holy angels over one repenting sinner, the man who feels himself a sinner may well be encouraged to rest his whole burden on Christ as his Saviour, Sanctifier and Glorifier.

We have seen how excellent a warrant the convinced sinner has to embrace Christ as his Saviour in the picture which Christ makes of himself as the shepherd seeking the lost sheep. Let us now see what an accession of encouragement there is in the picture which he now gives of his Father and the angels, as entering into his joy and rejoicing along with him over the recovered wanderer. But the very essence of the encouragement depends upon our marking well the kind of recovery they rejoice over. From what has been said it is evident that it is not every kind of recovery that would call forth the jubilee of heaven. When I read how solemnly God says, 'I have no pleasure in the death of him that dieth', I cannot but think that both God and angels would rejoice in the deliverance of any creature from pain, but of this I am very sure, for the existence of a hell bears awful testimony to the truth that though they rejoice in the happiness of every creature where it can be had consistently with the honour of the Godhead, the sustained honour and majesty of the divine Government are dearer to them than the happiness of worlds.

The repentance then which gives joy in heaven is a repentance which gives all the honour to the Saviour. The reason why such joy is said to pervade the uncreated Mind, and thence to spread through all the holy created minds of the universe upon the conversion of a sinner, is that the conversion of a sinner and the honour of the Saviour of sinners are inseparably united and must be to all eternity. Two mighty elements contribute to swell the full tide of joy. It is not that a creature is saved from pain, that a never-dying spirit is snatched from never-dying sorrow, that a soul and a body are rescued from the worm and the fire, the weeping and wailing and gnashing of teeth. It is not that only, nor that chiefly, that sends a thrill of joy through all the holy universe, but that you are redeemed from all this not with corruptible things but with the precious blood of Christ; that you are sanctified by no earthly power but by the precious Spirit of Christ; that you are a ransomed captive, borne off in triumph on the mighty shoulders of the Spoiler of Principalities. All heaven rejoices in the felicity of a creature but they rejoice in the brightening glory of the Redeemer more.

Take heed, then, in embracing the Saviour that you take him as a complete Saviour. You can no more find the way to heaven by yourself after Christ hath found you than you could find yourself when lost. You need to be sanctified by the same power which justified you. Too many are walking in heaviness this day because they are seeking to share in the honours of their own salvation. It may be you are convinced you have no righteousness and have been made willing to give the Saviour all the glory of that. 'How can man be just with God?' you rightly say, and therefore you willingly take the Lord for your righteousness, for, 'God hath made him to be sin for us who knew no sin, that we might be made the righteousness of God in him'.

But then, perhaps you think you have honoured the Saviour sufficiently by embracing his righteousness and think that this is all he can do for you – the moulding of your temper; subduing your evil habits, overcoming the world, the devil and the flesh, this must be all your own. Ah, the proud heart of man! How unwilling it is to give up all the credit of salvation to another. How loathe we are to be nothing that God may be all in all. Many a hard battle you will have to fight with your sins. Good resolutions and indomitable lusts will join issue in many a desperate struggle. All the devices of a self-sufficient soul may be tried by you. All earthly assistances may be brought into the field. But though you may again and again be flushed with hopes of victory, again and again sin will come off the conqueror. Perhaps you fly to retirement, to the desert, yet sin pursues, ascends the galley with you and rides behind the flying horseman.

This day the greatest cause of all your heaviness may be this, that you thought yourself saved and yet you are not sanctified. 'It is hard for thee to kick against the pricks.' How merciful is God that he does not suffer you to win the victory whilst you are fighting thus in your own strength. You yourselves must feel that it is no encouragement to you to know that angels rejoice over the returning sinner for you feel that you are not returning. You are no nearer than you were, the shame of defeat is more congenial to your feelings than the triumph of victory.

Learn from this parable more distinctly the economy by which you are saved and must be sanctified. We are saved by grace and sanctified by grace. Ascending to that most precious of all the promises. Sin shall not have dominion over you, for you are not under the law but under grace. 'Come unto me,' says Christ, 'all ye that are weary and heavy laden and I will give you rest.' All your disquiet arises from this that you are trying to give rest to yourself, robbing Christ of his honour. The shepherd must have all the glory of finding and bringing back the sheep. The Saviour must have all the glory of redeeming his own and purifying them to himself a peculiar people. He died to justify. He reigns to sanctify. On the cross and on the throne we must always look to Jesus as the Author and Finisher of our faith, whilst we run the race set before us.

Pray then that you may be so emptied of all glorying in yourself, that you may be convinced so thoroughly not only of your own utter sinfulness but of your own utter weakness. As to be willing no longer to go about establishing your own holiness any more than your own righteousness, but to take the Lord for your righteousness and strength, to look on Christ as made unto you sanctification and complete redemption. In a word, so as to be willing to be carried 'on the shoulders' of the great shepherd of Israel. And then indeed you will know what encouragement there is in the truth that all the holy angels are turning their golden harps to a new hymn of praise, and that there is joy in the presence of these angels of God over a sinner persuaded to cast all his care on the Saviour. 'There is joy', for none can pluck you out of the Saviour's hand. 'There is joy,' for principalities and powers are spoiled of one victim more. And whilst the Saviour makes a show of them openly, triumphing over them by bearing you in safety to the very gates of the heavenly Jerusalem, the attendant angels without and the white-robed choirs of the spirits of just men made perfect within shall join in the responsive song:

> Lift up your heads,
> Oh ye gates;
> And be ye lift up,
> Ye everlasting doors;
> And the King of Glory shall come in.
> Who *is* this King of Glory?
> The LORD strong and mighty,
> The LORD mighty in battle.

> Lift up your heads,
> Oh ye gates;
> Even lift *them* up,
> Ye everlasting doors;
> And the King of Glory shall come in.
> Who is this King of Glory?
> The LORD of Hosts,
> He *is* the King of Glory.

Preached before Dr. Welsh, April 1835. (written Edinburgh, March 30 1835).

22. Christ Came to Save the Lost (Luke 19:10)

For the Son of man is come to seek and to save that which was lost.

The Son of man is come to seek.
The salvation of Christ is for those who are lost.

Some remarkable points in the salvation of Zaccheus:

(1) Chief among the publicans; the publicans were a sad, dishonest, race. This was the chief and ringleader, the captain of Satan's army.

(2) He was rich. Christ had said that it was easier for a camel to go through the eye of a needle than for a rich man to enter the kingdom of God (Matt. 19:24).

(3) He was not seeking Christ. He was moved only by curiosity. Yet Jesus spied his eye on this man and brought him down in a moment. He that saved Zaccheus is able and willing to save you. When the Pharisees murmured, Jesus gave this recital, 'The Son of man is come to seek and to save that which was lost.' All lost sinners should now prick up their ears and attend with all their might to the loving declarations of Christ. You should press near him as did the publican. Come forward to where he stands in the midst of us, for he stands waiting for such as are lost.

1. Show who they are that Christ came to save – the lost
(a) Open sinners
(b) Unconverted
(c) Sinned against light
(d) Those that are not seeking Christ
Christ is come to seek and to save such.

2. Why?
(a) They have most need
(b) His gracious nature
(c) They will be most at praise.
Oh! When the thief in Paradise casts his crown at his feet, then you will see why the lost will praise.

3. Apply:
For awakening. What will you say as to why you have not come to Jesus? Many as did John Bunyan have no hope, therefore they live as

in sin. There is hope and you will be without excuse. You will see a great company saved, many of your own companions. Up then and seek him.

For drawing. Some are heavy laden. Christ points over the crowd to you.

Encouragement to backsliders.

The lost

The meaning of Christ's words seems to be, 'You murmur because I have saved this notorious sinner, but you do not know the principles upon which I am come. I am come in such a way that if there be a man more lost than another, I am willing to be his Saviour; that is the man for me.' Great sinners suit a great Saviour.

1. Show who are peculiarly lost

1. Open sinners. God has an awful abhorrence of open sin, because it is so dishonouring to his majesty. He notes all sin and the wages of all sin is death; but open sin exposes to his wrath in a dreadful manner. This was the brand on Sodom's forehead.

Isaiah 3:9: the show of their countenance doth witness against them.

Jeremiah 3:3: whore's forehead.

Jeremiah 6:15: were they ashamed?

Jeremiah 5:3: they have made their faces harder than a rock.

Philippians 3:19: glory in shame.

2 Peter 2:13: count it pleasure to riot in the day time.

Something exceedingly hateful to God in open sin
1. Because it shows great seardness of conscience. It shows a soul far gone in sin.

2. It spreads the infection so far and wide, as if a man with a plague were to run into the midst of a crowd.

3. It affronts the majesty of God. If a rebel were to come into the King's court and in his presence spit in his face, or aim a sword at him, such is the conduct of open sinners.

Such was Zaccheus, such many of you, well known as sinners, notorious, open drunkenness, that are well known as drunkards and Sabbath breakers. Oh! put in today for Jesus Christ.

2. Sin against light. Many that sin not so openly, yet live an unconverted life against light, against godly parents, teachers, convictions, prickings of conscience, yet have gone and plunged deeper into the world. You stopped your ears and ran, you avoid the truth and keep far from the sound of the gospel. This was the sin of Judas. He sat at the feet of Christ, heard his words, saw his love, yet kissed and betrayed him. This was the sin of Capernaum. This was the sin of Jerusalem. This I believe is the sin of many here. You know the gospel. You could preach the gospel. Yet you are not saved by it. You have loved the world. Still Jesus says, begin at Jerusalem.

3. Not seeking Christ. Many go through this world with no wish to find Christ. Many want to be rich, or their thoughts are there. Many seek pleasure. Some sit still and are at ease in Zion. Fearful sin and condemnation of such. Many in this place have seen others cry after the Lord Jesus, yet they never had a thought of seeking him. Yet he is come to seek. Some are like the sheep that goes further away the more it is sought. Christ is seeking the lost.

2. Why?

1. They have most need. They that are whole have no need of a physician, but they that are sick. On a battlefield where many are lying sick and wounded, the merciful physician looks not after those that are whole, but after the wounded. He bends over them. Lost sinners, you are the wounded, dying men the Lord Jesus has come to seek.

2. Because of his gracious nature. There is something in the very nature of God that makes him delight to show mercy to the vilest. He delighteth in mercy. The Lord is gracious. True, he is a consuming fire and the more a man sins, the more fire of God's anger flames against him. Yet it is as true that he delighteth in mercy, that his bowels move over sinners and move most over those who are the vilest. It seems a contradiction and yet I believe it is true that the more God is angry with a sinner, the more he has compassion towards him.

(a) Perhaps it was for this, God passed by the angels and came to men. There is reason to think that man has fallen lower than devils.

There are more lusts in the heart of man than in the heart of Satan. Yet God passed them by and came to us.

(b) This made him come to the Jews. Of all places the heaviest load of guilt rested there. Yet, 'Begin at Jerusalem'. These were the firstfruits of the gospel, 3000 and then 5000.

(c) This made him pity the woman of Samaria and the dying thief, he had pity on them. He had compassion on Corinth more than on Athens; so Dundee, passing others by. Some of you may feel that you are very vile in the eyes of Christ, worthless, worthy of his wrath; yet he came for the vile, the lost. His heart yearns over souls. Oh! if the woman of Samaria came to him, press you forward too. The heart that had pity for her has pity for you. Christ is the image of God. He is God and not man, you judge for yourself.

3. He has most glory from such. To the praise of the glory of his grace. 'This people have I formed for myself.' Sinners must be to the praise of his glory in one of two ways: either in being firebrands to show his wrath, or in being brands plucked out of the fire, to show his grace. The greatest monuments of grace are those that have been brought from the lowest depths.

The love of God is most conspicuous in such a one; when God loves a vile wretch; then it is seen to be free, unbought love. The blood of Jesus is seen to be precious blood. The Spirit is seen to be almighty. Many are drawn to come. Paul was saved as a pattern. Satan's kingdom is weakened (if you wish to weaken an army, carry off the captain).

Building pillars. There are some among you that are pillars of Satan's kingdom in this town. Oh, if you were saved, it would be to the praise of Christ's glory. Therefore Christ is most willing to save souls.

3. Application

Most awakening truth in the Bible. If Christ has come to seek the lost, he has come to seek you. There is one seeking your soul, the almighty Son of God. You say there is no hope, only that you had turned in youth. There is hope! You are lost, but one is seeking you. Oh! put in for him now. Today. How it will stop your mouth in the judgement, when you see in glory the Samaritan woman, Mary Magdalene and the thief and many from this town, friends and neighbours, companions in sin, casting their crowns at his feet and you cast out. Come then to his feet because you are lost, the chief of the publicans.

Drawing. Who are they in this congregation that Jesus most invites? Those that are most heavily laden, with sins of many years, aggravated against light and convictions. He points over the heads of the whole congregation to you, and says, 'Come to me and I will give you rest.' Oh! if you knew how Christ pities you, what willingness there is in Jesus to take you, and wash you, you would run unto him.

Backsliders more lost. Come freely to him. Oh! come as readily as Zaccheus. Had he not come down that day he had never come at all.

23. We Must be Born Again (John 3:3)

Jesus answered and said unto him, Verily, verily, I say unto thee, Except a man be born again, he cannot see the kingdom of God.

1. The necessity of being born again

(1) From the words of Christ, 'a man'
It does not say, except an angel be born again. They need no second birth, for they are as holy as when they came from the hand of God. It does not say, except an old man or a young man or a rich man or a poor man, but, 'except a man be born again'. This word applies to all of you, without any exceptions. Whatever be your age or talents or wealth or acquirements, you must be born again. If you have the human members, a human body and a human soul, if you have got the human features and the human faculties, you must be born again.

(2) From the guilt that is lying upon every man
'All have sinned and come short of the glory of God.' Mountains of sin are, at this moment, lying upon every unconverted soul.

The sin of Adam, 'by one man's'. Just as the blood of the Son of God is still lying upon the guilty Jews, so the guilt of Adam's sin is lying upon every Christian's soul.

The sin of your nature: you were shapen in iniquity, by nature a child of wrath even as others. You are as sinew to the backbone.

The sins of your life: every member you have used as an instrument of sin.

The sins of your heart: You are naked and laid open to the eyes of him with whom you have to do. If God were to judge you by what you are feeling at this moment, you could not stand.

Consider the nature of God, 'of purer eyes than to behold evil' (Hab. 1.13). Our God is a consuming fire. It is God's nature to consume sinners. You cannot go to God then, as you are. Either God must change or you must change.

One part of the new birth is bringing the soul to the blood of atonement and washing it clean. You must be brought there if you would be saved. You must be born again.

(3) From the natural heart that is in everyone
In every natural man there is a carnal mind, a mind set upon earthly things, a mind at enmity to God. Such a man is an enemy of the cross of Christ.

Now there is a law of our nature that a man can be truly happy only among kindred spirits. A child of God when placed in an unholy family feels desolate indeed; he longs for the wings of a dove. I remember Brainerd once saying, when he was obliged to live with some wicked worldly men, 'It would be hell to me to live in the company of wicked men.' Therefore, the children of God love to keep together, the lambs in the midst of the wolves.

An ungodly man in the midst of God's children feels unhappy, especially if they are freely opening their minds, humbly and joyfully speaking the praises of Christ. He is quite chop fallen, out of his element; he turns to the one side, then to the other. He rises and leaves the room. He calls it cant and hypocrisy. There is too much of the name of Jesus to suit his taste.

Dear friends, many of you must know that this is your case. Then suppose you were taken this night into heaven, with your present tastes and passions. Let the angels carry you to Abraham's bosom, into the midst of the holy society there. First, you would try and join yourself to the redeemed. All have white robes and palms in their hands, but as you drew near you would hear them saying, 'Thou wast slain and hast redeemed us to God by thy blood.' You could not bear their company, you could not join their song, you would turn away with disgust.

Next, you would try the angels, but behold every one of them is singing, 'Worthy is the Lamb that was slain.' Every harp is tuned to play no other name than 'Jesus'. Holiness is the atmosphere of heaven, you would be utterly miserable. 'Well, if this be heaven,' you would say, 'I must be down in hell.'

The wicked shall 'go away' into everlasting torment, they will not need to be driven. They shall be in a dreadful condition between two hells. They cannot bear to lie down in the lake of fire, still less can they bear the company of the redeemed, the presence of God and of the Lamb, the songs of glory; the holiness of heaven. Ah, you will 'go away'. In the nature of things, either heaven must become a place of sin or you must be born again.

2. The workman in the new birth is the Spirit

Nicodemus made this objection, that the thing was impossible (v.4). 'How?' Christ answered this in two ways: (1) by showing him that it was the work of the Almighty Spirit – 'Is anything too hard for the Lord?' (2) that it was not a birth of the body but of the soul. The Almighty Spirit is the workman in this amazing change.

(a) No sinner needs to despair. Some are awakened so far as to desire to be converted. If you ask, their chief desire is to be convinced of sin and get an interest in Christ; they come up to the house of God longing for conversion. But then they say, 'I am too old, how can I be born again when I am old? If I had listened when young, but there is no use in thinking of it now.' One said, 'I have been an old rebel, thirty-nine years I have served Satan daily.' Others say, 'I am too far gone in sin. My heart is so hard, filthy, impenetrable. I feel that I do not feel.' Now do not despair, it is the Almighty Spirit's work. He is able to do it and willing to do it. I have seen him melt hearts as hard as any here. He can turn the rock into a fountain of water, the flint into a standing water. Cry unto him.

(b) We do not need to despair of friends. Doubtless many of you have friends whom you would like to see brought to the feet of Christ. But then they despise the means of grace, they do not read, nor pray. They are freelivers or freethinkers, or they have a name to live and are dead. You despair. Why should you, as long as there is an almighty Spirit? He can make the weakest means reach their heart – jawbone of an ass; sling and stone. Only pray that he will come like rain on mown grass.

3. The manner of his working, 'Wind'.

(1) Unseen
You hear the sound through the bells, whistling through the rigging. You see the effects, curling the waves, filling the sail, melting the frozen lake, opening the rose. But still you do not see this wonderful visitor, 'thou canst not tell'. Such is God's Holy Spirit, almighty yet unseen. The world cannot receive because it seeth him not.

Learn the folly of the world. Are there not some who venture to work at the new birth? Such cannot comprehend it. How can these things be? Did you ever see a frozen lake when the thawing wind came over it? Ice gradually dissolves. So the frozen heart of your child. You have seen a garden. When the first breathings of spring come over it, green buds, snowdrop, crocus. So a soul beside you, from death to life.

(2) Sovereign where it listeth
Any one who has been at sea knows the sovereignty of the wind. It ceases, the sails flap, pennants hang. It wakes and fills the swelling sail. It chops about. So is everyone born of the Spirit. The wind only seems to be sovereign, the Spirit is sovereign. 'He hath mercy on whom he will have mercy.' He visits one soul in a family and leaves the rest. He touches the heart of Jacob and leaves Esau hard. He visits one city and leaves another dry.

(a) Unjust! Who art thou that repliest against God? May he not do what he will with his own.

(b) Use the Spirit while you have the Spirit. Sailors, when they have a favourable wind, spread every sail, for it may lull. Some of you may have the Spirit now breaking on your heart, striving with you. Oh! yield to him. I have seen many lost because they did not come to Christ when the Spirit was striving. If the Spirit is now convicting you of your sin and misery, of the emptiness of the world, oh, do not vex him. Do not rest till you can say, 'My beloved is mine and I am his.'

Many have undergone changes that are not by the Spirit of God.

(1) By time. Time makes great change. It makes the hair turn white, the hand tremble, the eye dim; the heart also changes, the passions lose their fire. This is a natural change, the same takes place in a tree, in a beast of the field.

(2) By education. The mind is expanded, faculties quickened; still this is natural.

(3) By fashion. One fashion to be irreligious, to swear, not to go to the house of God.

(4) By afflictions. Disappointments often embitter the world, bereavements make great change.

All these are natural changes. Seek a supernatural change. Whatever other changes you have, you must be born again. How shall I know? Answer, the Spirit leads you to Christ. He makes you to look to Christ and to grow like him.

24. Lydia and the Jailer (Acts 16:12-36)

And from thence to Philippi, which is the chief city of that part of Macedonia, *and* a colony: and we were in that city abiding certain days. And on the sabbath we went out of the city by a river side, where prayer was wont to be made; and we sat down, and spake unto the women which resorted *thither*. And a certain woman named Lydia, a seller of purple, of the city of Thyatira, which worshipped God, heard *us*: whose heart the Lord opened, that she attended unto the things which were spoken of Paul. And when she was baptized, and her household, she besought *us*, saying, If ye have judged me to be faithful to the Lord, come into my house, and abide *there*. And she constrained us. And it came to pass, as we went to prayer, a certain damsel possessed with a spirit of divination met us, which brought her masters much gain by soothsaying: The same followed Paul and us, and cried, saying, These men are the servants of the most high God, which shew unto us the way of salvation. And this did she many days. But Paul, being grieved, turned and said to the spirit, I command thee in the name of Jesus Christ to come out of her; And he came out the same hour. And when her masters saw that the hope of their gains was gone, they caught Paul and Silas, and drew *them* into the marketplace unto the rulers, and brought them to the magistrates, saying, These men, being Jews, do exceedingly trouble our city, and teach customs, which are not lawful for us to receive, neither to observe, being Romans. And the multitude rose up together against them: and the magistrates rent off their clothes, and commanded to beat *them*. And when they had laid many stripes upon them, they cast *them* into prison, charging the jailer to keep them safely: Who, having received such a charge, thrust them into the inner prison, and made their feet fast in the stocks. And at midnight Paul and Silas prayed, and sang praises unto God: and the prisoners heard them. And suddenly there was a great earthquake, so that the foundations of the prison were shaken: and immediately all the doors were opened, and every one's bands were loosed. And the keeper of the prison awaking out of his sleep, and seeing the prison doors open, he drew out his sword, and would have killed himself, supposing that the prisoners had been fled. But Paul cried with a loud voice, saying, Do thyself no harm: for we are all here. Then he called for a light, and sprang in, and came trembling, and fell down before Paul and Silas, and brought them out, and said, Sirs, what must I do to be saved? And they said, Believe on the Lord Jesus Christ, and thou shalt be saved, and thy house. And they spake unto him the word of the Lord, and to all that were in his house. And he took them the same hour of the night, and washed *their* stripes; and was baptized, he and all his, straightway. And when he had brought them into his house, he set meat before them, and rejoiced, believing in God with all his house. And when it was day, the magistrates sent the serjeants, saying, Let those men go. And the keeper of the prison told this saying to Paul, The magistrates have sent to let you go: now therefore depart, and go in peace.

God's ways are not like our ways, neither are his thoughts like our thoughts. When God sent Paul the vision of a man of Macedonia praying him and saying, 'Come over and help us?', who would have guessed that Lydia the seller of purple and the heathen jailer of Philippi were to be the firstfruits of Macedonia unto Christ? Or when these apostolic men hearing the commission, 'Go ye into all the world and preach the gospel to every creature', entered the gates of Philippi, a Roman colony, and the chief city of that part of Macedonia, who would have guessed that the homes of Lydia and the house of the jailer were the only two marked out by God for a blessing?

Lydia, we find, was a seller of purple from Thyatira, a city of Asia Minor, who had settled in Philippi, as we find she had a house and a household. That she was a Jewess or at least a Jewish proselyte is evident from her being one of those women who on the Sabbath day resorted to a place by the river-side for prayer. And it is said she worshipped God. She was then by no means a profligate or profane woman but one who waited on the Jewish ordinance of prayer – and yet she was unconverted. Oh, my friends, how many of you who, like Lydia, are far from being profligate or profane, how many of you who live honest and respectable lives, who wait on the ordinances of God and mingle with the worshippers of God, are yet, like Lydia, unconverted and need, like Lydia, to have your hearts opened by God to receive the truth of the love of God?

The jailer again was evidently a heathen man whose dark mind had never been enlightened by the knowledge of God or the promise of the Saviour. A man of force and of cruelty. The cruelty of his disposition is particularly remarkable in that when he was charged to keep them safely, he made that an excuse for keeping them cruelly. He *thrust* them into the inner prison. He might have kept them safely without thrusting them in. And not only so but as if the innermost prison were not sufficient to hold them fast, he made their feet fast in the stocks.

Such were the two whom God chose to be the firstfruits of Macedonia, a formalist professor and a hard-hearted heathen. How true the saying that is written, 'Many are called, but few are chosen.' Paul and his companions were many days in that city and no doubt preached the gospel to all that would listen. But we are only told of two houses where the hearts were opened, two of the most unlikely perhaps in the whole place, a foreign woman and a heathen jailer.

As it was then, so it is now: 'Many are called, but few are chosen.' We come this day with the message to all. There is not one of your houses that we are not anxious to enter with the message of salvation; there is not a man, woman or child to whom we do not this day offer Christ. Yea, there is not one of you, however dead and formal in your religiousness, however ignorant and cruel and profane, of whom the Lord permits us to despair. We know not to which one of you the Lord may this very hour bring the message, opening your heart to attend to the things that are spoken. To one and all do we this day anew offer Christ and all his benefits. We bring in the blood of Jesus and the righteousness of Jesus, a full and free salvation, and we lay all down at your feet. And we invite everyone to take Christ and have life as we say, 'Why will ye die?' Yea, and if you can tell me any way by which we can get at your hearts with greater plainness and power, we are ready to take that way of laying Christ before you. But will you all accept? Will all your hearts be opened? Will you all go back to your houses changed men, rejoicing in the free forgiveness of sins as those who have found great spoil? Alas, no! God will act differently from his normal way of dealing if he does so. For though he wishes you all to be saved and has no pleasure that one man, woman or child should perish, yet he tells us plainly that we are not to expect that the many will listen to us. He tells us that most of you will go on in your hardness, one going to his farm and another to his merchandise, that the most of you will hear and wonder and perish. And if he this day open the heart of some poor Lydia among you, some stranger whom you know not of and care not for, or if he bring some stout-hearted cruel man to cry out, 'What must I do to be saved?', this is all the reward that he bids us expect for our pains.

Let us now attempt briefly to trace the different steps in conversion as they are shown us in the conversion of the jailer, which is the fullest of the two. Conversion is always the same work and though there are many differences in time, place and circumstances, yet the main features of all conversions are the same:

1. Conviction of being a lost sinner is the first feature in this conversion

And it is the first feature in all true conversions. We find that Paul and Silas, though their backs were furrowed with stripes, and though thrust into the innermost dungeon, with their feet made fast in the stocks, yet at midnight prayed and sang praises unto God. Being afflicted they prayed, yet being merry they sang psalms. The black dungeon walls of that heathen prison-house, that had till now resounded only with the cries and groans of the prisoner, or the still more hideous grating of heathen oaths and profaneness, now resounded through all its vaults for the first time with the praises of Jesus. And the prisoners heard them and suddenly, as a token that their prayers were heard and their praise accepted, there was a great earthquake so that the foundations of the prison were shaken and immediately all the doors were opened and everyone's bonds were loosed. And the keeper of the prison awaking out of his sleep and seeing the prison doors open, drew out his sword and would have killed himself supposing that the prisoners had fled. But Paul cried with a loud voice, 'Do thyself no harm, for we are all here.' Then it was that the work of grace was begun in this hard-hearted man.

What was the exact train of thought that brought him to the conviction of sin, it may be hard to explain. The prison doors being thus wonderfully opened may have convinced him that God was on the side of these men; their patience in suffering and their calmness in their hour of danger also convinced him that God was in them of a truth. His own harsh treatment of the servants of the Most High God, his ignorance of that God, how he had been fighting against God, and how near he had rushed by his own hand into hell, all this seems to have flashed across his mind and to have awakened the complete conviction that he was a lost sinner. For he called for a light, and sprang in and came trembling and fell down at the feet of Paul and Silas and brought them out and said, *'Sirs, what must I do to be saved?'*

My dear friends, have you ever asked this question, What must I do to be saved? Not with the lips only but with the heart. Have you ever asked it with the intense anxiety of one who could not rest without an answer? Have you ever asked, as the Jews did, the way to Zion with their faces thitherward? Oh my friends, if you have never had any bosom-anxiety upon this subject, then you have never been convinced of sin, and it is all in vain that we preach Jesus to you. You can see no sense in a Saviour, for you do not feel any danger from which you are to be saved. Then the work of grace hath never been begun in your heart and you are as far from the kingdom of God as it is possible for any man to be who is not in hell.

Let us stir you up, if it be possible, to ask this question now, 'Did you ever think or believe that if you had no more than one sin you would be worthy of hell?' You know that God is a being of infinite loveliness and beauty, all perfection dwells in him. Whatever is lovely or amiable in any creature dwells infinitely in God. But the more amiable any object is, the more are we under obligation to love that object. We are more under obligation to love the children of God than the children of the world, for they are far more amiable and worthy of our love. But God is infinitely amiable or infinitely worthy of our love, therefore we are under infinite obligation to love him. And if we do not love him, then we are breaking an infinite obligation.

But every sin we commit proves that we do not love God, for if we loved him we would love to do his will. Therefore every sin is breaking an infinite obligation and, therefore, every sin deserves an infinite punishment. But an infinite punishment is hell. Therefore every sin deserves hell. Suppose then that there were but one sin lying on you; that one sin, my friend, is heavy enough to sink you to the lowest hell, and angels and men and devils and your own conscience would be found to say it was just and right it should be so. Just as one millstone tied round the neck will sink you to the bottom of the sea, so one unpardoned sin lying on your conscience is enough to sink you to the depths of hell.

But oh, my friends, is there no more than one unpardoned sin lying on you? Is not every faculty of your nature perverted by sin? The whole head is sick and the whole heart is faint. Is not your judgement perverted by sin? Do you not call good evil and evil good? Do you not put sweet for bitter and bitter for sweet? Is not your memory perverted by sin? How easily you can store up anything that will do the devil service in your heart. What a memory you have for worldly business or worldly pleasures, but you have no memory for the things of God, for the Word of God. Is not your imagination perverted? Is not every imagination of your heart only evil and that continually? How constantly have you abused that noble faculty to serve the basest sins. What a sick fancy you have for calling up scenes of folly and pollution and wickedness. What horrid imaginations crowd through your mind in the night watches. And then is not your heart perverted? Have you not loved the creature more than the Creator who is blessed for evermore? Have you not thrown away your best affections upon things that perish in the very using? And when you have been brought off from one object of your affection, has not your heart just given away after another as vain and vile and contemptible?

Look back over the history of your affections. Oh, what a scene of mad idolatry. Does it not show to you, as poor and contemptible as that of the Hindu that worships wood and stone, that the only Being in the Universe worthy of your supreme love has been trodden under foot. Truly the whole head is sick and the whole heart faint, from the sole of the foot to the crown of the head; there is no soundness in you but wounds and bruises and putrefying sores. Think then what mountains of sin are lying on you. It is not one sin that hangs like a millstone about your neck but whole mountains of sin are piled over you, more than the hairs of your head in number, all crushing you down to the lowest hell. And there is nothing between you and that place of woe but the thin thread of life which may be snapped by the scissors of disease in one night.

It is quite true you do not feel this load. You do not feel a featherweight upon your soul, you are not like men who have a burden on their backs. But that makes your case all the more horrible and dangerous. Just as the sick man's case is all the more dangerous if he does not feel that anything ails him, just as the slaves were all the more hopeless slaves because they did not feel the weight of slavery, so your case is all the more dangerous and terrible because you do not feel the weight of God's wrath that is pressing upon you. There are mountains of sin upon you, yet you feel them not. Oh, will none of you awake to feel the reality? Will none of you be alarmed by the awful burden of the Almighty's wrath? Will none of you be persuaded to cry out, 'Sirs, what must I do to be saved?' Oh, if we could get one of you to have a true sense of your sin, of the weight that is abiding on every Christless soul, I know well for I have seen it, how quickly you would run, trembling like the jailer, to ask of the weakest child of God, 'What must I do to be saved?'

2. But I hasten, secondly, to the answer of the apostles
This awakened the second grand conviction in his soul, the conviction of righteousness (vs. 31-32).

To the awakened soul asking, What must I do to be saved?, the gospel is the simplest of all contrivances that any mind could have imagined. To a soul that really feels mountains of unpardoned sin lying upon it; to a soul that feels that nothing he can do, no prayers, no tears, no works of penance can ever lift off the burden; to a soul that is really emptied of all self, of struggles, who says as one poor soul did, 'It is done, it is done, I never can do anything to save myself;' to that soul nothing can be plainer, simpler, more apt and fitting, than the offer of Jesus to bear the whole load, to suffer the whole curse. The soul slips from under the oppressive mountain and leaves it weighing down upon the shoulder of the almighty Redeemer. For it is written, 'On him were laid the iniquities of us all.' The soul chooses Christ as a sin-bearer, cleaves to him, and is at peace for eternity.

But there are many of you to whom the answer of the apostle is utter foolishness. There are many of you who attach no meaning to the words, 'Believe on the Lord Jesus Christ....' There are many of you who would have given the jailer a very different answer. You would have said, 'Be an honest man, put away drunkenness and swearing and cruelty; live decently and respectably in the world and so you will be saved?' Or at least there are many of you who, if you were honest, must frankly confess that you do not see how believing on Jesus would save the man.

Another consequence of conversion here given us is love and hospitality to the saints. It was thus with Lydia (v.15) and it was thus with the hard-hearted jailer. That same night he was cruel and harsh to them: thrust them into the inner prison; put their feet in the stocks, nay he was cruel to himself and his wife and children for he drew his sword and would have killed himself. But he is now a believer in Jesus, the lion is turned into the lamb: 'he took them...' (v.33).

This is a sure and unfailing feature of the children of God. Examine yourselves by it, I beseech you. If you be of the unconverted world, you will have one of two characters: either you will be covetous and greedy and grasping and hoarding and hard-handed and never running the least risk of entertaining angels unawares; or else your profuse hospitality and gentlemanly generosity will be poured out alike upon the pious and the profane.

But if you be the children of God, your hospitality and your charity will be quite different. You will have bowels of compassion for the unconverted world as Jesus had, who loved them and gave himself for them. But the bosom friends of your heart will be the children of God. Toward them you will show hospitality indeed without judging. When they are naked you will clothe them; when they are hungry you will feed them; when they are sick and in prison you will visit them; for you know that inasmuch as you do it unto the least of these Christ's brethren you do it unto Christ. Yea, you will give even a cup of cold water with peculiar joy to a disciple because he is a disciple of Jesus, and you shall in no wise lose your reward.

In conclusion

I return to what I said at first, that many are called but few are chosen. We this day call to every one of you. We have laid before you the reason why you should flee from the wrath to come – because of the mountains of sin that are lying on you. We have laid before you the completeness and all-sufficiency of Christ to bear all that load. And there is not one of you too cold, too hard, too careless that we despair of your conversion this day. May the Lord grant that some poor formalist like Lydia may have her heart opened, that some cruel man like the jailer may be brought to cry, 'What must I do to be saved?' And so God shall have all the praise in time and in eternity!

29th June 1836, preached in Barrowhall
3rd July 1836, preached in Dunipace
4th July 1836, preached at Blackmill Canon
1836, preached in St. Peter's

25. The Prayers of Paul

1. Romans 10:1: For Israel: Brethren, my hearts desire and prayer to God for Israel is, that they might be saved.

2. Romans 15:5, 13, 33: To the God of patience, hope and peace:

(a) That we may be made like Christ: 'Now the God of patience and consolation grant you to be likeminded one toward another according to Christ Jesus' (v.5).

(b) That we may be filled with peace, joy and hope: 'Now the God of hope fill you with all joy and peace in believing, that ye may abound in hope, through the power of the Holy Ghost' (v.13).

(c) That we may have his presence, so 15:24: 'Now the God of peace *be* with you all. Amen' (v. 33).

3. 2 Corinthians 9:10: Now he that ministereth seed: 'Now he that ministereth seed to the sower both minister bread for *your* food, and multiply your seed sown, and increase the fruits of your righteousness.'

4. 2 Corinthians 13:14: The blessing: 'The grace of the Lord Jesus Christ, and the love of God, and the communion of the Holy Ghost, *be* with you all. Amen.'

5. Ephesians 1:16-20: Spirit of wisdom, to know Christ; hope of his calling; riches of glory; his power: 'Cease not to give thanks for you, making mention of you in my prayers; That the God of our Lord Jesus Christ, the Father of glory, may give unto you the spirit of wisdom and revelation in the knowledge of him: The eyes of your understanding being enlightened; that ye may know what is the hope of his calling, and what the riches of the glory of his inheritance in the saints, And what *is* the exceeding greatness of his power to usward who believe, according to the working of his mighty power, Which he wrought in Christ, when he raised him from the dead, and set *him* at his own right hand in the heavenly *places*.'

6. Ephesians 3:14-21: For this cause I bow: 'For this cause I bow my knees unto the Father of our Lord Jesus Christ, Of whom the whole family in heaven and earth is named, That he would grant you, according to the riches of his glory, to be strengthened with might by his Spirit in the inner man; That Christ may dwell in your hearts by faith; that ye, being rooted and grounded in love, May be able to comprehend with all saints what *is* the breadth, and length, and depth, and height; And to know the love of Christ, which passeth knowledge, that ye might be filled with all the fulness of God. Now unto him that is able to do exceeding abundantly above all that we ask or think, according to the power that worketh in us, Unto him be glory in the church by Christ Jesus throughout all ages, world without end. Amen.'

7. Ephesians 6:24: 'Grace *be* with all them that love our Lord Jesus Christ in sincerity. Amen.' 'Grace be with you' (2 Tim. 4:22).

8. 1 Thessalonians 3:1: For increase of love: 'Wherefore when we could no longer forbear, we thought it good to be left at Athens alone.'

9. 2 Thessalonians 2:16,17: Comfort and stablishing: 'Now our Lord Jesus Christ himself, and God, even our Father, which hath loved us, and hath given *us* everlasting consolation and good hope through grace, Comfort your hearts, and stablish you in every good word and work.'

10. 2 Thessalonians 1:11,12: Count you worthy of this, fulfil all the good pleasure: 'Wherefore also we pray always for you, that our God would count you worthy of *this* calling, and fulfil all the good pleasure of *his* goodness, and the work of faith with power: That the name of our Lord Jesus Christ may be glorified in you, and ye in him, according to the grace of our God and the Lord Jesus Christ.'

11. 2 Timothy 4:16: Forgiveness of Stephen also: 'At my first answer no man stood with me, but all *men* forsook me: *I pray God* that it may not be laid to their charge.'

12. Hebrews 13:20: Make you perfect: 'Now the God of peace, that brought again from the dead our Lord Jesus, that great shepherd of the sheep, through the blood of the everlasting covenant.'

13. 1 Thessalonians 5:23: The very God of peace sanctify: 'And the very God of peace sanctify you wholly; and I *pray God* your whole spirit and soul and body be preserved blameless unto the coming of our Lord Jesus Christ.'

Remarkable: His remembering individuals (2 Timothy 1:3)

26. Justified by Faith we have Peace, Access and Hope (Romans 5:1,2)

Therefore being justified by faith, we have peace with God through our Lord Jesus Christ: By whom also we have access by faith into this grace wherein we stand, and rejoice in hope of the glory of God.

It is plainly the intention of Paul in the beginning of this chapter to show the blessed privileges of the justified man that he might stir up the affections of the Roman converts to rejoice in that most precious of all doctrines, the doctrine of imputed righteousness. Paul knew well enough that men could understand arguments about imputed sin and imputed righteousness a thousand-fold more readily if only their affections were interested in the matter. He knew that love is the best lamp for exploring the recesses of grace and accordingly he here encourages believing brethren to consider the privileges which they had received and were now enjoying, and reminds them of the peace that passeth all understanding; and the joys unspeakable which they had received by believing.

And truly, my believing friends, you carry about in your own bosom the most powerful arguments in defence of the doctrine of imputed righteousness. The world may sneer at the doctrine and say it is false, but you *feel* that it is true. And many a cottage believer, who cannot argue the matter with the wise disputant of this world, can yet weep over his unbelief and, laying his hand upon his bosom, say with a power which no arguments can shake, 'If this faith be false, whence is this peace with God? This joyful access to his presence? This having hope of glory?'

Let us now then, my believing friends, stir up our hearts to a higher esteem of the blessed way of salvation by Jesus, by going over in order the blessings of the justified man as they are here described to us.

1. The first advantage of the justified man is peace with God

That there is no peace to the wicked is a truth which the whole of the Bible proclaims. At the same time it is a truth which needs to be guarded and explained.

(a) Wicked men have often much of earthly peace and prosperity. This is plain not only from observation but from Scripture: 'I have seen the wicked great in power and spreading himself like a green bay tree' (Ps. 37:35).

'They are not in trouble as other men; neither are they plagued like other men' (Ps. 73:5). Their eyes stand out with fatness. They have more than their heart could wish. These are the ungodly which prosper in the world. They increase in riches.

(b) Wicked men have often much inward peace as well. They often live very serene lives, being much at peace with their own consciences. So that I believe there have been men found so much past feeling that they have sat for years under the most rousing ministrations of the Word without having had one storm of conscience during all that time. Indeed many seem to be lulled into a fatal repose by the very preaching which is intended to awaken them. Through long habit the preacher's voice is no more than an accustomed noise, and they sleep like the wet sea-buoy, rocked into deeper slumber by the storm.

(c) The wicked are very often, I believe I might say generally, at peace when they die. As it is written, 'There are no bands in their death: but their strength is firm.' There is a widely spread delusion upon this point which it would be well to dissipate. It is generally thought that if men have lived lives of wickedness and ungodliness they will die a death of great horror and agony. Whereas it has been the testimony of all experienced ministers that there are no bands in the death of the wicked, that they die as a dog dieth – that they slip away deceiving and being deceived, unconscious of the hell that is awaiting them. No doubt there have been notorious instances of the reverse, where for wise purposes God hath given the dying sinner a foretaste of hell. And some of you may have seen the look of unspeakable despair or heard the cry of fiendish anguish that betokened a soul awakened on this side of the grave to know its coming fate. But in general it is not so. The crust of unbelief that has been gathering through their whole life is then so hard, so impenetrable, like the scaly skin of the crocodile, that the sword of the Spirit cannot penetrate. The Spirit perhaps has ceased to strive and they are let alone.

In these three ways then there is a kind of peace to the wicked, but mark this one thing, *It is not peace with God or peace toward God.* On the contrary it is a peace without God. The very essence of the false peace of the wicked consists in God not being in all their thoughts. If the man who now lives so securely and so much at peace with himself, though unconverted, if he were but confronted with the God with whom he has to do, the God of infinite justice, the jealous God, the consuming fire, his peace would shrivel up like a withered leaf, his countenance would change, his knees knock one against another, his appetite would fail him and his sleep go from him. And he would understand then the word that is written, 'The wicked are like the troubled sea that cannot rest. There is no peace saith my God to the wicked.' And if the dying man who is slipping away so calmly, surrounded by all the attentions of his anxious friends, did but know the God into whose presence he is rushing, the Searcher of hearts, he would shrink back as from a serpent. He would feel that the very presence of such a holy God would be hell to him. His sick body and its remedies would be all forgotten in his agony of spirit. And thrusting aside his unholy friends, he would say, 'Miserable comforters are ye all. Which of you can minister to a mind diseased? Which of you can give a ransom for my soul?'

Then is brought to pass the saying which is written, 'Justified by faith, we have peace with God through our Lord Jesus Christ.' Ah, my believing friends, is this your experience? Have you undergone this transition from deep anxiety to a peace that passeth all understanding? Your heart was like the troubled sea that cannot rest. Now is it not like the calm sea of Galilee when Jesus said, 'Peace be still.' Your heart was more like Jerusalem besieged with armies when the Assyrian came down like a wolf on the fold. But now it is like Jerusalem delivered when her enemies melted like snow in the flame of the Lord.

Take this one direction with you: Take nothing but Jesus for your peace. You found peace at first not by *looking in* upon everything that is in yourself, but *looking out* to Christ, a full and free and a fitting Saviour. That gave you peace at first, let that give you peace ever to the last. If you suffer your peace to rest on your own selves and feelings, it will shift and carry like the face of an April sky. But if your peace and rest are on Christ alone, then it is founded on a rock, for Christ is the same yesterday, today and forever.

Oh, it is a blessed thing when it pleases God to awaken a soul before it be too late to know himself utterly lost, when God puts the man's sins in the light of his countenance, like spots in the sun, and convinces him that he is immutably condemned in himself, that he never can do anything to justify himself.

And it is a still more blessed thing, when the same Almighty Spirit takes him aside and reveals Jesus to the despairing soul; when he shows how Christ hath done all, obeyed the whole law perfectly, not for himself but in the stead and room of sinners; when he shows him how Christ hath suffered all; unveils the wounds of Immanuel, the points of the nails and the mark of the spear and shows that these were borne not for himself but in the stead and room of sinners. The Word whispers in his ear, 'Believe on the Lord Jesus.' He believes and is at peace. He hides in these words and cries out, 'My Lord and my God.'

2. The second advantage of the justified man is access unto grace wherein he stands

The unjustified soul has no access into the gracious presence of God. He does not dwell in the secret place of the Most High.

1. The unawakened soul does not seek or desire such access. If he prays, his prayers are the prayers of the formalist; the prayer of the lips, while the heart is far from God. Or they are prayers to an unknown God. If he sings praise it is the melody of voice without any melody of heart.

2. The awakened soul longs for access but cannot, dare not, find it. He feels polluted with the stains of sin, but not knowing the freeness of the fountain opened in the side of Immanuel, he does not come to wash, and he cannot draw near with a guilty conscience. He feels shut out from the Holiest of all and, not knowing that the veil has been rent from the top to the bottom, he dares not to enter through the rent veil of Christ's flesh into the presence of the blessed One whose very preserve is blessedness.

3. The believing soul however – knowing the perfect freeness of that fountain and the perfect openness of the way in to the Father, sprinkled and justified from all things – enters with boldness into the Holiest of all; enjoys access into the gracious presence of God.

And there he stands:
(a) Of all he has access. He has as it were an introduction into the audience chamber where God manifests himself to his own in another way than he does unto the world. The robe of the Redeemer's comeliness is put about the naked soul and he is led in by the Spirit

into the holy presence. As it is written, 'We hath have access by one Spirit unto the Father.'

(b) There he stands; he does not fall down or faint away, but stands upright. Although he is now in the very audience chamber of the heart-searching God, him who charged his angels with folly and in whose sight the very heavens are not clean and from whose look of anger the heavens and the earth are one day to flee away till there be found no place for them, yet clothed in the righteousness of God *he stands* pardoned, accepted in the Beloved. He abides under the shadow of the wings of him that is Almighty. It is the one thing that he desires, the only thing that he seeks after, that he may dwell in the house of the Lord all the days of his life, to behold the beauty of the Lord and to enquire in his temple.

Ah, my believing friends, is this your experience? Why then do you not continually make use of this privilege? Oh, have you not many a time, when your soul was vexed like Lot's with the filthy conversation of the wicked, longed to have the wings of a dove that you might flee away and be at rest? Or have you never wished that you had the wings and the blamelessness of a holy angel, that you might leave the cold atmosphere of the earth where all are busy in search of gold-dust or vain honours or polluting pleasures, that you might pass through these heavens and breathe an atmosphere where all is kindness and purity and love in the very presence of God? Behold here is your wish more than gratified. In the righteousness of Christ you have a covering nobler and more heavenly than that of angels. By Jesus a way is opened for you through these heavens and, hovering like the lark on the wings of believing praise and prayer, you may abide in the gracious sunlight of God's face, like the very angels of the Presence.

It was said by one many ages ago when he heard the Gospels read, 'Either this is not the gospel or we are not Christians.' Had that man lived in our day, I fear he would have said of most of us, 'Either access to God is not the privilege of believers or you are not believers.' For alas, how few of us live in continual access to God! How few of us ever seem to shine like those who have been in communion with God! Enoch walked with God. Alas, how few Enochs have we now! And yet we have greater light and greater encouragement than ever Enoch had.

And think my unbelieving friends, what you are losing – access into the favour of God. You cannot pray, you cannot praise, you are without the tabernacle. And if you have no access to God here, be sure you will have no communion with him hereafter. True, you do not now feel your loss, but neither does the man who was born blind feel the loss of his eyesight. Neither does the home-born slave who hugs his chains feel the loss of his liberty. Yet the one is in darkness and the other in slavery notwithstanding. You will feel your loss one day when you begin to knock and hear only the sad answer, 'Depart, ye cursed.'

3. The third advantage of the justified man is joy in the hope of glory

The Bible tells us plainly that they that are without Christ are without God and without hope in the world. Yet this truth also must be guarded and explained. Man is a creature of hope and even the wicked often live upon the hope of tomorrow more than upon the enjoyments of today. You know how much the peace of the farmer depends upon hope: he sows his fields and hopes for an abundant harvest. The weather threatens to blight the crops, yet still he hopes it will improve or should they fail he hopes another year will make up the loss. You know how much the peace of the merchant depends upon hope: his wealth is all floating upon the treacherous seas, but he hopes his vessels may escape the gales or should one ship be lost, he hopes another may make up for it. You know how much the peasant lives upon hope. The mother, while she presses her infant to her bosom, hopes that her boy will yet live to be her staff in declining years. The father, looking at the olive plants around his table, hopes they will one day be as arrows in his quiver, that he shall not be ashamed but speak with the enemies in the gate. Or if their favourite child be taken away they hope that the remaining ones will live to fill his place.

In all these things the wicked have their hopes and generally far more lively than the righteous. But observe, all these hopes are of earthly things; they have all their objects on this side of the grave and they do not penetrate beyond these skies. They are hopes of gain or hopes of riches or hopes of pleasure and peace in this world or hopes of the glory of man, but they are not the hope of the glory of God. But again, it is true also that the wicked have often times religious hopes. You will seldom meet with any man that thinks so ill of himself as not to hope that God will forgive him at last, that God will prove better than his Word, that God will somehow or other yet pardon and save him. These are what the Bible calls the hopes of the hypocrite which shall perish. But observe, the wicked never rejoice in the hope of glory. They are driven to a false hope when there is nothing else for them to do. But the justified have this hope within them as a continual feast of joy. Even when the world is at the brightest, they are whispering to their own souls, 'To depart and be with Christ is far better.' When men travel in great, sandy deserts they know not what to do. We are told that they are often delighted with the distant view of broad, clear lakes that reflect every object in their bosom. They advance to drink but the mirage is gone, the vision was all desert and they are left parched and desolate. Such is the hope of the wicked. But the hope of glory is to the justified man like a cool, perennial fountain in a secluded garden, to which ever and anon he retires from the busy, noisy world and, sitting down by its holy stream while he meditates on the freeness and perfectness of the right he has to the fountain of immortality, drinks in with holy meditations new foretastes of the blessedness which is to come.

Ah, my believing friends, let us retire far oftener than we do, to taste of the fountain of the hope of the glory of God. And then we shall live with a far holier contempt for the paltry possessions of time. What is gold and silver, what is the praise of man, what is food and raiment to a man that has the hope full of immortality?

And you, my unbelieving friends, you are right to hug these earthly things close to your bosom, for they are your all in all. You are right to eat and drink and be merry, for tomorrow you die. You are quite right to make the most of the pleasures of the present hour if you have made up your mind to reject the Saviour. For as sure as the Bible is true, these are the only heaven you will ever see and you will find none of these things in hell.

And now in summing up these three privileges of the justified man – peace, access and hope of glory – there is just one remark which I desire to leave impressed upon your consciences: that these are not distant but immediate privileges. The Bible does not say that if you believe the gospel and live a holy life for so many years, then you shall have peace, access and hope of glory, though this is the religion of too many. But it says if you will receive Jesus this day you shall this day receive these gifts along with him – peace, access and hope of glory. Justification must go before sanctification. What, am I, who have always been a sinner, offered Christ and pardon and access and hope of glory this day before I make myself holy? Yes, sinner, thou art offered all these this day because it is only by accepting these that thou canst be made holy. Ah, how little you know, my friends, of the freeness of the gospel of Jesus. His gold, his raiment, his eye-salve, are all offered freely to the poor, the naked, the blind. And however little many of you will believe it, every watchful minister has seen many a case in which a soul has been brought from the agonies of the pretaste of hell into the peace and access and hope of a child of God *within one little day.*

Commencement
When the spouse in the Song of Solomon compares Jesus to the apple-tree among the trees of the wood, under whose shadow she sat down with great delight and whose fruit was sweet to her taste, she points to our view sweetly and pleasantly the advantages to be had by believing in Jesus. It is evidently the intention of Paul to do the same thing in the passage we have read, only in plain language without a figure. Paul knew that men would understand arguments about imputed righteousness.

Preached
28th February 1836 in Dunipace
6th March 1836 in Larbert
29th August 1836 in St. Peter's, Dundee

27. Fencing (1 Corinthians 3:10)

According to the grace of God which is given unto me, as a wise masterbuilder, I have laid the foundation, and another buildeth thereon. But let every man take heed how he buildeth thereupon.

The work of the ministry is two-fold: (1) to lay the foundation and (2) to build the temple of God thereon.

1. To lay the foundation (v.10): 'As a wise masterbuilder, I have laid the foundation.' It is true that in one sense God alone has laid the foundation: 'Behold I lay in Zion for a foundation a stone, a tried stone, a precious cornerstone, a sure foundation.' When God sent his Son into the world he laid the foundation of the church and no man can lay it again.

Still, it is equally true that ministers lay this foundation when they carry the glad tidings concerning it to different places. When a minister comes into any place and lays down cleanly the great way of pardon and acceptance through the blood of Christ, he lays the foundation in that place on which the souls of men may rest. This I have attempted to do among you.

2. To build thereon (v.10): 'But let every man take heed how he buildeth thereupon.' In building a house, when you have laid the foundation, the next part of the work is to build the stones of the house upon it. So the minister's work is not always to be laying the foundation but building souls upon it, adding to the church daily. Now he does this when he brings into the church those who seem to be converted under his ministry.

Now dear friends, before proceeding to the holy ordinance of this day, I would have you briefly examine whether you have been rightly built upon the one foundation. For three weighty reasons:

1. Ministers are often mistaken

In building up the church of God, ministers not only build gold, silver and precious stones, but sometimes wood, hay and stubble. Ministers frequently bring into the church of God those who have only the appearance of stones, but are in reality rotten wood.

The apostles were frequently mistaken in admitting men into the church. They admitted Ananias and Sapphira, though both turned out to be mere stubble, empty hypocrites. They admitted Simon Magus for he really seemed to be a believer. Demas is twice recorded among the saints by Paul. Is it to be thought then that poor ministers nowadays, with such inferior gifts and grace, are to be able to exclude all mere pretenders? *The reason* is obvious: we do not know your hearts. We judge by your life, by your knowledge and by your experience, but God judges by the heart.

If then ministers are so often mistaken, how awfully solemn and binding is the duty of your examining whether you be silver, gold or precious stones, or wood, hay and stubble. Do not be satisfied that a minister has admitted you; Ananias and Sapphira were admitted by the apostles. But lay your heart in the light of God's countenance and say, 'Examine me.'

2. The day shall declare it

There is a solemn day coming (v.13), when every man's work shall be made manifest, for the day shall declare it. There is a day coming when you and I shall stand before the judgement seat of Christ. And then it will be manifest to the whole universe whether you are a true believer, or merely a hypocrite; whether you have oil in your vessel with your lamp; whether you truly feed on Christ; and whether you be silver, gold or precious stones, or wood, hay and stubble.

At present you come only before your fellow-men and you know well that none of them can see below your mouths, therefore you come with unblushing countenance. But in that day Christ's eyes will be upon you like a flame of fire. You will be exposed. Oh, wretched creature that shall continue to deceive ministers and be found out in that day a piece of rotten wood, painted like a stone of the temple. I charge you now to pass that sentence on yourself which will be pronounced upon you in the judgement day.

3. The fire shall try it

Christ is to be revealed in flaming fire. *Awful destruction of hypocrites.* Hypocrites in that day will be like rotten wood and stubble before the fire. If any man defile the temple of God, *him* will God destroy:

(i) Because they defile the temple of God. The wicked defile the world, the air, the blue sky that looks down upon them, but hypocrites defile the temple of God. Therefore their loss will be dreadful. They bring reproach upon the church and cause many to stumble.

(ii) The nearer they have been to Christ the more dreadful will be their destruction. Hypocrites in a sense are very near to Christ. They are built upon him, they are introduced into the church by professing saving faith in him. How dreadful will their disappointments and destruction be.

April, 1842

28. Heirs of God (Galatians 4:4-7)

But when the fulness of the time was come, God sent forth his Son, made of a woman, made under the law, to redeem them that were under the law, that we might receive the adoption of sons. And because ye are sons, God hath sent forth the Spirit of his Son into your hearts, crying, Abba, Father. Wherefore thou art no more a servant, but a son; and if a son, then an heir of God through Christ.

Introduction
In these words you have a brief compendious view of the way in which God saves a sinner from first to last, how he brings him from being a sinner to be an heir of God.

1. What God did for our salvation (v.4)

1. God sent to them his Son
How much there is in these words. This shows the fountain of our salvation, the heart of God. Sometimes an anxious sinner asks, 'Does God really want me to be saved?' Here is the answer, 'God sent forth his Son.' If God had wanted to destroy you, would he have provided a lamb for a burnt offering? Salvation is of the Lord.

This also shows that Jesus is a sufficient Saviour. He is of God's choosing. It was needful that a divine person should die for us. No creature was able to bear the creation, or to bear the Creator's frown. God chose one equal to the work. He laid not his hand upon man or angel or flaming archangel, but upon his own Son. God sent forth his Son.

It needed one of infinite compassion, one that had the same feeling of tenderness toward sinners that God had, else he might turn back. Therefore did God send one who would say, 'I and my Father are one', and, 'He that hath seen me hath seen the Father.' It needed one infinitely dear to God, that his dying would be accepted in the stead of sinners, that his sacrifice would be of value in the sight of God, equal to that of millions of sinners.

God sent forth his Son, his well-beloved Son. Oh, what confidence may you have in Christ as a Saviour. If you had seen him in his Father's bosom; adored by angels; creating all things by his word; upholding all things by the word of his power; had you been told that this was he who was to stand surety for sinners, to undertake for sinners, oh, would it not have satisfied your soul? It is all as true as if you had seen him. Rest in him. God sent forth his Son.

2. The incarnation

'Made of a woman.' Had it been revealed that the Son of God was to be the Saviour of sinners, who would have contrived the way?

(a) Will he come as at Sinai in lightning and storm?

(b) Will he come with a flaming sword as at Eden?

(c) Will he come in a pillar of cloud and fire as in the wilderness?

(d) Will he come in the clouds of heaven as at his second coming?

Ah no! God devised a far more wonderful method. 'Behold a virgin shall conceive and bear a Son and thou shalt call his name Emmanuel.' He is made of a woman. The God of glory becomes a worm and no man. Jehovah, who is incapable of suffering, becomes capable of pain and agony and death.

3. The substitution

Still, when Jesus stood on earth, a rod out of the stem of Jesse, the plant of renown, who would imagine the way in which he was to redeem lost sinners? The difficulty still remained. How would this glorious one pluck brands out of the burning? Will he lead them to glory? Will he reign over them? No, but he will come under the law in their room; the Son of God in our nature obeyed his own law. He showed it to be holy, just and good.

Never did the law appear so great, so broad, so good, as when Emmanuel obeyed it. He bore its curse, the curse came on him. Never did God's law appear so strict, so awful. Had millions of angels and men suffered under its curse, it would not have changed what Calvary showed. He magnified the law.

2. The purposes

1. To redeem them that were under the law

Who are under the law? All who have this law written on their hearts. All who have it written in their Bibles. All who have broken this law. All who have an accusing conscience. All who are seeking to justify themselves by the works of the law, who are trying to bring their lives and frames into agreement with the law. This glorious substitute is free to you all. To everyone of you who is groaning under this law. Here is a substitute freely offered.

Speak to various classes.

(a) To those of you who are happy because you think you have found righteousness by the law. Here is enough to break up your false peace. You are frustrating the grace of God. If righteousness came by the law then Christ is dead in vain. Do you think God would have sent forth his Son, if you could have got righteousness in your own way? The very fact of a perfect righteousness being offered shows that you are wrong.

(b) To those who are groaning under an accusing conscience, under legal terrors, under conviction of sin, there is enough to give you peace. God wishes you saved. The Son of God was incarnate for this, died for this. This glorious one is free to you as a substitute.

Today, before you rise, before you move, he asks your consent to be your redeemer. Nothing but your consent is requisite. Say yes and you have peace with God. If you will live on and die without Christ, that conscience will accuse forever. It will turn into the gnawing worm.

(c) To those who are slack. Oh, why are you slack? Is the curse of the law so easily borne? Is hell so easy a place that you are so slow in converting, or is Christ so common, so cheap, that you can turn him round and round like careless buyers. Oh, there is infinite madness in the world, living on at ease while Christless. But there is greater madness in you who know of Christ and yet consent not, rejoice not in him. Time is short. Death's scythe is mowing down many.

2. Adoption

We are adopted sons. There is matter of infinite wonder here. We are by nature a generation of vipers, children of the wicked one. Yet the moment we consent to take Christ we are adopted sons of God.

An awakened soul is seeking only peace, rest, forgiveness, but Christ is offering far more – adoption, the child's place in the Father's love. His finished work is free to us, but his finished work was not dying only but also the doing also of the Lord Jesus, gloriously perfect obedience in thought, word and deed. All this is free. To whom? To sinners, even the chief. Christ's all is free to you all.

Address sinners

You do not know what you are refusing. It is the glorious gospel, the glad tidings of great joy, that though you are vipers and under the curse of God and your hearts more like Satan than God, yet the holy God offers you a place in his bosom. He sent forth his Son to take you in. He cast out his dearly beloved Son, that he might enfold you, that you might receive the adoption of sons.

What are all the joys of sin compared with this? What are earthly titles but high-sounding nothings, sounding brass and a tinkling cymbal? Oh, surely you are deluded by Satan when you are willing to remain children of the devil, when you might be sons of God.

3. God's further dealings with adopted sinners (v.6)

When a rich man adopts a beggar boy into his family and takes him for a son, he not only clothes him and feeds him as his own son, but he educates him. He puts him under a teacher, to rid him of old habits and to put a new spirit into him, the spirit of his own son.

This is what God does when he receives a sinner. He not only puts the best robe on him and seats him at his table, but he sends forth the Spirit of his Son into his heart, the same almighty Spirit that rested in his own bosom and that of his Son. The Spirit that was in Christ Jesus, he sends him into the poor sinner's heart to make him a son indeed.

1. Observe the order

First he adopts, then he sends the Spirit into the man. Many are for reversing God's order. Many seek the Spirit of Christ in order that they may be adopted into God's family. They say, if I could only get the Spirit to change my heart and make me holy, if I could get more like a child, then I would go to Christ. That is, you would buy Christ. But that is contrary to God's order. God first redeems and adopts, and because you are sons sends the Spirit of his Son into your hearts.

Oh ungodly soul, if you are waiting till the Spirit comes into your heart and makes you holy before you will go to Christ or consent that Christ be your righteousness, you will wait for ever. You must consent to take Christ as you are, for all your righteousness. Consent now before there is any change in your life and then God will send the Spirit of his Son into your heart.

2. Observe what Spirit

The Spirit of his Son crying, 'Abba.' No natural man cries, 'Abba.' It is not the cry of nature. Children naturally cry 'father' to their earthly parent, it is one of the first things they learn. They do not thus call upon God. A sinner naturally distances God and dislikes God, but when he comes to Christ he feels the Father's smile, the Father's arms, the Father's love. He cries, 'Abba.'

Often it is little more than a cry. Many of God's children are not fluent in prayer, they have not many words, often they can only cry, 'Father.' The soul in Christ can cry, 'Father.' This runs through all he says to God, 'Abba.' In the multitude of words there wanteth not sin, but this one word is the believer's prayer, 'Abba.' In Romans 8, groanings. It is the breathing of perfect confidence.

'Believe in God and believe in me,' said Jesus. 'Thou wilt keep him in perfect peace.' In time of danger when the waves run high, when the winds are howling, the sails are torn, when the waves are breaking into the ship, the believing sailor can look above and whisper, 'Abba, Father.' In time of bereavement, when the dearest are taken away by a stroke, when we are left alone in this wide world, the child of God can meekly say, 'Abba, Father.'

Dear friends, have you this Spirit? It is this that will carry your soul above the world, its tossings, its cares. If you have it not, you may behold now when the sea is calm and the wind is fair, while all things go well with you, but that will stop when the breakers come. Your heart will die within you.

4. Future Prospects of God's Children (v.7)

'Wherefore thou art no more a servant, but a son, an heir of God.' God will never die and therefore a Christian is not an heir of God in that sense that we shall inherit what God leaves behind. No, but the meaning is we shall come into full possession of all that God has, as if we were really inheriting all things.

1. *We are no more servants.* When the prodigal was in a far country he said, 'I will say, Father, I am no more worthy to be called thy son, make me as one of thy hired servants.' But when he came to his father he could not say it. He felt that he was no more a servant but a son. 'Henceforth, I call you not servants, for the servant knoweth not what his lord doeth.' Yea, after, he calls us 'brethren' – 'go tell my brethren and Peter'; we are Christ's brethren and God's sons.

2. *Heirs of God.* God will never die and therefore a Christian is not an heir in the common sense of the word.

(a) All that God has is ours. 1 Corinthians 3.21: 'All things are yours', writes Paul; and they that wait upon God shall not lack any good thing; 'having nothing and yet possessing all things.' When a soul comes into Christ, rich or poor, he inherits all things, even in this world. He is an heir under age; Christ is his infinitely wise guardian and gives him just so much as is good for him. But he cannot want anything that is good. None that trust in God shall be desolate. Take courage, afflicted soul, thou art a lion of God.

(b) God is your inheritance. God said to Levi, 'Thou shalt have no inheritance in the land. I am thine inheritance.' True Christians are Levites, they have no other profession, on earth or in heaven. 'Whom have I in heaven but thee?' God hast been my dwelling-place.

1. A true saint prefers his God to everything else. The robe of Christ's righteousness he prefers to the finest clothing. The smile of the Father to the smile of all the creation. The adorning of the Holy Spirit to jewels of silver and gold. Half an hour spent with God, he feels worth an eternity spent with men. God is his treasure. It is to God he calls continually.

2. 'In heaven whom have I but thee?' God is the sun of heaven. If there were no God or Christ there, the true Christian could not be happy. It is to have God for his God, that he longs for heaven, to have his smile, to feel his love, and to love him back again. This is the portion of an heir of God.

Are you an heir of God? You may be always calm and happy for your inheritance changes not. The merchant trembles for his ships upon the sea. The director worries, not sure if his bank may break, his bonds fail. The nursing mother lives with anxiety for her child, for death may snatch it from her grasp. But your portion is indestructible. God is your portion. You are an heir of God. Once an heir of hell, now an heir of God.

3rd May 1840

29. The Marks of True Belief (Philippians 3:3)

For we are the circumcision, which worship God in the spirit, and rejoice in Christ Jesus, and have no confidence in the flesh.

Paul here tells you what it is to be a really converted man, one who is a Jew inwardly, an Israelite indeed in whom is no guile. There were some in Paul's days who taught that men must keep the law if they would be saved. Paul says of these men, 'Beware of dogs, beware of evil-doers, beware of the concision.' He calls them concision because they were unworthy to be called the circumcision, Jews unworthy to be called sons of Abraham, not having the faith of Abraham.

Let us now then notice the marks of one who is a true Israelite, 'We are the circumcision'. Three marks are here given, let us take the last first:

1. We have no confidence in the flesh
What it is to have confidence in the flesh you may learn from the example of Paul (vv. 4-6). It means that a man trusts that he can appear before God as he is in himself without being covered with another's righteousness. Every one of you who refuses the Lord Jesus Christ as your surety is having confidence in the flesh.

(a) Some think they can stand in their innocence before God. Like the young man who came to Christ, 'Good master, all these things have I kept from my youth up.' If you are walking in the dark in miry places, you may look at your garments and you will see no defilement on them. But the moment you come to the light you will see your filthiness. So it is with sinners; you are walking in darkness and you do not see your stained garments, but when you come before God you will be discovered.

(b) Some acknowledge their sins but think they can cover them. The poor Jews think they cover their sins by repeating their prayers over the graves of the dead. Alas, are there not Jews in this congregation who seek forgiveness in the same way? This is confidence in the flesh.

(c) Some think they are justified because they are anxious about their souls. Some when they feel their hearts melted under the Word begin

to think themselves on the sure way to heaven. This is confidence in the flesh. These convictions may be merely natural piercings of heart. There is often much more of nature than of grace in awakened consciences. And remember to be afraid of a storm is a different thing from being sheltered from it.

(d) Some look to their faith. They hear that we are saved by believing on Jesus, therefore they are trying to get that good thing 'faith' and they are striving to work it into their minds. That soul is gazing at itself, trying to discern faith. Alas, this is confidence in the flesh.

(e) Some look to their holiness. They are watching their own hearts to see if Christ be formed in them. If they could only see Christ in their hearts they would be glad, but they refuse all peace till then. Ah, this also is confidence in the flesh. Study sanctification to the uttermost but see thou make not a Christ of it, else it will come down one way or another. It is the hardest thing in the world to trust to Christ alone for righteousness. It is not Christ in us but Christ *for* us that must be our righteousness. Christ in us is an imperfect Christ and therefore cannot justify. Christ *for* us is a perfect Christ and therefore justifies fully.

What shall we do with this confidence in the flesh?
Answer: Have it not; renounce it; cast it away; do what Paul did in verse 7: 'What things were gain to me, those I counted loss for Christ.' When Paul's ship was nearly wrecked by the great storm in the Mediterranean Sea, the vessel was laden with corn and they cast the wheat into the sea. The wheat was good but they counted it *loss*. It was dragging them to the bottom of the sea.

So dear friends, you have much in your own righteousness which you think good while it is sinking you to the bottom of hell. As long as your eye looks inward for righteousness you are a perishing soul. Cast out all wares into the sea and then when you feel that you are empty of all good in the sight of God, the Lord make you willing to put on the righteousness of Christ.

When a beggar has nothing but his rags, he will hold them fast around him to keep out the rain and the cold. But if you give him a warm covering, all fresh and new, he casts away his rags as loss. So those of you who are natural men are clinging to your rags. All your righteousnesses are as filthy rags. Nothing you have will do to stand in before God. Yet you hold them fast for dear life. They are your all. But were the Lord Jesus to reveal himself to you, his fine linen white and clean, you would count all that but loss. Oh, cast confidence in the flesh away! Have no confidence in the flesh.

2. Rejoice in Christ Jesus

This is the finest and most lasting joy in the universe, when Christ is fully revealed to the soul and the excellency of the way of salvation by him. The heart is so often so full that the tongue cannot speak. It is joy unspeakable and full of glory. Hear what Paul says, 'Yea doubtless, and I count all things but loss for the excellency of the knowledge of Christ Jesus my Lord.'

(1) A Saviour provided by God

When a sinner is awakened, he trembles for fear of the wrath of God, but in Christ he is brought to see a Saviour provided by God.

(a) Chosen by God: 'Behold my Servant whom I have chosen, mine elect in whom my soul delighteth.' God laid his hand upon his own Son and said, 'I have found a ransom.' Now we are quite sure God would choose a sufficient Saviour, one who could well be surety for sinners.

(b) God's gift: 'If thou knowest the gift of God'; 'God so loved the world that he gave his only begotten Son...'. Ah, you may be sure indeed that the Saviour he gave will cover your soul in the day of wrath.

(c) Furnished for his work by God: 'A body hast thou prepared me.' The Father prepared the body in which Jesus should live and die for us. 'The Spirit of the Lord God is upon me because he hath anointed me.' The Father furnished him for the work given him to do.

(d) He is the Plant of Renown: which God raised up. 'I will raise up for them a Plant of Renown.' God knows the power of his own anger, therefore we may be quite sure the shield he has provided is a complete one.

(e) Christ is the foundation stone which God hath laid: 'Behold I lay in Zion a foundation stone.' Foolish men are always for building their eternal all upon a foundation of their own. But here is the God-provided One. This is the sweetness of Christ, that he is the refuge appointed by the Father. Oh, flee to him and you will find rest.

2. His work is finished

If Christ had yet to come and die, we might say perhaps he will not go through with it. But he has done it. It is more than 1800 years since he agonised in Gethsemane, since he poured out his soul upon the cross. It is finished! It is finished! His whole work as a Surety in the place of sinners is finished. The whole undertaking is completed. The whole obedience to the law is done. The bearing of the curse is fully accomplished. Nay more, God has accepted it. He has declared from heaven, 'This is my beloved Son in whom I am well pleased.' God has declared that he is satisfied with the death of his Son and that any sinner may come near by Jesus. Oh, it is this that ravishes the soul that believes. 'Oh, I am willing to be found in Christ,' the anxious soul cries. 'I am willing to all eternity to stand under the shelter of his finished work. What satisfies God, satisfies me. I am content for Christ hath died.'

3. He is a most suitable Saviour

There is a supply in him for every need. Sinner, you have broken the law and are under its curse. Well, but Christ was made a curse for us. You have no lifetime of obedience to offer to God. Well, but Christ has a lifetime of holy obedience which he offers you. You have divine wrath over you, but he is a divine Saviour to shelter you. You have a world of sins upon you. Well, but behold the Lamb of God that taketh away the sins of the world. You need one who can save you from sin and from hell. He is able to save to the uttermost. You need one who can save the chief of sinners. Well, he came into the world to save sinners, even the chief. Oh, he is a most sweet and precious Saviour. To you that believe he is precious. 'My God shall supply all your need out of his riches in glory.' He has a supply for every need of the soul.

4. He is a most free Saviour

The righteousness of God which is by faith of Jesus Christ is *with all* and upon all them that believe, for there is no difference, for all have sinned and come short of the glory of God. Some have sinned more, some less, yet all have sinned, so that the curse is over all, therefore the righteousness is free to all. 'As by the offence of one, judgement came upon all men to condemnation; even so by the righteousness of one, the free gift came upon all men unto justification of life.' By the offence of the first Adam the curse of God was laid at your door, so by the righteousness of the second Adam the free offer of justification is laid at your door. Oh, is there a burdened soul in all this assembly that will refuse to rejoice in such a Saviour as this, or take his own Word, his last message to a guilty world, that whosoever will may take of the water of life freely? If any one has the desire to be justified in this way you are welcome. Rejoice freely in Christ Jesus.

3. Worship God in Spirit

This is the great end for which Christ died: 'For Christ also hath once suffered for sins, the just for the unjust, that he might bring us to God' (1 Pet. 3:18). Some are contented to rejoice in Christ Jesus. They feel the joy and say, 'This is enough for me.' There must be something wrong in that soul. God brings us unto Christ that he may bring us to himself. 'This people have I formed for myself.' They shall be as the stones of a crown lifted up. 'Thou shalt be a diadem in the hand of thy God.'

1. Adoration

When a sinner is really brought unto Christ Jesus, his iniquities carried away, then he is brought near to the Father. He feels in the presence of God more than in the presence of the creatures. The soul then sees God in some degree as he is. As a sick person coming into the rays of the sun is revived by them, so the soul is enlightened, warmed, refreshed by the smile of a reconciled Father. The soul-piercing eye of God is felt to be resting on the soul. He feels the infinite love of God. He feels the awful majesty and greatness and holiness of God. The soul is thus brought to a calm posture, lying infinitely low yet without fear, rejoicing in God and adoring him. Like the seraphim in Isaiah 6, crying, 'Holy, Holy, Holy.'

Dear friends, have you been brought to adore God? When the sunbeams fall upon the sea they may draw forth the mists and exhalations which rise continually to heaven; and so when your soul is brought fully under the sweet, shining beams of the love of God, there should rise up the sweet return of constant adoration. Oh, it is sweet to spend life in holy intercourse with God. Enoch walked with God 300 years. He walked more with God than with his wife and children. Let us do the same and we shall know what heaven is upon earth.

2. Praise

One great part of the priest's office long ago consisted in the burning of incense upon the golden altar. And so when we are made priests to God, one great part of our duty is by Jesus to offer the sacrifices of praise continually. *By him* – we must put all our incense into the hand of Christ that he may offer it, perfuming it with his own merits and washing it in his own blood. Oh, it is sweet to know that even the sin of our holy things he is willing to take away.

Be much in praise, this is the truest worship of God. Adoration consists in beholding the glorious perfections of God. Praise is the showing them forth. Much of your eternity will be spent in this. Oh, it is a sweet and heaven-like employment. Make this life one continued song of praise. Begin the song of Moses and of the Lamb which you shall carry on eternally before the throne. Dear Christians, who seek the sweetness of glory, be much in praise. Unconverted souls, you may know how far you are from glory by your having no taste for praise.

'I would long to sit and sing this life away,' one dear soul said.

3. Self-dedication

This was shown by offering the whole burnt offering to God upon the altar. So those that have come to Christ offer themselves up to God upon the altar. As the animal went up in smoke, so that soul desires to spend and be spent for God. This was shown by the feast of first-fruits. The first ripe sheaf was brought to the temple and offered to God, to show that the whole was given to him. So Christians now love to give to God the best hours of the day, the best of their talents, to show that all are his. This is shown by the redeemed in glory casting their crowns at the feet of the Lamb. The crown is the noblest part of the dress and when they lay it down at his feet, it is laying their all down before him. Such is the worship of a soul in Christ.

Dear friends, be persuaded of this, to give your all away to him. Seize upon the moment when you fully rejoice in Christ Jesus, when you can say, 'My beloved is mine and I am his'; when you draw nearest to God and have freest access, then give yourself sweetly and freely away to him. Make full surrender of your *everlasting all* into his hands. 'Lord, into thy hand I commit my spirit. Thou hast redeemed me, Lord God of truth.' If you feel that God has redeemed you then give your spirit into his hand; 'yield yourself to God as one who is alive from the dead.' Resign *all temporal things* into his hand. 'Commit thy way unto the Lord; trust also in him; and he shall bring it to pass.' Resign your *dearest possessions* to his hand, such as dearest earthly relatives, so that when he takes away you may say, 'It is well. They were not mine but his.' This is real spirit worship of God.

Ah, how sweetly should we spend our few days, how far above the pains and troubles of this world if you would thus live upon Christ and live to God. Dear friends, before you rise to pray, give yourself all away to God. Is there any Christian within these walls that has not given his all away? It will be heaven to spend eternity thus!

29th February 1840

30. Enemies of the Cross (Philippians 3:17-21)

Brethren, be followers together of me, and mark them which walk so as ye have us for an ensample. (For many walk, of whom I have told you often, and now tell you even weeping, that they are the enemies of the cross of Christ: Whose end is destruction, whose God is their belly, and whose glory is in their shame, who mind earthly things.) For our conversation is in heaven; from whence also we look for the Saviour, the Lord Jesus Christ: Who shall change our vile body, that it may be fashioned like unto his glorious body, according to the working whereby he is able even to subdue all things unto himself.

1. Ministers should go before the flock, as shepherds in the East not only call upon the flock by name, but walk before them. So Paul. So all true shepherds. In what things?

(a) In counting everything loss for Christ, ministers should visibly show that they leave all other things for Christ, and their people should follow them in this.

(b) Pressing toward the mark (v.14). Seeking salvation from all sin as much as before conversion.

(1) Pray that God would make your ministers holy gospel ministers and keep them so; and that he will raise up such, that the vine shall flourish and the pomegranate bud in Scotland.

(2) Be followers of such. Many are willing to hear the shepherd's voice who are not willing to follow his steps. But both are means of

grace. Follow their lives as far as they follow Christ (1 Cor. 11:1), especially in gospel faith and gospel holiness. God makes ministers types or examples, that he may preach to the eye. God afflicts us that we may go before you in suffering; tries us that we may go before you in enduring temptation; comforteth us that we may comfort those who are in any trouble, see 2 Corinthians 1:4-6.

2. Many professors are enemies of the cross of Christ

1. Observe Paul's manner of speaking concerning them

(a) He had told them often. I have told you often. When Paul preached at Philippi he had often warned them against this, against appearing to be Christians and living an earthly life.

Many of you may think that we dwell too often and too plainly upon this, but observe what Paul did. Oh! we cannot speak too plainly, too urgently to those who are receiving an unholy gospel. If we do not speak plainly, many will reproach us in hell. 'You flattered me because I seemed to be converted, because I went through singular experiences, had deep impressions and lively affections and tears flowing in prayer. You flattered me that all was well, while all the time I was living a carnal life in secret, making a god of my belly and glorying in my shame.'

(b) Ever the necessity and great frequency and urgency in speaking to those who have a name and are dead. I could not bear your reproaches in hell.

(c) He told them weeping. Paul was a man of a very noble spirit. When he stood before Felix, Felix trembled; Paul did not tremble. When he stood before Agrippa, Agrippa was abashed before him. When he stood before the Caesar, no man stood with him (2 Tim. 4:16). Still he felt strengthened. But now he sat weeping like a woman, weeping like a child. Ah! what a tender thing is a Christian heart. It was the sight of unholy professors which moved the dauntless apostle. We have hard hearts that we can weep so little. I can truly say I weep inwardly over those that seem to know Christ, yet by works deny him.

2. Their character

(a) Their *general* character. 'They mind earthly things.' This is the great work of unconverted souls. If you have this you may know yourself Christless. The other points may be or may not be, this is invariably in every unconverted soul. In some of the deep valleys of Switzerland, I have heard of the children growing up without knowing that there was any world beyond the snowy mountains that met the blue sky above. Their thoughts and wishes all were confined to their valley where they were born. So it is with unconverted souls. They have not a thought or wish beyond the horizon of this world.

I have sometimes compared faith to a telescope by which we look beyond visible things into a world of eternal realities. Those that have no faith never see into that world. The unconverted is a man of one world. The child of God is a man of two worlds. His feet are in this, his head above and heart also. Examine where do your thoughts run? Your wishes? To money and all within the horizon! Alas, you mind earthly things. Have you no times like Jacob at Bethel? No times when there is a broad pathway opened into heaven?

(b) *God is their belly.* That is your god which you like best, from which you draw your greatest comfort. God is called the fountain of living waters, because he is the fountain of all life, of all pure living pleasures. But those who derive their chief pleasures from their appetites, make their belly their god. They find their chief joys flowing from sensible things, from what they see and hear and touch and taste and handle. They have no joys flowing from Christ, or from God, or from the pure Spirit that proceedeth from the bosom of the Father. They have forsaken the fountain of living waters. All their joy is from the things of sense and time. The Bible is a plain book, dear friends, it suffers no concealment of the truth. You may have much talk and many experiences, but if you find your chief joy in things of sense, then your god is your belly. Take that away and they have no more.

How plainly those are in an unconverted state whose chief joy it is to eat and drink. Not for the strengthening of the body, to serve God with, but for the gratifying of their lusts. Oh! it is enough to make all men to think how those can deceive themselves, by thinking they are on the way to heaven, who are making their belly their god.

(c) *Glory in shame.* A Christian should be ashamed of all sin, for Christ died to put it away. Yet how many that name the name of Christ, sit down at sacraments and bring children to baptise, glory in sin which is and will be their eternal shame. Either it is that which they ought to be ashamed of, or that which they will one day be ashamed of, when they shall rise to shame and everlasting contempt.

I shall take notice only of two points:

The forsaking of ordinances. In such a place as this where there has been such an evident work of the Spirit of God, many snatched from the fire, it is a shame that any should neglect ordinances. Yet how many do so? Glorying in their shame. This will be their eternal shame.

Sinning in day time. 2 Peter 2:13 sets a brand upon these persons, they declare their sin as Sodom, they hide it not. Lo! I fear it amongst ourselves. I have been in many heathen cities, but I never saw such sin in the day time as I have seen in this town. Is it not very dreadful in such a place as this, to see people playing cards in the open day and yet this I believe is to be seen? Is it not very dreadful in such a place as this, where the presence of God has been and where it becomes everyone to walk with a holy solemnity, to see young people meeting together as some do? Is it not enough to make us wonder that God spares the place? Does it not recall the words of Jeremiah, were they ashamed when they had committed iniquity? Thou hadst a whore's forehead, thou refused to be ashamed. Oh! my friends, if any such be here, this is glorying in your shame.

(d) *End destruction*. There is an indissoluble connection between these two, minding earthly things and destruction, an unholy life and hell. Some things are indissolubly joined, setting sun and darkness; reaping and sowing; the wages of sin is death; sometimes smooth to the end but their foot shall slide in due time, their path is dark and slippery, Psalm 35.

(e) *Enemies of the cross of Christ*. The cross is the way of salvation by Christ crucified for us. These persons are the great enemies of the cross. They bring scandal upon the cross, more than all heretics, Socinians, Arminians. Unholy professors are the greatest blasphemy of the cross. They hate it. Oh! be an enemy of anything rather, for the cross is pardon, holiness, all.

3. Case of the believers

Our conversation is in heaven. Our citizenship. Our life is spent among heavenly objects. Our feet on earth, our head and heart in heaven. Heaven is opened over every true believer as over Jacob.

(a) His eye rests upon Jesus. He sees Christ as he entered into heaven.

(b) The presence of God. He is hid in the secret of God's presence.

(c) He looks for the coming of Jesus. He looks forward to a time when Christ will come unto salvation and his glorious kingdom be established.

(Many were deeply affected during the preaching of this discourse, especially when that head on being enemies of the cross was given, many sobbed aloud, *Gloria Deo in excelsis*).

Thursday evening, 2nd July 1840

31. Be Careful for Nothing (Philippians 4:6,7)

Be careful for nothing; but in every thing by prayer and supplication with thanksgiving let your requests be made known unto God. And the peace of God, which passeth all understanding, shall keep your hearts and minds through Christ Jesus.

Believers should be careful for nothing

This is a singular command in such a world as this, 'Be careful for nothing.' If I were to denominate this world by any single name, I would say it is a world of care. 'Man that is born of a woman is of few days and full of trouble'. The grave is the place of rest: 'there the wicked cease from troubling; and there the weary be at rest' (Job 3:17). But this world is one of continual care. We came into it by the agonies of childbirth. We leave it by the agonies of the deathbed. It is a world of perpetual toil: 'cursed is the ground for thy sake; in sorrow shalt thou eat of it all the days of thy life. In the sweat of thy face shalt thou eat bread' (Gen. 3:17,19). The most have to rise early and sit up late to earn a scanty living. Many have want staring them in the face.

It is a selfish world. Everyone struggles for himself. No man cares for his neighbour. Everyone looks to self. You see a man reclining on a bed of money, faring sumptuously every day, heeding not the groans and the curses of the poor that starve at his gate.

It is a world of enemies. Full of enmity and strife. Men stab at one another's character and peace; all for sport.

It is a world of sickness. Most people carry some disease in their bodies. Those that know the human frame are amazed when this curious machine of the human body does not go wrong. Sickness goes round every family, groans rise in turn from every bed.

It is a world of death. His arrows fly day and night. Fresh tears are gushing every day. The work of the gravedigger is never done. It is a trade that never wears slack. Yet in this world of care, God says to believers, 'Be careful for nothing.'

Believers have more causes of care than other men. I will mention some that are peculiar to believers:

1. Care for their own soul. This is their care night and day, to make sure that their soul be truly saved. They never cease to examine with the greatest strictness into the reality of their conversion. They try themselves night and day. They never cease to examine whether they have received the Spirit; whether they are losing ground or gaining it; leaving their first love or increasing therein; whether they are becoming like Christ in all things. This is a deep-rooted, ever-pressing care.

2. Hatred of the world. If any man live godly in Christ Jesus he must suffer persecution. A man may be a moral man and much esteemed by the world. But you cannot be godly in Christ Jesus, you cannot be like the Lamb of God, cannot show that you are united to Christ and your holiness derived from him, without suffering persecution. Ah, this is a deep, deep care and sorrow.

3. Care for the souls of others. Hast thou an unconverted husband or wife or child? Thou hast a new cause of care of which our world knows nothing. To look day after day upon their much-loved faces and yet not to be able to speak the burden of the heart, ah, this is a grief the world never knew.

4. Care for the cause of Christ. It is said when Eli was 98 years old, he sat by the gate of Shiloh, 'and his heart trembled for the ark of God'. And when he heard that the ark of God was taken, 'he fell from off the seat backward and his neck brake and he died' (1 Sam. 4:18). So Paul says, 'that which cometh upon me daily the care of all the churches. Who is weak and I am not weak? Who is offended and I am not offended?' Those of you who are eminent in grace have much of this. These are what remain of the sufferings of Christ. Deep, solemn, heavy, constant care for the ark of God in this land, for the headship of Christ, for the cause of the Sabbath.

Yet even to believers in such a world is this word sent, *Be careful for nothing.* It is the duty of believers to live without anxiety, to live holy, calm, unmoved by the distresses, reproaches, bereavements of this perishing world. How is this?

1. Look on Christ

'The blood of Jesus Christ his Son cleanses us from all sin.' Guilt of all things burdens the soul most. It is that that gives a gloomy brow and an uneasy restlessness of soul. 'Justified by faith we have peace with God.' It is guilt that makes labour a toil; that gives the tongue of enemies all its piercing sharpness; that gives sickness its gloom and draws its sting. But have you looked to Jesus? Then your guilt is done away.

2. We have a Comforter

It is the wicked heart within that makes us so full of care. But we have the Holy Spirit. He began the work and will finish it.

3. We have a compassionate Father

An infant rocked in its mother's arms sleeps securely, it knows a mother's eye watches over it. So you in Christ. The boy in the storm said smiling, 'My father's at the helm.'

(a) Is it poverty that makes you anxious? Matthew 6, 'Consider the fowls of the air'; 'Consider the lilies of the field'. He that saved you from hell will save you from poverty. Seek ye first the Kingdom of God. The birds without barn or storehouse are fed.

(b) Is it hatred of men you fear? Matthew 10, 'fear not them that kill the body.'

(c) Is it your soul's salvation? 'He that hath begun a good work....' (Phil. 1:6).

(d) Is it the souls of others? 'Even so, Father.'

(e) Is it for the cause of Christ you tremble? 'Upon this rock I will build my church.' The cause of the world may seem to flourish like a green bay tree. Be careful for nothing. Invite the people to come and taste the sweetness. Unconverted men should be careful – they are all guilt and sin.

Remedy

Two-fold: prayer and thanksgiving.

1. Prayer

Prayer is the remedy against carefulness [anxiety], unbosoming of all to God. Do not allow it to lie upon your heart.

(a) In everything. Hannah said, 'I poured out my soul' (1 Sam. 1–2; cf. Psalm 62)

(i) In every great thing Jacob (Gen. 32); Hezekiah (Is. 37:14) spread the letter before the Lord, did not hide any part of it, told all his fears, all his sin, all his dangers. Often when calamity comes a believer says, 'This is too great a thing to ask God. There is no hope that he will hear me.' But is anything too hard for the Lord? Psalm 50:15: 'call upon me in the day of trouble.'

(ii) In every little thing. Life is made up of little things. Seldom great occasions occur. Small things discompose the soul just as much as great things. A stye in the eye; a thorn in the foot. Therefore if you are to live a life of holy peace you must make these all known, pour them out to God. God created little things, insects in walls, he feeds them all. *It shows true confidence in God to make known little things. A sick child asks to have its pillow smoothed.*

(b) Made known. He does not say, Fill your mouth with arguments, plead hard, etc. But, make known, show your wants, hold up your wounds, your weaknesses, your empty soul. Isaiah 65:24: 'Before they call I will answer.' Daniel 9:20-21: 'While I was speaking.'

2. Thanksgiving

In all things giving thanks to God.

32. If you are risen with Christ, you will seek the things of Christ (Colossians 3:1)

If ye then be risen with Christ, seek those things which are above, where Christ sitteth on the right hand of God.

If a company of blessed angels were to come and settle upon the earth, if they were to walk to and fro through our streets on their errands of mercy, if the light of their heavenly countenances were to appear amid the minds of our busy men of the world, oh, how remarkable they would be, how everyone would stand to gaze at them and little children in the streets would follow after them just to see the bright eyes that had looked on the glories of the better world.

Now there are at this day in the midst of us a company of men who are far more remarkable. True, they are not many; they are a little flock and it is true they do not catch the eye of the multitude, they have no bright wings nor do they always look like the children of a king. Most of them are very meanly dressed. Some are passing away on a sickbed. Only one or two have the riches of this world but, oh, they are a people to be wondered at for they are risen with Christ, they seek the things which are above where Christ sitteth on the right hand of God. They set their affections on things above, not on things on the earth. Oh Christians, you are this wonderful company! This is what you must be if you are Christians at all. Yet where do we find Christians who are risen with Christ? Oh, if you would live a life of faith you would be like jewels in a heap of rubbish. You would be a royal priesthood, a peculiar people, a kind of first-fruits of God's creatures.

1. Believers are risen in Christ as their surety

Everything that Christ did and suffered in this world he did and suffered not for himself but as a surety in the stead of sinners. Had he come to this world for himself, oh, what a different person he would have appeared. The beams of his divine glory would have burst through the thin tabernacle of flesh. You might as well have covered the sun with a curtain as have veiled his divine glory. Sinners would have fled away from his presence and cried on the rocks to hide them. But he did not come for himself; he came as a surety, as a man in the stead of other men.

1. He lived as a surety
Through his whole life Christ was fulfilling all righteousness. For this reason he was subject to his parents when a child. He was baptised in Jordan. For this reason he went about continually doing good, making it his meat and drink to do the will of his heavenly Father. He was holy, harmless, undefiled and separate from sinners. Now, it was not on his own account that he went through that life of willing

obedience, delighting to do the will of God. He did not need to earn heaven for himself for he was in heaven before he came. Why did he do all this? *Answer*: As a surety in the stead of sinners, that any sinner may clothe himself with his obedience and have a right to eternal glory. Oh sinner, you know not what you do when you refuse Christ as your surety!

2. He died as a surety

Through his whole life Christ was a suffering surety, but he was especially so in his dying. Had he stood for himself he would have had no sufferings, for he knew no sin, neither was guile found in his mouth. But though he knew no sin, yet God made him to be sin for us. God made him as if he were all sin from head to foot. And no wonder, for God counted as his the falsehoods of Abraham, the adultery of David, the murders of Manasseh. God charged him with the ten thousand thousand sins of all that ever had believed, of all that would believe on him, aye more than this, for the Bible says, 'He is the propitiation for our sins and not for ours only, but for the sins of the whole world.'

Question: Did Christ not refuse them and say, 'I did not commit these sins, I will not bear the punishment of them?'

Answer: No. He was like a lamb led to the slaughter, and as a sheep before her shearers is dumb, so he opened not his mouth. He called the iniquities his own. 'Mine iniquities have taken hold upon me so that I am not able to look up; they are more then the hair of my head, therefore my heart faileth me.'

Oh sinners, you know not what ye do when you refuse to take Christ as your surety. Though you had all the sins of David and of Manasseh on your own head, yet surely you might have boldness to take Christ as your surety and to have peace.

Oh believers, you are unified with Christ; hold fast your confidence in him unto the end. The devil will often try to bring the guilt of past sins against you, but, remember, carry you them all to Christ and heap them upon his head. Behold, the Lamb of God that taketh away the sin of the whole world.

3. Christ rose as a surety

Had Christ stood for himself he never would have lain down in the grave, neither would he have continued under the power of death for a time. In himself, heaven was his natural place and all the powers of hell could not have kept him from returning thither. But he lay in the grave as a surety. During these three days that word was fulfilled in him, 'Thou shalt surely die.' But the moment the God of infinite justice had received sufficient satisfaction, that moment our surety rose; he rose not for himself but for us, as a man in our stead.

Is there any among you awakened to feel that you are under the curse of God? Oh, be persuaded to accept of Christ as your surety. Believe the love in the bosom of God which provided such a surety. Do not doubt and in the moment of believing, you are crucified with Christ, you are justified with him, you are risen with Christ.

(a) You are risen from under the wrath of God. Just as Jonah when he was cast out on the dry land was risen from under the waves, so Christ, our great Jonah, is risen from under the waves of God's anger and so are you if you are with him. Wrath will never more come upon Christ, wrath will never more come upon you.

(b) You are risen into the favour of God. When Christ ascended from the dark sepulchre he entered into the light and the glory of heaven. And those who believe in him are translated from darkness into marvellous light. You are as much in God's favour as Christ is. Arise and shine for thy light is come and the glory of the Lord hath risen upon thee.

2. Believers are risen with Christ in their new nature

As long as a man is unconverted he is dead and lying at the utmost distance from God. God is the life of the soul just as much as the soul is the life of the body. When Adam walked with God in Paradise, God dwelt in him and walked in him and therefore Adam was holy and happy. But when Adam sinned, God departed from his bosom, he no more dwelt in that temple. Ichabod was written on the brow of man; the glory is departed. Man has become a dead thing, dead in trespasses and sins. He is lying in a grave of corruption and abomination; without and within all is loathsome.

Oh, that God would waken some of you who are thus dead to feel the dreadfulness of this dead condition. But the dead feel not, the dead cheek blushes not, the dead soul trembles not. Oh, that is the reason why so many of you are insensible under the preaching of the Word.

But the moment the ear hears the glad tidings of God having pitied dead, lost, depraved sinners, the moment the eye of faith is opened to behold Christ crucified for us and raised for us, the moment the heart is made willing that Christ be his surety, the moment the tongue cries out, 'He is my wisdom, my righteousness, my sanctification, my redemption,' in that moment the soul is justified before God. He is never justified till then. But in the moment of believing, the soul is as much justified and risen into the presence of God as Christ is. In that moment God says, 'I will come back to my dwelling place.' God sees no hindrance to his again coming to dwell in the heart of the justified sinner. God the Holy Ghost says, 'I will dwell in him and walk in him.' And just as it was said of the second Temple of Jerusalem, 'The glory of this latter house shall be greater than of the former' – so may it be said of the heart of the justified sinner. God the Holy Ghost comes to abide with us for ever and he lifts the soul up far nearer to God than unfallen Adam was. *Just as we have* a better righteousness than unfallen Adam had (he had only his own righteousness, the righteousness of a creature, but we have on the righteousness of Christ, the righteousness of the Creator), *so we have within* a far better holiness than Adam had. There was no certainty about his holiness for he fell, but there is covenant certainty about our holiness. It shall abide for ever, for the Spirit shall abide with us for ever.

Ask a question: Have you received the Holy Ghost? Has God really come to dwell in you, like a fountain, like a well, like a river? Some of you startle at such a question. Ah, how plain that you are not believers if God has not come to dwell in you. Read the Acts of the Apostles through and through and you will see that the gift of the Holy Ghost always followed on believing. Now, if any man have not the Spirit of Christ he is none of his. Some of you know what it is. He came like the wind – unfelt, unheard and unseen. He came like the golden oil from the green olive tree and now he dwelleth with you and shall be in you. He comforts you with sweet views of Christ. He lifts you up to have fellowship with the Father and the Son. You live in the Spirit and pray in the Spirit and are in the Spirit on the Lord's day. Oh, then you are risen with Christ and to you God sends the message this day, 'Seek those things which are above where Christ sitteth. Set your affections on things above, not on things of the earth.'

3. Show that risen souls should seek the things that are above where Christ sitteth and should set their affections on things above, not on things on the earth

1. Risen souls should seek God and set their affections on God
God is one of 'the things above where Christ sitteth'. Christ is on the right hand of God, on the same throne with God. God is the chiefest object then for the risen soul to seek. God is the true portion of the soul. Man was made at first that all his affections might embrace God. Just as the seashore with its thousands of creeks and bays was made to be filled up by the ocean, so the heart of man with its thousands of clasping affections was made to be filled and satisfied with God. When man fell, this was reversed. As if the creeks and bays of the seashore were to turn round and exclude the sea from their bosom, so did fallen man turn away from God and shut out God from his bosom. The affections that were made to embrace the Creator began to embrace the creatures and herein is our sin and misery summed up; we have been lovers of pleasures more than lovers of God. We have loved the creature more than the Creator who is blessed for ever. But if you be risen with Christ then your case is changed. If you be risen by the indwelling of the Holy Ghost then you cannot but seek God and set your affections on God. God the Holy Ghost loves God the Father with an infinite love. Wherever he dwells he will be always lifting himself heavenward, just as a flame always burns upward. Does God the Holy Ghost dwell in you? Then he will be constantly lifting your heart to burn upward as a holy flame toward the Father. You cannot but seek him who is above where Christ sitteth, you cannot but set your affections on him who is above. 'Whom have I in heaven but thee, and there is none on earth whom I can desire besides thee?' Some of you cannot love God. Why? Because you have not the Spirit.

2. Risen souls should seek heavenly occupations
Man was never made for idleness. An idle man is a monster in the universe. When Adam was put into Paradise he was put there to dress it and to keep it. When man fell he lost all his heavenly activity. True, there is much activity about unconverted men but then it is toward the earth; it is about money or eating or drinking or fleshly lusts. Look into a grave when corruption has begun its work, do you

see no activity there? Do you not see the activity of the worms? Such is the activity of unconverted men. But risen souls seek things above. If you be risen with Christ you will seek heavenly occupations and love them.

Look at God, he is always giving; like the sun which never wearies of shining, so God never wearies of giving out blessings.

Look at Christ, he is always busy, praying to the Father or walking among the golden candlesticks.

Look at the angels, are they not all ministering spirits sent forth to minister to them that shall be heirs of salvation? They have six wings; with twain they cover their feet, with twain their face, and with twain they do fly.

One thing is peculiar about all the occupations of heaven. They are all unselfish. On earth it is said, all seek their own; in heaven none seek their own. If ye be risen with Christ, seek those things which are above. If God the Holy Spirit be within you, ah, then I know you will be lifted up to seek not your own but the things that are Jesus Christ's.

Idle Christians

Some have the speech of Christians and yet do nothing for Christ. Oh, how is this? It is because you have not received the Spirit of Christ. If the Spirit of God dwelt in you, do you really think you would seek only your own things? Would an angel live in idle nothingness or that life of slavish labour only for himself which so many of you do? Awake, I beseech of you! Stir up the gift that is in you. Are there none naked to be clothed, no poor to be fed, no children to be taught, nothing to be done for Christ? Oh, how soon these days will be past. The night cometh. Seek those things which are above where Christ sitteth. Set your affections on things above, not on things on earth.

3. Risen souls should seek heavenly pleasures

Man was made to seek pleasure. Fallen men find pleasure in earthly things. It is their very nature to do so. But though there is much pleasure in sin, yet the pleasures of sin are but for a season, they last but a little while and then comes an eternal hell. But when God the Holy Ghost dwells in a soul he lifts the soul up to enjoy the pleasures at the right hand of God. It is the very nature of a risen soul to seek heavenly pleasures. A person that has always lived in the close atmosphere of a crowded factory is happy and contented with its pestilential vapours. But if he were lifted away to the free atmosphere of the glens and mountains he would acquire a taste for the fresh breeze and the sweet odour of the upland flowers. And just so, the soul that is justified and dwelt in by the Spirit acquires a taste for the fullness of joy that is in the presence of God and the pleasures that are at his right hand for evermore.

Are you risen with Christ? Then you will love praise. It is one of the sweetest pleasures of heaven. Are you risen with Christ? Then seek the knowledge of God, to know him more, to adore him more, that is the all in all of heaven.

4. Risen souls seek the possessions of heaven

'I will give her her vineyards from thence,' God says by the prophet. Even in the wilderness God appoints us our mansion and our vineyard above. Are you risen with Christ? Then seek the possessions above. Do not set your affections on riches. You will pierce yourselves through with many sorrows. Do not set your affections on friends, they will die when they are dearest. Hold yourself loose from all. Set your affections on things above.

You ask, 'How is this possible? I cannot help loving everything I see: my home, my books, my friends.' *Answer*: With man it is impossible but with God all is possible. Be filled with the Spirit and lean on the promise. If the Spirit dwells in you he knows the glories of the heavenly inheritance, he will lift your heart toward heaven, so that you shall say, day by day, 'Now is our salvation nearer than when we believed.'

Dear Christians, we are nearer glory than we were last Sabbath day.

St. Peter's, 1837

33. Election through Sanctification (2 Thess-alonians 2:13)

But we are bound to give thanks always to God for you, brethren beloved of the Lord, because God hath from the beginning chosen you to salvation through sanctification of the Spirit and belief of the truth.

In the preceding verses the apostle describes the fearful delusions of Popery, and the miserable end of all who are deceived by it.

1. He tells who is *the grand mover* of that scheme of iniquity in verse 9: 'Whose coming is after the working of Satan.' No enlightened mind who has studied the subject of Popery, who has observed their widespread influence, their imposing ceremonies and their mingling of truth with error, can doubt for a moment that the whole machine of Popery is animated and impelled by the prince of the fallen angels. Popery is Satan's greatest trap for catching the souls of men.

2. *That papists perish* 'because they received not the love of the truth that they might be saved' (verse 10). The truth is shining all round them, in the Bible, in the preached gospel, in the lives of the believers, but they do not like it; they turn away from it.

3. *That God gives them to believe a lie* (verse 11). It is often noticed that a Papist holds his creed more firmly than many a Protestant. Why? Because God has given them over.

4. *That they will surely perish* (verse 12), 'That they all might be damned.' When travelling through Popish countries, where we saw the people bowing down to images of wood and stone, and where God's Word is forbidden, these fearful words often come upon my mind, creating a feeling of unutterable sadness. But sometimes my mind wandered from the desolate scene around to the little flock of dear believers in happy Scotland, and then I understood something of Paul's feeling in these words in verse 13, 'But we are bound to give thanks.'

Electing grace alone makes you to differ.

1. That God is sovereign in choosing men to be saved

1. In choosing men and not devils

We read in the Bible of two great apostasies from God. There may be many more in the universe but these are all that have been made known to us. The first was in heaven. Lucifer, one of the brightest of the angels that stood round the throne of God, rebelled against him through pride, along with many more of the bright angels. God did not spare them but 'cast them down to hell and delivered them into chains of darkness, to be reserved unto judgement' (2 Pet. 2:4). The next rebellion was in Paradise. Man believed Satan rather than God and ate of the forbidden fruit, so that by one man's disobedience many were made sinners. Both families had sinned against the same God, both had fallen under the same curse, both were condemned to the same fire.

Now, it pleased God to show his free grace in providing a way of pardon for some of these lost creatures. He did not save all, for he wished to show his justice, but he determined to save some.

Whom shall he save, devils or men? Perhaps the holy angels pleaded that their brother angels should be taken and men left. They said the angelic nature was higher and nobler, that man was a weaker and more worthless worm. But ah! who by searching can find out God? Oh the depth of the riches both of the wisdom and knowledge of God! How unsearchable are his judgements and his ways past finding out. Behold he spared not the angels, he passed by the gate of hell. He took not on him the nature of angels. He did not lay on Christ the sins of devils. He raised no cross of Calvary in hell. He passed them by and came to the manger at Bethlehem. Now this is free, sovereign grace.

2. In choosing one nation and not another

If we look to the past this is remarkably shown in the choosing of Israel. All nations of the world were equally lost in the sight of God, yet God chose Israel. Not that they were more righteous than other nations; Deuteronomy 9:6: 'Understand therefore, that the LORD thy God giveth thee not this good land to possess it for thy righteousness; for thou *art* a stiffnecked people.' Neither did God choose them because they were greater in number; Deuteronomy 7:7-8, 'The LORD did not set his love upon you, nor choose you, because ye were more in number than any people; for ye *were* the fewest of all people: but because the LORD loved you....' So that they could sing Psalm 147:20: 'He hath not dealt so with any nation: and *as for* his judgements, they have not known them. Praise ye the LORD.'

When Israel sinned and were scattered, then God showed his sovereign mercy in sending the gospel to the Gentiles. The Gentiles did not deserve it any more than the Jews, but God had free mercy upon them. If you take up the map of the world it is singular to mark the sovereign election of God. Why has China with its teaming millions been walled around for centuries, left to the darkness of its vain idols? Why has Hindustan with its millions been left for ages under the cruel chains of Hinduism? Why has the rest of Asia been given over to the dreamy delusions of Mohammed? Why has Africa been given over to its dark superstitions? Why has the fair face of Europe been given over to delusion to believe a lie? And why has our bleak island been chosen for so many years to be the brightest repository of the truth in all the earth? Are we better than they? No, in no wise. There are sins committed amongst us that would make the heathen blush. This is free sovereign grace. I defy any man to give a reason why God has brought him into this land except the divine sovereignty.

3. In choosing the most unlikely persons to be saved

In general, God has passed by the rich, the wise and the virtuous. You would have expected that most of the rich would have been saved. They have most time to study divine things, they are not harassed by the fears of poverty, they can purchase the best books etc. But what says the Word? 'Hath not God chosen the poor of this world, rich in faith and heirs of the kingdom?' And again, to the poor the gospel is preached. Again, you would have thought God would have chosen the wise and learned. The gospel is a subject of very deep wisdom involving some of the most intimate questions in all philosophy; the Bible is written in ancient languages which are hard to be acquired. And then the wise and learned are generally free from many prejudices that darken other minds. But what says the Lord Jesus? 'I thank thee, O Father, that thou hast hid these things from the wise and prudent.' And again, 'not many wise, not many mighty, not many noble are called.' The most of those who will be in heaven will be poor, illiterate persons whom the world despised.

Again, you would have thought, surely God will choose the most virtuous people of the world. He is a God of purity who loves what is holy. And though none are righteous, no not one, yet some are much less stained with sin than others, surely he will take these. What says the Lord Jesus? 'The publicans and harlots do enter heaven before you. They that be whole have no need of a physician but they that are sick. I will have mercy and not sacrifice, for I am not come to call the righteous but sinners to repentance.' In all these the King of Zion takes his own way, that he may get all the glory, to stain the pride of all human glory, and to the praise of the glory of his grace.

4. In saving some that seek salvation and not others

All awakened persons who seek salvation are equal in the sight of God. Some have sinned more, some less, some have a heavier burden in the sight of God than others; still all are infinitely vile and lost. Yet Scripture and experience both show that some of these are taken and some are left. Some in this congregation who were once deeply awakened have, I trust and believe, been brought to Christ and saved, and some such are, I believe, this day in glory. Oh, there are some whose story I would tell you that was all grace from beginning to end. But ah, there are some in this congregation who were awakened at the same time and have been turned aside by a temptation, a persecution, or the world of sin and now you are left. Many are called but few are chosen. Has not this happened in children of the same family? You were brought up together, played together, sinned together, were awakened together, wept together, prayed together and yet one has gone back to her people and her god and another has followed the Lamb. Ah, how is this? 'He hath mercy on whom he will have mercy. He will have compassion on whom he will have compassion.'

Learn to give thanks. Ministers are bound to give thanks for yourselves. The very sight of your soul in heaven will call forth rapturous praise to God and the Lamb from all the holy angels. You are no better than a devil to yourself. Devils never rejected Christ as you have done; you have sinned in many ways that devils have not and yet you will be taken to heaven and they left in hell. You are no better than the heathen, no better than a Chinese or a Hindu, you have the same enmity to God, nay, you have sinned more than they, yet they will sink under the idolater's doom and you will mount to glory. You are no better than the sinners around you, indeed you have sinned, many of you, far more than they and yet he has passed them by and chosen you to salvation. You have more reason to praise him than all the angels in heaven. Many set out to seek the Lord with you but have turned back, you he has brought through! Oh, praise him while you have any being. Some have been hardened and offended under the very ministry under which you have been saved. 'Not unto us, Lord, not unto us....'

34. What we were without Christ (Titus 3: 3-6)

For we ourselves also were sometimes foolish, disobedient, deceived, serving divers lusts and pleasures, living in malice and envy, hateful, and hating one another. But after that the kindness and love of God our Saviour toward man appeared, not by works of righteousness which we have done, but according to his mercy he saved us, by the washing of regeneration, and renewing of the Holy Ghost; Which he shed on us abundantly through Jesus Christ our Saviour.

The apostle Paul was the first to carry the gospel into the large island of Crete, among a dark and wicked people of whom one of their own prophets had said, 'The Cretans are always liars, evil beasts.' He left Titus there to ordain ministers in every city and to set in order the things that were wanting. He wrote this epistle to encourage him in his different labours and here he tells him to bid the Christians of Crete to speak evil of no man, to be no brawlers but gentle, showing all meekness unto all men. And the reason he gives is – 'for we ourselves also...'

If Christians would remember their former condition and how they were saved out of it by mere grace, it would make them gentle and meek to all men, especially to sinners.

If Christians would remember their former condition

1. *Foolish* – the word means senseless, having no mind. This is very expressive of the condition of all unconverted persons.

(a) They are senseless about God. They have no mind with regard to God. Although they live and move and have their being in God, although they meet God in every blade of grass, in every pore of their body, although they meet God in the Bible and hear about him from ministers, yet they are quite senseless about God. God is not in all their thoughts. The fool hath said in his heart, 'There is no God.'

(b) They are senseless about their own soul. Although they are told their soul is perishing and quite ready to drop into hell, they are quite senseless, as if they had no mind. They stare with the vacant eye of a poor idiot boy. Although they know life is short yet they are quite senseless; though others die around them and they would drop into hell if they die, still they do not care, like a flock of silly sheep when one of them is carried off to the slaughter. They look up for a moment and then bow down the head to the pasture once more.

Unconverted, this is your condition. You think yourself wise and prudent but the Bible says you are senseless. The world thinks you a shrewd, sensible man and so you are in worldly things, but God says you are a fool, you have no mind at all. 'Thou fool, this night thy soul may be required of thee.'

Converted, this was your case. You were once thus senseless about God and your soul. Oh, how much need then have you to be humble and never open your mouth any more. To be gentle, showing all meekness to all men. Remember Christ and the Samaritan woman, and be you Christlike in gentleness.

2. *Disobedience* is another part of the natural character and it is very expressive of unconverted persons.

(a) They are disobedient to parents. Unconverted children are always disobedient children. If they do what they are bid to, it is out of fear, not out of love; for we never truly love our parents till we love Christ.

(b) Disobedient to God. God has set up his law in the heart and in the Bible. He says it is his own mind and will and never can be broken. Yet natural men delight to disobey God. Natural men disobey God just for the pleasure of doing it, as in swearing where there can be no other pleasure but just the pleasure of disobeying God. As some people choose the Sabbath day to sin upon in preference to other days, just for the sake of sinning against God.

(c) Disobedient to the gospel. They obey not the gospel. 'They believe not on me, they have forsaken me, the fountain of living waters.'

Christ is crying after simple, senseless sinners, but they stop their ears and will not hear.

Christ stretches out his hands to self-murdering sinners, but they are a gainsaying and disobedient people.

Christ offers his blood and righteousness to perishing sinners, but they trample both under their feet.

Christ makes some souls anxious to be saved from hell, but they are proud and will not come to Jesus Christ to be saved. They are disobedient sinners.

Unconverted, this is your case. You have all your life long been a child of disobedience, and if not born again you will be till you die.

Converted, this was your case. Should you not be meek and gentle toward poor hell-deserving sinners? Those who are just what you were. Should you not speak gently to them? Should you not remember the meekness and gentleness of David? 'Rivers of waters ran down mine eyes because they keep not thy law.'

3. *Deceived.* This also is very expressive of the condition of all unconverted persons.

(a) That they believe a lie
They think themselves right at the very time when they are wrong. Like the sheep that went astray, it did not at all feel lost.

(i) They believe that they are not yet condemned, that even if they were to die, God would have mercy upon them.

(ii) They believe that they shall be able to run to Christ whence they please to be saved and so they live on in sin. This is believing a lie, and being deceived.

(b) Some one deceived them
The devil is the great deceiver of the nations, the deceiver of souls. He flatters them and keeps them cosy in mind. All unconverted persons are under the power of the devil; they are his children and he works in them.

Unconverted, this is your case. You are deceived by the devil to believe a lie.

Question: If I be in an unconverted condition and under the wrath of God, why do I not feel it?

Answer: Because the devil deceives you; he flatters you, lulls you asleep. The Bible says you are deceived. All that have been saved feel that they were deceived before. You think you are safe because you are so confident; that is the very thing which shows you are unsafe. None are so confident as those who are deceived. Your eyes are blinded, the devil leads you by the hand, and you walk with a bold, confident step. But remember that is the way deceived persons always do.

Converted, this was your case. You were sometimes foolish, disobedient children. Tremble lest you be again deceived. I am jealous over you with a godly jealousy, for I fear that as the serpent beguiled Eve through his subtlety, so he should beguile you away from the simplicity that is in Christ. Be gentle to all. You were but yesterday in their case. Do not be proud toward them as if you were of a different race. Get the lamb-like spirit of the Saviour, say, 'Father, forgive them, for they know not what they do.'

4. Serving diverse lusts and pleasures. This also is most expressive of the condition of every natural man.

'Serving' should be rendered 'slavishly serving'. When a young person sets out in life he thinks he will make all his passions his servants. He will make them all minister to his pleasure. He will say to one, 'Go and he goeth, to another come and he cometh, to a third, do this and he does it.' And so he begins to sin, but when he hath sinned no more than once, he becomes a servant to that passion. Whosoever committeth sin is the servant of sin, the slave of sin. It is true he doth not find this out but thinks still that he is the master and sin the servant. Still, it is not a whit the less true. The tables are turned. His lusts now are the master and he is the miserable bond-slave. They say, 'Go and he goeth; Come and he cometh; Do this and he does it.'

Unconverted, this is your condition. You often boast of your liberty, yet there is not a more miserable slave in all the earth.

(a) A slave is often obliged to work *against his conscience*; his master may make him work on the Sabbath day. So it is with you. How often are you driven on by your lusts against the outcries of your conscience? How often are you driven by your cruel master to work sin on the Sabbath day?

(b) A slave is often obliged to work *against his reason*. So are you. Even when you see sin to be most unreasonable, contrary to all that you have heard, still when passion says, 'Do this', you are a poor, crouching slave, you run to sin against reason.

(c) A slave must often work *against his own interest,* against his own health. So are you. Often you know sin to be against your interest, against your good name, against your reputation in the world, but does this keep you back? Ah no! The slave must not dispute his master's commands. You are a poor, trembling slave, and you run greedily to obey your lust.

(d) When a slave is working, *the lash will often be applied.* So it is with your sin. It often lashes you at the very time you are doing its bidding. Which of you does not know that there are the pains of sin as well as the pleasures of sin? The cruel gnawings of remorse? The sickening disgust with your own self? The guilty tremors which make you often tremble?

(e) A slave *gets no wages* and is often killed at last. And so it is with you. Sin gives you no wages; he is a most cruel master. The only wage he gives is a place in hell, for the wages of sin is death.

(f) A slave *serves but one master,* but your case is much more dreadful than that. You are a slave of diverse lusts and pleasures. To be a slave to one would be bad enough, but ah! to be slave to many, how terrible. Yet this is your case if you be Christless. You are torn many ways at once, you are drawn asunder, you are distracted. The lust of the flesh cries out, 'Come here.' The lust of money cries out, 'Go yonder.' The lust of praise cries out, 'Do this.' Alas, if it be dreadful to be torn limb from limb by hungry, ravening wolves, just so dreadful is it to be the slave of diverse lusts and pleasures. There is not one lust that ever racked the bosom of a sinner, but it hath its place in your breast and its place is that of a master.

Look over all the annals of pollution and of crime since the Fall, and you will read only the history of your own heart. Look around you at the unblushing evil, the brazen-browed profligacy that is not even afraid of the sins and you will see as in a mirror your own unconverted heart, serving diverse lusts and pleasures.

Converted, this was your condition. Oh, bless God if you are redeemed out of it. Tremble lest you should again fall into it and be hardened through the deceitfulness of sin. Be gentler than you were. Oh, why does it become you to be proud and bitter over others, when you were in the same case but yesterday? Rather pray for them and weep for them and say with the lamb-like gentleness of Christ, 'Neither do I condemn thee, go and sin no more.'

5. Living in malice and envy, hated and hating one another.

As long as man was unfallen these hateful affections could not possibly exist in the human breast, for the greatest happiness of an unfallen creature consists in giving and not in receiving, in being least of all, in being a servant to others.

(a) The angels are unfallen creatures of far greater dignity than man, yet are they not all ministering spirits? They love to do it. It is their pleasure; they all try who will give up most and serve lowest in sweet happy service to one another and to the children of God.

(b) So it was with Jesus Christ. He was far greater than angels. By him they were all created, yet he came not to be ministered unto but to minister and give his life a ransom for many. He felt it sweetest and happiest to stoop down low – for others.

(c) So it is with God the Father. His happiness seems to consist very much in giving, far more than in receiving. As the sun is continually giving out rays, it is its very nature to give out blessings and to take nothing back, so it seems to be God's very nature to seek the good of others, to give out blessings and to receive none. This word is an eternal law of the universe, it is more blessed to give than to receive.

(d) So it would be with unfallen man. He would have loved to be the lover of all and to give up everything for others. He would have felt it his sweetest happiness to be like God and Christ, to be like the angels, to be a ministering creature. So that malice and envy could not have existed in the nature of things.

But the case is quite reversed; all men in their natural condition seek their own. I put it to the conscience of every unconverted person now hearing me: do you not just reverse the Word of God? When the Bible says it is more blessed to give than to receive, you say it is more blessed to receive than to give. All seek their own. Every one grasps at a portion for himself. Hence comes malice, envy, hatred.

Observe, 'living in ...' You say of a fish that it lives in the water. It is the very element in which it lives and moves. So it is with unconverted men. They live in malice and envy and hatred and hating. It is the very elements in which they live; take them away and they would die!

Converted, this was your case. Blessed be God who hath brought you out of it. Be gentle, showing all meekness to all men. Who made you to differ and what have you that you did not receive? Now, if you received it, why should you glory as if you had not received it?

When a sailor has been brought away from a wreck and saved from a watery grave, oh, it would be hideous to see him stand upon the beach and rail at his drowning comrades. If a man were saved from a house on fire, carried out of his bed and placed in safety, oh, what gentleness of spirit should he have toward those that remain in the burning pile. So be you who have been redeemed by the free mercy of God. Do not rail at your perishing brethren, but be filled with a tender spirit toward them. Pray for them. Weep for them. But, oh, be not bitter against them. Be like him who wept over Jerusalem saying, 'If thou hadst known, even thou.'

St. Peter's, 27th August 1838

35. Amen (Hebrews 1)

God, who at sundry times and in divers manners spake in time past unto the fathers by the prophets...

1. The law and gospel agree in this that God is author of both. God the Father is here meant.

2. The law, '*in time past*' (*palai*); the gospel, '*in these*

(a) *last days*'. The *palai* is from the giving of the law from Sinai to Malachi, 1100 years. 'In these last days': the last days of the Jewish church as 2 Peter 3:3; 1 John 2:18; Jude 18; not the same as 1 Timothy 4:1; 2 Timothy 3:1.

(b) '*To the fathers*, to us': Jews, Christ's and the apostles' day.

(c) *By many parts* – made a gradual discovery of his will, adding new lights and promising Messiah to complete it (Deut. 18:18); in Christ all complete at once. By dreams, visions, etc; in Christ by simple preaching

(d) *In the prophets,* especially Moses, in intimating the presence of God with his word. *In his Son,* the Son appeared to the prophets. But in a different way when he came in flesh.

(i) From the womb he was filled with perfect light, being God. But this is not the way in which the Father spoke to us in the Son.

(ii) The preparedness of the Son to declare the Father's will was all from the Father, 'the tongue of the learned'.

(iii) How? The endowment of the Spirit; so had the prophets, but Christ more.

(a) Fullness – John 3:34, Col. 1:9, John 1:16, Col. 2:3, Is. 11:2. He dwelt in those treasures, seeing to the bottom of them.

(b) At all times

(c) Other prophets but hewers of wood and drawers of water; they had to meditate on their own prophecy (1 Pet. 1:10), not so Christ.

(d) In the fullness of communication.

Learn

(1) The revelation of the will of God is eminently *of the Father*

1. *It was hid in God* (Eph. 3:9)

2. *Given out* according to his purpose

3. *The Father* sends the rod out of Zion

4. The Son speaks only what he heard of the Father: 'The doctrine is not mine,' he says; God beseeches (2 Cor. 5:20). Hence

(a) *The authority* of the gospel

(b) *The love* that is the spring of it

(c) *The call*, the Husbandman.

(2) The *gradual* revelation of God's will shows his infinite grace and wisdom.

(3) The perfection of the revelation by Christ.

Christ heir of all things

It may refer

1. To the eternal purpose of God

2. The Covenant

3. The promises to him, but most of all to the actual committing of all things into his hands declared by his resurrection, ascension and sitting: (i) for the consolations of the church; (ii) to strike terror into the ungodly

(a) *Over angels*. Being their creator and confirmer in holiness

(b) *Over devils*. Being fit to rule and by conquest

(c) *Over elect men*. Called and to be called

(d) *Over reprobates*

(e) *Over all grace*, pardon, regeneration, perseverance.

(f) *Over all gifts*. Natural and gracious and eternal

(g) *Over ecclesiastical things*

(h) *Over political things*

(i) *Over all the rest of creation*

Christ, the Maker of the world

1. Testimony to the eternal Godhead of Christ

    2. Unto the equity of his being made heir of all

    3. Hence we may have a sanctified use of the greatness of Christ

The brightness of glory

He is God manifest in flesh. Divine perfections shining through a human body, like the Shekinah through the veil. The express image of his person, like the gold plate on Aaron's forehead.

    1. All the perfections of God are in the Son

    2. The manifestations of God are by the Son: (a) Creation: (b) Providence

    3. Revelation

Upholding all: Like him in Ezekiel foreseeing all the wheels.

Learn: The folly of using the creatures in opposition to Christ (Dan. 5:23).

Priestly office: Having made atonement, by himself.

1. Holy admiration of this product of wisdom and rights

    2. The love of Christ

    (a) The need

    (b) The greatness of wrath

    (c) The way, by himself, not by his word

Sat Down

    1. Pledge that his work is perfected

    2. His blessedness and glory. His security and majesty. Different from Aaron, Christ sat down.

    Folly of Satan opposing Christ.

36. God Sent the Gospel (Hebrews 1:1-3)

God, who at sundry times and in divers manners spake in time past unto the fathers by the prophets, Hath in these last days spoken unto us by his Son, whom he hath appointed heir of all things, by whom also he made the worlds; Who being the brightness of his glory, and the express image of his person, and upholding all things by the word of his power, when he had by himself purged our sins, sat down on the right hand of the Majesty on high...

1. God the Father is eminently the author of our salvation

The rise and spring of the gospel was in the bosom of the Father. It was he who spoke to the fathers in time past by the prophets. It was he that spoke to us in these last days by his Son. He was the householder who sent his servants to gather the fruit of the vineyard, and last of all sent his Son.

1. It was hid in God

In Ephesians 3 it is called a mystery, from the beginning of the world hid in God. The Son joined in this plan, being one with him, 'Then I was by him.' The Spirit, who searcheth all things, even the deep things of God, was also there. Still, the Father's bosom was the spring and source of the gospel.

2. He sent the prophets and then his Son

All the prophets held their commission from God. God put his words in their mouths, he rose up early and sent them. The Father sent the Son into the world, gave him the work to do.

Siloam: Behold my servant.

'*My doctrine* is not mine but his that sent me.'

'As thou hast sent me into the world – even so have I sent them.'

3. He brings sinners to Christ

Psalm 110: The Lord shall send the consequence – 'Thy people willing.'

'No man can come unto me except the Father draw him.'

'All that the Father giveth me.'

'As many as thou hast given me.'

'*Thine they were* and thou gavest them me.'

The Spirit proceedeth from the Father.

Learn the love of God: God so loved the world. Christ did not die to make God love sinners. But God loved sinners and gave Christ to die for them. God is a consuming fire and yet God is love. He naturally destroys and devours sinners, and yet he naturally pitied and compassionated them. Oh, let him melt and attract you.

Learn: how shall you escape if you neglect?
He that spoke in Christ spoke in the prophets and now in us. We are ambassadors for God as though God did beseech you. Take heed, worms, your God is beseeching you. I am but a worm and yet Christ saith, 'He that refuseth you, refuseth me, he that refuseth me...'

2. The greatness of Christ

1. Maker of worlds
All worlds. To show his eternal power and Godhead. See John 1:3; Colossians 1:16. So here, he is the property of God, yet Maker of world. How amazing that the Maker of the world should be a babe, not have anywhere to lay his head. Yet more amazing than that, the world received him not.

2. Upholder
By him all things consist. He holds the sun in his journey, and all that grows; he gives life to every plant. He is the God of providence. In him you live. What madness in men to resist such an one (Dan. 5:23).

3. Brightness of glory and express image
Brightness, some suppose taken from the sun's rays. Better the Shekinah. Words of great depth to be studied in eternity. God manifest in the flesh. *From this learn* what a prophet he was. Other prophets had but sparks of light from God, they gave us a little of his mind which they often did not understand. But Jesus was God manifest, so that he that hath seen him hath seen the Father. He showed forth evidently God's heart toward sinners. Look to him to learn about the Father.

4. Heir of all (Gen. 3.15; Matt. 28). All power is given, even over angels. Worship him.

5. *Come with him to judgement.* Over devils, bruised head, took captivity captive; over saints, his sheep, his body, his spouse; over reprobates, his footstool; over kings, prince of kings of earth. Comfort to believers, dismay to enemies.

3. The priesthood of Christ
This was the great work he came to do. This is a faithful saying.

1. What it was. He purged our sins, made an atonement for them.

2. How? By himself. He through the eternal Spirit, not by his word, not by his power, not by silver, not by bulls and calves, but by his own blood. Behold the love of Christ, though he was so great and high. And this is what sinners are despising.

Question: But has God accepted the work of Jesus?

Answer: Yes, he has sat down – the high priest went in every year, but Christ has once offered himself.

Preached 28th June 1840

37. Christ is Pre-eminent because he is the Mediator (Hebrews 1:4-5)

Being made so much better than the angels, as he hath by inheritance obtained a more excellent name than they. For unto which of the angels said he at any time, Thou art my Son, this day have I begotten thee? And again, I will be to him a Father, and he shall be to me a Son?

The law was given through angels (Acts 7:53; Ps. 68:17-19). To show the pre-eminence of Christ above these is now his object, not the pre-eminence of his divine nature which was needless, nor of his humanity which was not true, but of his person and office as mediator.

(1) The Lord Jesus is exalted above angels.

(2) At his resurrection, as in Matthew 28:18, Acts 13:33.

(3) As much above them, as the name given to him excels the name given to them.

(4) This name he inherited, came to it on account of the discharge of his office.

Learn that all pre-eminence depends on the supreme will of God.

1 . The manner of his producing the testimony (v.5)
   1. He goes to Scripture
   2. Argues negatively, 'To which'
   3. He grants a distinction among angels

2. The testimony – from Psalm 2
   1. It applies to Christ (Acts 4:25; 13:33; Heb. 5:5).
   2. The name 'Son' is here appropriated to him.
   3. This name so given proves his pre-eminence. Angels are called sons (Job 1:6; 2:1; 38:7; Ps.89:6); as are believers (Rom. 8:16; Gal. 4:6; 1 John 3:1) and magistrates (Ps. 82:1,6; John 10:34). But God never peculiarly called one of them, 'my Son,' especially with the reason annexed. God here declares him to be his eternal Son by the resurrection and ascension. Therefore, if you would have listened at Mt. Sinai to the law given by the ministry of angels, much more should you listen to the voice of Christ!

Many say, 'I would believe if an angel stood beside my bed, if he told me of heaven and the way to glory.' But you have more than the testimony of angels – you will find when you die that you have been resisting greater testimony than that of angels, by refusing to hear the voice of the Son speaking in his Word and through ministers.

1. Because he is called 'My Son'
It is true that *angels* are called *sons of God* three times (Job 1:6; 2:1; 38:7), perhaps also Psalm 89:6. *Believers* also (Gen. 6:2, Gal. 4:7, a son; Rom. 8:16, 1 John 3:1, *tekna*, children). Magistrates too (Ps. 82:1,6; John 10:34). They are so for two reasons: (i) because they are the work of his hand; (ii) they partake of his likeness. But never did God say to one of them, 'Thou art my Son, this day have I begotten thee.'

(a) *Not in eternity.* Then he was 'my Son, my well beloved Son', equal with God. One with the Father. Still he was not man set as king on Mount Zion. God could not say, *'This* day.' Every day he was alive, though eternally begotten.

(b) *Not what he was in Bethlehem,* the babe, or the carpenter in Nazareth. He had not where to lay his head. True, he was then declared to be God's Son at Jordan and Tabor, but these were by anticipation.

(c) *Not on Calvary,* then God's wrath fell on him to the uttermost.

(d) But God raised him from the dead and then his word was fulfilled (Acts 13:33). When Jesus entered into heaven, having accomplished his errand – magnified the law, obeyed all its demands, borne all its curse to the full, revealed the heart of God to poor sinners. When he had made full exhibition to men and angels that God is inflexibly just and holy and yet infinitely merciful to sinners. Then as he entered, amid the hallelujahs of angels, the gates were lifted up so that the King of glory might enter in. God said, 'Thou art my Son, this day have I begotten thee. Never till this day could I declare it. Thou hast now maintained fully the character of God, shown to men and angels and devils what a God I am. A consuming fire and yet love.'

'I will be'. God says, 'Thou shalt now be peculiarly dear to me.' How amazingly this shows the greatness of Christ. No angel or archangel ever heard such a word. They too are faithful servants but as they come in after their errands, they say, 'We are unprofitable servants,' after their swiftest journeys and most burning adorations.

Learn the amazing value and glory of the work of Christ. God hath highly exalted him and given him a name that is above every name. Things are truly great according as God thinks of them. If God says a thing is glorious then we may be sure it has a true divine glory. But nothing was ever so glorious in the eyes of God as the work and person of Christ. 'Thou art my Son.' Never had the courts of heaven heard such words as when Immanuel entered, carrying the crucified thief on his shoulder and leading Satan captive.

Oh, what a cruel, low, devilish mind have you if you see no glory in the work of Christ. Learn your blindness.

2. Because God bids the angels worship him

This quotation is from the 97th Psalm. It seems plainly to refer to the second coming of the Lord Jesus. When the Lord again brings the first begotten into the world he says to all the angels, 'Worship him.'

(a) When he came the first time angels adored him. The angels of the Lord came upon the shepherds of Bethlehem. They sang glory to God, 'a multitude of the heavenly host'. Never did the world ring with sweeter melody.

(b) They attended him through life. One ministered to him at his agony. Twelve legions were ready to come at his bidding.

(c) They rolled back the stone from his sepulchre. They said, 'Come and see the place' (Matt. 28). Two angels one at the head, the other at the feet, like sentinels to watch the spot where the Lord of glory lay.

(d) They stood by the disciples, when he ascended to glory.

1. In heaven John saw many angels round about the throne and saying, 'Worthy is the Lamb' (Rev. 5:12). But when Christ shall come a second time this word shall be peculiarly fulfilled. He shall come with 'the voice of an archangel' (1 Thess. 4:16), 'with his mighty angels', (2 Thess. 1:7), 'when the Son of man shall come in his glory and all the holy angels with him' (Matt. 25:31). All will accompany him from heaven, all will sing their sweetest songs of praise. The archangel, the prince of the angels, will shout for joy.

(a) They will then see the plan completed. At present they desire to look in to these things; they do not understand the afflictions of God's children. The church in the wilderness, the rise of Popery, they cannot set to the holiness of God. But when Christ comes as head over all to his Church, they will see God's glory in the everlasting salvation of the redeemed. Heaven will re-echo with the thunders of their praise.

(b) They will themselves be confirmed. Christ will then gather all things together in one. Angels will be greatly advanced and confirmed by the work of Christ, therefore they will cast their crowns before him.

How highly should we honour him. Oh redeemed ones, the angels know not what it is to have been hell-deserving, to be lying under mountains of sin, to be plucked as brands. They know not what it is to be washed in his own blood and carried on his shoulders. We can say, 'Slain for us, he loved me and washed me.' Oh, if angels adore him, what should we do? If the praises of angels are like many waters, ours should be like ten thousand thunders. Oh, prize him who has made such a difference, who has glorified God in saving you.

How glad are those who give glory to Jesus Christ. The angels adore him, the very devils tremble before him. The redeemed sing their sweetest songs in his praise, they rest not day nor night.

The damned wail because of him. You are unconcerned at the name of Jesus. It is an awful truth that unconverted souls are more insensible to the glory of Christ than devils or damned spirits.

3. Because angels are servants and Christ is God over all, blessed for ever (7-12)

In those verses he compares three different Scriptures together and out of them shows the infinite superiority of the Lord Jesus. If one were taken this day into the realms of glory to see what John saw in the Revelation, you would see this very demonstration of the apostle before your eyes. Round about the throne you would see the angels, ten thousand times ten thousand and thousands of thousands. Some veiling their faces with their wings, some casting their crowns at his feet, some flying swift as the winds, some burning with love like a flame of fire, but all *serving* him that sitteth on the throne and the Lamb for ever and ever. Then you would see the meaning of that Scripture, 'He maketh his angels spirits' (v.7).

Again, if you looked toward the *throne* you would see the Lamb slain in the midst of the throne. You would see him who was laid in a manger, who slept on a pillow, who had not where to lay his head, who hung upon the cross, now sitting on the throne for ever and ever. His dominion is an everlasting dominion and his kingdom that which shall not be destroyed. *The hand* that was stretched out in love to heal the sick, to invite the sinner, that was stretched and nailed on the accursed tree, you would see that hand with the golden sceptre in it. *The head* that was buffeted, spit upon, crowned with thorns, sprinkled with blood, you would see anointed with the oil of gladness, for Christ has now obtained the fullness of the Spirit to bestow on all his members.

You would hear the Father confess him Creator and Lord of all. He who had no place on earth where to lay his head, being worse off than the foxes and birds of the air which have holes and nests. He who was condemned because he made himself equal with God. He who was hung up between earth and heaven. As Maker and Lord of all, himself unchangeable, Jesus Christ, the same yesterday, today and for ever. Ah, how soon you would learn that Christ is greater than the greatest angels, for he is Lord of all.

Learn the completeness of the work of Christ

He that was once on the cross for sinners is now on the throne. He undertook to bear our wrath and to fulfil the law for us. He said, 'Let the law take its course upon me.' Now if he has not suffered enough, why is he on the throne? Why has infinite justice let him go if he has not paid the uttermost farthing?

Nay, he is not only let go, but he is raised to the throne and become Lord of all angels. Oh then, breathing souls, flee to him! If any soul takes refuge in him he will in no wise be cast out, for justice has no more to demand of that soul.

Learn the joy of being under his sceptre

'Fear not, daughter of Zion, behold thy king cometh unto thee. He is just and having salvation, meek and riding upon an ass.' Some may be discouraged at hearing that Christ is a king, and begin to tremble. But see what kind of king he is! He is all kindness and gentleness, just and having salvation.

You may tremble to hear that Christ has got a sceptre, but, oh, it is a sceptre of righteousness. His commandments are not grievous, for he gives grace along with them. He gives grace to obey. When he stretches out his sceptre saying, 'Do this,' he drops a little of his oil into our heart and makes us willing. Oh, give up your hearts to be ruled by him. Let his dominion be from sea to sea.

Christ is an unchangeable portion

Everything in this world is like a garment getting old. The very mountains are crumbling down, the sun itself growing dim with age. Our bodies are frailer than they were. On how many of you is decay laying her fingers? How many teeth are gone and hairs turned grey? One thing alone abides the same, the Lord Jesus Christ, the sinner's friend. Thou art the same, *the same* through every scene of life – in affliction and in joy; in health and in sickness. You may always find in him the same peace, grace and guidance. *In eternity* when this world is passed away, 'Regions unknown are safer to you when I your friend am there.' One will be the same to us through all eternity. In him we shall have peace, in him grace, in him glory.

How truly wretched are those of you who have no interest in Christ. You literally have nothing. Your present possessions are your all and you will soon be turned out of those. A houseless soul for eternity. Look upon everything you have; it will die, it is changing in your grasp. It is like your garment, getting old. Soon all will be folded up and you must go naked into eternity. Oh, that you were wise! One thing is needful.

38. More heed (Hebrews 1:13,14)

But to which of the angels said he at any time, Sit on my right hand, until I make thine enemies thy footstool? Are they not all ministering spirits, sent forth to minister for them who shall be heirs of salvation?

In my last lecture I began to show you how much greater Christ is than angels. Our minds are so feeble that we cannot rightly estimate the greatness of a thing but by comparison. When a traveller comes in sight of the pyramids of Giza, he is generally disappointed. He thinks they are not high at all and wonder that people have written and spoken so much about them.

But if a man or camel or a tree be seen alongside of a pyramid, then those objects appear so small that the traveller is amazed at the sight of these stupendous masses of stone. It is for the same reason in this passage that the apostle Paul compares the holy angels with the Lord Jesus Christ. In our last lecture we were taken into the very courts of heaven and we saw the angels of God all casting their crowns at the feet of Jesus. We saw that he that was once hung by nails on the cross is now seated on the throne, that the hands that were pierced now hold the sceptre, that the head that was spit upon and crowned with thorns is anointed with oil above his fellows. Who is there among you all that did not feel inclined to cry, 'My Lord and my God'? Oh, that that glorious one may be my Saviour, may wash me, and rule over me, for ever and ever.

We now come to one comparison more between Christ and angels.

1. Let us consider the employment of the angels

1. They are all busy
'Are they not all ministering spirits?' Every glimpse which we get within the veil shows us that that glorious world is a world of never-ending activity. When Daniel beheld the Ancient of Days, 'thousand thousands ministered unto him and ten thousand times ten thousand stood before him.' And when Isaiah saw the Lord upon his throne, he saw the seraphim; each one with six wings; with twain each covered his feet and with twain his face and with twain he did fly; and they cried continually, 'Holy, holy, holy.' It is in respect of this they are compared to a flame of fire. For as a flame of fire is continually

active, flaming and burning upward, so these blessed spirits are always burning and flaming in the service of God. The rest of heaven will not be a rest from service but a rest from sin and pain. We shall rest from our labours but not from all service. We shall be as the angels of God. We shall serve him day and night in his temple.

Let none of you who are on the way to glory be idle now. The highest angel is not idle. You pray in the Lord's Prayer that you may do God's will like the angels. Do not contradict your prayers. Be diligent in business, fervent in spirit, serving the Lord. Be not weary in well doing, for in due season we shall reap if we faint not. Be not slothful but followers. Whatever your duty is, do it with all your might, do it heartily as unto the Lord and not unto men.

2. They are all busy for the sake of the heirs of salvation
I shall now enquire what the angels do for the children of God.

(1) They keep them in their conversion
When Lot and his wife and two daughters were lingering in Sodom, the two angels laid hold upon their hands, being merciful unto them, and they brought them forth out of the city and said: 'Escape for thy life, look not behind thee, neither stay thou in all the plain, escape to the mountain lest thou be consumed.' There can be no doubt that this was recorded to show us the interest which the angels take in the conversion of poor lingering sinners.

Is there any of you lingering, unwilling to leave all for Christ? Is there any of you trembling? Feeling your need of Christ and yet not willing to part with some worldly friend, some idol, some lust? Ah, the very angels are laying hands on you. They have seen the torment of hell, they have often heard the wailing and the weeping and the gnashing of teeth. This makes them anxious. They have tasted the sweetness of heaven, they bask in the smile of God, they feel the deliciousness of holiness and eternal life. These are their words to you, 'Escape.'

(2) They keep back judgements till God's children are saved (Rev. 7:1-3).
Here you see how anxiously the angel coming up from the east cries to the others to hold back the winds of judgement. And how willing they are to do it, for they are all ministering spirits. It is probable that in Scotland at present the angels are holding the winds till some of God's children be sealed. Many clouds are on the horizon,

but they seem all to be held back for a short time till we get more souls sealed. Oh, come and get Christ's mark on your forehead before the angels let go their hold and the winds of persecution lay our country desolate.

(3) They rejoice in the conversion of a sinner (Luke 15:10). No words in the Bible show more plainly the hearty interest which the angels take in the redeemed man. They sing a new song of praise. They cast their crowns afresh at the feet of Jesus. Oh, my friends, do you rejoice in the conversion of a soul, does it quicken you in praise, does it make you sing hallelujah? If not, you are more of a devil than an angel. None but devils and unconverted men on earth grieve over the conversion of a sinner.

(4) They watch the conflicts of the believer: 'When Jacob went on his way the angels of God met him (Gen. 32:1, 2), and when Jacob saw the men he said, This is God's host and he called the name of that place Mahanaim.' So when the converted soul goes on his way the angels of God meet him and go with him.

Paul says in 1 Corinthians 4:9: 'We are made a spectacle unto the world, and to angels and to men.' The holy angels watch the progress of a child of God with intense anxiety. They are present in our assemblies. They often join us in our songs of praise. Often a believer feels lonely and desolate. You think you are alone. Your family against you, your friends and neighbours against you, the whole world lying in the wicked one. Oh, do but look beyond things seen, put on the glass of faith and you will see the mountain round you full of horses of fire and chariots of fire. There are more that be with us than they that be with them. Only believe and you may call this place Mahanaim.

(5) They keep the believer from accidents: 'he shall give his angels charge over thee to keep thee in all thy ways. They shall bear thee up' (Psalm 91:11; see Psalm 34:7). He that knows the mechanism of the human body is not amazed that man should move unhurt through this world. But here you see plainly in the case of God's children that the gentle arms of the angels are round about them. They break your falls many a time and watch beside your bed.

(6) They stand beside the dying bed: 'Lazarus died and angels carried him to Abraham's bosom.' The proud world may despise the dying

beggar. Even God's children may not care to watch beside such. But, poor believer, do not be discouraged; the angels will wait on you as much as if you lived in a palace. They will shelter you with their wings. They will carry you to the feet of Jesus.

(7) One office more – The reapers are the angels. They shall gather the wheat into God's barn. In the great day of the coming of the Son of man, the angels will shout for joy. Then they shall be sent into the four corners of the world to gather the saints of God. They shall gather the jewels for Christ's crown, from their graves and the deep, deep oceans. They shall return with songs and everlasting joy upon their heads.

Learn from all this the love of God to his own. Not only did he give up his own Son for us all, but now he has given up his highest creatures to be our ministers. He that spared not his own Son but freely gave him up for us all, now gives us all things.

Learn wherein consists the true happiness of heaven. It does not consist in idleness, nor in labouring selfishly for our own gratification. The happiness of heaven consists in ministering to others. Every angel without an exception is a ministering spirit. The angels that behold the face of God go down and serve the weakest child that believes in Christ. The angel Gabriel comes down to the cottage of the virgin of Nazareth. The higher any angel is in glory, the lower he descends in humility. So it should be with ministers (they are all called angels in Revelation 2–3). Their true happiness is in ministering to all, in being the servants of all, that by all means they may save some. As it should be with you who hope to be in heaven. You who have heaven in your heart now, you should be like the angels, ministering spirits. This is not only your duty, but your true happiness. Let this mind be in you which was also in Christ Jesus, who being in the form of God took upon him the form of a servant. He girded himself with a towel. Ye ought also to wash one another's feet. 'If ye know these things, happy are ye if ye do them.' Let this be your habitual mode of life till you die, to seek the good of others, to stoop to the least of Christ's brethren, always to seek the good even of his enemies. It is more blessed to give than it is to receive.

2. The greatness of Christ
Turn we now from beholding the angels to behold the Lord of angels.

To which of the angels said he at anytime, Sit thou at my right hand?

Observe the greatness of Christ in two things:

1. Sitting at the right hand of God
This is the place of favour, power and authority. See Bathsheba (1 Kings 2:19). When the Son of man shall come, his sheep will be on his right hand. So in Psalm 45, the Queen shall stand on his right hand in gold of Ophir. This is a place that never was given to any angel or highest archangel. When they come in from their errands of love and mercy they are hailed with a smile of ineffable love and they hear this welcome sound, 'Well done, good and faithful servant.' And they cast their crown at his feet and say, 'Amen, hallelujah.' But when the Lord Jesus had finished the work given him to do, when he had lived and died for us, had shown to all worlds the infinite grace, purity, justice and love of God, when he came along the ranks of the wondering angels, this was the word addressed to him, 'Sit down at my right hand.' So that he may be sure of two things: (1) that his work is finished, accepted and rewarded; (2) that all power is given to him in heaven and in earth.

Learn, dear friends, how complete the work of Jesus is. It is not only done but also rewarded. However great and many your sins have been, you do not need to fear fleeing to him. He is at the right hand of God as a public person, as head over all things to his church, and if the head be there the body must follow! An old divine says, 'The body would be incomplete if it wanted a toe.' So the smallest member of Christ must sit upon the throne at the right hand of God. Only abide in him and he will bring you through every difficulty to the throne.

2. Until I make thine enemies thy footstool
Herein appears the amazing greatness of Christ, that all his enemies are to be made his footstool. Just as Joshua and the captains of Israel put their feet on the necks of the five kings of Canaan, so Christ will put his feet on the necks of all his enemies.

Two things are implied here:

1. That Christ will destroy all his enemies. Satan is the great enemy of Christ. Christ has already bruised him many times, especially in his cross. But Christ will yet finally triumph over him. Popery is another great enemy of Christ, but it shall be cast like a great millstone into the sea and shall never rise any more (Rev. 18:21). All kings that have persecuted his true servants, all that have not used their sceptre and crown for Christ in extending his kingdom, must be trodden in the winepress of his wrath. All families that have not called on his name, that have not worshipped Christ at the family altar and have thus cast him off, shall be trodden down under him. All persecutors, haters of God's children, mockers at prayer, scoffers at the righteous, all the fearful and unbelieving, will be trodden under his feet of burning brass.

2. They shall be made his footstool. He shall stand high and be exalted in their destruction. The Lord Jesus would be exalted in the salvation of sinners, in washing and carrying them to glory, but if they will not have that, the Lord Jesus will be exalted in their destruction. He will stand high upon them as a footstool. He will tread them in his anger and trample them in his fury – and all heaven will cry, 'Hallelujah, true and righteous are his judgements.'

   Learn the madness of being an enemy of Christ. How madly some of you are living, hating the word of Christ, despising his ministers, angry at the way of salvation by him. Some of you are angry when you see Christ working in the midst of us, displeased to see souls fleeing from the wrath to come. Some of you persecute God's children, speak slightingly of those whom God has wounded, and offend the little ones that believe in Christ. Ye know not what ye do. You will lose your own soul. Be an enemy of any man, angel or devil, but be not an enemy of Christ. Alas, he is the sinner's friend. To whom can you go for salvation. You will be made his footstool. As sure as you are now sitting at your ease, you will one day writhe under his feet. 'I will tread them in mine anger.' If you would flee to him now he would hide you in his bosom, but if you abide where you are he will trample you beneath his feet.

39. Give the more Earnest Heed (Hebrews 2:1-4)

Therefore we ought to give the more earnest heed to the things which we have heard, lest at any time we should let them slip. For if the word spoken by angels was stedfast, and every transgression and disobedience received a just recompence of reward; How shall we escape, if we neglect so great salvation; which at the first began to be spoken by the Lord, and was confirmed unto us by them that heard him; God also bearing them witness, both with signs and wonders, and with divers miracles, and gifts of the Holy Ghost, according to his own will?

We now come to a practical improvement of the argument. If God has spoken to us by so great a person in the gospel, we ought to give the more earnest heed, lest at any time we let them slip.

Christians are in danger of letting the gospel slip
Nothing more woeful than the history of professors, and even true Christians often degenerate.

Times of letting slip
(1) A time of worldly prosperity. 'Quails often make a lean soul.' Think of Demas (2 Tim. 4:10). Often a man is a happy believer in a time of poverty, but when he launches out into business he loses his relish, loses his hold. He is not so single in seeking the salvation of his soul, becomes keen after other things, attention is diverted. At one time it was his all, but now he is overcharged with surfeiting and drunkenness. He begins to neglect prayer, etc.

(2) Persecution. Parable of the Sower, when the sun was up (Matt. 13:5-6, 20-21). Some hold fast and grow stronger; some are in danger of letting slip. When Peter looked at the waves he began to sink. They did not count the cost. Peter denying Christ.

(3) Temptations. By sore temptation they fall into sin, ashamed to go back to Christ or to their godly companions. They abandon their hold of Christ or give way to their lusts.

1. Attend more; receive more; believe more; cleave more; follow fully. Increasing diligence in means of grace, hear for eternity. It is the Word of the highest. If you would listen to an angel, much more to Christ. Feed more on Christ alone. Do not let your interest in divine things be wrapped up with the creatures. March against occasions of letting slip, against the voice of strangers.

2. The greatness of the gospel salvation makes it certain that the neglecters of it will perish. The greatness of the salvation appears:

    (a) In the author of it – it came out of the heart of God.

    (b) In the messenger – not angels, but the Lord.

    (c) In the great hell from which it delivers.

    (d) In the great heaven to which it brings.

    Consider how impossible that you can escape.

1. The neglecters of it, not the opposers of it.

    2. It is sinning against love. You have already sinned against the justice of God, against his majesty. Now you are sinning against his mercy.

    3. No other name; the last offer.

40. Christ is Greater than Angels (Hebrews 2:5-9)

For unto the angels hath he not put in subjection the world to come, whereof we speak. But one in a certain place testified, saying, What is man, that thou art mindful of him? or the son of man, that thou visitest him? Thou madest him a little lower than the angels; thou crownedst him with glory and honour, and didst set him over the works of thy hands: Thou hast put all things in subjection under his feet. For in that he put all in subjection under him, he left nothing that is not put under him. But now we see not yet all things put under him. But we see Jesus, who was made a little lower than the angels for the suffering of death, crowned with glory and honour; that he by the grace of God should taste death for every man.

Christ is greater than angels because he is crowned over the world to come.

1. The world to come

Same as the gospel dispensation. The Jewish church, we, the world, the gospel.

    (a) *The same as* the kingdom of heaven. The glorious, perfect state of the church which is yet to come. Daniel's stone, the kingdom given to saints of the Most High.

(b) *The kingdom of glory*. This last I take to be the meaning here. Certainly a future and more glorious state of the church than we see at present, when everything shall be subject to Christ. All crowns and magistrates, geniuses, devils, all evidently below his feet which we do not yet see.

2. This world to come is not under angels

They are ministering spirits under the gospel; they will attend Christ at his coming; they will be gathered together in one in Christ, to form part of his glorious family.

3. This world to come will be under Jesus

He is Lord of all now, but then he will be seen to be such. He will reign over all things, nations, during the millennium; the 8th Psalm will be fulfilled then. He will rule over devils and enemies in the judgement. His name will be excellent in all the earth.

4. God's love to man in the work of Christ should fill us with admiration, as it did David.

Consider what God is, maker of all these. *Consider what man is*, a frail, vile worm. *Consider the work*, the diminution of Christ and setting above all, with all below his feet. All in love to man.

5. All this has been or soon will be fulfilled in Christ

(a) His diminution has been fulfilled. He was made lower, for a little while, to die; by the grace of God to taste death for everyone.

(b) He is crowned

(c) Soon all will be under his feet

2. Enquire what is the world to come

1. Some understand by it the gospel dispensation. They think that the Jewish dispensation was like an old world and the gospel a new world. The Jewish was a world of types, shadows, in which men come to Jesus through sacrifice, etc. But this is a new world in which we have boldness and access with confidence.

The objection to this is that Paul would never have called the gospel day a world to come, but a *world already here*. The shadows were gone. Christ had died, and risen. The Spirit was given, the gospel fully preached. Who could say it was a world to come?

2. The glorious kingdom of Christ which is yet to come. When Nebuchadnezzar dreamed of the great image he saw a stone smite the image and become a great mountain and fill the whole earth. This is the kingdom to be set up by the God of heaven. When Jesus came he preached that the kingdom of heaven was at hand. It is the same kingdom spoken of in the 72nd Psalm, when the kings shall fall down before him and all nations shall serve him. The kings of Tarshish and of the Isles shall bring presents, the kings of Sheba shall offer gifts. Men shall be blessed in him and all nations shall call him blessed. I am far from totally understanding the nature of that glorious kingdom that we pray for, but that I believe in the world to come, when all kings and magistrates shall obey Christ and when all crowns and sceptres shall be laid at his feet, all controversies as to church headship shall be hushed for ever, infidels and devils shall kiss the dust before Christ, and Christ's name will be exalted in all the earth.

3. It is possible that the words may refer to the kingdom of glory, the everlasting kingdom of blessedness and grace when this world and all its concerns are passed away. If any shall thus understand it, I shall not object. So it speaks in chapter 6, of tasting the powers of the world to come, which I believe means the eternal world, and in chapter 10, it speaks of a kingdom that cannot be moved, which I believe to be the kingdom of glory. So these words may refer to that glorious, everlasting kingdom which shall know no changes.

Are you living for this world to come? Or only for the world that now is? What a fleeting shadow is this present evil world. What a fool is the man that has no portion, but in this world.

41. Captain of our Salvation (Hebrews 2:10)

For it became him, for whom are all things, and by whom are all things, in bringing many sons unto glory, to make the captain of their salvation perfect through sufferings.

1. Many sons. Although few find the narrow way, yet many when you look at them. Look while we live. All who are saved are made sons.

2. To glory. To the other side. Whom he justified, then he glorified. When he cometh home. Joshua, the type, led them into Canaan.

3. The perfect captain
(i) One who is captain goes before, commands, leads, cheers them on. One of themselves.

(ii) Perfect through sufferings. It was needful he should die for his men. In this way he consumed our enemy, opened the way.

(iii) All this becoming to God.

It gracefully fits Christ, answers God, the author and end of everything. It would have been unsuitable to bring any to glory except by such a Captain. Those who are trying to get to heaven some other way are dishonouring God. It is glorifying to God for poor sinners to follow this Captain to glory. God is greatly glorified and you saved.

1. Many sons

1. Jesus said few there be that find it (Matt. 7:13,14).
This is true. Your experience must prove it. After all the awakening that has been in this place, few have found the gate. Many were left unawakened, some sought but did not find. Few there be that find it. Still when all are looked at in glory, they will be a great many. Revelation 7:9: 'I beheld and Lo! a great multitude', ten thousand times ten thousand will wear the white robes and wave the eternal palm. Psalm 110:3: the dew of the youth shall be more than from the womb of the morning. Genesis 15:5: 'Look now, tell the stars, so shall thy seed be.' The spiritual seed of Abraham are all that believe as he did. Oh! it is sweet to think that God will have many sons out of this world of prodigals. Christ shall see of the travail of his soul and be satisfied. 'They shall be mine in that day when I make up my jewels' (Mal. 3:17). Often the heart is likely to fail when we look on the ways of this country, living without Christ and without God. Sweet to think a time is at hand when our utmost desires will be satisfied. Christ shall be satisfied and so shall we. With regard to our unconverted friends in that day, we shall say, 'Even so, Father, for so it seemed good in thy sight', as did the Lord. Hallelujah. Worthy is the Lamb. Zaccheus the publican; the woman who was a sinner; the poor woman of Samaria; the dying thief, they will be there. And why not you?

2. All that company are sons (must be sons before glory).
Are we not all sons of God? No! Luke 15:32 – dead, lost. We once belonged to God's family but we have died out of it, we are lost prodigals. We become sons by believing on Christ: to as many as received him... (John 1:12). God sent forth his Son, so that we might receive the adoption of sons (Galatians 4:5). By regeneration (Romans 8). As many as are led by the Spirit of God they are the sons of God. By this you may know whether you are among Christ's 'many'. Are you a son? Have you found the child's place? Have you the child's spirit? No sonship now, no glory after.

2. To glory
By coming to God, the source and ocean of all things.
   (a) Implied that by sin men are fallen from glory.
   (b) That sonship is the way to glory.
   (c) Many: not all, not few.
   (d) God the bringer.

3. Captain
In antiquity, as Joshua. He is actual leader. A leader and commander, forerunner. The cause or author of salvation, implying difficulties in the way. He is the captain with care, with tenderness and with power.

God then is the bringer of many sons to glory and he chose who they were to be. As many as were ordained. He hath from the beginning chosen some to salvation (2 Thess. 2:13). He has chosen us in him (Eph. 1:4). We were chosen to believe, chosen unto sanctification. God gave his Son by the grace of God. God hath given to us eternal life. Him hath God the Father sealed (John 6:27). Christ is the sent of God, his servant doing his will. The Father draws to Christ: 'All that the Father giveth me shall come to me' (John 6:37); 'No man can come to me, except the Father which has sent me draw him' (John 6:44); 'Blessed art thou, Simon Barjona: for flesh and blood hath not revealed it unto thee, but my Father which is in heaven' (Matt. 16:17). Unless you know God as an absolute sovereign God, you do not know him as he truly is. This should humble you who are his children to think that this God chose you, drew you. Converted persons should have faith in God (1 Pet. 1:21). 'The Father himself loveth you' (John 16:27). The Father is bringing us to glory.

All whom God brings to glory, he makes sons first. Unconverted

are not sons of God: 'If God were your Father ye would love me....
Ye are of your father the devil' (John 8:44); dead, lost (Luke 15:32).
He makes them sons by adoption (John 1:12; Gal. 4:5); by
regeneration (Rom. 8).

He brings *many* sons – not all, not few – to glory. Election, sonship
and glory are three links of a golden chain that cannot be broken.
'Whom he justified them he also glorified' (Rom. 8:30). Joshua
brought all Israel over Jordan; so does Christ. Many tremble because
of temptations, afflictions, death. Do not fear; every son he brings to
glory. Rejoice that your names are written in heaven.

He is the perfect Captain

*1. One who is captain goes before, commands, leads, cheers them
on. One of themselves.*

(a) We need a Captain – implied. We live in our enemy's land,
passing through. The curse of the law, the devil, the much indwelling
sin. How shall we ever get to glory without a Captain?

(b) We have a Captain of salvation, a prince, the same that appeared
to Joshua (5:1). Isaiah 55:13-14: a leader and commander. Forerunner.

(c) He subdued our enemies. He is the Lord, strong and mighty,
Psalm 24.

2. Perfect through sufferings

He goes before them in obedience and in suffering. And in going to
glory he guides and gives strength. He subdues enemies for them
and in them. Therefore betake yourself to him and seek guidance
from him.

(a) He subdued the curse of the law, by bearing it, by letting it
pierce himself. He subdued Satan (v.14), bruised his head, made a
show of him openly. He subdued death by dying, to do away its
sting. 'Oh death, I will be thy plagues.'

(b) In us. Satan no more dominates over us. Sin shall not have
dominion. Fear of death removed.

(c) He goes before us in the way of obedience, suffering and
entering in as a forerunner.

(d) He cheers us on. Like weak sheep still he cheers us on – daily
supply, prospect of a throne and a crown.

3. All this is becoming to God

God is fountain and ocean of all. From the nature of God, sin must be punished. God a fire, of purer eyes than to behold iniquity. The righteous Lord loveth holiness. The Judge of all the earth must do right.

(a) What a dreadful thing sin is, how surely it will be punished.

(b) Those that seek salvation any other way are dishonouring God.

(c) It is glorifying to God to follow Christ; to enter in, under his shield.

42. The Amazing Love of Christ in the Incarnation (Hebrews 2:11-15)

For both he that sanctifieth and they who are sanctified are all of one: for which cause he is not ashamed to call them brethren, saying, I will declare thy name unto my brethren, in the midst of the church will I sing praise unto thee. And again, I will put my trust in him. And again, Behold I and the children which God hath given me. Forasmuch then as the children are partakers of flesh and blood, he also himself likewise took part of the same; that through death he might destroy him that had the power of death, that is, the devil; And deliver them, who through fear of death were all their lifetime subject to bondage.

In the last sermon, we saw that our Captain must die if he is to be a perfect Captain to lead us to glory. But how could he die? Was he not the brightness of the Father's glory and Lord of all? God of angels? Yes, but he became flesh. God was manifest in flesh. *This is here shown.*

1. The names here given to Christ and his people: 'He sanctifies' and 'the sanctified'

The name 'Sanctifier' is generally given to the Holy Spirit, because he is the immediate agent in making the soul holy. He is the living water springing up within the soul. But Jesus obtained the Spirit by dying, and gives the Spirit unto his own. So that he is now called the Sanctifier.

Or this part of salvation is put for the whole, the author of our whole salvation. His people are the sanctified: separated from the womb (as Paul was in Galatians 1:15, though many years a blasphemer), brought to Jesus; called; justified; the Spirit dwells in them; and they are sanctified, made truly holy.

Learn that none are brought to glory but the sanctified. No holiness now, no heaven hereafter. No grace, no glory. For the Saviour is he that sanctifies. Every sheep he finds he carries.

2. The Incarnation

They are all of one (v.14), he took part of the same. Great is the mystery of Godliness. He was the Son of God, equal with the Father, yet he took our flesh and blood. In two respects he was different:

1. He was not mere man. He was God also. We are mere men; we have no other nature and never will have, but he was Jehovah. He did not lay aside his Godhead, he only veiled it.

2. He was without sin. A holy being, separate from sinners yet without sin. He had no taint thereof. Spotless pearl, a holy lamb in this world of wolves. *But in all other respects* he was one, of one mass. He had our flesh and blood. The blood of David flowed in his veins, his bones were such as ours. Therefore he was weary and thirsty and hungry (John 4); he slept (Matt. 8). In Gethsemane he was exceeding sorrowful. He was grieved, he cried, he wept, he groaned and he died. His heart was melted, broken; he was distracted; his throat dried through crying. His eyes failed, etc.

3. See the amazing love of Christ in his Incarnation

It was mere love that moved him to this, to become united to human nature, so as to bear its agonies and distresses and weaknesses and curse. To be so united as forever and ever having our flesh and blood and bones even on the throne of heaven. Therein is love.

See Proverbs 8:30-31 '...my delights were with the sons of men.' See Galatians 2:20: he 'loved me and gave himself for me.' See Hebrews 10:7: 'Lo I come to do thy will...' This is the love you are despising, you that have never come to him.

Wise – grew in wisdom,

Mighty – worm,

Holy – made sin for us.

4. The consequences: He is not ashamed to call us brethren.

1. Show that he calls us brethren
He quotes three scriptures:

(a) In Psalm 22, where Jesus after his dreadful agonies says, 'I will declare thy name unto my brethren.' This he did after his resurrection. He opened their understandings, showed them the love and grace of God. Perhaps he raised the hymn in the midst of them as on the night after he was betrayed, acknowledging them to be brethren, mingling their voices together in unity. No doubt he will do this again when we meet. 'In that day I will show you plainly of the Father.' We shall drink the wine new with him and sing with him eternal praises.

(b) From Psalm 18:2; even in his lowest state he called us brethren. When like all of us he said, 'I will put my trust in a brother sufferer.'

(c) From Isaiah 8:18: at the last he will stand before God and acknowledge us. 'Him will I confess before my Father', as given to him, as his children, as worthy to be accepted by the Father.

2. He is not ashamed to do this
He might well be ashamed. Even when united to Christ and filled with his Spirit, yet what a vile wretch is man. That so great favours should be lavished upon him and yet he is unmindful of them all, he so easily forgets the grace of Christ bestowed on him. That the Spirit should be in him and yet such corruption, blindness of understanding, hardness of heart, such corruptions rising. Disciples forsook him, yet still brethren. But he is not ashamed to call us brethren.

Before conversion, we were utterly black and depraved, to do good we had no understanding. Yet Jesus comes stretching out his hands to such. Oh, this should encourage sinners to come to him. He will not be ashamed of you, he will confess your name. Backsliders should return. Believers should treat him as an Elder Brother. Go and tell Jesus, pour out all your sorrows there.

5. The purpose of his incarnation
That he might die. He took not on him our nature to taste glory in it, but to taste death in it. Not to be put on a throne, but to be nailed to a cross.

1. The state of sinners

Under sentence of death and the bondage of its terror. 'Thou shalt surely die', 'the wages of sin is death.' Most easy under it. But when God opens the eyes it is a dreadful bondage, terror of eternal death. It is an awful chain, to be bowed down under the frown of an offended God.

2. The power of the devil over death

He has not the keys of death. To God belong the issues from death. But the devil brought death into the world and he is the executioner of death eternal upon the souls that perish. He is their tormentor and to all eternity himself enduring torment.

3. Jesus died

He came in the stead of many and bore the very curse:

(a) So that Satan lost his power. He has no more right to torment or hurt a hair of the head of one that believes in Jesus. He is judged. In the very moment when Satan thought he had succeeded in putting an end to their Saviour, he himself was slain. Christ triumphed over him in his cross.

(b) So that all believers are delivered from the bondage of the fear of eternal death. If Jesus has borne my curse, there is no more for me to bear. The chain is broken that bound our soul to woe.

Learn the dreadful state of the unconverted in this congregation. You are under sentence of death, condemned already. Satan the executioner stands ready at this moment to spring upon your soul. He will torment you for ever. God has given him the power of death because of your sins and the will of the law. You do not feel this, you are at ease in Zion. But very soon you may be made to feel it all. You are perhaps brutishly ignorant. You do not wish to know or you have steeped your soul in lusts; or you have got a refuge, your own cloak of self-righteousness.

Learn the truly happy state of those that have fled to Christ. The bondage was terrible but sweet is the liberty. Sweet to be freed from fear of death, by the dying of Jesus. Satan has no more condemning power over you. He may torment and fire fiery darts, but he cannot destroy. Death has no more its curse for you.

43. Christ greater than Moses (Hebrews 3:2-6)

Who was faithful to him that appointed him, as also Moses was faithful in all his house. For this man was counted worthy of more glory than Moses, inasmuch as he who hath builded the house hath more honour than the house. For every house is builded by some man; but he that built all things is God. And Moses verily was faithful in all his house, as a servant, for a testimony of those things which were to be spoken after; But Christ as a son over his own house; whose house are we, if we hold fast the confidence and the rejoicing of the hope firm unto the end.

Before Moses died he left this prophecy behind him, 'A prophet shall the LORD your God raise up unto you of your brethren *like unto me.* Him shall ye hear in all things whatsoever he shall say unto you. And it shall come to pass that every soul which shall not hear that prophet shall be destroyed from among the people' (Deut. 18:18; Acts 3:22-23). Accordingly when John the Baptist came they said this question to him, 'Art thou the prophet?' And when Jesus came, some said he was Elijah, some Jeremiah or one of the prophets. In this passage Paul shows that Christ was the prophet like unto Moses and far greater than he. He had shown in chapter one that Christ was greater far than angels, and then that he was a greater captain than Joshua. Now, that he is a greater prophet than Moses.

1. Christ is greater than Moses because he is the builder of the house. Moses is only a stone of the building.

There is a house of God being built in this world. The *tabernacle* of old was a house of God in the wilderness. It must have been an amazing sight to see it standing in the vast sandy plain: its boards and bars, its curtains of badgers' skins, the veils of fine-trimmed linen; the court with its pillars and its hangings, and above all the cloudy pillar that rested on the tent by day and the fiery pillar that dwelt on it by night, marking it out as the dwelling place of God. Surely the wild Arab scouring the wilderness often stopped to gaze on that amazing sight. This was but a shadow of the church that is now being built in the midst of us.

The temple of Solomon was grand. Its marble pinnacles towered 500 cubits above the valley below. Its courts were spacious. Its brazen gates were beautiful and most of all the bright light of the Shekinah that shone through the veil showed that God was true. But all this is nothing to the temple of God that is now being built.

The church of Christ is the most wonderful thing in the universe. It has been nearly six thousand years in building and is not yet finished. The angels are wondering at it. The devils are trembling at it. If you have spiritual eyes you will see its glory.

(1) It will last for ever

All other houses and temples will decay. The tabernacle has long sunk into dust. The temple of Solomon was been ploughed over so that not one stone was left upon another. The house of prayer where we are met will soon become a ruin and the passing traveller will stop to ask the name of the grey, mouldering stones buried under ivy. Our bodies have the seeds of death and decay in them. The fairest and best loved head shall soon be a round white skull with hollow openings where the eyes have been and worms shall move within. This world on which we walk shall stagger soon like a drunken man. The mountains are already crumbling down. 'They shall perish... they all shall wax old as doth a garment; and as a vesture shalt thou fold them up, and they shall be changed' (Heb. 1:11-12).

What shall remain? The church of Christ. It is indestructible. It has no seed of decay or death in it. The older it grows, it grows the more perfect. Every stone of it becomes more perfect every day. The world is but the scaffolding round it. When the world is blazing, the church of Christ shall shine forth, clear as the sun and fair as the moon.

(2) It is a living temple

All other temples are dead. The tabernacle was one of boards and curtains. The temple of Solomon was splendid but was still dead. The church of Christ is a living temple. The foundation is a living one, the life of the world. Every stone of it is a living stone. Ah, there are many dead professors in the world but there is not one dead stone in the true church of Christ. The whole temple is alive. It is one body, all united together for eternity, and none of them can die. 'Because I live, ye shall live also' (John 14:19).

(3) It is dwelt in by God

'Know ye not that ye are the temple of God?' In whom ye also are builded together an habitation of God through the Spirit? (1 Cor.

3:16). Did you ever pick up a shell on the sea-shore and examine it? How amazing its beauty, the lines, the delicate colouring. Well, that is the dwelling God has provided for one of the meanest of his creatures. What shall his own dwelling be? Oh, look at this world, its hills and valleys, its trees and plants, at the lamps hung in the sky. All this is a house for man, a worm who is to live for a few years and die. What shall God's own house be like? Ah, my friends, you may see no glory in a poor, broken-hearted Christian, poor and neglected. You may pass him by. You may think it foul scorn to look at the side of the road he is on. But he is a stone of Jehovah's place for eternity.

2. Christ is the builder

This is plainly said by Zechariah (6:12-13): 'Behold the man whose name is the Branch... he shall build the temple of the LORD and he shall bear the glory.' And again, 'His hands have laid the foundation of this house, his hands shall also finish it' (4:9). Every stone from first to last is Christ's building. Ye are God's building. 'For every house is builded by some man but he that built all things is God.' When all is done he shall bear the glory. Angels and the redeemed will all sing, 'Worthy is the Lamb.'

(1) He laid the foundations

He became himself the foundation stone. Other foundations can no man lay.... 'Behold I lay in Zion for a foundation a stone, a tried stone, a precious cornerstone, a sure foundation.' Every stone of the true temple rests all its weight upon this foundation. He poured out his soul unto death in order to be a foundation. He made his soul an offering for sin. Not one sinner in the world can be a stone of this temple except by resting on this foundation.

Is this your foundation? Does all your peace and comfort flow from what Christ has done and suffered 1,800 years ago? A stone may be well carved and yet not on the foundation. There are many moral men who are not resting on Christ. Oh, see that ye be founded rightly. Some rest something on Christ and something on themselves. Ah, you will not stand. Other foundations can no man lay. Christ will be all your righteousness or none at all.

(2) He brings the stones

When Moses built the tabernacle, God told him to speak to the children of Israel that they bring an offering, 'of every man that giveth it willingly with his heart ye shall take my offering'. No one was compelled, all brought freely and willingly. So it is in Christ's church, every one that becomes a stone there becomes so willingly. We cannot force men to be concerned, to pray, to seek Christ, to believe and be saved. No, they must come willingly to Christ or not at all. But who makes them willing? Unconverted men are like stones: speak to them, they hear not; warn them, they feel not; beseech them, they move not. Sooner shall the rocks start from the caves of the ocean or from under the load of the mountains than unconverted men come of themselves to Christ. Ah, there is a load of guilt over them heavier than the ocean. There are bands of sin above them more binding than the ribs of the mountains.

How do any come? Christ makes them willing. Christ sends the rod of his strength out of Zion and then the people are willing in the day of his power. Christ says to the rocky hearts, 'Melt', and they melt; he says, 'Follow me', and they follow him. Have you been brought by Christ? Has your rocky heart been broken and made to run after him? Has the wedge of convictions ever severed you from the world? Has the hammer broken the rock in pieces? Ah, I sometimes fear lest God should have taken all the stones he means to take out of this place and that you may be left like a deserted quarry. Soon, perhaps, there may be no more sound of the hammer of God's Word among you. Sinners will be left to their lusts and formalists to their dead formality. 'My Spirit will not always strive with man.'

(3) He gives life and beauty to all

'To whom coming, *as unto* a living stone, disallowed indeed of men, but chosen of God, *and* precious, Ye also, as lively stones, are built up a spiritual house' (1 Pet. 2:4-5). The moment a soul rests on Christ it becomes partaker of a *new life*. Christ liveth in it, he gives it spiritual life. It still remains *a stone* but it is a *living stone*. A worm, helpless, a clod in itself, but the partaker of eternal life the moment it rests on Christ.

He becomes united to all believers. As the stones of a building are cemented together, so are Christ's people; they are cemented by love, holy love. This is Christ's doing. He makes men grow; other buildings do not grow, they grow old or ruinous, but Christ's temple grows larger and more beautiful every day. It groweth unto an holy temple in the Lord. Have you got this life and beauty from Christ?

Moses was a stone of this temple. Once he was dead but Christ made him willing. By faith Moses refused to be called the son of Pharaoh's daughter. A happy day for Moses' soul. Are you a stone? This question reaches into eternity. You will either be a stone of this temple or a brand in an eternal hell.

3. Christ greater than Moses because Christ is the Son over his own house

(1) Moses was a faithful servant
(a) A remarkable trust was committed to him. He was appointed mediator between God and Israel. He went up into the mount and spoke with God face to face as a man speaketh with his friend. He heard God's words and carried them to the people and he returned the words of the people unto the Lord. He received the law from God on tablets of stone. He was also a prince and judge over the many thousands of Israel. His chief honour was that he was a type.

(b) He was very faithful in his trust. In Exodus 40 when Moses set up the tabernacle it is said over and over again that he did it, 'As the Lord commanded Moses'. Moreover he carried himself very humbly in his office, not seeking his own. He was the meekest man upon the face of the earth. And when God offered to destroy Israel and make of him a great nation, Moses sought that God would rather blot out his name out of the book of the living.

All ministers are servants in the house of God and when faithful are worthy of honour. Consider: (i) the unsearchable riches which they handle; (ii) who works with them; (iii) their reward.

(2) Christ as a Son over his own house
Christ is not only the builder of the church but the Son and Lord over it. It is his own house because he built it. He keeps alive every stone in it. It is the monument of his own eternal glory. He is the only Lord over it in three respects:

(a) He gives pastors and teachers. He has the raising up and sending of his own servants into the house. He is the Lord of the harvest who alone can send labourers into the harvest. He has the hiring of the labourers into his own vineyard.

Learn that it is not right to take up the work of the ministry at our own hand. This is to leap over the wall of the vineyard, and we must take heed that such do not rather break down the vines than prune them. There are many I fear who run unsuccessfully because they run unsent, who have no commission from Christ and will receive no reward.

Learn that our church is engaged in a righteous struggle, maintaining that Christ should have the hiring of his own servants in his own house.

(b) He gives them all their supplies. Ministers are stewards but all our supplies come from Christ. If we get little we can give little. Pray that your ministers may get much from Christ, the Lord of the house, to feed his sheep and feed his lambs.

(c) To him all the servants must give account. Christ is to be judge of his own people and of his own ministers. We watch for your souls as they that must give account that we may do it with joy and not with grief. The master of the house is away on a journey to the highest heaven; soon he will come again. We know not the day nor the hour. But he will come. Then must you and I be summoned before him.

What account shall I give? Shall it be one of joy? 'Here am I and the children which God hath given me.' Or of everlasting guilt. 'Lord, who hath believed my report and to whom has thine arm been revealed?'

4. A bold profession in the face of trial to the end is the great mark of Christ's house

(1) All that truly come to Jesus are not only filled with peace but with a holy confidence and an exulting hope, for with the heart man believeth unto righteousness and with the mouth confession is made unto salvation.

(2) But many fall away in the day of trial. There are many trials that will try professors: (a) *persecution* because of the Word; either from friends or foes persecution will come, then many fall away from their profession; (b) *temptation,* the pleasures of this life; a snare is laid for them; sin appears sweet; they go back and walk no more with Jesus; (c) *heresies:* sometimes there spring up heresies in the Christian church and many seeming professors are led away.

(3) *There is the time to prove that we are the house of Christ.* When we pass through the waters and Christ is with us, then we are sure that Christ is ours and we are his. Remember Daniel's three friends. Stephen, when they gnashed on him with their teeth, looked steadfastly into heaven and said, 'Behold, I see the heavens opened and the son of man standing on the right hand of God. And they

stoned Stephen calling upon God and saying, Lord Jesus, receive my
spirit.'

Learn not to be surprised when many fall away. They went out
from us but they were not of us. There is many a byway to hell from
the narrow way.

Learn that untried faith is unsure faith. We are made partakers of
Christ if we hold...

Learn to commit the keeping of your soul to Christ. You choose
him because he chose you. You keep him because he keeps you.

44. Persevere to the End (Hebrews 3:12,13)

Take heed, brethren, lest there be in any of you an evil heart of unbelief, in
departing from the living God. But exhort one another daily, while it is
called To day; lest any of you be hardened through the deceitfulness of sin.

There are two great desires which fill the heart of every faithful
minister whenever he thinks about the flock committed to him: (1)
he desires that those of them who are in a Christless condition may
be brought to join themselves to Jesus Christ; (2) he desires that
those of them who have joined themselves to the Lord may hold fast
the beginning of their confidence firm unto the end. It was this second
desire which filled the bosom of Paul when he wrote these words.
The Hebrews to whom he wrote had been really awakened and brought
nigh by the blood of Jesus, but Paul's great anxiety for them was that
they might fall back and not persevere in the same faith to the very
end. In order to this he bids them do two things:

1. Watch over their hearts (v.12)
'*Take heed*, brethren, lest there be in any of you an evil heart of
unbelief, in departing away from the living God.' As if he had said,
'Remember that unbelief will drive you away from God.' The moment
you forget that God has loved sinners and provided a Saviour, that
moment you will depart from God. And remember that unbelief comes
out of an evil heart. It is the heart that is at enmity and suspicious
towards God which is the foundation of all unbelief. Take heed then,
watch over the heart. Keep the heart with all diligence for out of it
are the issues of life.

2. Exhort one another daily (v.13)

'Exhort one another...' As if he had said, 'You are not to care for your own perseverance only, care for the souls of one another. Speak to one another daily. Soon your days together will be ended; days of faith and prayer and exhortation will soon be over. Speak daily lest any of you be hardened in unbelief through the deceitfulness of sin.'

Someone may ask, Why all this care about holding fast our confidence to the end?

Answer: Because this day we can all be partakers of Christ. But are we all? Ah, there is need of all your watchfulness and all your exhorting of one another, for the end to be gained is the highest that any soul can be directed unto. We are made partakers of Christ, partakers of the Son of God, sharers in grace and glory.

1. We are partakers of Christ's sufferings and obedience if we hold fast the beginning of our confidence firm unto the end.

When a heavy-laden soul is first brought to believe on the Lord Jesus, to look upon the wounds of the Lamb of God with an eye of faith, he is brought to peace because he feels that the sufferings of Christ are his. He is a partaker of the sufferings of Christ.

Question: Does a believer really feel any of the pain of Christ's sufferings?

Answer: No. The sufferings of Christ are all past 1800 years ago, so that it is not possible a believer nowadays should feel any of the pain of them. But then Christ in suffering was the substitute for sinners; he did not suffer for himself but in the room of sinners. So that when any sinner believes on the Lord Jesus, Christ is in that hour counted his substitute so that the sufferings of Christ do, as it were, belong to him. He becomes partaker of the sufferings of Christ.

Just as in a mercantile house when one partner gains or loses, all the other partners gain and lose along with him. The losses and gains of one partner in the firm stand good for every other partner of the firm. So it is with Christ: he became partner with our flesh and blood that he might transact with God on our behalf, if we acknowledge him as our partner and Elder Brother. Thus all his gains and losses stand good for us. His sufferings are ours, his obedience is ours. Oh, this is the true happiness – of a sinner to be a partaker of Christ.

A word to the unbelieving

Why will ye refuse to become a partner with Christ? If a rich merchant were to offer a poor bankrupt to take him into partnership, what would you say if the poor man refused? But your case is far more foolish. The Lord of Glory offers himself to you. He has already laid down money enough – the fine gold of heaven – to pay all your debts. How shall you escape if you neglect him, if you turn away from so great salvation?

Question: How may a person continue a partaker of the sufferings of Christ?

Answer: By holding fast the beginning of his confidence firm unto the end. I trust that some of you were last Sabbath day brought to the beginning of your confidence, that for the first time you obtained a full and soul-reflecting view of Christ. You looked upon the silent wounds of Christ and could not doubt that they were your own. Ah, was it not sweet to God that you have suffered all that a just God would lay upon you? Did it not give you an awful peace to stand within view of the Cross and to feel that every groan and every tear and every drop of blood was your own? Ah, it is the sweetest, calmest peace that can fill the troubled bosom.

A word to those who are still enjoying it

Take heed, it is easily lost. Hold fast the beginning of your confidence firm unto the end. Remember it is not a sight of Christ on a sacrament Sabbath that will give you a constant peace. Feed on the manna day by day if you would live. You will find it the hardest thing in the world to be constant to Christ. Watch over your heart and exhort one another daily.

Some have lost their peace already

One little week has taken you away from your peace and fellowship with Christ in his sufferings. Ah, you have cause to be ashamed and to blush and to weep. But you have no cause to despair; if you have fallen, get up and run. But remember, the devil will persuade you to come to new peace in a new way. He will bid you look to your past experiences in Christ. I sat with joy at the table of the Lord, surely I may have peace. Ah, take heed, you cannot live upon yourself. You might as well think of satisfying your hunger by remembering how well you fed some days ago. Will that fill you? No. Neither will it give you true peace to remember how you fed on Christ. You must feed on him again, just as you did at the first. Go again to the cross, oh, heavy-laden sinner. Look again upon his wounds. Hold fast the beginning of your confidence unto the end.

2. We are made partakers of Christ's Spirit if we hold fast the beginning...

When a weary soul is brought first to believe in Christ, he becomes a partaker of Christ in receiving the Holy Spirit. He is brought into union with Christ so that he has communion with Christ. When a branch is grafted into the tree it becomes partaker of the sap and richness of the tree. Every member of the body partakes of the same living blood which flows to the head. So does every soul united to Christ become partaker of Christ, so that he can say, 'I live, yet not I but Christ liveth in me.' Just as the eyes and ears and all the organs of the senses are in the head, not for its own use but for the use and guidance of the members, so anything that is in Christ, all his treasures of wisdom and knowledge, all his treasures of grace and of the Spirit, are in him not for his own sake but for the use and guidance of all who are united with him.

Ah, it is the true blessedness of the soul to be a partaker of Christ, for it is to be partakers of infinite fullness. We beheld his glory as of the only begotten of the Father, full of grace and truth, and of his fullness have we all received, even grace for grace. When a rich man takes a poor man into partnership it is a happy thing for the poor man. The rich man says, 'All that I have is at your service. I have large sums of money in the bank; draw on my name as much as you will.' Even so is it when Jesus takes a poor sinner into union with himself, when we become partakers of Christ. He says, 'All things are yours. All that I have is thine. I have wisdom and grace and the Spirit of love and prayer and power and a sound mind. I have infinite treasures laid up in heaven. Draw in my name as much as you will. Hitherto have ye asked nothing in my name. Ask that your joy may be full.'

We shall wonder at two things in eternity: (1) that Christ should offer us such infinite fullness, unlimited supplies of wisdom, of grace, and of strength; (2) that those who are united to Christ should draw so little out of that fullness.

I speak to those who joined themselves to Christ last Sabbath day and know what it is to be partakers of Christ in receiving the Spirit. You know and feel what it is to draw out of his fullness, to have his power resting on you, to have his Spirit dwelling in you. Remember to hold fast the beginning of your confidence firm unto the end. You remember when first you had a soul-reflecting view of Christ, when you looked believingly on the wounds of the Son of God and felt that all had been borne. Now, then, keep up the same look of faith – your peace hangs on it. You remember when first your eye looked upon a risen Saviour, when he was revealed to you as a praying Saviour, as giving the Spirit without measure. This filled you with joy and peace. Keep up the same look at a risen Christ.

Hold fast the beginning of your confidence firm unto the end. It is by abiding in the vine that the branch bears any fruit. It is only by abiding in Christ with a branchlike faith that you can become a partaker of Christ. Take heed, and exhort one another. Some of you have not yet been made partakers of Christ's Spirit.

Some of you have lost it already. Some who last Sabbath day did truly join themselves to Christ and received the Holy Spirit have lost all already. You have lost the spirit of prayer, or the spirit of love has left you. You have been led into sin. You have cause to be ashamed and to blush and to weep. How true is that word, 'I was shaped in iniquity.' But you have no cause for despair. Remember the devil will persuade you to seek holiness some other way. He will drive you to promises and vows and self-contrivances which will make you proud as if you could change your own heart. But remember this word of God, 'We are made partakers.' You must come in the same humble way, as a thirsty sinner to the smitten Rock.

3. We are made partakers of Christ in glory if we hold fast

To be made partakers of Christ in his sufferings is wonderful. To be made partakers of Christ's Spirit is also wonderful. But to partake of Christ in glory is more wonderful than all.

When a poor sinner on earth is brought to lay hold on Jesus as a Saviour, he is filled with Christ's peace. 'My peace I leave with you, my peace I give unto you.' But when he enters into glory he is filled with Christ's joy. 'Enter thou into the joy of thy Lord.' He sits with Christ upon his throne. 'To him that overcometh will I give to sit with me on my throne.'

Question: Shall every believer be made a partaker of Christ in glory?

Answer: Yes. Every one of them in Zion appeareth before God. They shall never perish. Of all the souls that ever believed on Jesus, there shall not one perish. For though they be sifted like as corn is sifted in a sieve, yet shall not a grain fall to the earth.

Objection: What is the use then of bidding believers hold fast the beginning of their confidence firm unto the end, since they be saved whether they hold fast or no?

Answer: It is not true that they will be saved whether they hold fast or no. Every one that truly believes will be kept believing to the very end. For we are told that the inheritance is reserved for you who are kept by the power of God through faith unto salvation. If you are not kept holding fast the beginning of your confidence, you may be quite sure you will never be a partaker of Christ in glory.

Learn 1. That a believer in death finds peace in the same way as when he first believed. Even after having lived a life of faith and patience and love and good works, still upon his dying bed he holds fast the beginning of his confidence, finds peace in what gave him peace at first, he looks to the Cross. As one dear child of God said in dying, 'I just take all my good works and all my evil works and put them into a heap and bring all to the blood of sprinkling and there I find peace.'

Indeed, my dear friends, I believe the longer a believer lives a life of faith, the more he will draw his peace not from his own experience, his having tasted that Christ is precious, but from the testimony of God, that Christ is indeed enough for his soul.

Yes, dear brethren, that testimony really believed, not because you have found it but because it is the testimony of God, will shed a sweet, calm light through the dark valley of the shadow of death.

Learn 2. The unspeakable joys of the believer in glory. We shall partake with Christ. Oh, who can tell what meaning is wrapped up in that short phrase, partakers of Christ? I observe that when the wicked are sent away into their eternal dwelling place, it is said, 'Depart from me, ye cursed, into everlasting fire, prepared for the devil and his angels.' But when the saints are spoken of, it says, 'Well done, good and faithful servant, enter thou into the joy of thy Lord.' So that the joys of heaven are far more intense than are the pains of hell. The pains of hell are but the fires prepared for creatures, the devil and his angels. The joy of heaven is that of being partakers of Christ, entering into the joy of our Lord.

Oh, persevere then, dear Christian, by faith not by sight and you shall surely live in glory.

45. Persevering to the End (Hebrews 3:12-14)

Take heed, brethren, lest there be in any of you an evil heart of unbelief, in departing from the living God. But exhort one another daily, while it is called To day; lest any of you be hardened through the deceitfulness of sin. For we are made partakers of Christ, if we hold the beginning of our confidence stedfast unto the end...

A faithful minister has a two-fold concern for his people: (1) to get them brought into Christ; (2) to get them kept abiding there.

1. He has a deep concern over the unconverted. He sees them sleeping under the wrath of God. He knows how short their time is, how awful their misery will be. How precious their souls are, and he cries aloud, 'Flee from the wrath to come.' Like the angels of Sodom he would fain lay merciful hands upon them. Ah my friends, it is a wonder to me everyday that I can live and eat and sleep in the midst of you and see such multitudes perishing and yet not do more to warn every one and teach every man to flee to the Lord Jesus.

2. He has a deep concern over those that are saved. He knows the weakness of their hearts by his own. He knows the power and unwearied activity of the devil and the world. He is anxious lest the branches should decay or bear little fruit; lest they should leave their first love; lest they should return again to folly.

Ah dear friends, you little know how anxious we are not to lose the things which we have wrought, that the name of Jesus may not be blasphemed through you. This last was Paul's anxiety over the Hebrews, 'Take heed...'

1. The warning here given

1. What is this evil heart of unbelief? I have often of late showed you that unbelief or not coming to Christ proceeds from the heart. 'Ye will not come to me that ye might have life.'

(a) A God-hating heart

The natural heart is enmity to God. A natural man does not like God. He does not like to think of God, God is not in all his thoughts. If something be told him of God he soon casts it out of his mind. He does not like to pray to God in secret. It brings him too near. He does not relish the attributes of God, his holy nature is very contrary to a natural man. But Jesus came out from God. God anointed him and sent him into the world. Yea, Christ is himself the Son of God, having every attribute of his Father. He gave himself for us that he might bring us to God. Now this, the natural man cannot bear, therefore he knows not the way of salvation by Jesus. He sees no beauty in Christ that he should desire him. This is what keeps the unconverted among you from believing in Christ. You have an evil heart of unbelief.

Oh, take heed, dear believers, lest this evil heart should come back to you. It will drive you away from Christ.

(b) A self-righteous heart

Every natural heart is a self-righteous heart. He is proud of his own natural goodness, or of his amendments, or of his religious performances. He says, 'I thank thee, oh God, that I am not as other men are – adulterous, unjust, extortioners, nor yet as this publican. I fast twice in the week, I give tithes of all that I possess.' And accordingly when one comes in all covered with stripes and wounds and bruises saying, 'I was wounded for your transgressions and by my obedience many shall be justified,' the heart rises against him, casts him out of the vineyard and kills him. This is the way with all of you who will finally perish. You see so much beauty in yourselves that you see no beauty in Christ.

Take heed, believers, lest this evil heart rise up again in you. This is always what Satan is driving at, to get you to have confidence in the flesh that you may lose your joy in Christ.

(c) An idol-loving heart

The natural heart is given over to idols. In the Greek churches abroad the walls are painted round and round with idols. And you will often see the people choosing out their favourite idol and bowing down to it. Such is the natural heart. In every cell of it there is a different idol. And the soul bows down to each in turn. Sometimes it worships money, sometimes praise, sometimes dress, and sometimes sensual pleasure.

Christ comes to save us from our idols, to cast them all out of the heart and to fill it with his own Holy Spirit. This thought makes the natural heart hate and despise Christ. Ah, how many of you might have been saved souls this day but you cleaved to your idols. You went back to your people and to your gods.

Take heed lest this evil heart of unbelief be in you. It will drive you from Christ. If your heart cleaves to an idol you will soon bid farewell to Christ. Christ and idols cannot abide in the same heart.

2. The awful consequences: departing from the living God.

(1) It will make us depart from his presence and favour

When a soul first believes, he comes into the presence and favour of the living God. Jesus is our rent veil; we come through the veil into the holiest of all and draw near to God. Jesus is our Mercy Seat, where we have a meeting place with God. 'I will meet with thee, and I will commune with thee from above the Mercy Seat' (Exod. 25:22). Jesus is our way to the Father; no man cometh unto the Father but by Jesus. It is the chief joy of our life to come to God, to the living God. In him we find peace, rest, joy and satisfying pleasure, 'as the heart panteth...' (Psalm 42).

But unbelief is leaving all this. It is like Cain who went out from the presence of the Lord God. It is turning our back upon the Mercy Seat, the holiest of all, the rent veil, the way to the Father.

Oh my friends, would you lightly forsake all the peace and joy you have tasted in the smile of a forgiving God? Would you like to go back to the tents of wickedness? To be without God in the world? Take heed, then, of the evil heart of unbelief, for it will make you depart from the living God.

(2) It makes you depart from the life which he gives, from the living God. When you came first to Christ you were made partakers of divine life. You came to the life-giving God. You began to live. It was all death before that. But now Christ began to live in you.

You asked of him and he gave you living water. But unbelief is leaving all this. It is breaking your union to the vine tree. It is cutting off the communication between the living God and your soul. It is going back to death, to the death you were in before. Oh, do you love so much to be a dead soul that you would choose to go back to that condition? 'Take heed...'

This is your greatest danger. All other dangers are nothing compared with this. The devil knows well that if he can get you to lose hold of Christ he can easily lead you into any sin, and therefore all his craft and all his power is directed to this point.

As long as you keep your eye on Christ, as long as you keep a sense of pardon and acceptance with God, it is vain for Satan to tempt you. But put away faith and a good conscience and you will soon make shipwreck. By faith ye stand. This is the victory that overcometh the world even our faith. Be not afraid, *only believe.*

3. A means of avoiding unbelief: exhort one another daily.

(1) The spring of this duty

Holy Christian love. When God asked Cain, 'Where is Abel thy brother?', he said, 'Am I my brother's keeper?' He had not a spark of that holy love which is put into the heart of all Christ's people. He was a murderer and hated his brother. So it is with the world still. They have got Cain's heart. They will not be their brother's keeper. An ungodly father has no care over the soul of his child. An ungodly brother has no care for the soul of his brother. Am I my brother's keeper?

But when the soul is united to Jesus the head, it becomes united to all the members. Washed in the same blood, filled with the same Spirit, journeying to the same heaven, they love one another.

Christ is the precious corner-stone, uniting all the stones of the building into one. Christ is the head from which every member receives the same grace, love and strength. And here it becomes a clear mark of conversion: 'we know that we are passed from death unto life because we love the brethren' (1 John 3:14). See if you have it. If you can bear to see believers falling away into sin, if you can see them decaying and leaving their first love without holy grief, you are not Christ's at all. If one member be honoured, all the members rejoice with him or her. If one member suffer, all the rest suffer with him or her.

(2) The duty itself
Exhort one another daily – now.

(i) This is not the duty of ministers only. It is plainly their work to a remarkable degree. 'I charge thee before the Lord Jesus Christ...' (2 Tim. 4:1). 'Give thyself to reading, to exhortation, to doctrine...' (1 Tim. 4:13). It is my heart's desire that I could give myself more entirely to it, to speak to you publicly and from house to house with all plainness and affection. And may the Lord put it into your hearts to bear with me in doing it.

(ii) It is not to warn the unconverted. This also is a duty to speak to them as Lot did to his sons in law, 'Up, get you out....'. This is not the duty here spoken of.

(iii a) The duty of Christians speaking to Christians at all fitting opportunities, so as to stir them up to persevere in faith and holiness. We should *reprove sin* in one another. 'Thou shalt not hate thy brother in thine heart: thou shalt in any wise rebuke thy neighbour and not suffer sin upon him' (Lev. 19:17). 'If thy brother trespass against thee, go and tell him his fault between thee and him alone' (Matt. 18:15).

Ah, how little this is done among you who are Christians. You can notice one another's faults easily enough. You can speak of them to others. You can defame them behind their back or laugh at them or swear at them. But do you go with love to themselves to tell them their fault?

(iii b) We should instruct ignorant brethren. Thus did Aquila and Priscilla; when they heard Apollos preach they took him and instructed him in the way of God perfectly. How little is there of this.

(iii c) We should urge them to cleave to Christ. Thus did Barnabas, who, when he had seen the grace of God, was glad and exhorted them that with purpose of heart, they would cleave unto the Lord. Like apples of gold in a network of silver is a word fitly spoken. A word in season, how good it is. Ah my friends, I would like to see you living as a holy society, loving one another, helping one another.

3. *The manner of the duty*

It must be done:

(i) With love. If you have not holy love to their souls flowing in your bosom, then let it alone. Many of you know well how to reproach and accuse and cast up their sins to others. You have a secret pleasure in it. It would be a pain to you if you had no sins to reprove. Such men are like the birds that feed on rotten flesh. They have nothing of Christ about them. You must reprove as Christ did with a bleeding heart.

(ii) With self-amendment. Ah, how many there are that would pull the mote out of their brother's eye when a beam is in their own eye. Thou hypocrite. All your words will go for nothing if you do not back them with a holy example.

(iii) With urgency, daily while it is called today. Let it be your daily business to urge forward Christ's body to greater faith and love and holiness. The time is very short; soon it will be no more called today. Soon the morrow of eternity will dawn. Oh be diligent, be faithful unto one another. Exhort one another daily while it is called today....

4. Constancy in believing makes us partakers of Christ

1. We are partakers of Christ i.e. of his blood and righteousness, if we hold the beginning of our confidence firm unto the end. When a poor, lost worm condemns himself and consents to God's way of salvation, he becomes a partaker of Christ. Christ hath taken our sins and given us his righteousness. He has taken my mountains of guilt, sin and sorrow, and now he clothes me with his divine and lovely righteousness, thus I am a partaker of Christ. I share in the love of the Father with Christ. I share in the peace and justification which Christ now enjoys.

But how may you continue thus? *Answer*: by holding the beginning of your confidence firm unto the end. Come always as you came at first, with the same self-condemnation and the same looking to Christ for all. Cleave to the Lord with purpose of heart. 'Abide in me and I in you. If ye continue in my Word, then are ye my disciples indeed' (John 15:4; 8:31).

Some try to get back their first peace by remembering that they believed once, or by seeking out evidence of conversion. This is vain;

begin where you began before. As a lost sinner come heavy-laden to
Christ. Come devoid of goodness to be justified all by him.

2. We are partakers of his Spirit
In the hour of believing we become one spirit with Christ. His Spirit
is given to us and fills us so that we become holy partakers of Christ.

(i) For the Spirit comes from Christ. It is the same Spirit that is in
him.

(ii) He makes us like Christ. He forms Christ in us.

All that is in Christ is ours. Unsearchable riches, all the fullness
of the Godhead bodily. Would you continue thus? Keep your first
confidence. Come with the same sinner's grasp to lay hold on the
skirt of his garment.

3. Partakers of Christ in glory
Everyone that partakes of Christ's righteousness and Spirit shall
partake of his glory. Enter then into the joy of thy Lord. To him that
overcometh... Learn that even in dying you must believe as you did
at first. Even after a life of faith and devotedness you will still look
to Christ for all your righteousness. His blood and obedience alone
can fill the dying bosom with a calm delight.

Learn the joy of a believer: to partake of Christ now is blessed.
What will it be through eternity? To drink at the wellhead of being
and blessedness; to be perfectly filled with his Spirit; to have the
very being of sin rooted out and to reflect his holy likeness for ever
and ever.

'I shall be satisfied, when I awake, with thy likeness' (Psalm
17:15).

46. Do Not Provoke God (Hebrews 3:16-19)

For some, when they had heard, did provoke: howbeit not all that came out
of Egypt by Moses. But with whom was he grieved forty years? *was it* not
with them that had sinned, whose carcases fell in the wilderness? And to
whom sware he that they should not enter into his rest, but to them that
believed not? So we see that they could not enter in because of unbelief.

In these words the apostle goes back to the history of the unbelief of
Israel in the wilderness in order to draw out some more lessons of

heavenly wisdom. What a wonderful book is the Bible. Every time you read it, if the Spirit breathes over the page you will find new light – new nourishment to the soul. The Bible is the green pasture where he maketh his flock to lie down and feed, and every time the hungry flock return to it, they find the pasture has grown richer and more verdant than before. The Bible is the full waters of quietness by which the Shepherd leads his own, and every time they come to drink they find the river full as before of living water. An old divine compares it to a cabinet with many drawers-full of precious things. It may rather be compared to the ocean out of whose deep caves have been brought forth pearls and corals, but there are brighter things still beneath which no eye has seen and no hand searched out.

Learn to search the Scriptures; to lie down in these green pastures; to drink from those still waters. Take up your Bible with prayerful uplifted eyes. Turn its threatenings into confession; as dew draws out the odour from the flowers, so will the Holy Spirit draw out the fragrance of heaven from this garden of delights. All Scripture is given by inspiration of God....

1. Many hear God's Word only to provoke God (v.16)

So it was with Israel: God did great things for Israel whereof they where glad. He brought them out of the iron furnace, even Egypt. His way was in the sea and his path in the great waters and his footsteps were not known. He led his people like a flock by the hand of Moses and Aaron. He gave them bread from heaven to eat. He gave them water out of the rock to drink. He guided them by a pillar cloud. Nay, he spoke to them from heaven, as Moses says in Deuteronomy 4:33: 'Did ever people hear the voice of God speaking out of the midst of the fire as thou hast heard, and live?'

Nay, the gospel was preached to them as well as unto us. The lamb slain every morning and evening preached to them the Lamb of God. The scapegoat carrying their sins into the wilderness told them of him who bore our sins on his own body on the tree. The smitten rock which gave them water told them of Jesus the giver of living water, for 'that rock was Christ'.

Still even though they had heard they did provoke. They turned back like a deceitful people. They tempted God ten times. When the spies brought an evil report of the land, they lifted up their voice and cried and the people wept that night. They said, 'Would God that we had died in the land of Egypt, or would God we had died in this wilderness. Let us make us a captain and let us return unto Egypt.'

So in Isaiah's time: Often did Isaiah stand to preach beneath the shady rock – or the flowering fig-tree beside the fountain of Siloam. The old men and women of Jerusalem leaning on their staff, for they all would linger round, and Jewish boys and girls would leave their play in the streets of Jerusalem to go and hear the holy man. 'Ho! Every one that thirsteth, come ye to the waters.' But still at evening Isaiah often sought his lonely chamber or in secret retirement on the roof and poured out his complaint to God: 'Who hath believed our report?' The most heard and provoked God.

So in Christ's time: how often he stood by the lake of Galilee. The fisherman left his net to catch some of his gracious words. The shepherds from the brow of Naphtali came down to listen to him who spake as never man spake. And the crowd from the streets of Capernaum left their merchandise and ran down to the shore to hear the words of eternal life. How strange that the most of these men will yet hear these same lips say, 'Depart, ye cursed....' How sad regarding the men of Capernaum, that before he was done he could read in their faces that they despised his message.

Behold, ye despisers, and wonder and perish....
Some when they had heard did provoke.

So it is now: God has done great things for you. He has made you into a vineyard in a fruitful hill. He has sowed it and gathered out the stones and planted it with the choicest wine. He has built a lawn in the midst of you, and a wine press therein, and now he looks that you should bring forth grapes – yet most bring forth only wild grapes. 'What could I have done more for my vineyard that I have not done in it?'

God has done much for you as he did for Israel; yet doubtless most will provoke God and their carcasses will fall in the wilderness. We have come to you like Isaiah, bringing the same message. But like him we must go back complaining too. We try to bring you the very words of Jesus – but most will be down like Capernaum in hell. Like Paul we tell you, 'To you is the word of this salvation sent.'

'Through this man is preached unto you the forgiveness of sins.' Still the most of you will behold, despise and wonder, and perish. It will be worse for most that ever you heard a freely preached gospel. If you do not find a sanctuary in that Stone, it will be a stumbling block and you will fall and be broken and be snared and be taken.

Some will say, 'Then I will keep away from the church altogether.' *Answer*: it is too late now. You have heard the gospel and you must either receive it or reject it. You must either be one of those who believe and shall be saved or one of those who believe not and shall be damned.

2. God always has a remnant of believing people

Howbeit not all. When all the congregation of Israel murmured against God and wished to return unto Egypt, Joshua and Caleb were of another spirit and followed the Lord fully. They said, 'If the Lord delight in us then he will bring us into this land and give it us.'

There were 600,000 rebels whose carcasses fell in the wilderness and only two who followed the Lord fully. These were God's remnant. So it was at the flood: 'God looked upon the earth and it was corrupt for all flesh had corrupted his way upon the earth.' And yet God had a believing remnant in Noah and his family. Eight souls out of a world of sinners and one of the eight a traitor.

So it is now. God has his remnant. Although the world groans under the wickedness of its inhabitants, although millions are devoted to idolatry – millions to Mohammedanism and Popery – although the church of God is overrun with unconverted professors – whitewashed sepulchres, yet God has his own little flock. In almost every parish of our land there is a believing remnant.

Reasons:

1. To preserve the world from corruption: 'ye are the salt of the earth.'

If it were not for the children of God in this world it would become one putrid mass of living sin. Like meat exposed without salt, it would become one creeping crawling mass of hideous ants. A child of God is a preserving salt in a godless family. He may be very quiet and much persecuted, still God keeps him there as a salt. A believing family is a preserving salt in the neighbourhood where they live. A believing congregation are a salt in a town or country.

They preserve the world in three ways:

(a) By their prayers. When a child of God is within the veil he

obtains not only a full cup for himself but something for those around him. If he does not obtain converting grace, he gains at least restraining grace so that they are kept from much out breaking sin. Labour on, dear believers. Plead on for our town. God has given much in answer to your prayers and will give more.

(b) By their reproofs. A child of God has open grace given him to reprove sin. The heart of the unconverted is often made to tremble under the rebuke of a child of God. Sometimes the word of a little child believing in Jesus has been known to arrest the sinner in his headlong career.

(c) By their holy example. The very face and holy ways of a meek, humble child of God makes the world shrink back. His face is like that of Moses on which the children of Israel could not look. So there is something of heaven about every believer. This keeps the world in awe. What a hell this place would become if there were no children of God in it. Oh unconverted men, what fiends you would become if restraining grace were withdrawn, if there were no child of God to reprove you, no holy example to make you tremble.

2. To preserve communication with heaven

It is by means of his own that God keeps up the communication between earth and heaven. It was where Jacob slept that the ladder was set down. So it is still; God lets his ladder down and the ministering angels gladly descend to that spot where a believer dwells. The Holy Spirit, whom the world cannot receive, comes down and dwells in the believing breast, and God's eye and heart are continually over the spot where his own dear blood-bought people dwell.

Take away this remnant and this world would be quite cut off from heaven. As much as hell. The angels would fly round our world and find no spot for the sole of their foot to rest. The holy Dove would fly back grieved and quenched to heaven. And God could not bear to look on the world. A great gulf would be fixed, and this earth would become another hell. Learn to prize the children of God. Oh! unconverted men, it is they who keep this world from becoming a putrid mass, it is they who keep it from being an offcast world. Believers, give glory to him who chose you to be the salt and take heed you lose not your savour. Be not conformed.....

3. Unbelief is the sin that keeps the soul from God's rest

Unbelief was the grand sin of Israel, the root of all their provocations. It was on account of this that God was grieved with them forty years. It was this that made God swear they should never enter into his rest. It was for this that their carcasses fell in the wilderness.

Ah! my friends, this is still the damning sin. It is the only sin of which God swears that the man who lives in it shall not enter into his rest. He that believeth not shall be damned. There are a set of men who have risen up in our day who say that unbelief is no sin. They take the very sin which God says is damning and they say it is no sin. This is Satan again playing with men as he did with Eve. God said, 'Ye shall surely die.' Satan said, 'It is a tree to be desired to make one wise, the apple is sweet and good for food. Ye shall not surely die.' So Satan now says to the socialist, 'Unbelief is a harmless thing, an apple good for food and pleasant to the eye.' But God here said of it, 'The fearful and unbelieving shall have their part in the lake that burneth.' A little while will show whether God or the socialist is right.

But why is it so?

1. Unbelief springs from not attending to the gospel. Attention is the looking faculty of the mind. But unbelievers do not turn their attention to the gospel. When the Lord opened the heart of Lydia she attended to the things that were spoken. The natural heart does not attend to divine things. How many never come to the house of God, nor open the Word of God? They will be condemned because they would not come near the well of salvation. How many come to the church – but their days are filled with other things. Ah! unbeliever, you will know one day that it is a damning sin not to hear the voice of Christ, 'Whosoever shall not hear the voice of that Prophet shall be cut off from his people.'

2. Not attending to the gospel proceeds from love of sin. The reason why men do not come to hear the gospel or do not attend to it is that they know it would put them out of love for their sins. When a lively minister of Christ comes to a town, the people often flock to hear him for a little, but when they come to see the drift of the gospel – that it is a plan to turn them away from their sins – they soon drop away from the house of God or they seek a less faithful minister where they may sit and live in sin.

Ah! how many faces do I miss out of this church that once were here! And how many among you sit on but cover your hearts with a veil of unbelief because you know the gospel would save you from your sins. You would have come to Jesus long ago, if he would have let you live an unholy life. But you love the tinkling of the glass or the rattling of dice or the chink of your money better than holiness, therefore you are an unbeliever. This is the condemnation....

3. *Unbelief springs from the hatred of God.* A natural man hates God and therefore he cannot believe anything good of God. He that believeth not God hath made God a liar because he believes not the record. If you are unbelieving, you say God is not the holy God he says he is – that he must punish sin and that he has punished it in Jesus. Unbelief says God is not the God of love who gave up his only begotten Son. Unbelief says that he is not the God of grace who is willing to receive the vilest sinner that comes to him. An unbeliever sees that to come to Christ would bring him into the arms of God. This he cannot bear.

Ah! brethren, who can wonder that unbelief is the damning sin? 'He that believeth not is condemned already.'

To awakened souls. You believe one part of the testimony of God – that he is angry with your sin – but the other half you do not believe – that God is love, that he has provided a refuge for the vilest of sinners. You make God a liar as to the touchiest part of his nature – his free grace to sinners. Oh! that the Lord would open your eyes fully to see all the truth as it is in Jesus – for as there is no rest to the unbeliever, so true is it that we which have believed do enter into rest. There is peace and joy in believing. 'This is the work of God that ye believe on him whom he hath sent.'

47. Having therefore boldness, let us draw near (Hebrews 10:19-22)

Having therefore, brethren, boldness to enter into the holiest by the blood of Jesus, by a new and living way, which he hath consecrated for us, through the veil, that is to say, his flesh; And *having* an high priest over the house of God; Let us draw near with a true heart in full assurance of faith, having our hearts sprinkled from an evil conscience, and our bodies washed with pure water.

In the preceding part of the epistle, the apostle has gone through a long and most interesting argument to prove not only the superiority of the Christian dispensation to the Mosaic, but to show that the Christian was the full flower of which the Mosaic was the bud; the substance of which the Mosaic was the shadow. He had shown the superiority of Christ to angels, to Moses and the Jewish high priest. He had shown the superiority of the temple in which Jesus ministers – the true heavens; the house not made with hands – over the Jewish tabernacle which was but a shadow of it. He had shown the superiority of the one sacrifice of Christ over all the Jewish sacrifices, none of which could take away sin and which were only pictures of Christ's true sacrifice.

But now he comes to draw practical lessons from his argument, for what is the good of an argument if it does not lead us to peace with God and purity of life? It is a question, brethren, which some among you should often put to your own heart: what will all my knowledge, my power of arguing for Christ, avail me, if it do not lead me to the forgiveness of my sins? How often will a man, when he has come to the end of an argument, go away quite satisfied, nay, proud of his attainment?

Before explaining and enforcing these words, I am anxious that you should keep two things in mind:

1. That the words before us are addressed not to unbelieving, unconverted men, but to believers. This is evident:

(a) From Paul's classing himself along with them, 'Let *us* draw near,' *us* who have savingly believed; (b) it is evident from the qualifications which Paul bids them come with: 'a true heart and full assurance of faith, with hearts sprinkled from an evil conscience and bodies washed with pure water.' These are not the qualifications of unbelieving men but of those who believe to the saving of their souls. There are many passages in the Bible where unconverted men are entreated to draw near to God by Jesus, such as that in James 4:8: 'Draw nigh to God and he will draw near to you. Cleanse your hands, ye sinners; and purify your hearts, ye double-minded'; and that of Isaiah 55:6-7: 'Seek ye the LORD while he may be found, call ye upon him while he is near. Let the wicked forsake his way, and the unrighteous man his thoughts: and let him return unto the LORD, and he will have mercy upon him; and to our God, for he will abundantly pardon.' But the passage before us is not one of these, this passage is one addressed to believers, beseeching them to live habitually up to their privileges. *Let us draw near.*

2. The second thing which I wish you to bear in mind, is that Paul was writing to Hebrews, to converted Jews.

And accordingly he speaks to them in the language of the tabernacle and the Law of Moses. Every expression then will be best explained and this is the great secret in understanding this epistle, by looking back to the ancient tabernacle of the Jews, and by comparison with the ceremonial books of the Mosaic law.

Having premised these things, I wish now to explain the language of the passage, recalling to your minds the Jewish usages which are there expressed.

1. The first privilege which Paul makes encouragement to our drawing near to God is contained in verses 19 and 20: 'Having therefore *boldness* or liberty to enter', i.e. liberty of entrance into the Holiest (or the Holiest of all or the Holy of Holies), which was the innermost apartment of the Jewish temple. There was the Ark of the Covenant overlaid round about with gold, wherein was the golden pot that had manna (which was laid up there by the command of God that the descendants of Israel might recall the bread wherewith God fed their fathers forty years in the wilderness). And therein also was Aaron's rod that budded (which God commanded to be kept as a token against the rebellious princes of Israel who rebelled against Moses and Aaron). And the tables of the covenant were therein (the two tables of stone hewn out by Moses and written upon by the finger of God). Upon the Ark of the Covenant was a lid of pure gold, called also the mercy-seat, and over it the cherubims of glory shadowing the Mercy Seat with their wings. Above the Mercy Seat and between the wings of the cherubim was the Shekinah, a bright cloud by which it pleased God to manifest his presence, alluded to in Psalm 80. Now this innermost apartment, the most holy place, was separated from the outer apartment or holy place (wherein was two candlesticks and the altar of incense and the shew bread) by a veil or curtain of blue and purple and scarlet and fine twined linen, the same veil which, when Jesus yielded up the ghost, was rent in twain from top to bottom.

Into the most holy place no one was ever suffered to enter, lest he should die, except the high priest, and he only once in the year, not without blood which he offered first for his own sins and then for those of the people. How great and peculiar then was the privilege which Paul here brings before his Hebrew fellow-believers. 'Having liberty to enter into the holiest by the blood of Jesus.' The time was when we had no liberty to enter into the holiest, the high priest alone going in every year. But now by the blood of Jesus, it having been carried in by himself, we have liberty of access in before the Mercy Seat, into the presence, not only of the cherubim, but of him that sitteth between the cherubim. By a *new* way; new indeed, different from the old way when the priest entered in for us, but a living way that is a life-giving way. Had we gone in within the veil before, we should have died. But now to enter in this way giveth us life. 'A new and living way which he hath opened up for us through the veil, that is to say his flesh.' This is the first privilege to which he calls their attention.

2. The second privilege is that in verses 21-22: 'Having an high priest over the house of God, let us draw near with a true heart in full assurance of faith, having our hearts sprinkled from an evil conscience, and our bodies washed with pure water', which must also be interpreted from Jewish usage, i.e. an accusing conscience and having our bodies washed with pure water – soul and body cleansed by the blood of atonement – let us draw near to God.

Doctrine: Believers ought habitually to draw near to God
Because we have liberty of access, a new and life-giving way, let us draw near by it. If there were no way to the Father; if the veil had never been rent in twain; if the holiest of all had remained in inaccessible recess into which no sinful man might enter lest he die; then we would have wanted an encouragement to draw near. But since there is a way because the veil hath been rent from top to bottom, that is all the encouragement we need. And yet how many believing men are there who by the uncomfortableness of their religious life and the great hold which sin yet has over them, show plainly that they habitually keep away from God.

I am not now speaking to scoffers at religion, but to mere formalists in religion, men who have no religion but on the Sabbath day. I speak to those among you who have long been sincere and anxious in your religion, but never have got from it either the abiding peace of mind or the abiding purity of heart which it is intended to give. Now the simple reason of this distressing situation is that you do not obey the force of this argument, you do not habitually draw near to God.

Is there not a way into the presence of the living God? A way not for angels, but for sinners, even the chief? Is there any one thing you can state as an objection to that way? Is there any obstruction to its perfect openness and freeness? Is there any qualification required of you in treading it but merely that you be a miserable sinner? I know well why unconverted, unbelieving men do not draw near by it; they are proud and think they have a right to come before God in their own way without blood, in their own goodness, honesty and religiousness.

If nothing else will have you to draw near by this living way, think for a moment of the sinfulness of refusing. It is an awful sin for unbelievers to refuse this new and living way, it is the crowning lie of the world. But if it be awful in unbelievers, how much more awful is the sin in believers, in those who have once come near to God by Jesus?

When a child prefers a toy to some precious but less showy gift, when a savage prefers a piece of iron to a lump of gold, we do not wonder. We say they act thus because they do not know the value of what they are rejecting. Just so when the unconverted prefer some toy of their hearts, the gratification of some paltry lust, the pleasure of which perishes in the using; when the Customs man prefers his beloved money, which he cannot take with him beyond the grave, to the peace of God which lasts for eternity and passeth all understanding, we say, 'Alas, he does not know the value of forgiveness. He never tasted the sweetness of coming to God sprinkled from an accusing conscience, what wonder he should tread it down like the mire of the streets.'

But what shall we say when those of us who know the value of the blood of Jesus, who know the sweetness of the forgiveness of sins, who have tasted the good gift of God and the joy of the Holy Ghost, when we refuse again to taste of that blessedness? Be astonished in heaven at this, and be horribly afraid. Ah my believing friends, there is not one of us but has cause this day to lay our hand upon our mouth and put our mouth in the dust and to cry out, 'Unclean.'

For oh, if it be a damnable sin in unbelieving men to make God a liar by refusing to believe the record, to refuse to enter into the holiest by the blood of Jesus, and so it is written, he that believeth not shall be damned, they are condemned already, oh, how much more hateful a sin is it in us to tread our own dear Saviour underfoot, to count the blood of the covenant wherewith we were sanctified an unholy thing, and to do despite unto the Spirit of God? We are doing this every night we lie down to sleep without entering into the holiest, without drawing near to God with a true heart. We are doing this every night we lie down without making use of Jesus, without resting our weary head, like John, on the bosom of our Redeemer and God.

The second encouragement to which Paul points us as an encouragement for constantly drawing near to God, is that we have an high priest over the house of God. To have a way opened up for us into the holiest of all by which we may enter in before God, forgiven and accepted in the Beloved, is a great privilege, and if the apostle had had no other encouragement he might well have said on the strength of *that* encouragement, let us draw near. But there is an additional encouragement in our having a great high priest in our own nature at the right hand of God.

There is something awful in the thought of drawing near to the invisible God – God is a Spirit, we are frail worms of the dust. He is the Creator of all things, we are but miserable creatures of clay. It is true we cannot doubt his love, for God is love; he so loved us even when we were enemies, how much more now that we are reconciled. Yet there is something vast and overwhelming in drawing near even to this God of love. It is true he has all knowledge, yet how do we know that he can understand our feelings, our weaknesses of body, our weaknesses of mind, our temptations? No being can know these without having felt them. And therefore though God be all-powerful, all-wise, all-loving, yet is there something to fear and to keep us anxious in drawing near to him?

How blessed then the second encouragement here given, that we have an high priest over the house of God. Jesus stands at the right hand of God in our own nature, though without sin. The scars of suffering are still on his hands and feet, and on his wounded side; the marks of the crown of thorns may still be seen on his brow. He is still a man, though no longer a man of sorrows. He remembers all his pains; his weariness; his sitting down thirsty by the well; his temptations in the wilderness; his agony in the garden; the hour and power of darkness when the light of his Father's face was taken away from him. He remembers his strong crying and tears in Gethsemane; his bloody sweat; his prayer that the cup might pass from him. He is touched with a feeling of our infirmities. And here then is the strength of the encouragement, that coming into the holiest by the blood of Jesus we become partakers of the intercessions of One who knows by experience our feelings, our pains and trials.

Which of you who are believing men does not value the prayers of an experienced believer on earth, of one who can sympathise with your sorrows and enter into your griefs? How much more then should you value the intercession of Jesus, the great high priest of our profession, whose prayer on behalf of his own is never left unanswered. For it is written that the Father knoweth him always and heareth him always.

Now, my believing friends, I return to plead with those of you who are Christians, yet not like Christians, who have been brought to Jesus, yet are not happy and not holy. That unconverted men should live on in their sins, despising both the bloody way to the Father and the blessed Intercessor with the Father, is not to be wondered at. They never knew the blessedness of entering forgiven into the presence of God, and of saying from the heart, '*Our* Father, which art in heaven.' They never knew the blessedness of having Jesus, the high priest of the chosen family, to pray for them, though not for the world. When they turn away from the gracious offer of all these things, we say, 'Alas, they know not what they do.' They will one day weep over their blind folly with tears such as devils weep when distress and anguish come upon them.

But oh! when you who have once known the preciousness of having Jesus to pray for you, who have once received the answer to his prayer in the gift of the Holy Ghost giving you a new heart and a right spirit, when you refuse habitually to draw near to enter into the holiest to enjoy the same blessed privilege, then is it most of all that we are amazed at the long-suffering patience of God. Come, brethren, let us this day put away this unnatural unbelief and enter into the holiest by the new and living way.

Surely a day spent in the courts of the Lord is better than a thousand in the tents of the wicked. A day spent having the heart sprinkled from an accusing conscience is better than a thousand days of filth and terror. I had rather be a door-keeper in the house of my God than to dwell in the tents of wickedness.

Lastly, my unbelieving friends, I daren't go to judgement without this day putting the question to you, 'How do you think you are to go into the presence of God when you die?' It is true we stand beseeching you to enter in by Jesus, showing you how there is no condemnation to them that come before God in this way. But if Abram beseeching will not draw you into the presence of God as a forgiven and accepted child, be sure that death will drag you into that presence as a trembling criminal. And then how terrible shall be the vengeance of the God of love, how fearful your dream when the Intercessor is your accuser and your judge. How insupportable your weight of wrath, for it is the wrath of the Lamb.

31st January 1836 in Dunipace
7th February 1836 in Larbert
1837 in St. Peter's.

48. Whom do you belong to? (1 John 3:10-16)

In this the children of God are manifest, and the children of the devil: whosoever doeth not righteousness, is not of God, neither he that loveth not his brother. For this is the message that ye heard from the beginning, that we should love one another. Not as Cain, who was of that wicked one, and slew his brother. And wherefore slew he him? Because his own works were evil, and his brother's righteous. Marvel not, my brethren, if the world hate you. We know that we have passed from death unto life, because we love the brethren. He that loveth not *his* brother abideth in death. Whosoever hateth his brother is a murderer: and ye know that no murderer hath eternal life abiding in him. Hereby perceive we the love of *God*, because he laid down his life for us: and we ought to lay down *our* lives for the brethren.

1. There are only two classes in this world: the children of God and the children of the devil.

(a) There are two great families
One is the family of God. 'I bow my knees to the God and Father of our Lord Jesus Christ, of whom the whole family in heaven and earth is named.' They have all one Father, the arms of whose love are round them all. They have all one Elder Brother, the firstborn among many brethren. They have all one garment, fine linen white and clean. One Spirit fills all their hearts. They have all one home – in our Father's house are many mansions. Just as in families among yourselves, some of the children are at home and some abroad, some in Scotland, some across the ocean, so in the *one* family, some of the

children have gone home, some are still abroad seeking the better country. Still all are children of the same family.

The other is the family of Satan, the children of the devil. The enemy that sowed them is the devil. 'Ye are of your Father the devil, and the lusts of your father ye will do.' These also have one father, whose arms are round them all. They have one spirit also who dwells in them all, the god of this world. They have one home also with the devil and his angels.

Dear friends, to one of these families you must belong.

(b) There are two sets of vessels in the world
Hath not the potter power over the clay to make of the same lump one vessel unto honour and another unto dishonour? Just as you may have seen a potter out of the very same lump of clay making one vessel to be filled with sweet flowers and another broken and useless, to be cast away on the dunghill. So it is with God, he hath made two sorts of vessels in this world, of the same lump. Often two children that came out of the same mother's womb, that hung upon the same mother's breast, that sat on the same knee, the one is made a vessel unto honour, the other a vessel unto dishonour. You must be one of the two.

(c) Two flocks
When travelling in the east we used always to observe that the sheep and the goats were fed together. They used to mingle together the whole day long. So it is with Christ's people and the world. There is a little flock of sheep and lambs in the world; they are all white like sheep come up from the washing. The shepherd has found them and laid them on his shoulder. But the most are like goats, black in the sight of God. These are mingling together now. But the day is at hand when Christ will divide the sheep from the goats.

I exhort you all to *know on which side* you are standing. To one of these families you must belong. You must either be a child of God or a child of the devil. Some among you I observe who have not lived in *open glaring sins*; you have been kind, gentle, amiable. You have been an obedient child, a faithful wife and a kind mother; still you know that you are not in Christ, that you have never been born again. Then what are you? Consider there are but two families. If you are not in Christ, you must be out of Christ. If you are not a child of God, you must be a child of the devil.

Some awakened persons. Some among you have been made to seek Christ with great earnestness. You pray and wait on ordinances with great eagerness. You come up with desire to the house of God. Yet you know you are not come to Christ, you have not yet found him. Then where are you? There are but two places, either you are in the city of refuge or you are out of it.

Some well-disposed persons who seem to like good things; you like good ministers and good books and good friends. You like to hear awakening preaching, you like meeting for prayer, and yet you feel that you have not been converted, that you have no saving view of Christ. Then where are you? There are but two families, two flocks. Why halt ye between two opinions? If you are not Christ's you are Satan's. If you are not on the narrow way, you are on the broad way leading to destruction.

2. I exhort all who are of Satan's family to leave it

At present you may leave it. There is a way of passing from Satan to God. Many who were Satan's children in this place have left him and are now the happy children of God. There is a way in which the vilest sinner hearing me may be saved. Soon there will be an eternal separation of the godly and ungodly. Soon the door of God's house will be shut and no more will be invited in. Soon a great gulf will be fixed between the righteous and the wicked which no man can pass over. Soon you will be in the world of despair where there is no hope of any being saved, where there are no conversions. Now you are in a world of conversions, you are living in a very remarkable time when many are passing from death to life. You have a Bible now and a throne of grace, the Holy Spirit and a free Saviour. You have godly friends and willing ministers. Now is your time to say, 'I will arise and go to my Father.' Cleave to your godly friends as Ruth clave to Naomi, *'where thou goest will I go'*.

2. Hatred to God's children is the great mark of the children of the devil.

(1) *Shown by an example* (v.12), 'not as Cain' (read Genesis 4:2-8). Here were two vessels of the same lump, yet the one made unto

honour, the other to dishonour. They were carried in the same arms, they played before the same cottage door, and often when their gentle mother looked upon the sunny faces of the two boys, she thought that both might become heirs of glory. Yet the one was a child of God, the other a child of the devil.

When manhood came, Cain began to till the ground and Abel to feed a gentle flock of sheep. In the occupation chosen by Abel you may see already the work of a converted heart. It was from the flock that the tender lamb was taken to bleed upon God's altar. This, Abel delighted to think upon. And often when he led his flock beneath some shady grove or made them rest at noon beside some cooling fountain, he would joyfully say within himself, 'Behold the Lamb of God that taketh away the sins of the world.'

At the end of days, both brothers came to worship God. *See Abel's faith and love*. He felt his need of an atoning sacrifice, he felt that he deserved to die. He believed also in the promised Lamb of God. Therefore did he choose out the whitest and fairest lambs from his flock, one for himself, the other for his brother Cain. The one lamb showed his faith, the other showed his love to Cain. He led the two lambs after him, calling on them by name for they knew his gentle voice, till he came to the spot where God's altar was erected, perhaps at the gate of Eden. One of the lambs lay down at the door of the tent; the other he bound upon the altar, laid his hand upon its head confessing his sins and slew it. Abel next pleaded with his brother Cain, for he loved his soul, to offer the other lamb. But no. Cain felt no burden of sin, he did not feel his need of blood, he brought a bunch of fruits and laid it at God's altar. God burned up the lamb of Abel and left the fruits untouched and unaccepted.

Now Cain was angry and his countenance fell. He was angry with God, angry with his brother Abel.

God said, 'Why art thou angry and why is thy countenance fallen? If thou doest well shalt thou not be accepted? And if thou does not well the sin offering is lying at the door.' God pointed to the lamb that Abel had brought. This was more than Cain could bear. He saw that his brother was in the way of peace and he was not. He hated him and rose against him and slew him.

Have you got the mark of Abel or the mark of Cain? All our families are divided into Cains and Abels. You must be either a Cain or an Abel. Do you come to God through the blood of the Lamb? Do you stand before God only in that blood? And do you love the souls of others and try to bring them to the Lamb? Like Abel do you bring one lamb for yourself and another for your brother Cain? Then you have Abel's mark. You have faith in the Lord Jesus and love to all the brethren.

Do you not see your need of blood? Do you know that you have never come to Jesus and do you hate all that speak to you of Jesus? Do you call them hypocrites and turn away from them? Then you have the mark of Cain. You may wander from country to country, still this mark is upon you, the mark of the murderer Cain.

(2) *Because it is a mark of spiritual death*

There are marks of natural death with which you are all acquainted: the glazed eye, the blueness of the lips, the damp in the coldness of the limbs; these all show that the body is dead. In the same way, there are marks of spiritual death:

(a) Want of love is one of these. 'He that loveth not his brother abideth in death.' If there is any man who takes no particular interest in Christians, if any of his children have grace in them and he does not love them the better for it, if any of his servants are converted, it is no matter of concern to him. If any of his friends are brought to the foot of the cross, his heart does not warm to them anymore than before. Is there any such man here? That man is abiding in death.

Try yourselves, dear friends. Lay your hand upon your heart, tell me what you feel. Does it warm at the name of a believer in Jesus? Does it beat higher at the sight of one who has been washed in the blood? No. Do you feel no heat, no pulse? Alas, you are dead. Your soul is dead. You abide in death. If you saw your children getting rich or well-married or famous, your heart would beat high for them. But when they are becoming heirs of glory you have no interest. Alas, you have no part or lot in Christ.

(b) Hatred is a deeper mark. Many natural persons hate Christians. If they are children, they persecute them. If servants, they cruelly entreat them. If friends, they avoid their company, flee from them as from an adder. In the eye of God this is murder. This is the heart that was in Cain and 'no murderer hath eternal life abiding in him'.

Is there none of you conscious of this hatred to Christians? Do you not scoff at them in your secret thoughts? Do you not love to hear them evil spoken of? Have not some been guilty of direct acts of persecution against the poor lambs of Christ's flock? *Question*: Can we not read your hatred in your proud looks and bad behaviour? Go home and on your knees pray over this passage. In God's eye you are a murderer as much as any that ever died on a scaffold. Take heed lest ye offend one of these little ones.

3. Love is the great mark of God's children

1. This is the eternal law of God (v.11)
'This is the message'. This is the whole law comprehended in one word, Love. This is the law written in God's heart from eternity, for God is love. This is the eternal unchangeable law written on the heart of unfallen angels and unfallen Adam. This is the law which the Holy Spirit writes anew upon the heart of every believer. The nature of the Holy Spirit is love. The law he writes is agreeable to his nature; it is the law of love.

Question: Is this law written in your hearts?

Once you hated others, neglected others. If you were happy yourself, you cared not for the happiness of others. Is your heart changed? Have you received the Spirit of love? Do you breathe love all around, especially to God's children? When Christ was in this world, he walked in an atmosphere of love. Do you walk as he did? Is your life changed in this respect? Love worketh no ill to his neighbour. If you have the Spirit of love in you, you will not commit adultery, nor kill, nor steal, nor covet, for love worketh no ill to his neighbour.

2. Because it is the mark of life
'We know.' I have already shown that want of love is a sign of spiritual death. Now I would show that love to the brethren is a sign of spiritual life. There is no change half so wonderful as this. When a seed falls into the ground and dies and springs up green and fruitful, it is wonderful. When the trees seem to die in winter, it is wonderful to see them pass from death into life in spring, to mark the fresh green buds springing from the dead tree. When Christ said, 'Lazarus, come forth,' and the dead man awoke and came forth bound hand and foot with grave clothes, this was a glorious sight. When the trumpet shall sound and the voice of Christ shall raise the dead from their graves it will be a wonderful sight. But there is a wonder greater far going on

under your own eyes – a soul passing from death unto life; when Jesus comes to a poor dead soul and says, 'Live'; when he washes that soul and puts his Spirit within him.

Question: How shall we know that this change has passed upon us.

Answer: By this, that we love the brethren.

(i) It is a sure mark of spiritual life when you love Christians because they are like Christ. Do not deceive yourself, it is natural to love others for the natural qualities that are in them, such as a fair face. That is the law of nature. But to love them for the features of Christ in them, that is a gracious love.

(ii) It is a sure mark when you love others the more, the more they burn like Christ, when you love them all the more when you see the image of Christ growing brighter, plainer, fuller in their souls.

(iii) It is a sure mark when you love them as Christ loves them, with a sin-covering love. 'Thou art all fair, my love, there is no spot in thee.' When we can forget and forgive their faults, look on them in the blood of Christ, then we know that we are passed from death unto life. 'Search me and know my heart.'

3. It is like God (v.16)

'Hereby perceive we the love of God.' The remarkable thing about *the love of God* was that he laid down his life for us. 'God commendeth his love to us in that while we were sinners Christ died for us.' This was the greatest stoop love ever made; never did love lie down so low on behalf of its object – from the throne to the cross, from the light of heaven to the darkness of hell.

The angels are like him in this. They are all ministering spirits sent forth to minister. If their death could have satisfied for sin, it is probable that many of them would have offered themselves to die, for they have the same mind in them that is in Christ. Many divines believe that the highest angels are those who stoop the lowest, who minister to little children that believe on Christ.

If we have the Spirit of Christ we will be like him in this. I fear there are some among you who seem to be in Christ who yet are quarrelling who shall be greatest. You love to be most looked at, most spoken of, most praised. Some love to rule over others, yet Christ came to be a servant; he stooped and washed the disciples' feet.

It is using plain language, for I wish you to understand me. Are there not some who will not lay down a sixpence for the brethren? How dwelleth the love of God in you? Are there not some who will not bear a scoff or a taunt to save a soul? How dwelleth the mind of Christ in you? He bore a cross. Oh, see that you have Christ's Spirit in you. It is vain to talk of experiences and awakenings and joys and the opinions of ministers. If you have not the Spirit of Christ, you are none of his.

If you have that Spirit you will love to be the servant of all, to wash the disciples' feet. Like Lydia you will constrain them to abide at your house. Like the jailer you will wash their stripes and, if need be, you will lay down your life for the brethren.

15th March, 1840

49. Love to the Brethren (1 John 3:16-24)

Hereby perceive we the love *of God*, because he laid down his life for us: and we ought to lay down *our* lives for the brethren. But whoso hath this world's good, and seeth his brother have need, and shutteth up his bowels *of compassion* from him, how dwelleth the love of God in him? My little children, let us not love in word, neither in tongue; but in deed and in truth. And hereby we know that we are of the truth, and shall assure our hearts before him. For if our heart condemn us, God is greater than our heart, and knoweth all things. Beloved, if our heart condemn us not, *then* have we confidence toward God. And whatsoever we ask, we receive of him, because we keep his commandments, and do those things that are pleasing in his sight. And this is his commandment, That we should believe on the name of his Son Jesus Christ, and love one another, as he gave us commandment. And he that keepeth his commandments dwelleth in him, and he in him. And hereby we know that he abideth in us, by the Spirit which he hath given us.

God's love is a doing love

True love is like a fountain. It cannot rest. It cannot be confined. It must break forth upon all around it. So it was in the heart of God from all eternity. Even in eternity he says, 'My delights were with the children of men.' Now this love of God did not show itself in word and in tongue only, but in deed and in truth. If God had looked down upon this lost world and if he had spoken aloud from heaven and said, 'Ah, that these poor sinners had a Saviour,' this would have done no good. Had he sent messengers to say, 'I pity you from the bottom of my heart' and yet not reached out his hand to help us, it would only have been a mockery of our pain. Had he passed by like the Levite on the other side that he might not look upon our misery, still this would have been vain, empty love. But when he so loved us, he gave his Son for us. His was a doing love. He chose out the peerless Son of God, the matchless one, tore him from his bosom, gave him up to the death for us all.

Christ's love was a doing love

If Christ had merely come into the world to speak kind words he would have done little for us. Some men love to live at their ease, to recline upon a cushioned sofa, to pamper their bodies with every delicacy and then to speak a few sentimental words about the miseries of man. But this was not the love of Christ. Some men love to live as herewith, shut themselves out from the view of men, follow the pleasures of their own mind and weep in secret over the follies of mankind. This is not the love of Christ. If he had come merely to shed tears over Jerusalem or to weep at the grave of Lazarus, he would have left us where he found us, under the wrath of God. But ah no, he laid down his life for us. His whole career on earth was one great undertaking of love in the stead of sinners. His life was one of sacrifice. First he laid down his glory for us, then he laid down his life.

Christ's love is still the same doing love

When he ascended up on high, the Father said to him, 'Sit thou at my right hand.' But the whole Bible shows that he could not long remain there. He could not rest even in heaven. When Stephen saw Jesus he was standing at the right hand of God. He had risen up to catch the spirit of his dying servant. When John saw Jesus in Revelation 1, he was walking amid the seven golden candlesticks, marking his constant, active care – like the high priest with the oil vessel in his hand, trimming the lamps and supplying their flickering flame with fresh oil. When John saw him again he was standing beside the golden altar of incense with the censer in his hand, offering up the prayers of all his saints with much incense.

He is the very same in heaven that he was on earth in respect of the activity of his love. On earth he went about continually doing good, he made it his meat and drink. He does the same in glory. He is the same yesterday, and today and forever. He cannot rest. On earth he loved to be beside every sick-bed. So now, there is not a sick child that believes on him but Christ is there. On earth he was with his disciples always, when they taught the multitudes or when they prayed or when persecuted. So now he is with his ministers always. Oh, that I would feel his presence more. He is present at every meeting for prayer. He walks with his persecuted ones in the middle of the furnace. On earth they often leaned upon his gentle arms and John upon his tender bosom. So now he supports every one of his children, bears all their weight. 'His left hand is under my head and his right hand doth embrace me.' The winds never cease, nor the tides; so the love of Christ is unending.

1. Christians' love should be the same doing love

The world love in word and in tongue. Their love is lip-love. I do not say that unconverted men have no pity; but I say that it ends in words. How many are there in this town who never knew what it was to want a sleep on a down bed, and three meals in one day; who have every luxury at command, whose only effort to relieve the thousands that are starving is *a sigh*! Their love goes no further than a remark at a dinner table. They have some talk about it and show their fine feelings and that is all.

Some go further and give what they will never miss. If there is spare meat at the table which would be thrown away, the poor may have that if they care to ask for it. If their clothes are old and useless to themselves, some benevolent friend is allowed to carry them away to the poor. This is not the love that was in Christ.

1. Christ's was seeking love. He did not wait till we should go to him. If he had done that he would never have died. But he came to seek and save. He laid down the plan of mercy and came and executed it without being once asked to do it. When you have the spirit of Christ, you also will have a seeking love. You will not fold your hands till the poor come to your door, but you will seek them out. This is pure religion and undefiled. But some give with a curse.

2. It is self-sacrificing love. The world give what they will never miss. The Christian gives what he will miss; there is the difference. When Christ came to this earth he missed his throne, his robes of glory, his willing servants, his Father's smile. He exchanged them all for the crown of thorns, the bloody cross, the mockery of murdering priests and his Father's frown. If you have the spirit of Christ you will do the same. How many are there that never sacrificed a luxury from their table, a piece of finery from their dress, to save either the body or soul of another? Should you not write upon that gaudy dress, *the price of blood.* How dwelleth the love of God in you?

3. To the bodies of men. Christ was very tender to the bodies of men. His eye was full of tenderness to the sick. When they brought them to him in the sheets he went over every one and healed them all. He could not bear to see any poor person hungry for bread. He fed multitudes out of a few barley loaves and fishes. He bore our sicknesses and carried our sorrows. If the Spirit of Christ be in you, you should love the bodies of men.

Ah, how many giddy creatures there are that dance on through life's merry day and do not once remember how many are groaning upon sick-beds. How many to whom wearisome nights are appointed, who are full of tossings to and fro, till the dawning of the day. Remember them which are in bonds as bound with them and them which suffer adversity as being yourselves also in the body.

4. To the souls of men. Christ was still more tender to the souls of men. His love to men's bodies cost him but a word. His love to their souls cost him his life. He was at much pains to heal all that were diseased among the people, but to save their souls he gave up his life. Christ saw eternal things all in their reality. He knew the bliss of heaven and the dreadfulness of hell. He knew the shortness of time and the endlessness of eternity. And this made him seek above all things to save men's souls. If you are in Christ and have his Spirit abiding in you, you will do the same. *Your chief business* in this world ought to be to save the souls of others. Your chief business is not to make yourself rich or comfortable, or your children independent. Your chief business is not to be in your office, not to be in your shop, and not to be at your labour. Your chief business should be to save the souls of others.

Souls are the most precious things in the world. You should weigh them in Christ's balances. Then you will risk for them. Merchants risk a great deal often for some prize. People in a lottery often risk a great deal. If you are in Christ you will risk more than the merchant, more than the gambler. Plainly now, dear friends, a straw on the water will show what way the tide is going; a pennant at the mast head will show which way the wind is blowing; and so a very small thing will show whenever you have the mind of Christ in you. If there be a collection for the Infirmary and another for sending the gospel to perishing men, if you give half a crown for the one and sixpence for the other, that of itself shows that you have not the Spirit of Christ in you.

Ah, how is it you who have this world's good can see thousands in this town still without a minister to tell them of Christ? If you shut up your bowels of compassion from them, how dwelleth the love of God in you? Alas, alas, you know not the joy which Christ felt in his breast, that of laying down his life for others. Ah, how much happier you would be. You blindly grasp everything you have to yourself, you think to make yourself happy. Foolish man, 'he that saveth his life shall lose it.'

2. A further assurance will be granted to the doing Christian

In Romans 5, there are two hopes mentioned. When a sinner is awakened he is without hope, he sees no light, no way of forgiveness. God reveals to him the way of salvation by Christ, he draws near and now hope fills his breast. As he goes on in the divine life troubles come around him; these lead him nearer to God and bring out the experience of a child of God and now he arrives at a further hope of glory. One that walketh not ashamed.

In Matthew 11, there are two rests mentioned. When a soul is burdened with guilt, it is a burden heavier than the sand, sinking the soul into a desperate gloom. When that soul sees that Jesus is beckoning him, waving his hand for him to come to him, he finds rest; that moment the bands are loosed, the soul is free. But when he is sitting at the feet of Christ he learns the meek and lowly disposition of Christ, he gets a new nature whereby he knows that he has truly come to Christ, and now he finds a further rest to his soul.

So here there are two kinds of assurance. When a man is awakened he feels exposed to God's arrows, he feels that he is a mark for the sharp arrows of God's justice. But the moment Christ the Shield is revealed to him and he feels hid under that Glorious One, he feels safe, he sings, 'Hallelujah. I will praise thee.'

He lives on in the life of faith, he prays that his peace may not be false. The Holy Spirit dwells in him, changes his heart, writes the law of love there. His heart and life are changed, now he comes to a further assurance that he is really in Christ. When he sees the book of God's Word and the book of his heart agreeing, when he can have all the letters of God's holy law more and more brightly on his own heart, then he comes to a further conviction that all is well with his soul. When he sees the features of Christ appearing in his soul – as a calm lake reflects every cloud and feature in the sky, so his soul reflects every feature of Christ – he will have a growing resemblance. Then he says, 'I have fought a good fight, I have kept the faith.' This is the assurance that comes from sanctification.

1. Try yourselves by this

Does your heart condemn you? Try yourself at the bar of your own heart. You thought you were come to Christ; you have had wonderful experiences; your story was wonderful to hear; but does your heart condemn you? Does your heart say that you do not love the brethren? That you shut up the bowels of your compassion from them? That you are not changed into Christ's image? God is greater than your heart and knoweth all things. If you see yourself to be black, you must be ten thousand times blacker in the sight of God. Oh, flee to Christ without delay and do not live on deceiving your own soul.

2. Some whose heart condemns them not

Some of you feel that your heart condemns you, and yet it condemns you not. You feel infinitely vile and that in yourself you are perfectly unjustified before God. Yet you feel that God has brought you under the shadow of the Plant of Renown and given you his Holy Spirit. You feel, yes, you feel that your heart is a new heart, that you are not the being you once were. You feel that God is changing and renewing you into the image of Christ. You long for that above all things.

You have confidence toward God. Dear friends, would you have constant nearness to the Father? Would you approach to God as a child? Would you live in great intimacy with God? Would you be a consistent Christian? An unholy Christian has no nearness to God. Sometimes you envy men of God their nearness to God. Would you know the secret of it? It is a consistent life, resemblance to Christ.

Would you have answers to prayer? I have observed that some Christians are far more successful in prayer than others. Some are like Jacob, they do not let God go till he gives them the blessing.

Like Hezekiah and Daniel they are answered while speaking. What is the reason? They have this freedom of access, being not only in Christ, but having much of Christ in them. They are holy believers and they prevail. Oh, aim at this, dear children. When you know you are in Christ, you can put the finger upon the promise and say, 'Give me in the name of Jesus.' Amen.

50. Belonging to God (1 John 5:16-21)

If any man see his brother sin a sin *which is* not unto death, he shall ask, and he shall give him life for them that sin not unto death. There is a sin unto death: I do not say that he shall pray for it. All unrighteousness is sin: and there is a sin not unto death. We know that whosoever is born of God sinneth not; but he that is begotten of God keepeth himself, and that wicked one toucheth him not. *And* we know that we are of God, and the whole world lieth in wickedness. And we know that the Son of God is come, and hath given us an understanding, that we may know him that is true, and we are in him that is true, even in his Son Jesus Christ. This is the true God, and eternal life. Little children, keep yourselves from idols. Amen.

The Bible is a wonderful book. There are shallows where a lamb may wade and depths where an elephant may swim. This is one of the depths. The Lord carries us on his shoulder and then all will be sweet and easy.

1. Our duty when we see a Christian brother fall into sin
(a) The whole Bible bears witness that an old heart remains after conversion, sometimes called 'the flesh', or 'a law', or 'the body of sin', 'members on earth'. Every Christian feels that it is so. Indeed it seems one of the clearest evidences of a work of grace in the soul is the felt warfare, the wrestling.

(b) But this passage shows a Christian may visibly fall; he does not only carry a body of sin in his heart but he can fall into sin in his life. So the history of the falls of the saints: Noah, Lot, Abraham, Isaac, Jacob, Moses, David, Peter.

Learn to know your weakness and also fear God. A haughty spirit goes before a fall. Keep in the arms of Christ. Keep near to God. Live much upon the Holy Spirit. You are not away from falls. Learn not to be bitter against those who have fallen; consider thyself. Some indulge in a bitter censorious spirit; much pride in this; let it rather teach you to tremble. Pray for them believing. Set about their restoration. Remember you have seen evidence in them that it is the work of Christ. They should be restored. Plead Psalm 89 with God or that verse in Psalm 37: 'Though he fall he shall not be utterly cast down.' You may be quite sure God will hear your prayer. It is according to his will the sin is not unto death, it is worthy of hell but will not end there. In this way you will show that you have the same heart that Jesus has; you will bear one another's burdens, and so fulfil the law of love.

2. The world may sin in such a way that we cannot pray for them believing

'There is a sin unto death.' John was one of the disciples of Christ. He spoke not only as he was moved by the Holy Ghost, but no doubt also as he had heard Jesus speak. Let us compare some of the words of Christ:

Matthew 12:31,32: 'Wherefore I say unto you, All manner of sin and blasphemy shall be forgiven unto men: but the blasphemy against the Holy Ghost shall not be forgiven unto men. And whosoever speaketh a word against the Son of man, it shall be forgiven him: but whosoever speaketh against the Holy Ghost, it shall not be forgiven him, neither in this world, neither in the world to come.'

Mark 3:28-30: 'Verily I say unto you, All sins shall be forgiven unto the sons of men, and blasphemies wherewith soever they shall blaspheme: But he that shall blaspheme against the Holy Ghost hath never forgiveness, but is in danger of eternal damnation: Because they said, He hath an unclean spirit.'

Luke 12:10: 'And whosoever shall speak a word against the Son of man, it shall be forgiven him: but unto him that blasphemeth against the Holy Ghost it shall not be forgiven.'

And also:

Hebrews 10:26: 'For if we sin wilfully after that we have received the knowledge of the truth, there remaineth no more sacrifice for sins.'

2 Peter 2:20: 'For if after they have escaped the pollutions of the world through the knowledge of the Lord and Saviour Jesus Christ, they are again entangled therein, and overcome, the latter end is worse with them than the beginning.'

The sin I apprehend to be final unbelief. It can be no other sin, for the Scripture speaks so widely, for example:

Isaiah 1:18: Sin as scarlet and crimson can be forgiven. All manner of sin and blasphemy can be forgiven. 'The blood of Jesus Christ his Son cleanseth from all sin' (1 John 1:7). Whosoever cometh unto Christ he will in no wise cast out. The only one who will be cast out is he that does not come to Christ. The only sin the blood of Jesus will not cleanse is the heart that does not wash in his blood. There is no sin too scarlet.

Revelation 21:8: the fearful and unbelieving; these are they on the front rank of those who go away into everlasting punishment.

This sin shows itself in different ways:

(a) *Pharisees.* They said Jesus had an unclean spirit, that he did wonders by the devil, that he had not come to save. They would not believe, even when they saw others saved. Are there any such here?

(b) In those who have received much light and knowledge and yet who wilfully go away from Christ and will not come to him, nor submit after they have had much of the Spirit working in them. I fear these are on the brink of this sin.

(c) Especially those who have much knowledge and yet will not come to Christ. Warn them!

Question: Are we not to pray for such souls?

Answer: (1) The apostle does not appear to say so. But we cannot pray for such as we deem in this state with a certainty of being heard.

(2) If we know their hearts as Christ does, then we could say, 'I pray for them, I pray not for the world.' But Christ has not given this power of discerning hearts to us. Judge not that ye be not judged.

(3) Yet actually Christ often says, as in John 17:9: 'I pray not for the world.' When Christ is leaving a soul he bids his servants give over praying. Ah! dear friends, who do not like so many meetings for prayer, you do not know what may be depending on them. The giving up of prayer in this place will be the hell of your souls.

3. Those who are born of God do not then fall away

(a) There are some who are born of God. When we look at the world lying in the wicked one, when we read of some having much light and knowledge yet falling away, it is sweet there are some jewels after all, born of God. Can you say, 'I am of God, God has mastered me, drawn me by chords to Christ'?

(b) These keep themselves. God works in them and they work out their salvation.

(c) The devil toucheth them not. They were once his prey, lying in his arms or at his feet. One stronger came and snatched them into his arms. Now Satan cannot touch them.

(d) They sin not, they do not fall utterly away.

51. True marks of being born again (1 John 5:1-3)

Whosoever believeth that Jesus is the Christ, is born of God: and every one that loveth him that begat loveth him also that is begotten of him. By this we know that we love the children of God, when we love God, and keep his commandments. For this is the love of God, that we keep his commandments: and his commandments are not grievous.

1. If we believe that Jesus is the Christ.
2. If we love others that are born of God.
3. If we love God, or which is the same thing, keep his commandments, have a heart agreeing with God with regard to all his commandments.

1. Everyone who is brought not only to awakening, prayer, tears, conviction of sin, but to believe on Jesus Christ for righteousness, every such soul has had more than human teaching. He has been born of God. He has undergone the second birth. My Father in heaven has opened his eyes.

2. He cannot but love God who has done this for him; and if so, he must love every other that is born of God, for this is an invariable rule of our nature; when we love the Father, we love the children also.

3. So that we may easily know whether we have a genuine, biblical, divine affection to God's children – by finding out we are born again if we love God and keep his commandments.

4. For to love God and keep his commandments are joyous. If we are delighted in the contemplation of that glorious, pure, lovely One, our heart is changed into his image. Our holiness will be heart holiness, not grievous but delightful.

5. I said that the commandments were not grievous. The reason is that whatever is born of God overcomes the world. Everything that is born from above tramples the world beneath his feet. How? By believing. Keep the eyes on Christ and God. No other can overcome the world but the believer in Jesus.

Introduction
One Sabbath in Jerusalem, the sun had set behind the hills of Judah, the crowds attending the feast of Passover had retired to rest. There was silence in the streets of the city, except the word of the watchmen that go about the city and the songs of some pious Semites in the temple. Jesus had spent a day of hard labour, speaking as never man spake, and doing wonders of mercy. He had now retired to an upper chamber in some kind Israelite's house, for he had no house of his own, where to lay his head. His disciples had gone to repose. He alone sat waking, when suddenly there came a gentle knock upon the door. The Saviour rose, undid the bar and opened to the stranger. The stranger entered. His snow-white turban and elaborate mantle showed him at once to be a ruler of the Jews, although he had concealed his face. 'Rabbi,' he began with reverential air, 'we know that thou art a teacher come from God, for no man can do these miracles that thou doest, except God be with him.' Jesus knew the man, he knew his heart and said, 'Verily, verily, I say unto thee, except a man be born again he cannot see the kingdom of God.'

It was for no light reason that Christ broke so suddenly upon the mind of this man, with the startling declaration. The most important question in the world is, 'Are you born again?' You may be better than what you were; you may be a student of your Bible; you may wear your knees hard by constant prayer; you may forsake your work for the house of God; and yet if you are not born again, you will never see the kingdom of God. In the words of our text are the marks of regeneration.

1. Whosoever believeth that Jesus is the Christ

Many are awakened under a sermon; their case is described as if the minister knew their heart. They are pierced as with a dart; they are afraid to die. They weep, they tremble. Many say, 'There is a saved soul', and yet before a week is over, you may see that soul again in the midst of sin and hard against God's Word.

To be awakened is not to be born again. Many begin to pray. They find that they are dead and hear they need a divine Saviour. They say, 'Lord, help me, I perish.' They begin to pray in secret, greatly to labour after salvation. They do many things, like Herod. They give up many evil habits and companions. Many say, 'This person is born again', and yet in a little while he may be seen going back, like the sow washed to the mire. To seek salvation earnestly is not to be born again.

But is there any one awakened so as to feel like Isaiah, undone; anyone who has given up all hope of justifying himself by his own doing, by his own frame or state of mind, or by any change in his life? So as to feel helpless and curious? As to saving his soul, is that soul now brought to be unspeakably pleased with the way of salvation by Jesus Christ? Do you see a beauty in the person, offices and work of Christ, which steals away your heart, whether you will or no. So that you cannot but believe, you cannot but submit to the righteousness of God. Then thou art born again for 'whosoever believeth hath everlasting life'. 'Flesh and blood hath not revealed it unto thee but my Father in heaven.' Inquire solemnly whether any such event has taken place in your history.

'It pleased God, who separated me from my mother's womb and called me by his grace, to reveal his Son in me,' said Paul; so with you. The veil shall be taken away, as if from you. Have you had a saving sight of Christ? Soul-ravishing, contenting, comforting? Blessed are you. But if not, do not deceive yourself, you are not born again. He that believes and is baptised shall be saved. He that believes not shall be damned.

2. Love to the brethren (v.1)

Everyone that is truly a child of God has this love. 'We know that we have passed from death unto life because we love the brethren.' 'The fruit of the Spirit is love...' However quarrelsome, ill tempered, selfish they have been before, when a person is born again they begin to love. A new stream flows through their heart – love.

(a) They are saved from the same hell. Often you will find that seamen who have been saved from the same wreck have a peculiar love for one another. They have been snatched from the same watery grave. Much more those who have been saved from the same hell, by the same gracious hand. How can you but love one another?

(b) They have the same Spirit. In the world, persons of the same tastes love to be together. Those who love music, whose heaven is all in sweet sounds. Those who love nature, fields, and walking. But children of God have one heart and one Spirit. The same Spirit groans in them all, loves in all, works in all. They all love prayer and communion with God. They cannot but love one another.

(c) They see the features of God in one another. There is nothing so lovely to the eyes of a believer as the features of Christ. When he sees them in believers he loves them. But Christians have Christ found in them. Christ lives in me. The features of God are there. You cannot but love them. The more you are like Christ, the more you love them. Enquire if it be so with you. If not, you lack the true mark of one born again.

Are you offended at God's children, do you love the company of the world better, are your idols your after dinner friends, your companions in leisure hours, your inner friends? A person has inner and outer friends; some never get further than the tattle of the lips: 'How are you?' friends, and 'The weather is fine' friends. But who are your inner friends, those who share your inward thoughts, whose heartstrings are tuned with yours, who are bound by the mysterious tie of sympathy? Are they the worldly, sensual, earthly ones? Alas, many choose the world.

3. Love to God and his commandments (vv. 2,3)

It must be confessed that some do love the children of God who are themselves unborn again. There is such a thing as worldly love to God's children. I have known children of God who possessed fine natural qualities: a fine natural temper, fine tastes, powers of entertaining others. The world often loves what is natural to them. The crop is sometimes concealed beneath. I have known children of God who hid their cross below their mantle, so that the world loved them. How shall I know when I have true love to God's children? *Answer*: by this: when you love God and keep his commandments. No natural man loves God. He has not one thread of this love in his heart. The carnal mind is enmity against God. No natural man loves to think upon God, or to speak to God. He does not love to come near to God. The reason? The holiness of God. God as a being is so opposite from him. A natural man listens to the devil but not to God. The very presence of God condemns him, for he is not reconciled to God. He feels that God condemns him. When a sinner is brought to Christ he begins to love God. Two reasons:

(1) He feels the love of God to him. When the maniac sat at the feet of Christ he begged to go with him when he was stepping into the boat. He loved Jesus.

(2) He has the Holy Spirit in him. The Holy Spirit loves what is holy; as the flame tends upwards, so the Spirit in the heart. He loves God for his holiness. Loves the saints for the same reason. Loves heaven because it is filled with holiness. Loves the law of God for it is holy, the mark of God.

Do you feel this? Have you got this new spiritual relish?

(1) Do you love to be alone with God? To meditate on God? To speak to God? Do you love to adore him, to serve him?

(2) Do you love his holy law? All the commandments? Would you like it if there were no other in your heart?

(3) 'My burden is light.' Do you find that the Almighty Spirit makes his law easy, so that you mount up with wings as eagles, that you are kept from falling? Then you are born again.

3rd May, 1840

52. The Great Advantage of Being Born Again (1 John 5:4,5)

For whatsoever is born of God overcometh the world: and this is the victory that overcometh the world, *even* our faith. Who is he that overcometh the world, but he that believeth that Jesus is the Son of God?

In the last sermon we saw the marks of being born again: faith, love to the brethren and love to God! Now we have here the great advantage of being born again and the superiority of those who have received this benefit to all the world.

1. Whatsoever is born of God overcometh the world

Warfare will last as long as we are in this world. The world is all that within or without keeps down the life of God in the soul. On coming to Christ we are not wholly delivered from 'all that is in the world'.

The world *within* is where the flesh lusteth against the Spirit, the old man with his deeds. In natural men, it is all the world within and nothing more. In believers the old world remains, but the Holy Spirit dwells there and fights against it.

The world *without* has its frowns and smiles, and both tempt to sin. Some can stand the frown who cannot stand the smile. Some are proof against its smiles and such, but fall beneath its frown. The whole world lieth in wickedness. Satan's army is marching against the truth. he is against all the true flock. The world is a great battlefield.

The world unseen: we wrestle not against flesh and blood, but with the tempter and accuser of the brethren, the great deceiver Lucifer ('son of the morning'). He is full of devices, full of enmity, seeking to cast us down, to beguile us from the simplicity that is in Christ. Everyone that is truly born of God, from the strongest to the weakest, overcomes the world, be they the most enlightened saints like Edwards and Enoch, or the weakest believer, them that are weak, with faith as a grain of mustard seed, the weak brother for whom Christ died. Of all it is equally true, that they overcome the world.

Certain persons have been carried victoriously through this world. 'Rejoice not over me, oh mine enemy.' They had many sore conflicts and were often ready to die. Still they all overcame and are now singing the song of Moses. Who were they? Those who were born of God.

Reasons

(1) They are members of Christ's body. No member can wither or fall away. We are members of his body, of his flesh and of his bones. He gave himself for us, to deliver us from the present evil world. He that laid us over his shoulder will keep us there. 'Be of good cheer; I have overcome the world' (John 16:33).

(2) The Holy Spirit dwells in them. An almighty Spirit, he strengthens them with all might in the inner man. He renews and changes every part of the soul. He restores.

(3) God is faithful. He 'will not suffer you to be tempted above that ye are able' (1 Cor. 10:13). Often a tempted believer thinks his case is singular. No, it is common to man. God will suffer you to be tempted up to that ye are able. If another grain would rock the scale, he will not let that grain be put in. Sometimes you think no way of escape, but he will. God will not break the back of faith. He will lay on just as much as you can bear.

2. The way in which a believer overcomes the world – by faith

This is the victory. This is the meaning of victory. Believers make great mistakes.

(1) Some think they are to overcome the world by forever laying aside the very being of sin, by getting their lusts rooted out and being filled with the Spirit of God alone. Soon cast down from their joy, when they find the flesh lusting against the Spirit. The body of sin is a bottomless fountain of corruption. Victory is not by the clear removal of our lusts. These lusts remain till the fabric is taken down and moulded into Christ.

(2) Some think it is by what they call good principles within them. The graces growing till they fill the whole heart. And so they begin to lean upon their graces, such as their love to the Saviour, till they get an awful discovery of the nothingness of their graces and the infinite depths of corruption still in the soul. Be strong in the grace that is in Christ.

(3) The only way is by faith, believing all that is spoken concerning Jesus, especially verse 2.

(a) Believing in Christ crucified. God forbid that I should glory save in the cross. Keeping the eye upon the cross. Bearing about the dying of the Lord Jesus. This keeps the heart near to God and as the world dies away from our mind and our heart dies to the world, the world is on one cross and we are on the other, and both are dying. Keep your eye on the cross, if you would wear the crown. Realise Christ for us. Keep nigh by the blood of Jesus, if you would overcome the world.

(b) Believing in Christ glorified. He is able to save to the uttermost, seeing he ever liveth. Keep the eye upon Christ living and praying for us. Realise the power, the all-seeing eye, the all-prevailing intercession of Christ for all that come unto God by him. Only believe and thou shalt overcome. Keep your eye above. Live amongst unseen realities.

3. No other can overcome the world
Nothing short of a believer, a heaven-born soul, can gain the victory.

1. Some think that by education you may bring up a child to overcome. Now God has attached large promises to educating a child, 'train up'. Still, conversion is needful. If you train a crab tree ever so much, you will never make it bear sweet fruit. If you train a tiger and teach it to be gentle, still its fierce nature will break out again. A change of nature is required.

2. Keeping out of temptation. I have seen families brought up on this plan. They were never told that there was a wicked world. Their manners, so quiet and reserved. You would say, 'Ah, here is the victory over the world.' But an opportunity and sin breaks forth. Like gunpowder stored up, when the spark comes, it all takes fire. Like volcanoes, for a little while quiet and placid, so that you may go and look into the crater and say all is quiet. But soon it erupts out, scattering fire and lava and other flames. A lion sometimes sleeps and then it lies as quietly as a camel, you may stroke its lovely mane. The awful test is when it wakes and you will find it is a lion still. It has been said that the tiger's claws are concealed beneath soft downy velvet. Dear friends, if you would have your children overcome the world, rest not till they are born again. It is well to keep them out of temptation, to restrain them, to train them. But ah, rest not till you see the new birth in them. The child of many prayers will never perish. Rest not till you see that their eye falls upon the Son of God, till they are unspeakably pleased with Jesus Christ, till they believe on the Lord Jesus Christ.

3. Some think that moral people, good natured men, will overcome the world. There are some, who touching the law, are to the eye of men blameless. Your outward actions are fair to man's eye. You think there is no fear of you. Ah, you will find your morality nothing in an hour of temptation. Do you know that you are not born again? You will never overcome. The best natural man in the world can not get above nature. They that are in the flesh cannot please God. You have not the sweet laws of the gospel written in your heart. You have no heart-holiness. If days of trial shall come, you will be the first to fall away from Christ's cause.

Dispersed men

Caution. Have a good will toward divine things, love good ministers and pastors, speak well of them and take their side. Are you born again? For if not, you will not overcome. If you are not ready to believe in the Son of God, you will fall in the hour of trial. This world is a battlefield. Two great contending armies: one, the world, all opposed to Jesus Christ and his people; the other, a little flock, their sword is the Word of God. They are a praying army. Like our Covenanters of old, they kneel down on the battlefield and pray to the God of armies. They will overcome and will die, crying, 'Victory, victory, victory!'

9th May, 1840

53. The Warrant to Believe in Jesus (1 John 5:6-10)

This is he that came by water and blood, *even* Jesus Christ; not by water only, but by water and blood. And it is the Spirit that beareth witness, because the Spirit is truth. For there are three that bear record in heaven, the Father, the Word, and the Holy Ghost: and these three are one. And there are three that bear witness in earth, the Spirit, and the water, and the blood: and these three agree in one. If we receive the witness of men, the witness of God is greater: for this is the witness of God which he hath testified of his Son. He that believeth on the Son of God hath the witness in himself: he that believeth not God hath made him a liar; because he believeth not the record that God gave of his Son.

He had told them the only way of overcoming the world, namely, by believing on the Son of God. But are we warranted to believe? There are heavenly witnesses, all bearing record that Jesus is the Son of God in whom lies eternal life.

1. The Father

Our example. At John's baptism Jerusalem and all Judea had come out and were baptised. The work all over, then Jesus came, perhaps toward evening when crowds were listening to John preaching by the palm trees on the banks of Jordan. He comes out of the water. Lo! The heavens were opened to him, as later to Stephen and Saul. Every eye attracted to heaven. The Holy Ghost descended in a bodily shape, every eye watched whence it came. On the head of Jesus. A voice, probably full of majesty like the thunder, first to himself ('Thou art'), then to the crowds ('This is my beloved Son in whom I am well pleased').

This is the Father witnessing. Again at the transfiguration. Again at the grave of Lazarus. Again at his resurrection. 'I ascend to my Father,' the risen Jesus said. God hath highly exalted him. God has thus confessed him to be his Son, his elect, his servant, the Saviour of Sinners. 'The Father himself which hath sent me hath borne witness of me.'

2. The Word

He also bears witness to his being the Saviour bringing eternal life freely to sinners.

(a) By his miracles. 'The works, that I do in my Father's name, bear witness of me' (John 10:25) – wonders of mercy, done at his own command and will: 'I will, be thou clean', not like the apostles who had to pray that it might be done.

(b) By his divine person. He was God manifest. We beheld the glory. His veil of flesh could not hide the beams of his majesty that shone through. He showed the heart of God in every action and word so that the narrative of his life is a narrative of God's heart toward sinners.

(c) By his plain declarations. To the woman of Samaria, 'I that speak unto thee am he.' 'If any man thirst let him come unto me.' 'I am the bread of life.' 'I am the way.' Thus did these glorious words concur with the testimony of the Father, that Jesus is the Son of God and Saviour of the world, drawing every eye unto himself, inviting the gaze of lost souls to behold him.

3. The Holy Ghost
(a) By coming upon him at his baptism.

(b) By abiding on him, anointing him to preach, resting on him.

(c) By his glorious coming on the day of Pentecost and ever since then. Jesus had promised, 'If I go away I will send him unto you.' So when he came, he was the great witness that Christ was risen indeed. His great work and business is to testify concerning Christ. At Pentecost this was his great office. He came like cloven tongues of fire. Every tongue speaking of Jesus. So in a time of revival he comes to magnify Jesus, to reveal the Son of God as the Saviour of the world. It is his part to open the eyes to let sinners see the beauty of Jesus, as truly as if you saw him with the bodily eyes; to persuade men that it is all true, to show the glorious beauty of Christ; to give a clear, full view of the way of pardon by him, its reality and safety. So these three are one. They are three witnesses of one thing. The witness of two men is true, but here are three testimonies from heaven.

Do you receive the witness of men? The witness of God is greater. If you do not believe, you make God a liar.

4. There are three witnesses on earth, within the heart: the Spirit, the water and the blood. When Jesus had said, 'It is finished,' he bowed his head and gave up the ghost, the glorious work was now done. But as he hung dead and pale upon the cross, the soldiers came to see if they were dead. They broke the legs of the thief and the other, but when they saw that Christ was dead already, they broke not his legs. But one of the soldiers with a spear pierced his side and forthwith came there out blood and water. In insulting mockery he pierced the cold side of humanity, thrusting in the new spear through the leader's flesh.

Behold, what an answer of love to this insult. Out gushes a stream of blood and a stream of water, to show the murderers the way of peace and holiness. In the very same way, have I seen sinners among yourselves boldly insulting Christ, thrusting a spear into his side, and instead of vengeance, a stream of mercy has come forth to your own soul. This awful scene dwelt in the heart of John. He could not forget it, he got all his peace from it. Perhaps John then learned for the first time completely the way of pardon and holiness. These are the witnesses on earth to which he points the soul.

1. The blood. The grace-speaking blood of Jesus, the blood of sprinkling. In former ages, the alter which was sprinkled with the blood of lambs was the witness to Christ. (a) The blood of the great sacrifice is seen in the garden and on the cross. What does that blood testify? That Christ has died, finished transgression. (b) The blood is now within the veil. He has entered in with his own blood, scars still on him. Oh troubled soul, can you look on the blood of Christ, the Son of God? The work is finished, the wrath all borne, for the blood has been shed. The blood of Christ is grace-speaking, for it is the witness that God's wrath has fallen and is satisfied.

2. The water. The stream of water opened from the side of Christ is witness that he was the smitten rock, the fountain of living water, the only author of inward purity and holiness. The water from the side of Christ told his murderers that the only stream of holiness must flow from him. What say you to this witness? Have you tried him? Have you tried if Jesus really be a fountain of living water? If you do, you will have the witness in yourself.

3. The Spirit. He is not only a witness in heaven but on earth also. 'When he, the Spirit of truth, is come, he will bear witness to me.' The Spirit opens the eye to discern spiritual beauty in Christ. He convinces of righteousness, speaks through the minister testifying of Jesus. When ministers only speak, they may master all their ingenuity in exquisite descriptions of Christ, his love, work, person, offices and beauty. But when the Spirit is present he can make the very name of Jesus all full of light. He can show a glow of wisdom, beauty, and sweetness in Christ as attracts the soul, draws it to cleave to him. Ah, there is no witness like the Spirit.

3. Three Consequences

1. If we believe, we will have internal evidence
The moment a man really believes he has the witness in himself, in the peace in which the blood gives, and the purity which the living water gives, and especially in the struggle which ensues between grace and nature. Have you this inward evidence?

2. All most reasonable to believe

You receive the testimony of men; the testimony of God is greater. When two men bear solemn witness to any transaction, no reasonable man has any further doubts. How is it that you doubt God? You treat God worse than you do the vilest of men.

3. The awful guilt of unbelief

Making God a liar. If you do not believe a man, you say in your heart that he is a liar. So with God. You make each person of the Godhead a liar. You make God a liar when testifying of his love. Some believe God when he condemns the guilty; they believe that he is strictly just, an avenging God; but they will not believe that he has opened a way for them to be saved. When he speaks of his love and grace, then they say, 'No, I can not believe that!' You take the fairest jewel out of God's crown and tread it beneath your feet.

7th June, 1840

54. The Record (1 John 5:11,12) (I)

And this is the record, that God hath given to us eternal life, and this life is in his Son. He that hath the Son hath life; *and* he that hath not the Son of God hath not life.

In the past verses we saw that there are three heavenly witnesses and three on earth all testifying concerning Jesus and that it is most reasonable to believe their word and a fearful crime not to believe, even making God a liar.

Question. What is their testimony? What is the sum of their witness bearing? What is the purpose of it?

Answer. This is the record (v.11), that the Father, the Word and the Holy Ghost have been declaring, in the ears of the whole world ever since the Fall, the gospel, the joyful sound, the glad tidings of great joy. 'God hath given to us eternal life and this life is in his Son.'

1. What is the gift? Eternal life

(a) *Judicially.* A full pardon for ever. When the Queen pardons a criminal she is said to give him his life. When God pardons he gives eternal life, pardon for ever. We are entirely without it. God freely bestows it. He has put it freely within reach of the chief of sinners.

(b) *Actually.* Quickening or renovation of soul, life of the soul, eternal life. We are entirely dead in sins, but here is a wellspring of eternal life, a renovation of soul that will last for eternity. An infinitely precious gift.

(c) *The life of eternal felicity.* Perhaps this should not be separated as it is just the full fruit of which the foregoing is the fountain. Oh! most precious and blessed gift to sinners, to us irrespective of what we are and have been.

How many there are that turn away from the gospel. I venture to say there are thousands in this town who turn away with disgust from ministers and sermons, who do not know what is in the gospel. Oh, it is life: eternal life, pardon, holiness, felicity.

2. Where is the gift?

In his Son. All this life is in the hand of Christ and nowhere else. Christ is the great gift of God and in him is found all this eternal life. Christ with eternal life in him is laid down at every door.

(1) *Judicial life.* Men seek it elsewhere, in their own innocency, in works of reformation. They go about while it lies straight before them, treasure hid in their own field, when they are ploughing every day. It is all in Christ – in his work of redemption, in his work of suffering as surety.

(2) *Life of grace in the soul.* Again men wander far to seek it. They contrive a holiness that is not eternal, such as the holiness of monks and hermits. An earthly, carnal holiness. Have a kind of holiness from good resolutions and self-imposed restraints. But all is false and temporary. Living holiness is a gift of God and is all in Jesus. In him as a fountain inexhaustible, the Spirit dwells. Every member receives it freely and fully. We are like an infant carried by Christ.

(3) *Life of felicity.* God hath given us this also in Christ. For Christ will be our portion. He will fill our hearts full throughout eternity. Our heaven is to be with him where he is and to receive out of his fullness.

3. How is it given?

1. *Not in possessions.* Sometimes you send a gift to your friends. You send it to their house and put it into their hands. You leave it in their hands. Not so with God's gift.

(a) Some have it, some have not the gift.

(b) By experience, we know that we have it not till we believe. We know that multitudes never have pardon or the life of grace and that multitudes will die the second death.

2. *Still it is freely given.* The gift is out of God's hand and laid down in the midst of sinners. It is like the gift of a physician. If the queen were to send down a physician of great skill to this town, who was to heal all, rich and poor, that came to him without money and without price, this would be a free gift to all the people in the town. But multitudes might make no use of him; some might say, 'I like my own better;' some, 'I would rather pay.' So is it with the offer of Jesus.

Question. Have you the Son? Startling question. Not, have you a profession, a name to live, a religion, convictions, feelings? But, have you Christ? Have you believed the record and cleaved to the Lord? Then, you have all that is included in that wonderful word, eternal life. Can you say, 'My beloved is mine'? Does he mean more than if you could say, 'The wealth of the Indies is mine.' Know your estate. You have peace with God. Your life is hid with Christ in God. You have a glory that is to come. God will show you the path of life.

If your answer is, 'No', then you have not life. You have knowledge, character, convictions, good friends, books, serious thoughts, sentiments, talk. But you have not the Son. You have not a grasp on the Son of God. You are not a branch in a vital union to him. You have not had a heart cleansing. You have no pardon, no holiness, no glory. Death is your sentence. Death is your condition. Death will be your eternal portion.

55. The gospel is from God (1 John 5:11,12) (II)

And this is the record, that God hath given to us eternal life, and this life is
in his Son. He that hath the Son hath life; *and* he that hath not the Son of
God hath not life.

This record is the gospel; to believe it with the whole mind is to
believe the gospel and so be saved. To refuse to believe it is to be
guilty of unbelief, to make God a liar. There is much in this simple
record.

1. Something about God the Father
God hath given to us eternal life. We naturally hate God and cannot
believe that he has any kind thought toward us. Man always suspects
whom he hates. Therefore Adam hid from God. Therefore Cain built
a city. Therefore unconverted souls flee the thought and presence of
God. To some the presence of a true minister of Christ is revolting.
They cast out his name as evil. The record reveals something of God
and his heart, desires and work.

God hath given to us eternal life.

(a) That God does not want sinners to die the second death. 'As I
live saith the Lord, I have no pleasure in the death of the wicked...'
God's bowels yearned over self-destroyed sinners. His law condemns,
his nature abhors them. All that is true. The sentence is passed, they
are condemned and that justly. Still God mourns over their case. He
wondered that there was no intercessor.

(b) Not true feeling but a gift. Often some men pity a beggar but
give no help. This is a poor waste of feeling, not so God – 'God hath
given to us eternal life and this life is in his Son.' God has chosen his
only begotten Son and given him. He hath given to us eternal life,
put it freely within reach of sinners, laid it down at their feet. The
love of God toward polluted, condemned sinners is a gift, not mere
verbiage, not mere lip work, not the pity of words or of tears, but of
deeds. The record is a laying hold of the heart of Jehovah.

Look here, hardened rebels, and melt. The thing that keeps sinners
going on in their unbelief is that they do not know God. 'This is life
eternal to know thee...' Acquaint thyself with God and be at peace.
Believe this record! Oh! if you hear, sinner, how the infinite God
pities you, a drunkard or sailor. If you know how his large heart

yearns over you, you dare not keep on in your sins. At any moment you are most loathsome in his sight. He says, 'Oh! that you were wise.'

Here lies the peculiar guilt of unbelief, that it makes God a liar when he speaks of himself, of his love and gift and glorious plan of saving sinners. God says, 'I am holy and angry with the wicked every day. My curse is on every one that continueth not in all things.' 'Amen,' says the awakened soul, 'I believe this.' God says, 'My bowels yearn over the lost and condemned. I have made the greatest sacrifice to open a way of pardon and life to every sinner. I have given them eternal life in my Son. So that this way is free and complete to every soul.' 'No,' says the unbelieving soul, 'I dare not think it free to me.' Ah! This is unbelief, giving God the lie when he speaks of his own love to the hell-deserving and his own gift to bring them nigh to him.

2. Something about God the Son
This life is in his Son. The record tells us here plainly about Jesus, the reason of his coming into the world. God wants to give pardon and renovation to sinners and he put it all in Jesus, in his hand, in his blood. The record shows then that all eternal life is in the hand of Jesus (see previous chapter).

3. The freeness of the gospel
Given to us. Given freely to a guilty world. Show how he is not given, not in possession, but given in offer, laid down at every man's feet. The gift is at every man's door. His name is the Saviour of the world.

4. Implied in the record
That all men are dead. Under sentence of death, and condemned to die. In Adam all died, condemnation passed upon all. All are under God's wrath and curse, dead in sins, the heart has no vitality toward God. It is this that makes the gospel so nauseous to most men. It implies that they are condemned for all they do, that they are filthy and unable to live of their resolves. It is this that makes so many refuse Christ's counsel as an affront.

56. Our Confidence is in the Lord (1 John 5:13-15)

These things have I written unto you that believe on the name of the Son of God; that ye may know that ye have eternal life, and that ye may believe on the name of the Son of God. And this is the confidence that we have in him, that, if we ask any thing according to his will, he heareth us: And if we know that he hear us, whatsoever we ask, we know that we have the petitions that we desired of him.

Matters

1. To whom the apostle wrote, to believers. Pastors and teachers are for the edifying of the body of Christ, not for conversion only.

2. That the apostle wrote to believers these things. The record. The simple gospel, that which is converting much is edifying. Believers must not weary of the gospel, nor ministers of preaching the same gospel. To me not grievous, to you safe.

3. Why? Two reasons:

1. That ye may know that ye have eternal life

(a) The world think it impossible to know. Papists also. Why? Because they wish to remain in a doubtful place. Most do not wish to enquire. The truth is that few need to hesitate a single moment. They that have not the Son have not life.

(b) How we may know. There is an immediate way of knowing, namely by believing. The moment a man receives the truth, sees it with new eyes, that moment does he feel that he has eternal life. Every time the truth is brought to bear upon his mind, he feels that he has it. He that believeth hath the witness in himself. You may call this fancy, enthusiasm, or any other name you like, but it is fact, and every one that has the Son at this moment in the arms of his faith, has got a hold of Christ, feels that he has eternal life. Another way of knowing, by getting the seal of the Spirit, making calling sure (2 Peter 1).

(c) Advantages of knowing that you have eternal life.

(i) It gives rest to the mind. Return unto thy rest, Oh! my soul. The world have a kind of rest, it is the lull before the storm. It is the rest of the stupid ox before the axe comes down upon its head. True rest is pardon, nearness, and love of God.

(ii) To give boldness in prayer.

(iii) To make you willing to suffer all things for Christ. Moses counted the reproach of Christ. If sufferings are in store for us, who will bear them like our martyred forefathers, Hamilton and Wishart? Those that know they have eternal life. You took joyfully the spoiling of your goods. Make your soul dwell in a calm in midst of accidents and troubles. A rock in midst of ocean; love to those who have to settle their being in Christ when days of trouble come. Pray that ye may not only be in Christ, but know that you are in him. That ye may believe with so much clearness, fullness and simplicity as to know that ye have eternal life.

(iv) That ye may lay hold on the promises. All are yea and Amen in Christ. But if I know not whether I be in Christ, I know not whether any of the promises are mine. You will never get strength to overcome the world unless you place your interest in Christ. Christ is mine. I know it from the Bible. All that is in him is free to the believer.

(v) That ye may believe, increase and persevere in believing. Faith must be a constant thing with the believer. The object is constantly set before him, that he may constantly believe. Constant guilt coming upon the conscience needs constant washing. Constant corruptions, weakness and ignorance need constant supplies of grace from Christ. Heed the warnings in Hebrews as to letting slip at any time. Hold fast the beginning of your confidence, that faith may increase, that you may believe the record of God more firmly – and more of the record. Hold a firmer grasp and hold a grasp of more things. Some are shaken by a view of their enemies as the trials of life. Learn to believe more of what is in the record. What is in that eternal life? All needful supplies for every state.

What love in this gift! Can you not commit your spirit into that hand? We have the need of a constant exhibition of the record, of the prayer to increase our faith, and of preaching Christ to believers.

(d) Boldness in prayer is given to all that know they have eternal life. Confident asking is one of the consequences of knowing.

(i) Prayer is incumbent on all. Men ought always to pray. Simon Magus. Sailors in a storm. Do you ask, Shall I pray? Yea, call upon thy God. He that hears the ravens or the young lions may hear thee, although you deserve nothing at his hand.

(ii) But prayer is a sweet duty to a believer; he receives sweet answers. He can ask according to the will of God. He knows the will of God and wants it to be done. In things promised he knows the will of God by the promise, as in the gift of the Spirit, or in other things by other ways. The Spirit makes him love God's will and pray according to that (Rom. 8:14, 27).

(iii) He knows that the Father hears every breathing.

(iv) He knows that he is answered before the answer comes.

He knows the will of God from the Word and loves it – our sanctification, the gift of the Spirit. He loves the glory of Christ and his great name, and asks according to it. He asks for things which he sees to be plainly according to the will of God, the sanctification of his soul. He feels that he has it. His prayers are on the altar, the answer will come. Every believing prayer will be answered. Just as every particle of vapour that ascends comes down in rain, so every believing prayer.

Why no answers?
Because ye ask not! Because ye ask amiss, for wrong ends. Because ye ask without confidence. 'He that spared not his Son, but delivered him up for us all, how shall he not with him also freely give us all things' (Rom. 8:32).

May we ask particular things in that confident manner?
Answer. Yes, if you know them to be according to his will. If God in any way shows you that a thing is according to his will, then ask, and rise from your knees sure that you have it. But make sure that Christ is yours and that ye know it.

57. Song to Jesus (Revelation 1:5)

And from Jesus Christ, *who* is the faithful witness, *and* the first begotten of the dead, and the prince of the kings of the earth. Unto him that loved us, and washed us from our sins in his own blood.

Some have thought these words to be one of the songs of heaven. That even before the door was opened in heaven and John's eye penetrated into the wonders of the upper world, its song of joy and ecstasy burst upon his ear, 'Unto him that loved us...' This is evidently a mistake. It is the song of John, banished, poor, in trial and tribulation, an exiled man upon a lonely rock of the sea. A man who had his heaven begun on earth, 'Unto him.' It has got the fragrance and melody of heaven about it. Believers do not fear a suffering lot, do not fear though they be taken to a sickbed, or a lone rock dashed by the eternal waves of ocean.

If you really know Jesus, have tasted and seen the grace that is in Christ, you may begin the song now. It is the song of a redeemed soul and contains two things: (1) what Christ hath done for us; (2) what we must do for him.

1. What Christ hath done for us

1. He loved us
(a) *Eternity, with electing love.* When in heaven, his delight was with the children of men (Prov. 8:31).

They were no better than devils, no better than Hindus, no better than others in our town or family, yet he loved us. He planned our salvation, ordered all of it, wrote our names in the book of life. Nothing so wonderful as that Christ should love any, knowing how vile our hearts are, how black our lives, what depths of sin. Amazing that he should love any – an unconverted heart is so ugly, so frightful, so black, so disgusting.

Another wonder is that when he loved any, he loved *me*. Every believer knows more evil of himself than of any other. He knows that he is the chief of sinners and therefore every believer feels it an infinite wonder that Jesus loved him. The woman of Samaria said, 'Jesus loved me.' The thief said, 'Jesus loved me.' Zaccheus said, 'Jesus loved me.'. And we may say the same.

(b) *What he bore in time for us.* He left heaven for us. 'Greater love hath no man than this than that he lay down his life for his friends.' John had his eye on the garden and the cross when he said this. John had seen Jesus setting his face steadfastly while sweating blood. He had seen him bound, spit upon, buffeted. He had seen him nailed to the cross, the crown of thorns, bleeding, dying, the darkness, the frown. And this was what he learned from it: Jesus loved us. He saw Jesus bearing our sins in his own body, standing in our place, bearing our shame, made a curse for us. He loved us. Have you truly looked to Jesus Christ? You may say the same about Jesus.

(c) *How he followed our soul.* When the sheep went astray the shepherd came to seek it. So Christ seeks every soul he finds. None come unsought to Jesus. It was this John remembered. 'How I wearied him by my sins, hardness, ungodliness, unbelief. He sent John the Baptist, providences, he came to the Sea of Galilee and sought me. He came to Jordan, he invited me to follow him. Come and see. When I wearied of him he came to me again at Galilee.' So may every one of you say that has been saved, Jesus has tracked you. You have heard his footsteps, you have wearied him with your sins, yet he followed. He sent ministers, providences, sickness. He knocked on the door. He waited long. Oh! surely you have need to say, 'Unto him that loved me.'

2. Washed us from our sins in his own blood

There is nothing so defiling as our sins. Everyone that is now redeemed was all over stained and defiled with sin. We were plunged in the miry clay. 'An unconverted man is the most doleful of all creatures' (J. Bunyan).

One walking by the sea said, 'My heart would pollute all that ocean.' Sin is an infinite evil and therefore it leaves a mark on the soul that nothing human can wipe away. Oh! pray for a discovery of the filthiness of sin. One thing greater than sin – the blood of Jesus, his own blood, the blood of the Lamb. As the water was higher than the highest mountains, so the blood. Where sin abounded, grace did much more abound. It is atoning blood. There is a fountain filled with blood. He washed us. The fountain open will do no good unless we be washed in it. He washes all his own. Not only opens the fountain but plunges them in. Oh! the unspeakable grace of Jesus. He begins and ends. An unappropriated Christ is no Christ to me. If the Israelite had not put the blood on his door, he would have died. Is the blood of Jesus on the portals of your heart? Has he washed you from your sins? Some think that Jesus loved them though he has not washed them. Vain hope. It will perish. Some think they can wash without blood, an amended life. John Bunyan was always anxious to have sin dealt with in the right way. So be you.

'I found that unless careless guilt of conscience was taken off the right way, a man grew rather worse for the loss of his trouble.' Lord, let it not go off my heart but by the right way, by the blood of Christ. Oh! take care, dear friends. Some would wash and then come; get rid of their sins and then come to Jesus. Every one whom Christ finds is unwashed, vile, in their sins. You would need to sing a different song.

3. *Made us kings and priests*

Negative and positive holiness. By nature we are slaves to sin and priests to Satan. But when Christ washes the same, he makes us kings and priests to God and his Father.

These two are united in the Christian, two of the greatest offices in the world. They were united in Melchizedek. He was king of Salem and priest of the Most High God. United also in Christ: 'Thou shalt be a priest for ever after the order of Melchizedek. He shall sit and rule as priest upon his throne.' He has the white robes of the priesthood and the golden girdle of the king. So it is true of every one united to Christ. He hath made us kings and priests. Observe he does not say he will make us kings and priests, though that is true, but he hath made us, we are already made kings and priests.

(1) **Kings**. John was at this time in Patmos, a slave. Some think that he was working in the mines underground, perhaps loaded with a chain and yet he says, 'He hath made me a king.' This is true of every Christian in two respects:

(a) The vastness of his possessions. Kings in old times had immense possessions. Solomon gathered all the peculiar treasures of kings. But a soul united to Jesus has more. He has the pearl of great price, the clothing of wrought gold. He has God's lovingkindness, which is better than life. He can look on the hills and valleys and resplendent rivers, and say, 'My Father made them all.' 'All things are yours, whether Paul or Apollos, or Cephas, or the world, or life or death, or things present or things to come.' All are yours. Having nothing and yet possessing all things.

(b) Power of a king. He has the kingly spirit of Christ: 'uphold me with thy free Spirit.' He has power over his own soul. Once he was the slave of sin, he obeyed sin and was its slave. But now he has a new Spirit within him, so that he overcomes himself. This is more than if he took a city.

He has power over the world. He was once its slave. He yielded to its lead. He followed in the train, yielded to its pleasures, bound by its silver bands, the world's dread laugh.

He has power over the devil. Once he was like the maniac led captive by Satan at his will, sometimes driven into the fire, sometimes into the water. But when Jesus, the stronger than he, comes, he snatches the soul out of his grasp. Jesus makes us tread upon the lion and the adder.

Dear friends, this is what Jesus offers, not only to wash you but to make you a king. To give you peace now and glory after. To make you rule over your spirit now, to rule over the nations afterwards. A crown of righteousness, a crown of life, a crown of glory.

(2) **Priests to God and his Father**. A natural man is a priest of Satan. He offers continual sacrifice to the god of this world; time, health, body, soul all are sacrificed to his god. But when Jesus saves him, he makes him a priest to God.

(a) In access. The priests always came into the holy place, the high priest once in the year went into the holiest of all (Lev. 16:2). But now we are bid to draw near, to lean on the breast of Jesus, to come boldly to the throne of grace.

(b) In bearing up our heart. Just as the flame came down from heaven and kindled up the sacrifice, so the fire of the Spirit kindles our heart and makes it go up to God in flame.

Praise. One part of the priest's duty was to burn incense upon the golden altar; the golden altar represents Jesus; the incense our prayers and praises; these when put upon the golden altar rise sweetly up to heaven. Other prayers and praises never rise from the ground but these mount up to heaven.

Dear friends, has this change passed upon you? By this you may know whether you are truly washed. These two cannot be separated; he hath washed us and made us kings and priests. Are you still the slave of sin, led captive of Satan at his will? Does he reign over you? Has he his chain about your soul? Then you are not washed. Are you not a priest? Have you no access to God? Is your heart an altar without a sacrifice? Then you are yet in your sins.

Now glance at the whole history of Christ's dealings with a soul. He loved us, washed us, made us kings and priests to God and his Father. Is this your history? How happy are the souls for whom he has done all this. They have the broad seal of heaven upon their forehead. They are God's people. Oh! pray to be one of them. Happy is that people whose God is the Lord.

2. What we must do for him
I have done this for thee, what hast thou done for me?

1. To him be glory
The saved soul longs to give glory to Christ. He longs to give Christ all the praise of his conversion from first to last. He looks back over all the way by which he has been led and says from the bottom of his heart, 'To him be glory.' He looks to the love of Jesus, to his wakening, drawing, washing, renewing, making him a king and priest. Ministers may have been used as instruments. Still he looks far beyond them and says, 'To him be glory.' A true Christian will cast his crown nowhere but at the feet of Jesus. The true believer will say that it was Christ that welcomed him, it was Christ that loved him and that washed him. 'To him be glory.'

Try yourselves by this
It is the clear mark of a hypocrite that they are willing to cast their crown at the feet of a creature. Every jewel has its counterfeit. So there is a counterfeit conversion. Satan often changes people and makes them think they are converted. These will give the glory to man. They cast their crown at the foot of a fellow worm and say, 'To him be glory.' But one that is truly saved looks above man, to Jesus and says, 'To him be glory.' A man healed by the brazen serpent would never attribute it to the pole, or to the man that held it. He would look steadily to the blazing sign that God had set up. A man saved by Jesus will say to all eternity, 'To him be glory. Salvation to our God.'

And when he comes into the new Jerusalem, he will not stop to look at the angels, nor at the redeemed, but will hasten to where Jesus sits and fall down and worship and adore him; casting his crown at his feet and crying, 'Thou art worthy. Worthy is the Lamb that was slain.'

2. Dominion for ever
A saved soul gives himself away to Christ for ever. Before conversion, a man loves to be his own master, to do what he will with his time, his money, his all. But when Jesus lays his hand on him, washes and renews him, then he says, 'I am the Lord's. I am not my own but bought by him. To him be the dominion for ever and ever.'

Oh! Christians, come and give up your all to Christ. Give up your heart to him. Let his dominion be from sea to sea in your heart, from one corner to another. Is there any part of your heart where you do not wish Christ to reign? Then you have not seen him, neither known him.

Give up your all to him. Dear friends, say, 'They are not mine but Christ's,' and so you will part from them without a tear, but without losing your all. Your money, give all to him. If there is anything you are unwilling Christ should have, then you are not his. To him be dominion. Oh! it is sweet to have nothing of our own, but to give up all to Christ, to become his for ever and ever. Once you gave all to Satan, now give all to Christ.

58. Christians should be like Christ (Revelation 1:10)

I was in the Spirit on the Lord's day.

A child of God is the same at all times and in all places. He is not always equally happy, nor equally holy, nor equally near to God; far from it, but he has always the same desire to be like Christ and near Christ. A hypocrite changes like the chameleon. As long as he is under the eye of a minister, a godly friend, he appears to be a saint indeed, quiet, holy and demure in looks. But the moment this restraint is lifted off, corruption bursts out in all its power. How many of you here today sit with solemnity and hear God's Word with a holy, reverent look as long as you are in the eye of man, but perhaps tonight when darkness has shrouded you in its mantle and no eye but God's is upon you, you will talk and laugh and do things of which it is a shame even so much as to speak? Not so with John.

There is a rocky island in the Aegean Sea; two rocky mountains rise from its bosom; the inhabitants are few and poor; neither now nor in ancient times did they know the joy of a holy Sabbath. This island is Patmos. It was to this island John was banished by the Roman emperor Domitian in AD 94. Here he was allowed to wander, no eye of man to watch over him. And no doubt he often stood upon that shore and looking to the East, envied the waves that rushed past him toward his beloved Ephesus. Or standing on the northern shore he looked toward Macedonia where beloved Paul had planted so many churches. Or turning to the south-east he stretched his eye to see if he could catch a glimpse of the islands near to Corinth, where dear Christians dwelt.

From this little verse we learn two interesting facts:

(1) That even in Patmos, John remembered the Lord's day, 'I was in the Spirit on the Lord's day.' True, he could not that morning see out of his window the church of Ephesus, nor could he meet his little children; he had no words of warning or invitation to address that day, he was a prisoner and alone. Still he did not forget to keep the Lord's day.

(2) The Lord did not forget John upon his own day. 'I was in the Spirit on the Lord's day.' John was alone, far away from the courts of God's house and yet he that feeds the plants and wild flowers on the mountains' brow did not forget John. He chose his own day to send the Comforter to John. 'I was in the Spirit on the Lord's day.'

1. Prove that the first day of the week is the Christian Sabbath, and the manner in which Christians should keep the Lord's day.

We have already proved that the Sabbath was made for man, that it began in Paradise and was intended to last till there is no more sea. Some of you will say, What evidence have you that the day was changed from the seventh to the first day of the week?

Now, we have no express command to this purpose. This is admitted on all hands. The reason why we have no express command is very plain and very gracious. Christ revealed the truth to the disciples only as they were able to bear it. It was a long time before he told them he must die. And when he left them he said that the Comforter would teach them many things he had omitted. It was long before they knew that the Gentiles were to be saved as were the Jews. And so out of tenderness for the Jews who clung very much as they do still to their old Sabbath with all its ceremonies, Christ did not reveal to them till John wrote the Revelation, that it was to be changed for the Lord's day. Still he gave many proofs all along that it was to be changed.

1. The name, the Lord's Day

There can be no doubt that the Lord's day is the first day of the week. This name here applied to it by John is the name by which all the early Christians call the first day of the week. It is the same word which is used in 1 Corinthians 11:20, concerning the Supper, 'to eat the Lord's supper'. It is a word formed for the purpose and is nowhere applied to anything but to the communion table and the first day of the week. But this name clearly proves that the day was entirely devoted to the Lord.

(i) The gospel is called 'the Word of the Lord' (1 Pet. 1:25). 'The Word of the Lord endureth for ever', because it is all his. It is his planning, his executing, his ending.

(ii) The children of God are called the Lord's people; they are Christ's because he made them, he bought them, they are his, body and soul.

(iii) The Lord's Table is his table. He spreads the table and invites the guests. He says of the bread, 'This is my body', and of the wine, 'This is my blood.' He feeds his own people there.

(iv) In like manner, the Lord's day is his day. He instituted it. He set us an example on it by rising from the dead. Every hour of it is his, the morning and evening of it are his. It is all holy to him. It is as much his as the Bible is his Word, as the children of God are his people, as the Lord's table is his table. You cannot bear to hear a man blaspheme the Bible, it is God's holy book, very pure, more precious than gold. You cannot bear to hear a man reproach God's children, accuse them falsely and persecute them; they are the Lord's body. You cannot bear to see a man profane the Lord's table, sitting down at it as at a common meal. And no more can you bear to see a man profane the Lord's day. The blasphemer, the persecutor, the profane communicant and the Sabbath-breaker are on a level.

2. From prophecy – Psalm 118:22 – it was there foretold:
(a) That the builders would refuse this stone.

(b) That God would raise up the stone to be the head of the corner.

(c) That that day should be kept as a day of solemn joy and gladness.

Now all these things came to pass. The Jewish priests, who should have been the builders of God's church, refused Christ. They stumbled at that stumbling stone. But God raised him from the dead on the first day of the week, and that day is a day of joy and gladness to all believers to the end of the world.

3. It was the day Jesus blessed

The same day that Jesus rose from the dead, the disciples were assembled together and Jesus came and stood in the midst and said, 'Peace be unto you.' And after eight days again, the next Lord's day, his disciples were within and Jesus came and revealed himself to Thomas.

On the same day the Spirit was poured out at Pentecost; the first revival of the Christian Church began on the Lord's day. 'When the day of Pentecost was fully come, they were all with one accord in one place'. The same day John, on the lovely isle of Patmos, received the Spirit. How plain that Jesus wished to make us keep this day of blessing.

4. It was the day of Christian worship

Acts 20:6,7: 'And upon the first day of the week...' Here Paul waited over the Jewish Sabbath and preached and broke bread on the Lord's day. Upon the same day did Paul command religious contributions to be made (1 Cor. 16:1,2). The duty here enforced was that of collecting alms for the poor saints. The time, the first day of the week, as if no other day would do so well; and this command was not confined to Corinth, the churches of Galatia got the same command. It seems perfectly clear from these two examples that the early Christians did make use of the Lord's day as the Christian Sabbath.

From a Christian writer who lived fifty years after John, we learn that 'all the Christians that live either in the town or country meet together at the same place upon the day called Sunday, where the writings of the prophets and apostles are read. When the reader has done, the bishop makes a sermon wherein he instructs the people and animates them to the practice of such lovely precepts. At the conclusion of this discourse we all rise up together and pray. Bread and wine and water are offered, and the people conclude all with the joyful exclamation of Amen.'

2. How Christians should keep the Lord's day

1. Prepare for the Sabbath

I have showed you that it is the Lord's day, a day sacred to him, that it is the day when Jesus comes in, when Jesus breathes on his own, when the Spirit comes with power. Oh then, should it be carelessly entered on? Lay by your worldly business a little while before and seek preparation of heart for the coming day of blessing. I do not wonder at men of the world stumbling into the Sabbath in the midst of their work, but it shall not be so among you. Those of you that have shops, shut them up early on the Saturday evening. I know it is the way of the world to have them open till late that evening, but it shall not be so among you. Those of you that are believing servants, get your work well through early on Saturday evening that you may have leisure to prepare for meeting God.

A minister in Ireland arrived at a brother minister's house one Saturday evening. The night being cold, he asked leave to go to the kitchen fire to warm himself, but thought perhaps he may disturb the servants there. 'Oh no, no work is done after 6 o'clock.' He went and found it so. Some of you feel that you do not make much improvement of your Sabbaths; ask if this be not one reason? If you were going to meet a king, you would prepare yourself for the interview. How much more when you are about to enter the palace of the great King!

2. Give it all to God

It is common for worldly people to give part of the day to God and to give the rest to business or friends or pleasure. Many sleep longer on Sabbath mornings. Some come half the day to the house of God and the other half read the newspaper. Some come twice to church and spend the evening in visiting their friends, in idle walks, etc. It shall not be so with you. God does not say, Remember the Sabbath morning, or evening, or forenoon or afternoon, but *the day*, the whole day. Remember, 'A false balance is an abomination to the Lord.' The scant measure is abominable to him. He cannot bear cheatery between man and man. Will he bear it *between man and God?*

If you loved another and had a certain time to meet with them, would you steal half of the time out of their company? The Sabbath is Christ's trysting time with his church. If you love him, you will count every moment of it precious. You will rise early and sit up late, to have a long day with Christ.

3. Spend it cheerfully

'This is the day that the Lord has made; we will rejoice and be glad in it.' Call the Sabbath a delight. If a worldly man is forced to keep a strict Sabbath, he becomes dull and melancholy. He becomes sour and ill-humoured because he cannot laugh and talk, because he has no opportunity for carnal mirth and enjoyment. This shows plainly that he would be miserable in heaven. It is not so with you. Your joy is in the presence of Christ. All other joy is like the crackling of thorns, a short blaze ending in darkness. Your joy is to see much of Christ and be much filled with the Spirit. Be joyful then on the Lord's day. The Lord loveth a cheerful giver. Spend much of the day in praises, in a thankful remembrance of past mercies, in anticipation of glory.

4. Seek the Spirit on that day

'I was in the Spirit on the Lord's day.' From what has been said, there is nothing superstitious in believing that we may expect more visits of Christ and of the Spirit on the Lord's day than on other days. Thomas was absent the first Lord's day when Jesus came in, and we see he had almost lost his soul by it. If any of the disciples had been wandering on the day of Pentecost they would have lost his blessing. If John had been careless of the Lord's day, he would not have received such a full measure of the Spirit. How many of you lose a full blessing by a careless neglect of the Lord's day?

Many of you complain that you have little of the Spirit, that you have a hard heart, little love to Christ, frequent falls into sin, much coldness. See if this be not one main cause that you do not seek to be in the Spirit on the Lord's day. See if you do not grieve the Spirit by worldly cares and thoughts, by loose careless language, by mixing with worldly people in their talk on the Lord's day. See whether you prize every moment of holy time, looking up for a constant supply of the Spirit.

5. Spend it knowing that your Sabbaths are few

Spend it also as you will wish to have done when you are in heaven. Your Sabbaths are all numbered. You have a vast work before you and Sabbath is the best season for doing it in. You have lusts to crucify and the world to overcome and Satan to contend against. You have to fight a good fight, to finish your course, to keep the faith.

3. Warning

1. To awakened persons

God is at present dealing with some of you in a very gracious manner, pouring his Spirit on your heart and striving with you. Some of you are very much concerned to know what you must do to be saved. I have attempted to show you that you must get into Christ. But now I would show you another thing you should be careful of and that is, do not profane the Sabbath. It is common for Satan to beguile awakened persons back to their sins and he generally tries to do it on the Sabbath. Ah take heed, do not quench your convictions. Christ revealed himself to Thomas on the Sabbath and to the 3,000. It is precious time, all time is precious, but especially holy time.

2. To unawakened persons

(i) You have heard this day that the Sabbath was made for man, not for God's children only but for the benefit of all men. You have heard that it is a day when Christ often comes into the assembly of his people, and when 3,000 were converted in one day. Do not despise the Sabbath, I entreat of you. It is the day in which God is peculiarly seeking your salvation. Surely it is the devil that makes you hate the very season when Christ is seeking you. Oh! if you were wise, you would anxiously wait for God on the Sabbath. Although you are unconcerned, yet you know you must be converted or perish. Now there is no time so likely for being saved as the Sabbath. Do not join the ranks of the Sabbath-breakers then.

(ii) You have heard this day that it is the Lord's day, that it is not your own. Take heed then, how you steal any part of it. Remember all sin committed this day is double sins and will bring down double vengeance. If you steal this day, you both steal and break the Sabbath in one. God is dreadfully provoked by your sinning on the Lord's day. Some of you that talk lasciviously and indulge in wanton behaviour, you provoke God doubly when you do it on the Sabbath day. You that frequent the tavern and spend your nights in rioting and drunkenness, you doubly provoke God by doing it on the Lord's day. Oh! what a tormenting thought it will be in hell that God gave you a peculiar day for seeking conversion and these were the days when you sealed your damnation.

December 26th, 1841

Other Titles
of
Robert Murray McCheyne
published by
Christian Focus Publications

From the Preacher's Heart

This volume of sermons was originally published with the title *Additional Remains of Robert Murray McCheyne*. It contains sixty-four sermons and four sets of lectures (The Ten Virgins, The Family at Bethany, The Good Shepherd, and Capernaum. In the preface Maurice Roberts provides historical information about McCheyne and his ministry as well as an assessment of McCheyne's preaching style and content.

hardback   ISBN 1-85792-029-X   *536 pages*

A Basket of Fragments

This selection of 37 sermons was first published five years after McCheyne's death. They were compiled from the notes taken down by hearers but 'without the least view to publication'. One advantage of this is that they bring before us the extemporaneous pleadings with sinners in which few so greatly excelled as did Robert Murray McCheyne. These sermons are stamped with eternity; they are the expression of one upon whose heart the weight of perishing sinners pressed and who earnestly longed for their conversion. Subjects include

Adoption,
the Transfiguration of Christ,
the Call of Abraham,
A Faithful Ministry,
The Office of the Ruling Elder,
Future Punishment Eternal

large paperback   ISBN 0 906731 03 8   *194 pages*

The Seven Churches of Asia

The Seven Churches of Asia deals with the early church as seen in Christ's summaries and assessments recorded in Revelation chapters 2 and 3. The pictures given are powerful and relevant to the church today – and more particularly to the church of tomorrow.

ISBN 0-906731-51-8

Comfort in Sorrow

McCheyne's lectures on the family in Bethany – Mary, Martha and their brother, Lazarus. In particular, McCheyne focuses on events recorded in John 11, connected to the death and resurrection of Lazarus. He shows how Christ is especially sympathetic and near to those who sorrow and how the Saviour uses such occasions to develop the graces of his people.

This book is in Large Print.

pocket paperback   ISBN 1-85792-012-0   *160 pages*

Robert Murray McCheyne
Alexander Smellie

This biography of McCheyne provides a warm insight into the life of a most disciplined and spiritual servant of Christ. Smellie describes McCheyne's family background, his school and college days, his training for ministry, his role as a leading preacher in revival, and his pastorate in Dundee. The reader will discover the main features of McCheyne's balanced Christian lifestyle which helped make him the man he was, including his methods of personal devotion and his choice of spiritual friends. This volume also includes two additional sections: (a) an account of the revival in Dundee by Alexander Cumming, a ministerial friend of McCheyne's; (b) extracts from the diary of Jessie Thain, a close personal friend of McCheyne's.

paperback   ISBN 1-85792-184 4   *256 pages*

Christian Focus Publications publishes biblically-accurate books for adults and children. The books in the adult range are published in three imprints.

Christian Heritage contains classic writings from the past.

Christian Focus contains popular works including biographies, commentaries, doctrine, and Christian living.

Mentor focuses on books written at a level suitable for Bible College and seminary students, pastors, and others; the imprint includes commentaries, doctrinal studies, examination of current issues, and church history.

For a free catalogue of all our titles, please write to
Christian Focus Publications,
Geanies House, Fearn,
Ross-shire, IV20 1TW, Great Britain

For details of our titles visit us on our web site
http://www.christianfocus.com